OXFORD MONOGRAPHS IN INTERNATIONAL HUMANITARIAN AND CRIMINAL LAW

The Right to Life in Armed Conflict

OXFORD MONOGRAPHS IN INTERNATIONAL HUMANITARIAN AND CRIMINAL LAW

The aim of this series is to publish original and innovative books on fundamental, topical, or cutting-edge issues in international humanitarian law and international criminal justice. The primary purpose of the series is to publish books which, in addition to critically surveying existing law, also suggest new avenues for improving the law.

ALSO PUBLISHED IN THIS SERIES

Fairness in International Criminal Trials
Yvonne McDermott

The Special Tribunal for Lebanon
Law and Practice
Edited by Amal Alamuddin, Nidal Nabil Jurdi, and David Tolbert

Rwanda's Gacaca Courts
Between Retribution and Reparation
Paul Christoph Bornkamm

The Right to Life in Armed Conflict

IAN PARK

OXFORD
UNIVERSITY PRESS

OXFORD
UNIVERSITY PRESS

Great Clarendon Street, Oxford, OX2 6DP,
United Kingdom

Oxford University Press is a department of the University of Oxford.
It furthers the University's objective of excellence in research, scholarship,
and education by publishing worldwide. Oxford is a registered trade mark of
Oxford University Press in the UK and in certain other countries

First Edition published in 2018
Impression: 1

Published in the United States of America by Oxford University Press
198 Madison Avenue, New York, NY 10016, United States of America

British Library Cataloguing in Publication Data
Data available

Library of Congress Control Number: 2017960272

ISBN 978–0–19–882138–0

Printed and bound by
CPI Group (UK) Ltd, Croydon, CR0 4YY

Acknowledgements

The doctoral thesis that formed the basis of this book could not have been written without the support and guidance of some wonderful people. First and foremost, I am indebted to my supervisor Professor Dapo Akande, Professor of Public International Law at the University of Oxford. The support and guidance that Dapo provided was truly exceptional—he has a rare gift to inspire. After our meetings I always left enthused, despite not always submitting draft chapters that were entirely convincing. I am also extremely grateful to Balliol College, which is a wonderfully supportive environment to research students in law. Throughout my time there, Professors Timothy Endicott and Grant Lamond were outstanding mentors. For more than a decade, Dr Andrew Shacknove at the University of Oxford has been a source of inspiration and guidance. I am extremely grateful to Andrew for all that he has done for me. The Public International Law community and discussion group at Oxford provide the perfect canvas upon which to discuss ideas and engage in challenging debate. I am indebted to Professors Catherine Redgwell and Antonios Tzanakopoulos for allowing me the opportunity to present my work and receive valuable feedback in these fora. I am also particularly grateful to my DPhil examiners, Professors Guy Goodwin-Gill and Nigel White. The feedback they provided was extremely insightful and the viva, although challenging, was a fascinating and enjoyable experience.

During the writing of this book I benefited enormously from a year spent as a Visiting Fellow at Harvard Law School. I am extremely grateful to everyone at the Human Rights Program at Harvard for the support they offered. The Human Rights Program is an amazing environment in which to research and write, made possible by the fantastic people who work there. Very special thanks must go to Professor Gerry Neuman and Roi Bachmutsky, both of whom read and commented upon draft chapters. I am also extremely grateful to Dr Mindy Jane Roseman, Yale Law School, for the support she provided during my time in the United States.

My most sincere thanks go to the outstanding team at OUP who supported me throughout this project. I am particularly grateful to Natasha Flemming, Merel Alstein, James Baird, Arokia Anthuvan Rani, and Kristy Barker for all of their help and guidance. My thanks must also go to the series editors and the reviewers of the monograph proposal for the excellent comments and suggestions they made.

I could not have written this book without the unstinting support of my family. My parents, Alan and Sheila, have made innumerable sacrifices, over many years, to allow me to follow my career in the armed forces and the law, and I will always be grateful to them for everything that they have done for me. Equally, my brother Neil, his wife Julia, and their children Cameron and Megan have been wonderfully kind, supportive, and, in the case of Cameron and Megan, splendidly entertaining. I must also thank my parents-in-law, Margaret and Dave, and their family, David, Nicola, Blake, Elisabeth, and Liberty, for everything that they have done for me. Finally, and most importantly, I thank my wife Caroline and our daughter Emmeline—you are the world to me and this book is dedicated to you.

Contents

Detailed Table of Contents

PART II. APPLICATION OF THE RIGHT TO LIFE IN ARMED CONFLICT

Table of Cases

EUROPEAN COURT OF HUMAN RIGHTS

EUROPEAN COMMISSION OF HUMAN RIGHTS

INTER-AMERICAN COURT OF HUMAN RIGHTS

INTERNATIONAL COURT OF JUSTICE

UN TREATY BODIES

HUMAN RIGHTS COMMITTEE

Consideration of state party reports and general comments

COMMUNICATIONS

UNITED KINGDOM NATIONAL CASE LAW

OTHER JURISPRUDENCE

International Criminal Tribunal for the Former Yugoslavia

African Court of Justice and Human Rights

Table of Legal Instruments

UNITED KINGDOM STATUTES AND STATUTORY INSTRUMENTS

List of Abbreviations

ACHR	American Convention on Human Rights
AP I	Protocol Additional to the Geneva Conventions of 12 August 1949 and relating to the protection of victims of international armed conflicts
AP II	Protocol Additional to the Geneva Conventions of 12 August 1949 and relating to the protection of victims of non-international armed conflicts
CAT	Convention against Torture
CEDAW	Convention on the Elimination of All Forms of Discrimination Against Women
CIA	Central Intelligence Agency
CRC	Convention on the Rights of the Child
DCDC	Development Concepts Doctrine Centre (United Kingdom)
DRC	Democratic Republic of the Congo
ECHR	European Convention on Human Rights and Fundamental Freedoms
ECtHR	European Court of Human Rights
EJIL	European Journal of International Law
EU	European Union
FARC	Fuerzas Armadas Revolucionarias de Colombia
GC I	Geneva Convention (I) for the Amelioration of the Condition of the Wounded and Sick in Armed Forces in the Field (1949)
GC II	Geneva Convention (II) for the Amelioration of the Condition of the Wounded, Sick and Shipwrecked Members of the Armed Forces at Sea (1949)
GC III	Geneva Convention (III) Relative to the Treatment of Prisoners of War (1949)
GC IV	Geneva Convention (IV) Relative to the Protection of Civilian Persons in Time of War (1949)
HRC	Human Rights Committee
ICC	International Criminal Court
ICCPR	International Covenant on Civil and Political Rights
ICJ	International Court of Justice
ICRC	International Committee of the Red Cross
ICTY	International Criminal Tribunal for the Former Yugoslavia
IHL	International Humanitarian Law
IHRL	International Human Rights Law
ILC	International Law Commission
IRA	Irish Republican Army
ISAF	International Security Assistance Force (Afghanistan)
JDP	Joint Doctrine Publication
JFC	Joint Force Commander
JSP	Joint Service Publication
KFOR	Kosovo Force (NATO)
LOAC	Law of Armed Conflict
LTTE	Liberation Tigers of Tamil Eelam
NAC	North Atlantic Council
NATO	North Atlantic Treaty Organization
NGO	Non-governmental organization

OAS	Organization of American States
OEF	Operation Enduring Freedom
OHCHR	Office of the High Commissioner for Human Rights
OP	Optional Protocol
PMC	Private Military Company
RoE	Rules of Engagement
RAF	Royal Air Force
RN	Royal Navy
SAS	Special Air Service
SFIR	Stabilization Force Iraq
SIB	Special Investigations Branch, UK Military Police
TST	Time-Sensitive Target
UDHR	Universal Declaration of Human Rights
UK	United Kingdom
UN	United Nations
UPR	Universal Periodic Review
US	United States
VCLT	Vienna Convention on the Law of Treaties

Introduction

The application of the right to life in armed conflict has polarized opinion. Potentially irreconcilable positions have emerged between those who assert that human rights law generally, and the right to life specifically, have no place during armed conflict,[1] and those who argue to the contrary.[2] In domestic and supranational courts, the application of the right to life in armed conflict has generated considerable litigation, prompted scathing criticism of judicial decisions, necessitated government declarations in respect of the use of derogations in future armed conflicts, and is yet to be comprehensively analysed. Moreover, and as a natural corollary, it is submitted that the implications of affording right to life protections during future military operations, particularly those involving military coalitions, are not yet fully realized. Indeed, affording such protections could fundamentally, and adversely, affect armed forces' ability to achieve their military objectives.

With respect to the United Kingdom (UK),[3] only passing reference is made to human rights law in armed forces doctrine[4] and military legal publications.[5] Moreover, there is no reference made to the UK's right to life obligations in respect of those affected by the actions of the state's armed forces, or armed forces personnel themselves, during international and non-international armed conflict.[6] There

[1] See, for example, Richard Ekins, Jonathan Morgan, and Tom Tugendhat, 'Clearing the Fog of Law: Saving Our Armed Forces from Defeat by Judicial Diktat', Policy Exchange, London (2015), <http://www.policyexchange.org.uk/images/publications/clearing%20the%20fog%20of%20law.pdf>.

[2] See, for example, Daragh Murray, Elizabeth Wilmshurst, Francoise Hampson, Charles Garraway, Noam Lubell, and Dapo Akande, *Practitioners' Guide to Human Rights Law in Armed Conflict* (Oxford University Press 2016).

[3] When analyzing the application of the right to life in armed conflict, the approach of the United Kingdom will be used as the principal representative example. Where applicable, however, the practices of other states bound by human rights obligations will be considered.

[4] The principal UK armed forces doctrinal publications are: UK Defence Doctrine (JDP 0-01), UK Air and Space Doctrine (JDP 0-30), British Maritime Doctrine (JDP 0-10), UK Joint Operations Doctrine (JDP 01), Campaign Execution (JDP 3-00), Legal Support to Joint Operations (JDP 3-46), Captured Persons (JDP 1-10), Security and Stabilisation, The Military Contribution (JDP 3-40).

[5] UK Manual of the Law of Armed Conflict (JSP 383) and Amendments 1 (Jan 2004), 2 (Jul 2007), 3 (Sep 2010), 4 (Jul 2011), 5 (Aug 2011), 6 (Nov 2011), and 7 (May 2013).

[6] The lack of reference to human rights law generally and the right to life specifically in UK military doctrine is reflected in the UK's litigation strategy in the ECtHR and domestic courts. The UK government has only conceded that human rights law has extraterritorial effect in extremely narrow circumstances during armed conflict. See, for example, *Al-Skeini and Others v the United Kingdom*, Application no 55721/07 (ECtHR, 7 July 2011) 118, where the UK government only accepted that the ECHR had extraterritorial effect in respect of the sixth applicant's son, who died in a 'United Kingdom-run military detention facility located in a United Kingdom base'. The UK government asserted that the ECHR did not have extraterritorial effect in respect of the family members of the other five applicants. A further example of the UK's litigation strategy is *Hassan v the United Kingdom*, Application no 29750/09

is therefore no formal mechanism for human rights law to be considered by those responsible for planning and executing military operations. It is, however, indisputable that, following a number of binding judgments of the European Court of Human Rights[7] (ECtHR)[8] and domestic courts, human rights law can apply in such circumstances.[9] The extent to which human rights law applies, and how to apply it, remains widely debated[10] and in certain areas largely unresolved,[11] yet of potentially considerable significance to how military campaigns are conducted and resourced.[12] It has been argued by some that an adherence to human rights law principles during armed conflict adversely affects an operational commander's ability to achieve their military objectives[13] and that armed conflict ought to be governed exclusively by international humanitarian law. Conversely, others contend that 'the application of both bodies of law (human rights law and international humanitarian law) should be carried out in a complementary and mutually reinforcing manner'[14] and that 'over the years, the General Assembly, the Commission on Human Rights and more recently the Human Rights Council, have considered that, in situations of armed

(ECtHR, 16 September 2014) 70–73, in which the UK government again submitted that the ECHR did not have extraterritorial effect in this case.

[7] See, for example, *Isayeva v Russia*, Application no 57950/00 (ECtHR, 24 February 2005); *Isayeva, Yusupova and Bazayeva v Russia*, Application nos 57947/00, 57948/00, and 57949/00 (ECtHR, 24 February 2005); *Issa and Others v Turkey*, Application no 31821/96 (ECtHR, 16 November 2004); *Hassan v the United Kingdom; Al-Skeini and Others v the United Kingdom*, and *Al-Jedda v the United Kingdom*, Application no 27021/08 (ECtHR, 7 July 2011).

[8] The ECtHR is hereinafter also referred to as 'the Court'.

[9] See, for example, *Serdar Mohammed and Others v Ministry of Defence* [2017] UKSC 2, *Smith and others v Ministry of Defence* [2013] UKSC 41, and *Al-Saadoon and Others v Secretary of State for Defence* [2016] EWCA Civ 811.

[10] See, inter alia, Guglielmo Verdirame, 'Human Rights in Wartime: A Framework for Analysis' (2008) EHRLR 689; Noam Lubell, 'Challenges in Applying Human Rights Law to Armed Conflict' (2005) 87(860) *IRRC* 738; Louise Doswald-Beck, 'The Right to Life in Armed Conflict: Does International Humanitarian Law Provide All the Answers?' (2006) 88(864) *IRRC* 881; Orna Ben-Naftali, 'International Humanitarian and International Human Rights Law—Pas de Deux' in Orna Ben-Naftali (ed), *International Humanitarian and International Human Rights Law* (Oxford University Press 2011) 1; Louise Doswald-Beck, *Human Rights in Times of Armed Conflict and Terrorism* (Oxford University Press 2011); Peter Rowe, *The Impact of Human Rights Law on Armed Forces* (Cambridge University Press 2006); Heike Krieger, 'A Conflict of Norms: The Relationship between Humanitarian Law and Human Rights Law in the ICRC Customary Law Study', 11 JCSL (2006) 265; Cordula Droege, 'Elective Affinities? Human Rights and Humanitarian Law', 90 IRRC (2008) 501; Yoram Dinstein, 'Human Rights in Armed Conflict: International Humanitarian Law' in T Meron (ed), *Human Rights in International Law* (Oxford University Press 1985); Louise Doswald-Beck and Sylvain Vité, 'International Humanitarian Law and Human Rights Law', 293 IRRC (1993) 94; Cordula Droege, 'The Interplay between International Humanitarian Law and International Human Rights Law in Situations of Armed Conflict', 40 Isr Law Rev (2007).

[11] Daniel Bethlehem, 'The Relationship between International Humanitarian Law and International Human Rights Law in Situations of Armed Conflict', CJICL 2(2) (2013) 180–95.

[12] *Smith and Others v the Ministry of Defence* 66. Lord Hope considers the gravity of the issue thus: 'but subjecting the operations of the military while on active service to the close scrutiny that may be practicable and appropriate in the interests of safety in the barrack block or in the training area is an entirely different matter. It risks undermining the ability of a state to defend itself, or its interests, at home or abroad. The world is a dangerous place, and states cannot disable themselves from meeting its challenges. Ultimately democracy itself may be at risk.'

[13] Ekins, Morgan, and Tugendhat, 'Clearing the Fog of Law'.

[14] United Nations Human Rights Office of the High Commissioner, *International Legal Protection of Human Rights in Armed Conflict* (New York and Geneva 2011) 118.

conflict, parties to the conflict have legally binding obligations concerning the rights of persons affected by conflict'.[15] The purpose of this study is therefore to examine a discrete area concerning the applicability of human rights law during armed conflict that has not hitherto been considered in detail, namely, the recognition and scope of the right to life during international and non-international armed conflict.[16] Two issues will be addressed: first, when and how right to life obligations apply during armed conflict; second, the extent to which states can comply with these substantive and procedural right to life obligations by reference to current military doctrine and procedures.

The study is principally concerned with the applicability of the European Convention on Human Rights (ECHR), the International Covenant on Civil and Political Rights (ICCPR) and, where appropriate, national legislation relevant to the activities of armed forces. Despite the broad remit of most states' armed forces, the activities under consideration are limited to their participation in international and non-international armed conflict.[17] It is in these areas that a significant volume of litigation has arisen and that right to life issues are most commonly debated.[18] Both the substantive and procedural aspects of right to life obligations will be considered in respect of combatants and non-combatants in the area in which armed forces are operating, as well as members of the armed forces themselves. This study will not consider the relationship between the right to life and *jus ad bellum*, but rather is limited to an examination of a state's obligations once an armed conflict has commenced.[19]

In order to fully analyse a state's right to life obligations during armed conflict, the study is divided into four parts. Part I considers the nature of a state's substantive and procedural right to life obligations with reference to the ECHR and ICCPR. These obligations are considered in respect of both international and non-international armed conflict, and the positive and negative aspects of a state's right to life obligations are also determined. It is concluded that states have both substantive and procedural right to life obligations during armed conflict, although the ECHR and

[15] United Nations Human Rights High Commissioner's opening remarks at the Expert Consultation on the Protection of the Human Rights of Civilians in Armed Conflict, Geneva, 15 April 2009.

[16] The right to life obligations of states have been considered generally in Elizabeth Wicks, *The Right to Life and Conflicting Interests* (Oxford University Press 2010) chapter 4 and Peter Rowe, *The Impact of Human Rights Law on Armed Forces* (Cambridge University Press 2006). Discrete areas of the relationship between the right to life and international humanitarian law have also been considered in Stefan Oeter, 'Collateral Damages—Military Necessity and the Right to Life' and Vera Gowlland-Debbas, 'The Right to Life and the Relationship between Human Rights and Humanitarian Law' in Christian Tomuschat, Evelyne Lagrange, and Stefan Oeter (eds) *The Right to Life* (Nijhoff 2010) 167–94.

[17] For a consideration of the human rights obligations of peacekeepers see Kjetil Mujezinović Larsen, *The Human Rights Treaty Obligations of Peacekeepers* (Cambridge University Press 2014).

[18] This will include a consideration of cases that arose when UK armed forces were present in a country after the end of active hostilities. It is beyond the scope of this study, however, to consider the classification of armed conflicts and military occupation. These issues are addressed in detail in Elizabeth Wilmshurst (ed) *International Law and the Classification of Conflicts* (Oxford University Press 2012), specifically chapter 3 by Dapo Akande, 'Legal Concepts' 32–79.

[19] For a consideration of the relationship between the right to life and the *jus ad bellum* see William Schabas, 'The Right to Life' in Andrew Clapham and Paolo Gaeta (eds), *Oxford Handbook of International Law in Armed Conflict* (Oxford University Press 2013) 365.

ICCPR differ significantly in how these obligations are drafted, and the nature of the obligations thereby created. Equally, these obligations can be modified by reference to IHL—this issue is considered in Part II.

Part II considers the application of the right to life to situations of armed conflict. Despite the issue of the extraterritorial application of international human rights law treaties having been considered at some length both in monographs and in academic articles, it is submitted that this issue forms an essential prerequisite in a consideration of a state's right to life obligations during armed conflict. If jurisdiction could not be established then a state could not have any human rights law obligations when its armed forces operate overseas. All is far from settled, however, as even the briefest glance at the progression of *Serdar Mohammed v Ministry of Defence*[20] through the UK courts reveals. The specific contours of the circumstances in which jurisdiction arises when armed forces operate overseas continue to evolve through repeated judicial consideration. Chapter 3 therefore examines the current state of play in respect of the extraterritorial application of the ECHR and ICCPR.

Chapter 3 on the extraterritorial application of human rights law is followed by a detailed analysis of how the right to life applies during armed conflict. This begins with an analysis of a state's substantive right to life obligations. Implicit in this analysis is a consideration of the interaction between international humanitarian law (IHL) and international human rights law (IHRL) in respect of the use of lethal force. A structured approach to the analysis is taken in which the right to life obligations of states in the land, air, and maritime environments are considered. This includes the targeting processes employed, individual and collective self-defence (in the *jus in bello* sense), deaths during detention operations, and the right to life obligations of states during coalition operations, including when armed forces personnel are embedded with colleagues from other states. A determination is made in respect of the extent to which current NATO procedures comply with a member state's substantive right to life obligations. Once a state's substantive right to life obligations are analysed, the chapter turns to a consideration of the extent to which current state practice complies with the procedural element of the right to life. This analysis necessitates, inter alia, a consideration of states' military justice systems. The military justice system of the UK is used as a representative example.

Part II concludes with a consideration of the right to life obligations of states in respect of their own armed forces personnel during armed conflict. The specific details of when and how these obligations arise are analysed, and the level of compliance, based on current state practice, is determined.

Given the declaration of the UK government[21] in respect of the use of derogations to relevant human rights law provisions during future armed conflicts, Part III is dedicated to an analysis of this issue. The scope and limitations of the use of derogations are examined in detail, and it is submitted that entering derogations is far from

[20] *Serdar Mohammed & Others v Ministry of Defence* [2017] UKSC 2.

[21] The UK government's intention to derogate, subject to certain criteria, can be found at https://www.parliament.uk/business/committees/committees-a-z/joint-select/human-rights-committee/inquiries/parliament-2015/government-proposed-echr-derogation-16-17/ (accessed 6 November 2017).

a panacea to prevent the unwelcome encroachment, as some see it, of human rights law into armed conflict. The applicability of any derogation pursuant to Article 15, ECHR requires an analysis of the nature of the military activity undertaken and the relationship between IHL and IHRL, given that any derogation is only applicable insofar as it relates to 'deaths resulting from lawful acts of war', as determined and regulated by IHL.

The study concludes with Part IV, which considers how states can ensure compliance with their substantive and procedural right to life obligations during armed conflict. Moreover, it is submitted that while complying with the aforementioned obligations would have resource implications for states and armed forces during armed conflict, it would not adversely affect a military commander's ability to achieve their military objectives.

In analysing a state's right to life obligations the principal area of focus will be the ECHR, for two reasons. First, the jurisprudence in this area is well developed, has been considered during international[22] and non-international[23] armed conflict, and is being adopted by domestic courts.[24] Second, in related circumstances, the UK has adapted its military doctrine and procedures in light of ECtHR judgments indicating a willingness to comply with the judgments of the Court.[25] The Universal Declaration of Human Rights will be briefly considered by way of background, and right to life obligations pursuant to Article 6, ICCPR will be analysed both in isolation and in comparison to Article 2, ECHR.

Substantive right to life obligations, both positive and negative, will be considered and the extent to which states can ensure compliance during armed conflict assessed. In determining substantive right to life obligations, a structured approach is required that takes into account a number of factors. These include the classification of the armed conflict, a state's role in it, and the specific circumstances in which military personnel are operating. With respect to non-international armed conflict, there is considerable debate regarding the extent to which a human rights-based law enforcement paradigm or international humanitarian law is applicable to regulate the use of lethal force.[26] Equally, there is also debate as to what amounts to membership of an armed group and direct participation in hostilities, with the ICRC and certain commentators taking different positions.[27] It is submitted, therefore,

[22] See, for example, *Hassan v the United Kingdom*. Tarek Hassan was arrested by UK armed forces in April 2003, prior to the end of active hostilities in Iraq on 1 May 2003.

[23] See, for example, *Isayeva v Russia*.

[24] See, for example, *Smith and Others v Ministry of Defence* and *Al-Saadoon and Others v Secretary of State for Defence*.

[25] The entire courts martial system was amended following an ECtHR judgment in *Grieves v the United Kingdom*, Application no 31821/96 (ECtHR, 16 November 2004) and major modifications were made following an ECtHR judgment in *Findlay v the United Kingdom* [1997] 24 EHRR 221.

[26] A range of views can be seen in 'Expert Meeting: The Use of Force in Armed Conflicts: Interplay between the Conduct of Hostilities and Law Enforcement Paradigms', Report prepared and edited by Gloria Gaggioli, legal adviser, ICRC, November 2013, <https://www.icrc.org/eng/assets/files/publications/icrc-002-4171.pdf> (accessed 8 November 2017).

[27] To illustrate see ICRC, *Interpretive Guidance on the Notion of Direct Participation in Hostilities under International Humanitarian Law* (ICRC, May 2009) 34 and Sandesh Sivakumaran, *The Law of Non-International Armed Conflict* (Oxford University Press 2012) 360.

that it may not be possible to simply transpose to non-international armed conflict the conclusions reached regarding the relationship between international humanitarian law and the right to life obligations of states in human rights law in respect of the regulation of the use of lethal force in international armed conflicts. As a consequence, the relationship between international humanitarian law and human rights law in international and non-international armed conflict will be considered separately.

The interaction of international humanitarian law and human rights law must be assessed with reference to the use of lethal force across the spectrum of military activity in order to closely examine how the bodies of law interact and where any differences exist. Only then can the scope of specific obligations be determined. Put simply, where right to life obligations exist, there must be consideration of whether they are to be interpreted with reference to extant international humanitarian law principles governing the use of lethal force during armed conflict or if they create separate obligations beyond that required by international humanitarian law. Where right to life obligations arise following the use of lethal force by states, without explicit reference to international humanitarian law—as the ECtHR has asserted in certain 'Chechen cases'[28]—the extent to which adherence to international humanitarian law principles regulating the use of lethal force would have prevented a violation must be addressed. In other words: does a violation of the right to life also violate the international humanitarian law governing the use of lethal force, and vice versa? Addressing this issue will require a consideration of the interaction between the two bodies of law in specific scenarios. A range of military environments will be considered, including the air and maritime, but with a focus on the use of lethal force in land targeting and deaths in military detention. It is in these areas that right to life obligations most frequently arise and have been litigated. The relationship between the use of lethal force in self-defence and right to life obligations will also be considered.

The study will not be limited to substantive right to life obligations, but will also assess what procedural right to life obligations exist during armed conflict. As an illustrative example, the extent to which the UK's numerous investigatory procedures comply with this requirement will be considered. This involves a consideration of the scope of a state's procedural right to life obligations that exist beyond merely conducting an investigation and include, for example, prosecuting and punishing offenders. It will again be necessary to examine the relationship between international humanitarian law and human rights law in respect of the circumstances that necessitate an investigation following the use of lethal force, and this is done in Chapter 4. As the requirement to conduct an investigation pursuant to international humanitarian law is not as widely applicable, nor the investigation itself arguably as comprehensive, as the procedural element of the right to life, it may not be possible to simply interpret a state's procedural right to life obligations with reference to international humanitarian law. First, the extent to which international

[28] *Isayeva, Yusupova and Basayeva v Russia*, Application no 57947-9/00 (ECtHR, 24 February 2005; *Isayeva v Russia*.

humanitarian law requires an investigation following the use of lethal force in both international and non-international armed conflict must be determined as an essential prerequisite in analysing the state's procedural right to life obligations. Second, the extent to which procedural right to life obligations can be modified during armed conflict must be assessed before a comparison of the two legal frameworks can be undertaken.

Once the applicable legal framework regulating a state's obligations to conduct an investigation following the use of lethal force has been determined, it can then be used to assess the extent to which the UK can comply with this requirement. This will necessitate, inter alia, a consideration of the investigatory procedures employed by UK armed forces during armed conflict and by the military justice system in both its investigatory and prosecutorial functions.

Despite the significant volume of academic literature on the issue of the extraterritorial application of human rights treaties and its repeated consideration by the ECtHR and domestic courts, this topic still has the capacity to excite and is not entirely settled.[29] While the basic proposition of the general applicability of human rights treaties to armed conflict is now widely accepted, the exact nature of how individuals come within the jurisdiction of states remains keenly debated. In *Al-Saadoon*,[30] for example, Leggatt J devoted 85 paragraphs to the issue; he concluded that 'shooting someone involves the exercise of physical power over that person'[31] and, when combined with a situation where British forces were 'exercising public powers that would normally be exercised by the government of Iraq',[32] this would bring that person within the jurisdiction of Article 1, ECHR. By way of further illustration, the ECtHR was required, for the first time, to consider discrete issues[33] of military command and control in determining the jurisdictional scope of the ECHR in *Jaloud*.[34] As the first stage in assessing the extent of the UK's right to life obligations during armed conflict, it is necessary to resolve the question of the extraterritorial jurisdiction under the relevant human rights treaties. This must be determined with reference to those who come into contact with UK armed forces operating overseas and members of the armed forces themselves.

The focus of this study will be limited to the right to life obligations of the UK government, although the analysis of the extraterritorial application of the ECHR in Chapter 3 and the consideration of the relationship between international humanitarian law and human rights law in Chapter 4 will apply equally to other ECHR states parties. It is recognized that in certain circumstances, non-state actors may

[29] For an excellent consideration of the issues see Guy S Goodwin-Gill, 'The Extra-Territorial Reach of Human Rights Obligations: A Brief Perspective on the Link to Jurisdiction' in L Boisson de Chazournes and M Kohen (eds), *International Law and the Quest for Its Implementation/Le droit international et la quête de as mise en œvre, Liber Amicorum Vera Gowlland-Debbas* (Brill/Martinus Nijhoff, 2010) 293.

[30] *Al-Saadoon and Others v Secretary of State for Defence* 32–137.

[31] Ibid, 294.

[32] Ibid.

[33] This can be compared to overall military command and control that the ECtHR considered in, for example, *Bankovic and Others v Belgium and 16 Other Contracting States*, Application no 52207/99 (ECtHR, 12 December 2001) (Grand Chamber).

[34] *Jaloud v the Netherlands*.

have human rights obligations,[35] but such considerations are beyond the scope of this study. Similarly, it is also recognized that in directly applying human rights law to armed conflict, potential limitations exist in relation to the equality of belligerents, as human rights treaties bind only states.[36] It is therefore important to determine the extent of the UK's substantive and procedural right to life obligations and how, if at all, they differ from their obligations pursuant to international humanitarian law regulating the use of lethal force during armed conflict. A central pillar of the argument for the non-applicability of human rights law in armed conflict falls away if it can be demonstrated that substantive right to life obligations of states during armed conflict are not incompatible with their international humanitarian law obligations.

Derogating from a state's right to life obligations in times of war or where circumstances threaten the life of the nation has been cited as a viable option in order to limit the effect of human rights law and therefore avoid unnecessarily encumbering armed forces.[37] Following an analysis of the relationship between international humanitarian law and human rights law, Chapter 6 explores the circumstances in which a state can derogate from its right to life obligations and the effect that this will have. State practice and judgments of the ECtHR and domestic courts form an integral part of this analysis. Clearly, this analysis will be focused on the ECHR, given that the right to life in ICCPR (Article 6, ICCPR) is a non-derogable provision (Article 4(2), ICCPR).

Consideration of the relationship between international humanitarian law and human rights law is again necessary in order to determine the purported advantage that would be gained by derogating from a state's right to life obligations. If, during armed conflict, a right to life violation can only arise where there is a breach of international humanitarian law, derogating from a state's right to life obligations may have only limited effect. Equally, however, if it is asserted that killings in armed conflict that do not violate international humanitarian law also do not violate Article 2, ECHR then Article 15(2), ECHR, which provides for derogations with respect to lawful acts of war, may become redundant. This in turn may violate a principle of treaty interpretation that prohibits reading treaty texts such as to make clauses redundant.[38]

[35] Andrew Clapham, *Human Rights Obligations and Non-State Actors* (Oxford University Press 2006); Philip Alston, *Human Rights and Non-State Actors* (Oxford University Press 2005).

[36] Sandesh Sivakumaran, 'Re-Envisaging the International Law of Internal Armed Conflict', EJIL 22 (2011) 240.

[37] Ekins, Morgan, and Tugendhat, 'Clearing the Fog of Law'.

[38] Article 31, Vienna Convention on the Law of Treaties (entered into force 27 January 1980) is widely accepted to consider that meaning and effect must be given to all the terms of a treaty: 'an interpreter is not free to adopt a reading that would result in reducing whole clauses or paragraphs of a treaty to redundancy or inutility'. Appellate Body Report, *United States—Standards for Reformulated and Conventional Gasoline (US—Gasoline)*, WT/052/AB/R, adopted 20 May 1996, 21. Moreover, Article 31 VCLT is generally recognized as reflecting customary international law: see *Case Concerning the Territorial Dispute (Libyan Arab Jamahiriya/Chad)* Judgment [1994] ICJ Rep 21, 41; *Case Concerning Oil Platforms (Islamic Republic of Iran/United States of America)* Preliminary Objections, Judgment, [1996] (II) ICJ Rep 812, 23; and specifically in respect of Article 31.3, *Case Concerning Kasikli/Sedudu Island*, Judgment, [1994] ICJ Rep 1045, 48.

The effect of entering a derogation on a state's procedural right to life obligations must also be considered, and two possible scenarios emerge. First, the effect of derogating from the right to life in times of armed conflict may remove the requirement to conduct an investigation pursuant to the procedural aspect of Article 2, ECHR. This would not, however, mean the incident would not be investigated at all. Clearly, the requirements of UK criminal law, the military justice system, and obligations pursuant to the Rome Statute remain. Alternatively, however, if the derogation is only effective with reference to international humanitarian law, this may leave scope for the applicability of human rights law if the international humanitarian law provisions in respect of an investigation and other procedural requirements following a death during armed conflict are inadequate. In other words, there may be scope for the application of procedural right to life obligations where international humanitarian law does not provide an adequate investigatory framework.

In addressing the issues under consideration, the study will draw upon jurisprudential consideration of this area by domestic and supranational courts, international legal scholarship, proclamations of various United Nations human rights bodies, the International Committee of the Red Cross (ICRC), and, as an essential element in assessing compliance with its obligations, the practice of the UK government and armed forces in recent military campaigns. The analysis of the UK government's approach to its right to life obligations will be informed by, inter alia, state practice, military doctrine, rules of engagement, targeting and tactical directives, tactics, techniques, and procedures. The UK's litigation strategy in a number of cases emerging from the conflicts in Iraq and Afghanistan, as well as the establishment of public inquiries and the Iraq Historic Allegations Team and Iraq Historic Allegations Prosecution Team, will also be considered. In addition, the UK's contribution to NATO's Operation Unified Protector in Libya in 2011 and its ongoing contribution to the response to the threat of Islamic State in Northern Iraq and Syria will be considered where applicable.

In certain quarters,[39] the encroachment, as they see it, of human rights law into the hitherto exclusive domain of international humanitarian law has had catastrophic consequences on a state's ability to conduct military operations and has been to the 'benefit of our ... adversaries'.[40] One of the most significant areas of concern is in relation to a state's right to life obligations both in respect of those individuals in the area where armed forces are operating and of the armed forces themselves. This study seeks to assuage some of those concerns and argues that the effect of recognizing right to life obligations, when interpreted through the principles of international humanitarian law in armed conflict, does not impose a significant burden upon states and military commanders beyond that which already governs the use of lethal force. It is further contended that international humanitarian law and human rights law can mutually complement each other and enable military objectives to be achieved while ensuring the requisite protection for those entitled to it.

39 Ekins, Morgan, and Tugendhat, 'Clearing the Fog of Law'.

40 Ibid, 7.

Ultimately, this study advances three propositions. The first is that the states should adopt a general proposition that, as a matter of the extraterritorial application of the ECHR and ICCPR, the state has right to life obligations during international and non-international armed conflict. Second, substantive right to life obligations are modified by international humanitarian law principles governing the use of lethal force to the extent that a violation of the state's substantive right to life obligations can only occur in circumstances where there has been a violation of the applicable international humanitarian law governing the use of lethal force. Procedural right to life obligations cannot, however, be modified to the same extent, although it is submitted that procedural obligations are only applicable, in respect of those killed on the battlefield, where there has been an alleged violation of international humanitarian law. Generally speaking, deaths in custody from consequences other than enemy action or deaths of states' armed forces personnel geographically removed from the battlefield will invoke the state's procedural right to life obligations. Finally, as a consequence, recognizing a state's substantive right to life obligations pursuant to the ECHR or ICCPR does not have a dramatically adverse effect on the ability of armed forces to achieve their military objectives during armed conflict. In respect of a state's procedural ECHR right to life obligations, however, states will have obligations to investigate beyond those required by IHL. With reference to the UK, for example, current doctrine must be amended to both reflect the state's procedural right to life obligations and comply with them. Equally, the ability to conduct investigations during armed conflict ought to be sufficiently resourced as an essential prerequisite in ensuring compliance with the state's procedural right to life obligations. These requirements, it is submitted, are not unduly onerous and do not risk adversely affecting the ability of a state's armed forces to operate effectively during armed conflict.

PART I

THE SCOPE OF THE RIGHT TO LIFE

1

Substantive Right to Life Obligations

1.1 Introduction

The International Covenant on Civil and Political Rights (ICCPR) and European Convention on Human Rights (ECHR) both contain clauses recognizing the right to life. The clauses are, however, drafted differently. In respect of the substantive element, the ICCPR creates an exception to the right to life by stating that 'no one shall be *arbitrarily* deprived of his life'[1] without specifically identifying what amounts to an arbitrary deprivation of life. The ECHR, on the other hand, is more prescriptive. In Article 2(2), exceptions to the right to life are set out in detail and are exhaustive.[2] Additionally, unlike the right to life provision in the ICCPR, Article 2, ECHR is subject to a derogation clause contained in Article 15 that can be exercised by states 'in time of war or other public emergency threatening the life of the nation ... to the extent strictly required by the exigencies of the situation, provided that such measures are not inconsistent with its other obligations under international law'.[3]

The right to life clauses in the ICCPR and ECHR have also been interpreted to have a procedural as well as a substantive element. The Human Rights Committee and European Court of Human Rights (ECtHR) have reasoned that substantive right to life protections would be ineffective without a procedure for reviewing the lawfulness of the use of lethal force by states. The purpose of this chapter is to examine the nature of both the substantive and procedural aspects of the right to life clauses in the ICCPR and ECHR. This is a necessary prerequisite to an analysis of how the right to life interacts with the applicable international humanitarian law regulating the use of lethal force in armed conflict.[4] Equally, the ECtHR has considered alleged violations of a state's substantive[5] and

[1] Article 6(1), ICCPR.

[2] Article 2(2), ECHR:

> Deprivation of life shall not be regarded as inflicted in contravention of this Article when it results from the use of force which is no more than absolutely necessary:
> (a) in defence of any person from unlawful violence;
> (b) in order to effect a lawful arrest or to prevent the escape of a person lawfully detained;
> (c) in action lawfully taken for the purpose of quelling a riot or insurrection.

[3] Article 15(1), ECHR. [4] See Chapter 4.

[5] See for example, *Isayeva v Russia*, Application no 57950/00 (ECtHR, 24 February 2005); *Isayeva, Yusupova and Bazayeva v Russia*, Application nos 57947–49/00 (ECtHR, 24 February 2005).

procedural[6] right to life obligations during armed conflict[7] without any reference to international humanitarian law. It is important therefore to explore how the right to life is protected and when the use of lethal force would not violate a state's right to life obligations. Prior to an examination of the ICCPR and ECHR, the role of the Universal Declaration of Human Rights (UDHR) in establishing the foundations for the codification of the right to life will be briefly considered.

1.2 The Universal Declaration of Human Rights

Article 3 of the UDHR establishes that 'Everyone has the right to life, liberty and security.' While not designed to be legally enforceable, the UDHR was in the vanguard of recognizing and protecting the right to life.[8] Moreover, it provided the foundation for the legal enforceable right enshrined in both the ECHR and ICCPR. Given its status as one of the founding documents of human rights and its pivotal role in influencing the development and codification of subsequent international instruments, the UDHR is justifiably considered to form part of customary international law.[9] Of some significance is that it is a document borne out of conflict and therefore conceived of and drafted against a background of war and suffering. The UDHR drafting committee drew heavily upon the War Crimes Commission report[10] to elucidate the pivotal significance of the right to life and to reject the contempt in which it was held by the Nazi regime.[11] While no doubt aspirational, and thus not without criticism,[12] the UDHR places the right to life firmly at its core and considers it to be inherent for every human being.[13]

[6] *Al-Skeini and Others v the United Kingdom*, Application no 55721/07 (ECtHR, 7 July 2011); *Jaloud v the Netherlands*, Application no 47708/08 (ECtHR, 20 November 2014).

[7] It is recognized that in *Isayeva* the ECtHR did not specifically state the circumstances in which the substantive right to life violations occurred was an armed conflict, but it is submitted that a compelling case can be made that it was.

[8] Article 1 of the American Declaration of the Rights and Duties of Man (*Bogota Declaration*, April 1948) as agreed by the Organization of American States stated that 'Every human being has the right to life, liberty and the security of his person.'

[9] 'The UDHR was proclaimed by the General Assembly on 10 December 1948 and since then is widely regarded as forming part of customary international law'—unchr.org, Digital Record of the UDHR February 2009, <http://www.ohchr.org/EN/NEWSEVENTS/Pages/DigitalrecordoftheUDHR.aspx>. accessed 15 May 2014; JP Humphrey, 'The Universal Declaration of Human Rights: Its History, Impact and Juridical Character' in BG Ramcharan (ed), *Human Rights: Thirty Years After the Universal Declaration* (Springer 1979) 21, 37; I Sohn, 'The Human Rights Law of the Charter' (1977) 12 Texas Int LJ 129, 133; Myres S McDougal, Harold Lasswell, and Lung-Chu Chen, *Human Rights and World Public Order: The Basic Policies of an International Law of Human Dignity* (Yale University Press 1980) 273–74, 325–27; Anthony D'Amato, *International Law: Process and Prospect* (Dobbs Ferry New York 1987) 123–47.

[10] 'Information concerning Human Rights arising from Trials of War Criminals' (E/CN.4/W.20).

[11] Ibid.

[12] Simpson considers the UDHR to 'represent little more than an exhalation of pious hot air': AWB Simpson, *Human Rights and the End of Empire: Britain and the Genesis of the European Convention* (Oxford University Press 2001) 11.

[13] 'Recognition of the inherent dignity and of the equal and inalienable rights of all members of the human family is the foundation of freedom, justice and peace in the world': UDHR Preamble.

The rights enshrined in the UDHR are not all without qualification. The use of the term 'arbitrary' can be found in Articles 9,[14] 12,[15] 15,[16] and 17,[17] and will recur in the ICCPR to limit and qualify the hitherto unrestrained proclamation of the right to life in Article 3, UDHR. At this stage, however, the UDHR drafting committee did not consider it necessary to elucidate further on the right to life by affording special protection to specific groups or to in any way place restrictions or qualifications upon the right. With respect to its status as a non-legally binding document, the committee felt that its influence and effect would be more considerable if it was declaratory rather than purposive and binding.[18] As such, the language used is not as prescriptive and the articles not as tightly drafted as subsequent conventions and covenants. That said, as Lauren[19] contends, because the UDHR can be seen as the starting point for the development of international human rights law generally, and the right to life specifically, its significance cannot be understated. Nor can the assertion that it 'enormously accelerated the evolution of international human rights'[20] be convincingly challenged. The obvious similarities and common themes within the ECHR and ICCPR, as well as the mutually reinforcing nature of the documents, can be traced back to the UDHR. There are, however, distinct and notable differences between the ECHR and ICCPR with respect to the right to life.

1.3 The International Covenant on Civil and Political Rights

The International Covenant on Civil and Political Rights was adopted by the General Assembly of the United Nations in Resolution 2200 (XI) on 16 December 1966. The relevant provision on the right to life (Article 6) reads:

> 1. Every human being has the inherent right to life.
> This right shall be protected by law. No one shall be
> arbitrarily deprived of his life.

The basic concept of an inherent right to life as enunciated in the first sentence of Article 6(1) attracted significant support in the Third Committee of the General

[14] Article 9: 'No one shall be subjected to arbitrary arrest, detention or exile.'

[15] Article 12: 'No one shall be subjected to arbitrary interference with his privacy, family, home or correspondence, nor to attacks upon his honour and reputation. Everyone has the right to the protection of the law against such interference or attacks.'

[16] Article 15(2): 'No one shall be arbitrarily deprived of his nationality nor denied the right to change his nationality.'

[17] Article 17(2): 'No one shall be arbitrarily deprived of his property.'

[18] JP Humphrey, 'The Universal Declaration of Human Rights: Its History, Impact and Juridical Character' in Ramcharan (ed), *Human Rights* (Springer 1979) 37.

[19] PG Lauren, *The Evolution of International Human Rights: Visions Seen* (2nd edn, University of Pennsylvania Press 2003) 239.

[20] Ibid.

Assembly.[21] Analysis of the *travaux préparatoires*[22] reveals that the notion of an 'inherent' right to life proposed by the Colombian and Uruguayan delegations was considered attractive and not only reflected the UDHR and the American Declaration of the Rights and Duties of Man, but also recognized the right as a duty owed by society and states to the individual.

During the drafting process of the ICCPR, the right to life was considered to be the supreme human right,[23] as Nowak contends that 'without effective guarantee of this right, all other rights of the human being would be devoid of meaning'.[24] Taking a more expansive view, it has been considered by some to be *jus cogens.*[25] Notwithstanding the obvious difficulties in respect of such a *jus cogens* notion not only with reference to Article 15, ECHR derogation but also to state practice,[26] it is recognized that the right to life is of fundamental significance in the international legal arena. Such a view is further supported by the ICCPR in that it is the only right that is given the declaratory adjective 'inherent'[27] beyond the initial draft.[28] In turn, therefore—and reflecting the wishes of the Human Rights Committee[29] created by the ICCPR[30]—it is a right that must be positively enforced and protected.[31] Importantly, however, following considerable debate and redrafting,[32] the right to life was not considered by the drafting committee to be an absolute right, but rather one that was limited in certain circumstances. This therefore necessitated the committee's consideration of the circumstances in which individuals could be deprived of the right and, as a corollary, the mechanisms by which a state must take positive steps to ensure and enforce the right.

1.3.1 States' duty to ensure the right to life under Article 6(1)—a positive and negative obligation

Nowak's[33] analysis of the right to life reveals a desire on the part of the majority of delegates to give Article 6 horizontal effect. This reflects the significance of the right

[21] This was adopted by a vote of sixty-five in favour to three against, with four abstentions. The objections and abstentions were not due to the content of the proposal, but rather that, given that it was merely a declaratory statement, it ought not to be in a legal document. MJ Bossuyt, *Guide to the 'Travaux Préparatoires' of the International Covenant on Civil and Political Rights* (Martinus Nijhoff 1987) 119.

[22] Third Committee, 12th Session (1957), A/3764, section 112.

[23] Manfred Nowak, *United Nations Covenant on Civil and Political Rights CCPR Commentary* (2nd revised edn, NP Engel, 2005) 121. In its General Comment no 6 [16] adopted at its 378th meeting on 27 July 1982, the Human Rights Committee observed that the right to life enunciated in the first paragraph of article 6 of the International Covenant on Civil and Political Rights is the supreme right from which no derogation is permitted even in time of public emergency.

[24] Nowak, *United Nations Covenant* 121.

[25] BG Ramcharan (ed), *The Right to Life in International Law* (Martinus Nijhoff 1985) 297.

[26] For example, significant numbers of states, including the United States, retain the death penalty for a wide range of criminal offences.

[27] Nowak, *United Nations Covenant* 121.

[28] Cf Article 6 of the text enacted by the Human Rights Committee in 1954, in E/2573, 66; Nowak, *United Nations Covenant* 122.

[29] Dominic McGoldrick, *The Human Rights Committee: Its Role in the Development of the International Covenant on Civil and Political Rights* (Clarendon Press 1994) 329.

[30] ICCPR, Part IV.

[31] McGoldrick, *The Human Rights Committee* 329.

[32] Ibid.

[33] Nowak, *United Nations Covenant* 121.

and goes beyond what a number of states, including the United States, had envisioned for its recognition. Additionally, the committee stated that 'the protection of this right [Article 6(1), ICCPR] requires that States adopt positive measures',[34] and even at this early stage it was anticipated that breaches of the state's right to life obligations ought to result in a remedy and reparation for individuals.[35] Moreover, the relevance of international humanitarian law and its interaction with international human rights law was clearly contemplated in respect of a state's obligation to prevent war, genocide, and other forms of mass violence.[36] Equally, cognizance was given to the procedural element of the right to life with reference to a state's obligation to conduct an investigation where deaths are attributable to the state.[37]

While not explicitly stated, it is apparent that the right to life as conceived of by the ICCPR drafting committee consists of a substantive and a procedural element. The substantive element is the positive obligation on the state to protect the right to life and the negative element not to take life 'arbitrarily'.[38] The procedural element is ensuring an independent mechanism exists to investigate alleged violations and take remedial action if required. Nowak emphasizes the procedural element in the following terms: 'a violation of the obligation to protect flowing from Article 6(1) can be assumed only where state legislation is lacking altogether or when it is manifestly insufficient as measured against the actual threat'.[39] Dinstein[40] adopts a more restrictive interpretation of Article 6(1), stating that 'the right to life, in effect, is the right to be safeguarded against (arbitrary) killings'.[41] On either construction, however, it is necessary to consider, first, the precise scope and meaning of the term 'arbitrary'; second, if the activities of the armed forces that involve the taking of life can be considered *non-arbitrary* and, if so, what safeguards must be in place to ensure the actions of armed forces are not arbitrary; and finally, what mechanisms[42] the UK government has to give effect to the Article 6 right with specific reference to the activities of the armed forces.

1.3.2 Definition of the right to life

The right to life is considered to be an inherent right, one protected by law and which people are not to be deprived of, save for in exceptional circumstances. The Human Rights Committee has even found violations of the right to life in circumstances

[34] GenC 6/16, § 5.

[35] 'Basic Principles and Guidelines on the Right to a Remedy and Reparation for Victims of Violations of International Human Rights and Humanitarian Law', E/CN.4/2000/62.

[36] GenC 6/16, § 2, 4. [37] Ibid. [38] Article 6(1), ICCPR.

[39] Nowak, *United Nations Covenant*, 121.

[40] Y Dinstein, 'The Right to Life, Physical Integrity and Liberty' in L Henkin (ed), *The International Bill of Rights* (Columbia University Press 1981) 114.

[41] Ibid.

[42] As a minimum requirement, Nowak and Ramcharan contend that this will require prohibitive norms under criminal law.

where attempts have been made on the life of an individual that resulted in them sustaining life-threatening wounds, but ultimately surviving.[43]

1.3.3 The limitations of Article 6, ICCPR—a prohibition of the *arbitrary* deprivation of life

An analysis of the *travaux préparatoires*[44] reveals that in the drafting of Article 6(1), the committee encountered difficulties when endeavouring to define the scope of the right to life,[45] and in particular regarding the meaning of the term 'arbitrarily'. This issue was not unique, however, as similar difficulties had beset the main drafters prior to this when defining the terms of the UDHR. A number of states supported a notion that the ECHR should be considered a useful benchmark and the term '*intentional* deprivation of life' ought to be adopted as the term 'arbitrarily' was considered too vague. Conversely, it was contended that the term 'arbitrarily' was broader and therefore more encompassing than 'intentional' and, as Nowak contends, 'obviated the problem of having to list all cases of permissible deprivation of life'.[46] The debate continued into the Third Committee of the General Assembly,[47] where the term 'arbitrarily' was again criticized for being too vague and for containing elements of '*unlawfulness* and *injustice*, as well as those of *capriciousness* and *unreasonableness*'.[48] Ultimately, however, the committee attempted to resolve these drafting difficulties by providing guidance that the right to life itself, as opposed to the term 'arbitrarily deprived of his life', must not be interpreted narrowly.[49] Furthermore, the *travaux préparatoires* illustrate a desire on the part of some delegates to agree on a term that went beyond a strictly legal construct.[50] As Ramacharan contends, the term 'arbitrary was chosen with the intention to provide the highest possible level of protection and confine permissible deprivations to the narrowest of limits'.[51] This, however, did not obviate the difficulties in terminology, and an analysis of the relationship between the terms 'arbitrary deprivation' and 'unlawful deprivation' is required to further clarify the scope of Article 6(1).

1.3.4 The relationship between 'arbitrary deprivation' and 'unlawful deprivation' of life

In accordance with the guidance of the Human Rights Committee, it is contended that the term 'arbitrary deprivation' of life is a broader and more encompassing notion than that of 'unlawful deprivation' of life.[52] Support for such a view can be traced back to the UDHR, where the Third Committee considered that the term

[43] *Chongwe v Zambia*, Communication no 821/1998.
[44] Nowak, *United Nations Covenant* 121. [45] Ibid. [46] Ibid.
[47] A/C.3/L.651. [48] E/CN.4/SR.310, § 9; Nowak, *United Nations Covenant* 128.
[49] Nowak, *United Nations Covenant* 128.
[50] Third Committee's 5th (1950), 9th (1954), and 12th (1957) Sessions in Bossuyt, *Travaux Préparatoires* 123–24.
[51] Ibid, 19. [52] McGoldrick, *The Human Rights Committee* 343.

'arbitrary' had a broader meaning than the term 'illegal'.[53] Analysis of the text of the ICCPR does, however, reveal a contradictory picture and inconsistent use of the terms 'arbitrary' and 'arbitrarily'. In addition to Article 6(1), the terms 'arbitrary' and 'arbitrarily' are used on three other occasions in the ICCPR: Article 9,[54] Article 12,[55] and Article 17.[56]

In Article 9, having made reference to 'arbitrary arrest or detention', the remainder of the article further defines the scope and meaning of the right to liberty and security of person. This is not an exclusively legal construct in which the right is only enforced through the judicial process.[57] It is therefore evident that the term 'arbitrary' encompasses 'unlawfulness' within the context of the right to liberty and security of person, but goes beyond it to consider 'elements of inappropriateness, injustice and lack of predictability'.[58] In Article 12(4) the term 'arbitrarily' is also considered and defined beyond a strictly legal dimension when read in conjunction with Article 12(3):

> The above-mentioned rights shall not be subject to any restrictions except those which are provided by law, are necessary to *protect national security, public order* (ordre public), *public health or morals or the rights and freedoms of others*, and are consistent with the other rights recognized in the present Covenant. [my emphasis][59]

The reference in Article 12(3) to national security, morals, and the freedoms of others, it is contended, takes the definition of 'arbitrarily' beyond the strict dimensions of law and introduces further elements of morality and, significantly, the notion of conflicting human rights considerations. Further support for this proposition can be found in Article 17(1), where the terms 'arbitrarily' and 'unlawful' are used as alternatives in the following terms: 'No one shall be subjected to arbitrary or unlawful interference with his privacy, family, home or correspondence, nor to unlawful attacks on his honour and reputation.' The use of the term 'arbitrary' in this clause is not superfluous, but rather demonstrates that the right under consideration is to be construed beyond the strict legal dimension. The presence of the term 'arbitrarily'

[53] P Hassan, 'The Word "Arbitrary" as Used in the Universal Declaration of Human Rights: "Illegal" or "Unjust"?' 10 Harv Int LJ (1969) 243–46.

[54] Article 9(1), ICCPR: 'Everyone has the right to liberty and security of person. No one shall be subjected to arbitrary arrest or detention. No one shall be deprived of his liberty except on such grounds and in accordance with such procedure as are established by law.'

[55] Article 12(4), ICCPR: 'No one shall be arbitrarily deprived of the right to enter his own country.'

[56] Article 17(1), ICCPR: 'No one shall be subjected to arbitrary or unlawful interference with his privacy, family, home or correspondence, nor to unlawful attacks on his honour and reputation. (2) Everyone has the right to the protection of the law against such interference or attacks.'

[57] *Hugo van Alphen v the Netherlands*, Communication no 305/1988, UN Doc CCPR/C/39/D/305/1988 (1990) 5.8:

> The drafting history of article 9, paragraph 1, confirms that 'arbitrariness' is not to be equated with 'against the law', but must be interpreted more broadly to include elements of inappropriateness, injustice and lack of predictability. This means that remand in custody pursuant to lawful arrest must not only be lawful but reasonable in all the circumstances. Further, remand in custody must be necessary in all the circumstances, for example, to prevent flight, interference with evidence or the recurrence of crime.

[58] Ibid. [59] Article 12(3), ICCPR.

in Article 6 is therefore of considerable practical significance in specifying the scope of the right.

1.3.5 Arbitrary deprivation of life—international standards and national laws

In order to afford individuals the greatest protection with reference to Article 6 and recognize the intent of the Human Rights Committee when drafting the ICCPR, it is considered important that the term 'arbitrary deprivation of life' is defined by international human rights standards and not national laws.[60] Such an approach is advantageous in that a reliance on national laws to interpret the term risks the danger of vastly differing standards in the protections afforded by a supranational human rights instrument, the critical issue being a narrow interpretation of 'arbitrary deprivation of life' by national authorities. Such an approach is, however, not without difficulties, given the paucity of guidance provided by the Human Rights Committee. This inevitably leads to a consideration of the issue on a case-by-case basis in order to establish a degree of clarity and some overarching principles.

1.4 The Substantive Element of Article 6, ICCPR

Attempts have been made by commentators[61] to further define the exceptions to the Article 6 right to life and compile circumstances that would amount to an arbitrary deprivation of life. While many of the circumstances cited[62] are self-evident, such an exercise fails to recognize the subtleties and legal analysis involved in the assessment of whether, in all the circumstances, the actions of the state agents amounted to an arbitrary deprivation of life. By way of illustration, in a law enforcement scenario the assessment may turn on the perceived threat to life to the state agents based upon the actions of those under suspicion of criminal activity. Such a scenario depends upon an assessment of individual cases and the *reasonableness* of the actions of those concerned, and not a blanket determination of the activities that amount to *arbitrarily* depriving someone of their life. Further, when considering the substantive element of Article 6(1) the committee has applied a *proportionality* assessment with respect to, for example, the exigencies and requirements of law enforcement.

The Human Rights Committee has applied such a *reasonableness* and *proportionality* analysis in, inter alia, individual communications concerning state agents from Colombia, Suriname, Uruguay, Zambia, and Zaire.[63] By way of illustration, in

[60] Roland Otto, *Targeted Killings and International Law* (Springer 2010) 61.

[61] Ramcharan (ed), *The Right to Life in International Law* 316.

[62] For example, genocide, death following torture, or excessive use of force by state agents.

[63] *Maria Fanny Suarez de Guerrero v Colombia*, Communication no R.11/45, UN Doc Supp No 40 (A/37/40) at 137 (1982); *Herrera Rubio v Colombia*, Communication no 161/1983; *Baboeram, et al v Suriname*, nos 146, 148–154/1983; *Bleier v Uruguay*, Communication no 30/1978; *Dermit Barbato v Uruguay*, Communication no 84/1981; *Chongwe v Zambia*, Communication no 821/1998; *Miango Muiyo v Zaire*, Communication no 194/1985.

the case of Mrs Maria Fanny Suarez de Guerrero, the Colombian law enforcement authorities were acting following the alleged kidnapping of a former Colombian ambassador in Bogotá. Mrs Suarez de Guerrero and others were killed when the police, acting in the capacity of state agents, stormed the premises in which they believed the ambassador was held. The Committee found that there was a deprivation of the right to life for the following reasons:

> In the present case it is evident from the fact that seven persons lost their lives as a result of the deliberate action of the police that the *deprivation of life was intentional.* Moreover, the police action was apparently taken *without warning to the victims* and without giving them any *opportunity to surrender* to the police patrol or to offer any explanation of their presence or intentions. There is no evidence that the action of the police was *necessary in their own defence or that of others,* or that it was *necessary to effect the arrest or prevent the escape of the persons concerned.* Moreover, the victims were no more than suspects of the kidnapping which had occurred some days earlier and their killing by the police deprived them of all the protections of due process of law laid down by the Covenant ... For these reasons it is the Committee's view that the action of the police resulting in the death of Mrs. Maria Fanny Suarez de Guerrero was *disproportionate to the requirements of law enforcement in the circumstances* of the case and that she was arbitrarily deprived of her life contrary to article 6 (1) of the International Covenant on Civil and Political Rights. Inasmuch as the police action was made justifiable as a matter of Colombian law by Legislative Decree No. 0070 of 20 January 1978, the right to life was not adequately protected by the law of Colombia as required by article 6 (1). [my emphasis][64]

The following general principles can be determined from this communication. First, where lethal force will be employed, a warning ought to be given if feasible; second, self-defence may justify the use of lethal force; third, effecting a lawful arrest or preventing the escape of suspects may justify the use of lethal force; and finally, the actions of state agents must be proportionate to the requirements of law enforcement in the circumstances pertaining at the time. In each case, these general pronouncements require a further assessment of whether the actions of the state agents were reasonable and proportionate in the circumstances.

1.4.1 Arbitrary deprivation of life—definition and overarching principles

Nsereko has proposed the following as an overarching definition of the term 'arbitrary deprivation of life':

> Deprivation of life would be arbitrary if: (a) it is made without due regard to the rules of natural justice or the due process of law; or (b) it is made in a manner contrary to the law; or (c) it is made in pursuance of a law which is despotic, tyrannical and in conflict with international human rights standards or international humanitarian law.[65]

[64] *Maria Fanny Suarez de Guerrero v Colombia*, Communication no R.11/45, UN Doc Supp No 40 (A/37/40) (1982) at 137.

[65] Daniel Nsereko, 'Arbitrary Deprivation of Life: Controls on Permissible Deprivations' in Ramcharan (ed), *The Right to Life in International Law* 248; Nowak, *United Nations Covenant.*

While this definition is wide-ranging and sufficiently broadly drafted to recognize the main themes evident in the *travaux préparatoires* of the UDHR and the ICCPR, it is ultimately flawed as it does not accurately reflect the requirement to consider each alleged violation on a case-by-case basis assessing the factors present at the time. As Nowak,[66] Ramcharan,[67] Otto,[68] and others have advocated, assessing each case on its own merits with reference to the meaning of 'arbitrary deprivation of life' and a broad set of overarching principles may be a more productive approach. These overarching principles include the following:

> The term 'arbitrary deprivation of life' encompasses 'unlawfulness' and includes violations of the principles of international law, but is a broader and more inclusive term.[69]
>
> An assessment of whether the deprivation of the right to life is arbitrary should be considered with reference to international human rights law norms and not national laws.[70]
>
> An allegation of an arbitrary deprivation of life by a state agent is determined by the specific circumstances of an individual case.[71]
>
> An allegation of an arbitrary deprivation of life by a state agent ought to be subject to a reasonableness and proportionality assessment.[72]
>
> An arbitrary deprivation of life can be committed by a state agent either intentionally, recklessly or negligentlydelete.[73]

Such an approach gives primacy to human rights law, provides latitude in allowing a broader definition of 'arbitrary deprivation of life', and therefore, in turn, affords greater protection of the right to life by increasing its applicability or, more accurately, increasing the likelihood of actions by state agents being considered 'arbitrary' and therefore caught by the provision. Additionally, it addresses the reality of enforcement with a recognition that each case ought to be viewed on its own merits and based upon a reasonableness and proportionality assessment. This approach is still, however, far from perfect, as questions arise concerning the specific meaning of 'with reference to international human rights law norms' and what specifically amounts to 'an arbitrary deprivation of life'.

1.4.2 Individual self-defence

Individual self-defence, as opposed to states acting in self-defence pursuant to Article 51 of the UN Charter, is a relevant consideration for armed forces across the full spectrum of their activities. Whenever armed forces personnel are armed, they will be issued with their individual self-defence card. The specific details contained therein, the training armed forces personnel receive, and the validation of such training will be considered in Chapter 4. As a preliminary consideration, however, an assessment must be made regarding the extent to which individual self-defence amounts to a non-arbitrary deprivation of life with respect to Article 6. Unlike

[66] Nowak, *United Nations Covenant* 14. [67] Ibid, 19.
[68] Ramcharan, *The Right to Life in International Law* 61.
[69] Roland Otto, *Targeted Killings and International Law* (Springer 2010) 243–46.
[70] Ramcharan (ed), *The Right to Life in International Law* 61.
[71] Nowak, *United Nations Covenant* 14. [72] Ibid. [73] Ibid.

the ECHR, the ICCPR does not expressly state the exceptions to the right to life. During the drafting of Article 6, the representatives of states discussed the permissible exceptions to the right to life that included, inter alia, 'the killing of a person by officials in self-defence or defence of another person'[74] and concluded that using the term 'arbitrarily' would 'obviate the necessity of setting out the possible exceptions in detail'.[75] Actions in self-defence were clearly not considered a blanket exception, however, and in order for individual self-defence to amount to a non-arbitrary deprivation of life, strict criteria must be applied in assessing if certain actions by a 'state agent' amount to self-defence.

The following criteria have been identified in respect of the use of lethal force in self-defence:

> A State killing is legal only if it is required to protect life (making lethal force *proportionate*) and there is no other means, such as capture or non-lethal incapacitation, of preventing that threat to life (making lethal force *necessary*). The proportionality requirement limits the permissible level of force based on the threat posed by the suspect to others. The necessity requirement imposes an obligation to minimize the level of force used, regardless of the amount that would be proportionate, through, for example, the use of warnings, restraint and capture.[76]

An arguably more definitive and comprehensive proclamation is made by the Human Rights Committee in its draft General Comment 36 on the right to life:

> in order not to be qualified as arbitrary, the application of lethal force in self-defense must be reasonable and necessary in view of the threat posed by the attacker; it must represent a method of last resort after non-lethal alternatives, including warnings,[77] have been exhausted or deemed inadequate;[78] the amount of force applied cannot exceed the amount strictly needed for responding to the threat; the force applied must be carefully directed, as far as possible, only against the attacker;[79] and the threat responded to must be extreme, involving imminent death or serious injury.[80] The deliberate use of lethal force for law enforcement purposes which is intended to address less extreme threats, such as protecting private property[81] or preventing the escape from custody of a suspected criminal or a convict who does not pose a serious and imminent threat to the lives or bodily integrity of others, cannot be regarded as a proportionate use of force.[82]

[74] UN Commission HR, 5th Session (1949), UN Doc A/2929, Chapter VI in Bossuyt, *Travaux Préparatoires* 122–23.

[75] Ibid, 121–22.

[76] Philip Alston, 'Report of the Special Rapporteur on Extrajudicial, Summary or Arbitrary Executions', A/HRC/14/24/Add.6, 28 May 2010, 32.

[77] *Guiliani and Gaggio v Italy*, Application no 23458/02 (ECtHR, 24 March 2011), 177.

[78] Communication no R.11/45, *Suarez de Guerrero v Colombia*, Views adopted on 31 March 1982, 13.2.

[79] Ibid, 13.2–13.3.

[80] 'Report of the Special Rapporteur on Extrajudicial, Summary or Arbitrary Executions', 23 May 2011, 60.

[81] 'Report of the Special Rapporteur on Extrajudicial, Summary or Arbitrary Executions', 1 April 2014, 72.

[82] Cf *Kazingachire v Zimbabwe*, Report of the ACHR of 12 October 2013, 120.

While again only 'soft law', this sentiment is echoed by the United Nations Office on Drugs and Crime (UNODC) in its Handbook on the Rules for the Use of Force,[83] where it considers individual self-defence to include the use of pre-emptive lethal force provided that the force used is proportionate to the threat, necessary, and reasonable in the circumstances.[84] The UN also provides guidance on self-defence in the Basic Principles on the Use of Force and Firearms by Law Enforcement Officials:

> Law enforcement officials shall not use firearms against persons except in self-defence or defence of others against the imminent threat of death or serious injury, to prevent the perpetration of a particularly serious crime involving grave threat to life, to arrest a person presenting such a danger and resisting their authority, or to prevent his or her escape, and only when less extreme means are insufficient to achieve these objectives ... intentional lethal use of firearms may only be made when strictly unavoidable in order to protect life.[85]

In order for an assessment to be made regarding whether the use of lethal force in individual self-defence is considered a non-arbitrary deprivation of life, the following criteria must be satisfied: an imminent threat of death or serious injury must exist, and the use of force must be reasonable and necessary in the circumstances and proportionate to the threat faced.[86]

1.4.3 An imminent threat of death or serious injury must exist

The first precondition in any assessment of the use of lethal force in self-defence is that there must be an imminent threat of death or serious injury. Absent this precondition, the killing would be arbitrary within the definition of Article 6(1), as there could not exist any nexus between the act of killing and the justification for such action. This assessment is made with reference to an identifiable individual or individuals who face imminent threat to life within a human rights paradigm,

[83] UNODC Handbook on the Rules for the Use of Force for Private Security Companies (PSC) and Privately Contracted Security Personnel (PCSP) (2015).

[84] Ibid.

> It is both good law and common sense that a person who is attacked may defend themself. It is also good law and common sense that they may therefore do, but only do, what is reasonably necessary to respond to that attack upon them. Ultimately, no person may limit or stop another from acting in *individual self-defence* in the face of a *harmful act* or *imminent threat of harm.*
>
> Any use of force in *self-defence* must be proportionate to the threat.
>
> In the context of *self-defence*, 'proportionate' refers to the amount of force used in response to a specific threat. It is assessed in terms of its context and the people involved. It includes an assessment of the nature of the threat, whether the response was reasonable and necessary in the circumstances, and whether less harmful options were realistically available.
>
> The use of force in *self-defence* is generally authorised so long as the *harmful act* or threat continues. When force is used in *self-defence*, the degree and duration of force used should not exceed that which is required to deter, neutralise or stop the threat.

[85] *UN Basic Principles on the Use of Force and Firearms by Law Enforcement Officials*, UN Doc A/CONF.144/28/Rev 1 (1990) 112.

[86] See also Human Rights Committee, draft General Comment 36, 18.

as distinct from the notion of immediacy to justify military action in response to a terrorist threat.[87]

The Human Rights Committee considered the issue of imminence within a human rights construct in the *Maria Fanny Suarez de Guerrero* case[88] and it was determined that the resort to lethal force by the Colombian authorities was not in response to an imminent threat either to the police or to the kidnapped former ambassador. An assessment of imminence is not easy to define or quantify, but may be determined or clarified by actions on the part of the state agent. For example, the use of a warning that is not heeded or a resort to non-lethal means, such as CS gas or taser, that are ineffective may indicate that the use of lethal force will be the only effective response in the circumstances existing at the time. Put another way, the use of lethal force following an escalation in the use of force is more likely to be considered a 'last resort' and therefore justifiable, and, in turn, 'non-arbitrary' with reference to Article 6(1).

Within the context of protecting vessels at sea, the UNODC has provided the following guidance to assist with an assessment of the concept of 'imminence' and therefore the justifiable resort to the use of lethal force:

> Measures to Assist in Determining the Existence of an *Imminent Threat of Harm.*
>
> Time and circumstances permitting, vessels should take proactive measures to help them to determine the intent of the threatening entity. Such measures could include: Display of presence; Verbal query; Verbal warning and/or radio warning; Visual warnings; Noise warnings; The establishment of physical barriers; Changing course and speed to determine if the threat is continuing to maintain a hostile profile, position, approach or posture.[89]

There is no doubt that the concept of imminence is a high threshold to satisfy and, as such, affords individuals a necessary protection from the unrestrained use of lethal force by state agents. It must, however, be considered in conjunction with the other individual self-defence criteria, as the presence of an imminent threat to life alone may not always justify the use of lethal force if the threat can be neutralized without resorting to lethal force.

1.4.4 The pre-emptive use of lethal force is permissible

A natural corollary of the notion of imminence in the use of lethal force in self-defence is that of the use of pre-emptive action. It is axiomatic that a state agent does not have to wait until a lethal attack has occurred before they can use lethal force to intervene. A prohibition on such action would render the notion of individual self-defence ineffective. That said, any pre-emptive use of lethal force must be justified with reference to the nature of the attack and subject to a proportionality assessment. The state agent must be able to demonstrate that their resort to the use

[87] This issue has been considered in Michael Schmitt, 'Counter-Terrorism and the Use of Force in International Law' 32 (2002) Isr Yb Hum Rts 53–116, among others.

[88] *Maria Fanny Suarez de Guerrero v Colombia*, Communication at 137.

[89] Ibid, 35.

of lethal force was proportionate to the threat they faced and that other non-lethal alternatives were not applicable or appropriate in the circumstances.

1.4.5 The use of lethal force must be proportionate to the threat

There is support[90] for the legal test of proportionality being a central tenet in any assessment of individual self-defence. The obvious question is, of course, what must the use of lethal force be proportionate to? In the case of *Maria Fanny Suarez de Guerrero*, the actions of the Colombian police were considered 'disproportionate to the requirements of law enforcement'.[91] Equally, the use of lethal force can be considered with respect to the threat faced by state agents. There is a nexus between proportionality and the concept of imminence through the requirement to employ escalation of force measures short of a resort to lethal force, reflected in the reference made to the requirement for the use of a warning in *Suarez de Guerrero.*[92] Such statements do not, however, exclude the possibility of an immediate recourse to the use of lethal force if the circumstances necessitate such action. The UNODC rules on the use of force illustrate the notion of proportionality thus:

> If you are behind a solid barrier, and a person approaches the barrier waving their fist and shouting at you, it is neither necessary nor reasonable to respond with deadly force. In such case, the person poses no immediate ability to harm you. If, however, the person approaches the barrier with a grenade, a lethal use of force against that person may be lawful if you believe on reasonable grounds that the person poses an immediate threat to your life or the life of others. Where less than lethal use of force options are available to deter, neutralize or stop the threat, those lesser levels of force should be utilized.[93]

Ultimately, therefore, proportionality requires that the use of lethal force is proportionate to the threat faced.

1.4.6 The use of lethal force—reasonableness and necessity

The reasonableness of the actions of any state agent is measured against both objective and subjective criteria. The national laws, regulations, rules, protocols, or procedures under which the state agents acted will be subject to an objective assessment of their compliance with Article 6(1). For example, in the *Suarez de Guerrero* case the Human Rights Committee considered a Colombian 1978 statutory decree that established a statutory defence where killings were 'committed ... by the members of the police force in the course of operations planned with the object of preventing or curbing the offences of extortion and kidnapping, and the production and processing of and trafficking in narcotic drugs'[94] to be in contravention of

[90] Nowak, CCPR Commentary, Article 6, para 14 (p 129) and Human Rights Committee in *Maria Fanny Suarez de Guerrero v Colombia* at 137.

[91] *Maria Fanny Suarez de Guerrero v Colombia* at 137.

[92] Ibid, paras 13.2, 13.3.

[93] Ibid, 36.

[94] Ibid, and Nowak at para 15.

Article 6(1). A subjective assessment is made with respect to the actions of the state agents given the exigencies of the situation they face, and a margin of appreciation applied. Where the state agent faces an attack that threatens their life it would not be unreasonable to presuppose that their intention was to prevent the attack and not kill the assailant. As such, cognizant of their aim to prevent the loss of their life, the actions of the state agent would not be considered arbitrary, or, put another way, would be considered reasonable with respect to Article 6(1).

The notion of 'necessity' within an individual self-defence can be considered as the absence or lack of any viable alternative to the use of lethal force. In other words, the alternatives to the use of lethal force have been employed and have failed to halt the attack, or, given the exigencies of the situation, there are no alternatives to the use of lethal force and its use is necessary to prevent death or serious injury. The Human Rights Committee has endorsed this approach and established a particularly high threshold for the use of lethal force in self-defence, noting that 'before resorting to the use of lethal force, all measures to arrest a person suspected of being in the process of committing acts of terror must be exhausted'.[95] Examples of such alternative measures are set out in the UN Basic Principles on the Use of Force and Firearms by Law Enforcement Officials,[96] as is the option to immediately employ lethal force if required.[97]

1.4.7 Defence of others

It would be non-arbitrary to use lethal force in the defence of others provided that the criteria set out above are satisfied, namely, that there exists an imminent threat to the life of another person or persons and the force used by the state agent was proportionate to the threat faced. This approach finds support in the Human Rights Committee Concluding Observations and in the 'UN Basic Principles on the Use of Force and Firearms by Law Enforcement Officials'.[98] To illustrate, with respect to Israel, for example, the Human Rights Committee concluded that the use of

[95] Human Rights Committee, *Concluding Observations on Israel*, UN Doc CCPR/CO/78/ISR (2003), 15.

[96] Para 2: 'Governments and law enforcement agencies should develop a range of means as broad as possible and equip law enforcement officials with various types of weapons and ammunition that would allow for a differentiated use of force and firearms. These should include the development of non-lethal incapacitating weapons for use in appropriate situations, with a view to increasingly restraining the application of means capable of causing death or injury to persons. For the same purpose, it should also be possible for law enforcement officials to be equipped with self-defensive equipment such as shields, helmets, bullet-proof vests and bullet-proof means of transportation, in order to decrease the need to use weapons of any kind.' Para 4: 'Law enforcement officials, in carrying out their duty, shall, as far as possible, apply non-violent means before resorting to the use of force and firearms. They may use force and firearms only if other means remain ineffective or without any promise of achieving the intended result.'

[97] Para 10: 'In the circumstances provided for under principle 9, law enforcement officials shall identify themselves as such and give a clear warning of their intent to use firearms, with sufficient time for the warning to be observed, unless to do so would unduly place the law enforcement officials at risk or would create a risk of death or serious harm to other persons, or would be clearly inappropriate or pointless in the circumstances of the incident.'

[98] Ibid.

lethal force was permissible where individuals were 'suspected of being in the process of committing'[99] terrorist attacks that could result in the deaths of citizens. The Committee further commented that 'a stringent proportionality test must be applied and other safeguards respected when targeting individuals for their participation in terrorist activity (art. 6)'.[100] This reinforces the requirement that the use of lethal force ought to be a last resort when exercised in the defence of others. Further, it reinforces a high threshold test for the use of lethal force by state agents in defence of others.

The UN Basic Principles on the Use of Force and Firearms by Law Enforcement Officials consider the issue of the defence of others thus:

> Law enforcement officials shall not use firearms against persons except in self-defence or *defence of others* against the imminent threat of death or serious injury, to prevent the perpetration of a particularly serious crime involving grave threat to life, to arrest a person presenting such a danger and resisting their authority, or to prevent his or her escape, and only when less extreme means are insufficient to achieve these objectives.[101]

Ultimately, if the use of lethal force is to amount to a 'non-arbitrary' deprivation of life for the purposes of Article 6(1), then the state agent must demonstrate that the use of force was in response to an imminent threat (to another) and was proportionate to the threat the other person faced.

1.4.8 Effecting a lawful arrest

Resort to the use of lethal force when effecting an arrest is cited as permissible in the UN Basic Principles on the Use of Force and Firearms by Law Enforcement Officials.[102] The state agent must, however, be able to establish a nexus to an imminent threat to life and act proportionately to the threat faced. In reality, therefore, it is likely that the resort to the use of lethal force will be a last resort when other non-lethal measures[103] have been employed and have failed.

1.4.9 Preventing an escape

While preventing an escape[104] could amount to a justification for the resort to the use of lethal force, the threshold for such action is particularly high. It is extremely likely that all non-lethal methods of preventing the escape would have to be employed, including the use of warning prior to the use of lethal force.

[99] Human Rights Committee, *Concluding Observations on Israel*, UN Doc CCPR/CO/78/ISR (21 August 2003), 15.

[100] Human Rights Committee, *Concluding Observations on Israel*, UN Doc CCPR/C/ISR/CO/3 (29 July 2010), 10.

[101] Ibid, principle 9 [my emphasis].

[102] Ibid, principle 9.

[103] Non-lethal measures can include, inter alia, the use of warnings, tear gas, pepper spray, tasers, and batons.

[104] Human Rights Committee, *Concluding Observations on Israel*, UN Doc CCPR/C/ISR/CO/3 (29 July 2010), principle 9.

Where lethal force is employed, the state agent must be able to demonstrate that there is an imminent threat to life and the proportionality criteria must be satisfied.[105] In reality, this is only likely to occur when the 'escapee' is armed and there is a reasonable prospect of him or her using a weapon to endanger life. It is extremely unlikely that the mere prospect of a future attack by an unarmed escapee, based on their past behaviour, would justify the resort to lethal force. A strict approach to the use of lethal force to prevent an escape, requiring a nexus to an imminent threat to life, has also been advocated by the Human Rights Committee, citing *Kazingachire v Zimbabwe*,[106] in draft General Comment 36.[107]

1.4.10 Quelling a riot or insurrection

If the self-defence criteria are satisfied, then the use of lethal force to quell a riot or insurrection would amount to a 'non-arbitrary' deprivation of life. It is significant, however, that in the UN Basic Principles on the Use of Force and Firearms by Law Enforcement Officials, specific reference is made to the use of such force in the following terms: 'exceptional circumstances such as internal political instability or any other public emergency may not be invoked to justify any departure from these basic principles'.[108] It follows, therefore, that offensive force by state agents would not be permissible in quelling a riot or insurrection, and any action would be limited to self-defence only.

1.4.11 The right to life of those detained by the state

The Human Rights Committee[109] has asserted the right to life obligations of states in respect of those it detains in the following terms:

> states parties also have a heightened obligation to take effective measures[110] to protect the lives of individuals incarcerated by the State, since by arresting, detaining and imprisoning individuals States parties assume the responsibility to care for their life[111] and they may not rely on lack of financial resources or other logistical problems to reduce this responsibility.[112]

[105] Ibid, principle 16: 'Law enforcement officials, in their relations with persons in custody or detention, shall not use firearms, except in self-defence or in the defence of others against the immediate threat of death or serious injury, or when strictly necessary to prevent the escape of a person in custody or detention presenting the danger referred to in principle 9.'

[106] *Kazingachire v Zimbabwe*, Report of the ACHR of 12 October 2013, 120.

[107] Human Rights Committee, draft General Comment 36, 18: 'The deliberate use of lethal force ... [to prevent] ... the escape from custody of a suspected criminal or a convict who does not pose a serious and imminent threat to the lives or bodily integrity of others, cannot be regarded as a proportionate use of force.'

[108] Ibid, principle 8.

[109] Human Rights Committee, draft General Comment 36, 27.

[110] Communication no 546/1993, *Burrell v Jamaica*, Views adopted on 18 July 1996, at 9.5.

[111] Communication no 1756/2008, *Zhumbaeva v Kyrgyzstan*, Views adopted on 19 July 2011, at 8; Communication no 84/1981, *Barbato v Uruguay*, Views adopted on 21 October 1982, 9.2.

[112] Communication no 763/1997, *Lantsov v the Russian Federation*, Views adopted on 26 March 2002, 9.2.

The Human Rights Committee further asserts that the state's right to life obligations extend to those in 'military camps'[113] and 'refugee and internally displaced persons camps'.[114] It must be noted, however, that the term 'military camps' here relates specifically to armed forces personnel within military camps in Armenia in which allegations of ill treatment of soldiers had been made. Nonetheless, recognizing the ECtHR judgment in *Al-Skeini*, it could be asserted that a state's right to life obligations pursuant to Article 6, ICCPR apply equally to detainees during armed conflict. The precise contours of the relationship between human rights law and international humanitarian law in respect of the right to life protections afforded to detainees will be addressed in Chapter 4.

While detainees are in detention, the state must ensure they are provided with 'the necessary medical care to combat life-threatening diseases',[115] monitor their health,[116] and protect them from inter-prisoner violence.[117] The extent to which these right to life obligations interact with international humanitarian law provisions regulating the treatment of detainees will again be considered in Chapter 4.

The Human Rights Committee has further asserted that 'state parties are deemed to violate the right to life of persons who died while in their custody, unless it can be shown that there is no causal relationship between their death and their incarceration'.[118] As a consequence, the state has significant right to life obligations in respect of those it detains.

1.5 Armed Forces Activities and *'Non-Arbitrary Deprivation'* of Life in Article 6

To briefly recap, notwithstanding its status as the supreme human right, the right to life is not absolute. Individuals can, in certain circumstances, be deprived of their inherent right to life. With respect to the ICCPR, this is permissible as a consequence of the clause in Article 6(1), 'No one shall be arbitrarily deprived of his life', which leads to the inexorable conclusion that there are circumstances that constitute 'non-arbitrary' deprivations of life. Unlike the ECHR, the ICCPR is not prescriptive on this point, but state practice has established circumstances in which the deprivation of life is permissible. In broad terms, non-arbitrary deprivation of life in respect of Article 6, ICCPR includes deprivation of life during international and non-international armed conflict, in individual self-defence, in the defence of others, in effecting a lawful arrest, in preventing escape from detention, and in quelling

[113] Concluding Observations: *Armenia (2012)* 15.

[114] Concluding Observations: *UN Administration for Kosovo (2006)* 14.

[115] Communication no 1020/2001, *Cabal and Pasini v Australia*, Views adopted on 7 August 2003 at para 7.7 ('a failure to separate detainees with communicable diseases from other detainees could raise issues primarily under articles 6, paragraph 1'); Concluding Observations: *Moldova (2002)* 9; Concluding Observations: *Tajikistan (2013)* 9.

[116] Communication no 763/1997, *Lantsov v the Russian Federation*, Views adopted on 26 March 2002, 9.2.

[117] Cf *Edwards v the United Kingdom*, Application no 46477/99 (ECtHR, 14 June 2002) 60.

[118] Communication no 1473/2006, *Tornel v Spain*, Views adopted on 20 March 2009, 7.2.

a riot or insurrection. The broad range of activities undertaken by UK armed forces means they have historically acted, and will continue to act, in these areas.

1.6 Article 6, ICCPR and International and Non-International Armed Conflict

The detailed relationship between international humanitarian law and human rights law in armed conflict will be considered with reference to specific activities of armed forces in Chapter 4. For the purposes of assessing the exceptions to right to life as defined by Article 6(1) it is, however, necessary to consider the extent to which deaths resulting from international and non-international armed conflict amount to a non-arbitrary deprivation of the right to life.

As a starting point, the International Court of Justice provides a framework for considering the issue:

> In principle, the right not arbitrarily to be deprived of one's life applies also in hostilities. The test of what is an arbitrary deprivation of life, however, then falls to be determined by the applicable *lex specialis*, namely, the law applicable to armed conflict which is designed to regulate the conduct of hostilities. Thus whether a particular loss of life, through the use of a certain weapon in warfare, is to be considered an arbitrary deprivation of life contrary to Article 6 of the Covenant, can only be decided by reference to the law applicable to armed conflict and not deduced from the terms of the Covenant itself.[119]

The Court subsequently restated this view[120] and elaborated and refined its position thus:

> As regards the relationship between international humanitarian law and human rights law, there are thus three possible situations: some rights may be exclusively matters of international humanitarian law; others may be exclusively matters of human rights law; yet others may be matters of both these branches of international law. In order to answer the question put to it, the Court will have to take into consideration both these branches of international law, namely human rights law and, as *lex specialis*, international humanitarian law.[121]

As a general proposition, therefore, if a state or state agents act in compliance with the internationally recognized 'laws of war'[122] (international humanitarian law) during an international or non-international armed conflict then any loss of life as a consequence of their actions would not constitute an 'arbitrary' deprivation of life within the definition of Article 6(1). In order to avail themselves of the 'protections' afforded by international humanitarian law, the state would have to ensure that the various requirements and tenets thereof were complied with. In doing so, the

[119] ICJ, *Legality of the Threat or Use of Nuclear Weapons*, Advisory Opinion of 8 July 1996, ICJ Reports 1996, 225–593, at 240 (para 25).

[120] ICJ, *Legal Consequences of the Construction of a Wall in the Occupied Palestine Territory*, Advisory Opinion of 9 July 2004, ICJ Reports 2004 133–271, at 177–78 (paras 104–06).

[121] Ibid, para 106.

[122] UN Secretary General, Respect for Human Rights in Armed Conflicts, Report of 18 September 1970, 25th Session, Agenda Item 47, UN Doc A/8052 (18 September 1970) 104 (Annex I, para 46).

state would not contravene the protections afforded by Article 6(1). In respect of a state's procedural right to life obligations that analysis is not so straightforward, as the circumstances in which an investigation is required, pursuant to international humanitarian law, are arguably not as wide-ranging. As a consequence, there may not be applicable international humanitarian law norms through which a state's Article 6 obligations can be interpreted.

1.7 The European Convention on Human Rights

The protection of the right to life in the ECHR is not absolute.[123] Unlike Article 6, ICCPR, where unlawful violations of the right to life are those considered to be 'arbitrary'—thus allowing significant scope for interpretation of the provision—Article 2 of the ECHR is more prescriptive. It reads:

1. Everyone's right to life shall be protected by law. No one shall be deprived of his life intentionally save in the execution of a sentence of a court following his conviction of a crime for which this penalty is provided by law.
2. Deprivation of life shall not be regarded as inflicted in contravention of this Article when it results from the use of force which is no more than absolutely necessary:
   1. (a) in defence of any person from unlawful violence;
   2. (b) in order to effect a lawful arrest or to prevent the escape of a person lawfully detained;
   3. (c) in action lawfully taken for the purpose of quelling a riot or insurrection.

Notwithstanding the more prescriptive nature of the right to life provision, both the European Commission of Human Rights[124] and, latterly exclusively, the European Court of Human Rights have addressed both the substantive and procedural elements of the right to life. Additionally, they have considered a number of associated issues that are addressed below as preliminary considerations.

1.7.1 ECHR Article 2—Preliminary Considerations

1.7.1.1 Exhaustion of domestic remedies

Article 35(1)[125] has been applied by the Court with 'some degree of flexibility'[126] and 'without excessive formalism'[127] when considering allegations of a state's failure to

[123] This can be compared to Article 3 of the ECHR, 'No one shall be subjected to torture or to inhuman or degrading treatment or punishment', where the protection of the right is made without qualification and cannot be subject to any derogation, and can therefore be considered absolute.

[124] On the entry into force of Protocol 11 of the ECHR (1 November 1998), the European Commission of Human Rights was abolished. Prior to this date individuals did not have a direct right to petition to the Court and cases were referred by the Commission on behalf of individuals if they were considered to have merit.

[125] Article 35(1): 'The Court may only deal with the matter after all domestic remedies have been exhausted, according to the generally recognised rules of international law, and within a period of six months from the date on which the final decision was taken.'

[126] *Isayeva v Russia*, Application no 57950/00 (ECtHR, 24 February 2005) 153.

[127] Ibid, 153.

protect the right to life. This has enabled cases to be considered by the Court where the applicant may have not exhausted all the domestic remedies as a consequence of the contracting state not handling the matter expeditiously.[128] Similarly, the Court has also considered cases where the range of domestic remedies, albeit pursued to a conclusion, are deemed inadequate or ineffective,[129] or where the law enforcement bodies were not functioning properly at the material time, thus rendering their investigation ineffective or incomplete.[130] In every case involving an alleged violation of Article 2, the Court has asserted that it will apply a 'particularly thorough scrutiny'.[131]

1.7.1.2 Burden of proof

In the first instance, a conventional burden of proof applies to cases involving an alleged violation of the right to life by a state, namely, that the applicant must demonstrate to the required standard that the state failed in their duty to protect the right to life. In certain circumstances, however, the Court has repeatedly asserted that a 'reverse' burden of proof may occur when examining states' alleged violation of the right to life.[132] With respect to the activities of armed forces this arises, among other areas, in respect of deaths that occur in detention. The Court has characterized the circumstances of a change in the burden of proof thus:

> Where the events in issue lie wholly, or in large part, within the exclusive knowledge of the authorities, as in the case of persons within their control in detention, strong presumptions of fact will arise in respect of injuries and death occurring during that detention. Indeed, the burden of proof may be regarded as resting on the authorities to provide a satisfactory and convincing explanation [of the death].[133]

The circumstances that amount to 'exclusive knowledge of the authorities' and the extent to which this principle can be applied to other activities of armed forces will be considered in Chapter 4.

1.7.1.3 Standard of proof

The Court has repeatedly enunciated that the standard of proof is 'beyond reasonable doubt'[134] and provided further elaboration that 'such proof may follow from

[128] Ibid, 153.

[129] *Aksoy v Turkey*, Application no 21987/93 (ECtHR, 18 December 1996) *Reports* 1996-VI, 2275-76; *Akdivar and Others v Turkey*, Application no 21893/93 (ECtHR, 16 September 1996) 1210; *Isayeva v Russia* 144.

[130] *Isayeva v Russia* 158.

[131] *McKerr v the United Kingdom*, Application no 28883/95 (ECtHR, 4 April 2000); *Ribitsch v Austria*, Application no 336 (ECtHR, 4 December 1995) 32; *Avsar v Turkey* Application no 25657/94 (ECtHR, 14 October 1996) 283.

[132] *Bazorkina v Russia*, Application no 69481 (ECtHR, 27 July 2006) 105; *Salman v Turkey* [GC], Application no 21986/93 (ECtHR, 2000) 100; *Çakıcı v Turkey* [GC] Application no 23657/94 (ECtHR, 1999) 85; *Ertak v Turkey*, Application no 20764/92 (ECtHR, 2000) 32; *Timurtaş v Turkey*, Application no 23531/94 (ECtHR, 2000) 82.

[133] *Bazorkina v Russia* 105; *Salman v Turkey* [GC] Application no 21986/93 (ECtHR, 2000) 100; *Çakıcı v Turkey*, Application no 23657/94 (ECtHR, 1999) 85; *Ertak v Turkey*, 32; *Timurtaş v Turkey* 82.

[134] *Bazorkina v Russia* 106; *Avşar v Turkey* 391.

the coexistence of sufficiently strong, clear and concordant inferences or of similar unrebutted presumptions of fact'.[135] In this context, 'the conduct of the parties when evidence is being obtained has to be taken into account'.[136] This is a clear indication from the Court that where the disclosure of relevant materials is incomplete, or if a state's cooperation with the proceedings is limited in circumstances where, prima facie, a death has occurred within the 'exclusive knowledge of the authorities', the Court is more likely to find a violation of the right to life.

1.7.1.4 The scope of 'intentional deprivation of life'

It has been convincingly argued[137] that the clause 'Everyone's right to life shall be protected by law. No one shall be deprived of his life intentionally' in Article 2(1) includes negligent as well as intentional deprivation of life by the state. The scope of Article 2 was first considered in *McCann*[138] thus:

> The Court considers that the exceptions delineated in paragraph 2 (art. 2-2) indicate that this provision (art. 2-2) extends to, but is not concerned exclusively with, intentional killing. As the Commission has pointed out, the text of Article 2 (art. 2), read as a whole, demonstrates that paragraph 2 (art. 2-2) does not primarily define instances where it is permitted intentionally to kill an individual, but describes the situations where it is permitted to 'use force' which may result, as an unintended outcome, in the deprivation of life.[139]

Having clarified the scope of Article 2(2), the Court further considered that although the actions of the soldiers themselves, in killing three suspected terrorists in Gibraltar, did not give rise to a violation of Article 2(2), there was ultimately a violation of Article 2(2) by the state in that, inter alia, 'failure by the authorities also suggests a lack of appropriate care in the control of the organisation of the arrest operation'.[140] Further and compelling support for the notion that negligent deprivation of life may be contrary to Article 2 comes from, among other areas, the 'Chechen' line of cases. While not explicitly using the term 'negligent', the Court in *Isayeva*[141] considered the use of free-falling high explosive bombs in a populated area as

> impossible to reconcile with the degree of caution expected from a law-enforcement body in a democratic society . . . the massive use of indiscriminate weapons stands in flagrant contrast with this aim and cannot be considered compatible with the *standard of care* prerequisite to an operation of this kind involving the use of lethal force by State agents. [my emphasis][142]

It is implicit in these comments that while the military action may not have been intentionally designed to kill innocent civilians, such negligent actions would

[135] *Bazorkina v Russia* 106.

[136] *Ireland v the United Kingdom*, judgment of 18 January 1978, Series A no 25, 161; *Bazorkina v Russia* 106.

[137] Roland Otto, *Targeted Killings and International Law* (Springer 2010) 151–53.

[138] *McCann and Others v the United Kingdom*, Application no 18984/91 (ECtHR, 27 September 1995).

[139] Ibid, 148.

[140] Ibid, 213.

[141] *Isayeva v Russia* 158.

[142] Ibid, 191.

inevitably result in the loss of innocent lives and would therefore amount to a substantive violation of Article 2.

1.7.2 Article 2 ECHR—law enforcement and the substantive element of the right to life

Article 2(2) provides for circumstances in which the deprivation of life shall not be inflicted in contravention of the general proposition in Article 2(1) that 'Everyone's right to life shall be protected by law'. In order for the deprivation of life to be considered lawful, the use of force must be 'no more than absolutely necessary' in respect of the permitted circumstances in Article 2(2). The application of the circumstances established in Article 2(2) will be examined with respect to specific activities of armed forces in Chapter 4. Prior to this analysis, a consideration of the scope of the associated terms 'necessity' or 'absolutely necessary', 'proportionality', and 'precaution' or 'planning' is required to establish the legal foundation upon which the scope of Article 2(2) exceptions to the right to life can be assessed.

1.7.2.1 Use of lethal force is 'absolutely necessary' for achievement of legitimate purposes

The terms 'necessity' and 'absolutely necessary' have been used interchangeably by the Court and Commission.[143] Further, the term 'absolutely necessary' and the concept of proportionality have been regularly conflated by the Court thus: 'any use of force must be "no more than absolutely necessary", that is to say it must be strictly proportionate in the circumstances.'[144] Such a conflation does not hinder a structured analysis of the legitimacy of a resort to the use of lethal force, but any assessment of proportionality must be subject to a three-stage test. First, proportionality must be considered with reference to the achievement of the legitimate aim; second, the measures taken to achieve the legitimate aim must be necessary and no more than necessary; and finally, there must be a reasonable balance of proportionality between the effects caused by the measure and the harm sought to be countered. It is in this respect that the proportionality assessment goes beyond that of necessity.

The requirement of necessity (absolutely necessary) ought to be considered with reference to achieving a legitimate aim. Article 2(2) establishes what might constitute a legitimate aim, namely, the defence of a person from unlawful violence; effecting a lawful arrest or preventing the escape of a person lawfully detained; or action lawfully taken for the purpose of quelling a riot or insurrection. As Melzer,[145] in part citing Kretzmer,[146] contends, the concept of necessity consists

[143] A typical example can be found in *Nachova and Others v Bulgaria*, Application nos 43577/98 and 43579/98 (ECtHR, 6 July 2005), where in para 94 the term 'absolutely necessary' is used and in para 95 the term 'absolute necessity'.

[144] *Nachova and Others v Bulgaria* 94.

[145] Nils Melzer, *Targeted Killing in International Law* (Oxford University Press 2008) 116.

[146] David Kretzmer, 'Targeted Killing of Suspected Terrorists: Extra-Judicial Executions or Legitimate Means of Defence?' 16 (2005) *EJIL* 178.

of qualitative, quantitative, and temporal elements. This analysis, drawing upon the ECtHR judgments in *McCann*,[147] *Güleç*,[148] and *Nachova*,[149] simply amounts to addressing three questions with reference to the use of a firearm as the obvious example. First, was it absolutely necessary to employ lethal force, using the firearm, to achieve the legitimate aim? Second, was the minimum amount of force used, namely, no more rounds than were absolutely necessary? And finally, at the time at which the firearm was discharged, was it absolutely necessary, or could an alternative, non-lethal means of achieving the legitimate aim have been employed? In effect, a proportionality assessment is applied to the qualitative, quantitative, and temporal elements of necessity. Again, with reference to the use of a firearm, the proportionality assessment consists of the following. First, is the use of a firearm proportionate to the threat faced? In other words, how is the assailant armed and what are they doing? Second, was the number of rounds fired proportionate to the threat faced? Finally, at the exact moment the firearm was used, was this proportionate to the threat faced or had the situation changed? However, a further proportionality assessment is required with reference to the achievement of a legitimate aim as enunciated in Article 2(2). In other words, with respect to each of the sub-clauses in Article 2(2), the state agent must assess whether the resort to lethal force is justified notwithstanding that, for example, a lawfully detained individual is attempting to escape. Such a situation was specifically addressed by the Court in *Nachova*.[150]

1.7.2.2 An honest belief on the part of the state agent

The Court has been cognizant of the difficulties faced by state agents when having to make split-second life and death decisions. As such, a violation of Article 2 has not been found where the state agent(s) acted in the honest, but mistaken, belief that the use of lethal force was absolutely necessary in the circumstances.[151] In effect, the Court has established a two-stage test where the actions of the state agent must be subjectively honest and objectively reasonable.[152] Amplifying their remarks in *McCann*, the ECtHR in *Andronicou and Constantinou* considered that the Court

> cannot with detached reflection substitute its own assessment of the situation for that of the officers who were required to react in the heat of the moment in what was for them a

[147] *McCann and Others v the United Kingdom*, 212.

[148] *Güleç v Turkey*, Application no 54/1997/838/1044 (ECtHR, 27 July 1998) 71.

[149] *Nachova and Others v Bulgaria*, 108.

[150] Ibid: 'The Court considers that in principle there can be no such necessity where it is known that the person to be arrested poses no threat to life or limb and is not suspected of having committed a violent offence, even if a failure to use lethal force may result in the opportunity to arrest the fugitive being lost.'

[151] *McCann and Others v the United Kingdom* 200; *Andronicou and Constantinou v Cyprus*, Application nos 86/1996/705/897 (ECtHR, 9 October 1997) 192.

[152] *McCann and Others v the United Kingdom*, 200; *Andronicou and Constantinou v Cyprus*, 192; *McKerr v the United Kingdom*, Application no 28883/95 (ECtHR, 4 May 2001) 116; *Kelly and Others v the United Kingdom*, Application no 30054/96 (ECtHR, 4 May 2001) 99.

unique and unprecedented operation to save life. The officers were entitled to open fire for this purpose and to take all measures which they honestly and reasonably believed were necessary to eliminate any risk either to the young woman's life or to their own lives.[153]

In justifying this approach in *McCann*, the Court noted that 'to hold otherwise would be to impose an unrealistic burden on the state and its law-enforcement personnel in the execution of their duty, perhaps to the detriment of their lives and those of others'.[154]

1.7.2.3 The requirement of precaution and planning in the use of lethal force

A violation of Article 2 can occur in circumstances where the state has failed to properly plan, organize, or control an operation that has resulted in the use of lethal force.[155] Significantly, a violation can occur notwithstanding the Court's consideration that the use of force by the state agent was 'absolutely necessary' in the circumstances as the state agent perceived them to be. A failure to plan, organize, and control an operation incorporates the provision of insufficient training[156] to the state agents charged with undertaking the operation and an insufficient assessment of intelligence information.[157]

1.8 The Protection of the Right to Life in National Legislation

In order to comply with their obligations pursuant to Article 2, states must ensure that the right to life is properly protected in national legislation,[158] and that procedures exist to ensure that the potential use of lethal force by state agents exists within a 'framework of a system of adequate and effective safeguards against arbitrariness and abuse of force'.[159] In *Makaratzis*, with respect to law enforcement, a statute dating from 1943 that reflected the prevailing situation in the Second World War, supplemented by a presidential decree that stated that firearms should be used 'only when absolutely necessary and when all less extreme methods have been exhausted', was not sufficient to comply with Greece's obligations pursuant to this element of Article 2.

[153] *Andronicou and Constantinou v Cyprus* 192.
[154] *McCann and Others v the United Kingdom* 200.
[155] *Güleç v Turkey* 71; *Nachova and Others v Bulgaria* 108; *McCann and Others v the United Kingdom* 150, 194, 205, and 213; *Andronicou and Constantinou v Cyprus* 171.
[156] *McCann and Others v the United Kingdom* 211.
[157] *McCann and Others v the United Kingdom* 193 and 210.
[158] *Kılıç v Turkey* 62; *Makaratzis v Greece* 56–71.
[159] *Makaratzis v Greece* 56–71 and, *mutatis mutandis, Hilda Hafsteinsdóttir v Iceland*, Application no 40905/98 (ECtHR, 8 June 2004) 56.

1.9 Article 2(2) ECHR—Exceptions to the Right to Life

1.9.1 In defence of any person from unlawful violence

1.9.1.1 The scope of defence of any person

Implicit in the wording of the 'self-defence' exception to Article 2 is a recognition that the notion of self-defence extends to the defence of others. The Commission and Court have consistently defined the notion of the 'defence of any person' broadly, but have included a temporal element in their assessment of the level of risk or threat of unlawful violence. In cases where an immediate threat to life is perceived, the Commission and Court have, while noting other factors, accepted that state agents act in 'situation[s] in which split second decisions had to be taken to avert the real and immediate danger'.[160] As such, they have been more willing to find that a violation has not occurred where a state agent must make a split-second life and death decision.[161] Conversely, however, where there does not exist an immediate threat to life, the Commission and Court have been more likely—although not exclusively so[162]—to find a violation.[163]

1.9.1.2 The meaning of unlawful violence

The notion of 'unlawful violence' is not exclusively confined to loss of life. 'Unlawful violence' does incorporate the perceived threat of violence and, if the relevant criteria are satisfied, pre-emptive action is permitted to prevent it.[164] There is, however, no support in the judgments of the ECtHR or UK national law for a proposition that the defence of property, absent a nexus to a loss of life, justifies recourse to lethal force.

The Commission and Court have considered numerous cases where an assessment of the scope of the recourse to lethal force in 'defence of any person from unlawful violence' has been determined. In *Wolfgram v Germany*,[165] the Commission considered that the German police acted lawfully in opening fire and killing two suspected bank robbers when attempting to effect an arrest. In not complying with the orders of the police and detonating a hand grenade, the suspected bank robbers had created a situation in which, in the opinion of the Commission, the resort to lethal use of force was absolutely necessary to effect a lawful arrest and in self-defence. Despite making explicit reference to both exceptions, the Commission appears to place greater emphasis on the use of lethal force in self-defence as the relevant

[160] *Andronicou and Constantinou v Cyprus*, Application nos 86/1996/705/897 (ECtHR, 9 October 1997) 191.

[161] The Commission and Court have taken this approach in *Wolfgram v Germany, McCann v the United Kingdom*, and *Andronicou and Constantinou v Cyprus; Ahmet Özkan and Others v Turkey* 302.

[162] *Kelly v the United Kingdom*, Application no 17579/90 (ECtHR, 13 January 1993).

[163] *Ayetin v Turkey*, Application no 22880/93 (ECtHR, 18 September 1997).

[164] *McCann and Others v the United Kingdom; Andronicou and Constantinou v Cyprus*,

[165] *Wolfgram v Germany*, Application no 11257/84 (ECHR, 6 October 1996).

criteria—'the dangers to life and limb inherent in the situation'[166]—as opposed to effecting a lawful arrest.

In *McCann and Others v the United Kingdom*,[167] the Court held that the actions of a group of UK Special Air Service (SAS) soldiers in killing three unarmed suspected terrorists did not constitute a violation of Article 2(2). The Court accepted that the soldiers honestly believed the suspected terrorists had intended to remotely detonate a car bomb in Gibraltar; as such, their actions in killing them before they were able to do so were 'strictly proportionate to the achievement of the aims set out in [Article 2]',[168] namely, the protection of any person from unlawful violence. Ultimately, a violation of Article 2 was found by the Court as a consequence of failings in the planning, organization, and control of the operation. This does not, however, affect the legitimacy of the actions of the soldiers who used lethal force.

Further reinforcing the principles established in *McCann*, the Court again considered the actions of special forces operatives[169] in *Andronicou and Constantinou v Cyprus*. In this case, a rescue attempt by Cypriot special police forces was made in response to a hostage situation that resulted in the intentional death of the hostage-taker and the unintentional death of the hostage. The Court held that in planning and executing the operation, the state agents acted in a way that was 'reasonable in the circumstances'.[170] In relation to the intentional killing of the hostage-taker, the Court accepted that it was 'necessary ... to fire at him repeatedly in order to remove any risk that he might reach for his weapon'.[171] The Court also confirmed that the police officers were 'entitled ... to take all measures which they honestly and reasonably believed were necessary'[172] to protect their lives or that of another.

In *Makaratzis v Greece*,[173] the Court held that, following a prolonged car chase through Athens in which the driver passed through five road blocks and injured two civilians, the actions of the police in opening fire on the vehicle were 'reasonable in the circumstances',[174] as the car 'represented a lethal threat to innocent civilians'.[175]

The judgments of the Court in *McCann, Andronicou and Constantinou*, and *Makaratzis* can be contrasted with the Court's judgment in relation to the actions of a Turkish police special operations team in *Gül and Others v Turkey*.[176] Applying the same principles as established in *McCann* and *Andronicou and Constantinou*, the Court considered that the actions of the Turkish forces in firing 50–55 rounds through a door in a flat on a residential housing complex without any knowledge of who was on the other side could not be regarded as 'absolutely necessary'.[177] This was notwithstanding the fact that the Turkish forces were conducting a search and arrest operation against suspected PKK[178] terrorists. It was clear that, unlike in *McCann* and *Andronicou and Constantinou*, there was not a sufficient nexus to the

[166] Ibid. [167] *McCann and Others v the United Kingdom* 150. [168] Ibid.

[169] In this case police force officers rather than special forces soldiers.

[170] *McCann and Others v the United Kingdom* 183. [171] Ibid, 192. [172] Ibid, 192.

[173] *Makaratzis v Greece*, Application no 50385/99 (ECtHR, 20 December 2004).

[174] Ibid, 66. [175] Ibid, 65.

[176] *Gül and Others v Turkey*, Application no 22676/93 (ECtHR, 14 December 2000).

[177] Ibid, 83.

[178] Partiya Karkeren Kurdistan.

prospect of 'unlawful violence' to justify the actions of the Turkish forces, despite their assertion that they were responding to being fired upon by a PKK terrorist armed with a pistol.

1.9.2 In order to effect a lawful arrest or to prevent the escape of a person lawfully detained

When considering the facts of the cases before the Commission and Court, the justification advanced by states has often included both 'in defence of any person from unlawful violence' and 'to effect a lawful arrest'. In order to provide a degree of clarity with respect to the scope of the exceptions to Article 2, ECHR an attempt must be made to disaggregate the two criteria.

Notwithstanding the wording of the provision, recourse to lethal force to merely effect a lawful arrest, absent any nexus to an immediate threat of unlawful violence, cannot constitute a lawful deprivation of life. In *Nachova*,[179] the Court reasoned thus:

> the legitimate aim of effecting a lawful arrest can only justify putting human life at risk in circumstances of absolute necessity. The Court considers that in principle there can be no such necessity where it is known that the person to be arrested poses no threat to life or limb and is not suspected of having committed a violent offence, even if a failure to use lethal force may result in the opportunity to arrest the fugitive being lost.[180]

Similarly, in *Gül*[181] the Court held that, absent a threat of unlawful violence, the recourse to lethal force was not justified in a search and arrest operation.[182] In *Wasilewska and Kałucka v Poland*,[183] the Court reaffirmed the principle established in *McCann, Makaratzis, Nachova*, and *Andreou* that the 'legitimate aim of effecting a lawful arrest can only justify putting human life at risk in circumstances of absolute necessity'.[184] Further, the Court reaffirmed the requirement to ensure that the actions of state agents are 'authorised under national law ... policing operations must be sufficiently regulated by it, within the framework of a system of adequate and effective safeguards against arbitrariness and abuse of force'.[185] And finally, with respect to the planning, execution, and control of an operation, the Court held that it must have 'been planned and controlled so as to minimise to the greatest extent possible recourse to lethal force or incidental loss of life'.[186] This incorporates a requirement to ensure that state agents authorized to use firearms are trained to the required national and international human rights law standards.[187]

[179] *Nachova and Others v Bulgaria*, Application nos 43577/98 and 43579/98 (ECtHR, 6 July 2005).
[180] Ibid, 95. [181] Ibid, 83. [182] Ibid, 106.
[183] *Wasilewska and Kałucka v Poland*, Application nos 28975/04 and 33406/04 (ECtHR, 23 February 2010).
[184] Ibid, 44. [185] Ibid, 45. See also *Makaratzis* and *Andreou*.
[186] Ibid, 46. See also *McCann* and *Bubbins v the United Kingdom*, Application no 50196/99, 136.
[187] Ibid, 47: 'law-enforcement agents must be trained to assess whether or not there is an absolute necessity to use firearms, not only on the basis of the letter of the relevant regulations, but also with due regard to the pre-eminence of respect for human life as a fundamental value.'

The Commission conclusions in *Kelly v the United Kingdom*,[188] in which the actions of Ulster Defence Regiment soldiers in firing 14–15 rounds at a car passing through a checkpoint in Belfast were considered to be justified in order to effect an arrest of suspected terrorists, must be reconsidered in light of the Commission's subsequent finding in *Ayetkin v Turkey*[189] and other decisions of the Court.[190] As such, the reasoning of the Commission in *Kelly* can no longer be considered sound, in that the recourse to lethal force to effect an arrest, absent any threat of unlawful violence, will amount to a violation of Article 2.

1.9.3 In action lawfully taken for the purpose of quelling a riot or insurrection

In much the same vein as the Court's analysis of the use of lethal force to effect an arrest, the use of lethal force for the purpose of quelling a riot or insurrection, absent any threat of unlawful violence, will amount to a violation of Article 2.

By its nature, a riot[191] will involve a degree of unlawful violence, but this will not necessarily amount to unlawful violence for the purposes of justifying a recourse to the use of lethal force pursuant to Article 2(2). In *Kathleen Stewart v the United Kingdom*,[192] the Commission considered that 'a violent and hostile crowd attacking [eight soldiers] with stones and other missiles'[193] amounted to a riot. Consequently, the use of a baton round (plastic bullet) which unintentionally struck and killed Mrs Stewart's thirteen-year-old son was considered 'absolutely necessary'[194] in the circumstances. Conversely, in *Güleç v Turkey*[195] a violent demonstration involving around 3,000 people resulted in the Turkish police taking action to disperse the crowd. The police did not have 'truncheons, riot shields, water cannon, rubber bullets or tear gas',[196] which the Court considered to be 'incomprehensible and unacceptable because the province of Sirnak, as the Government pointed out, is in a region in which a state of emergency has been declared, where at the material time disorder could have been expected'.[197] Absent any alternative means, the police used firearms to disperse the crowd and, in doing so, struck and killed fifteen-year-old Ahmet Güleç. In finding a violation of Article 2, the Court considered that 'the force used to disperse the demonstrators, which caused the death of Ahmet Güleç, was not absolutely necessary within the meaning of Article 2'.[198] Clearly, a distinction can be drawn between *Kathleen Stewart* and *Güleç* in respect of the type of weapons used to

[188] *Kelly v the United Kingdom*, Application no 17579/90 (ECtHR, 13 January 1993).
[189] *Ayetkin v Turkey*, Application no 22880/93 (ECtHR, 18 September 1997).
[190] *Nachova and Others v Bulgaria* and *Gül and Others v Turkey*.
[191] In UK law the Public Order Act 1986 s 1 defines a riot as follows: 'Where 12 or more persons who are present together use or threaten unlawful violence for a common purpose and the conduct of them (taken together) is such as would cause a person of reasonable firmness present at the scene to fear for his personal safety, each of the persons using unlawful violence for the common purpose is guilty of riot.'
[192] *Kathleen Stewart v the United Kingdom*, Application no 10044/82 (ECtHR, 10 July 1984).
[193] Ibid, 29. [194] Ibid, 30. [195] *Güleç v Turkey*. [196] Ibid, 71.
[197] Ibid, 71.
[198] Ibid, 73.

quell the riot. The purpose of baton rounds (plastic bullets) is not to kill, although it has to be accepted that this can occur when used at close range.[199] Considered in the context of the Court's judgments in *Nachova* and *Gül*, any recourse to the use of lethal force to quell a riot would only be lawful with respect to Article 2 if there is an imminent threat to life.

Insurrection is not defined within UK law, although the term can be found in an Act of Congress of the United States.[200] It can be considered to be an uprising against the government characterized by acts of violence. The extent to which an insurrection may amount to a non-international armed conflict is considered in chapter 4.

1.10 Article 2 ECHR—Armed Conflict and the Substantive Element of the Right to Life

When it is determined that human rights law applies during armed conflict, it is necessary to consider both the substantive and procedural Article 2 obligations of states. The ECHR judgments in a series of cases concerning the armed conflicts in Cyprus, Chechnya, Turkey, and Iraq provide a framework against which the future activities of armed forces, in respect of their compliance with Article 2, can be assessed.

As a starting point, the Court has considered that the use of lethal force by state agents in armed conflict can, as a matter of principle, fall within 'paragraph 2 of Article 2'[201] and therefore not amount to a contravention of Article 2. This can include the use of a wide range of military weaponry.[202] Any use of lethal force must, however, be subject to a strict assessment of whether it is considered 'absolutely necessary' for the achievement of one of the purposes set out in Article 2(2),[203] and 'the force used must be strictly proportionate to the achievement of the permitted aims'.[204] As will be discussed in Chapter 4, when considering the use of lethal force in international and non-international armed conflict the provisions of Article 2(2) are, in effect, expanded to include legitimate targets as defined in, and subject to, the *jus in bello* of international humanitarian law. In other words, with respect to targeting of combatants in armed conflict, a contravention of Article 2 is only possible where the relevant rules of international humanitarian law have been contravened.

199 Detailed ballistics data was provided in *Kathleen Stewart v the United Kingdom* that concluded the use of plastic bullets could cause fatal injuries when fired at close range. Such information was not, however, known by the soldiers at the time.

200 Act of Congress 28th of February, 1795, 1 Story's LUS 389, provided: 'In the case of an insurrection in any state, against the government thereof, it shall be lawful for the president of the United States, on application of the legislature of such state, or of the executive, (when the legislature cannot be convened,) to call forth such number of the militia of any other state or states, as may be applied for, as he may judge sufficient to suppress such insurrection.'

201 *Isayeva, Yusupova and Bazayeva v Russia* 178.

202 Ibid, 178.

203 Ibid, 169.

204 Ibid, 169.

With respect to the non-international armed conflict in Chechnya, the Court, without explicitly stating so, has endorsed such an approach thus:

> The Court accepts that the situation that existed in Chechnya at the relevant time called for exceptional measures on behalf of the state in order to regain control over the Republic and to suppress the illegal armed insurgency. These measures could presumably include employment of military aviation equipped with heavy combat weapons.[205]

This statement must be read in conjunction with the following sentence: 'The Court is also prepared to accept that if the planes were attacked by illegal armed groups, that could have justified use of lethal force, thus falling within paragraph 2 of Article 2.'[206] It is contended that the fact that the Court makes reference to 'regain(ing) control over the Republic' and 'suppress(ion) of the illegal armed insurgency' clearly justifies and authorizes a degree of pre-emptive force beyond that authorized by the Court within a law enforcement paradigm. This is further amplified by the Court's subsequent reference to a 'self-defence' construct in respect of attacks on aircraft. Yet more convincing is the reasoning in the Chechen line of cases read in light of the Court's explicit reference to the interplay between international humanitarian law and international human rights law in, for example, *Esmukhambetov and Others v Russia*,[207] *Benzer and Others v Turkey*,[208] and *Hassan v the United Kingdom*.[209] Ultimately, where Article 2 is applicable to armed conflict, the criteria established within a law enforcement paradigm are applicable, with modifications, to reflect the nature of armed conflict.

1.10.1 Planning of a military operation

The Court has repeatedly asserted that states must ensure that an 'operation was planned and controlled by the authorities so as to minimise, to the greatest extent possible, recourse to lethal force'.[210] With respect to the planning of operations, given the explicit authorization by the Court to use 'heavy combat weapons'[211] and the concomitant possibility of significant loss of life, there is a commensurately high threshold for states to comply with when planning the use of such weapons.

[205] Ibid, 178. [206] Ibid, 178.

[207] *Esmukhambetov and Others v Russia*, Application no 23445 (ECtHR, 29 March 2011) 76.

[208] *Benzer and Others v Turkey*, Application no 23502/06 (ECtHR, 12 November 2013) 89 refers to Common Article 3 of the Geneva Conventions and IHL in para 184 thus: 'the Court considers that an indiscriminate aerial bombardment of civilians and their villages cannot be acceptable in a democratic society [see *Isayeva v Russia*, 191] and cannot be reconcilable with any of the grounds regulating the use of force which are set out in Article 2 § 2 of the Convention or, indeed, with the customary rules of international humanitarian law or any of the international treaties regulating the use of force in armed conflicts.'

[209] *Hassan v the United Kingdom*, Application no 29750/09 (ECtHR, 16 September 2014) 76, 77, and 100.

[210] Ibid, 171 and, inter alia, *Güleç, Nachova and Others, McCann and Others*, and *Andronicou and Constantinou, Khashiyev and Akayeva v Russia*, Application nos 57942/00 and 57945/00 (ECtHR, 24 February 2005) 159.

[211] *Hassan v the United Kingdom* 178.

For example, in *Isayeva, Yusupova and Bazayeva*, '12 S-24 non-guided air-to-ground missiles were fired, six by each [Russian air force] plane, which is a full load. On explosion, each missile creates several thousand pieces of shrapnel and its impact radius exceeds 300 metres'.[212] Not only was the use of such weapons considered to be disproportionate to the aim advanced by the Russian government, and accepted by the Court—namely, 'to protect persons from unlawful violence'[213]—but the mission planning was also considered inadequate.[214]

In planning a military operation, the safeguards employed by the state must be practical and effective in protecting the civilian population.[215] Inherent in this requirement is commanders' understanding of their human rights obligations, such obligations being incorporated into the military plan, and effective communication of the plan to the armed forces personnel charged with conducting the mission.

There is also a requirement to disclose military plans to the Court. In *Esmukhambetov*,[216] the Russian authorities' unwillingness to disclose any information regarding the planning of the mission that resulted in the deaths of five civilians was heavily criticized by the Court.[217]

1.10.2 National legal and administrative framework

Inextricably linked to the planning of a military operation is the requirement for states to establish 'an appropriate legal and administrative framework defining the limited circumstances in which law-enforcement officials may use force and firearms, in the light of the relevant international standards'.[218] The reference to law enforcement officials applies, *mutatis mutandis*, to armed forces personnel acting in a law enforcement capacity[219] in armed conflict, with the relevant international standards interpreted to mean, inter alia, the applicable elements of international humanitarian law.[220] This requirement is separate and distinct from the procedural element of the right to life in that it specifically refers to regulating the use of firearms in advance of the use of lethal force and not the establishment of an enforcement mechanism in respect of Article 2.

1.10.3 Training prior to a military operation

The Court has consistently criticized states for a failure to properly train armed forces before they embark on a mission.[221] This has specifically concerned a lack

[212] Ibid, 195. [213] Ibid, 181. [214] Ibid, 195.

[215] *Soering v the United Kingdom*, Series A no 161, para 87, 7 July 1989; *Loizidou v Turkey* (Preliminary Objections), Series A no 310, p. 27, para 72.

[216] *Esmukhambetov and Others v Russia.*

[217] Ibid, 144: 'The Court further finds unacceptable the Government's failure to provide any meaningful information and documentary evidence as to the planning and execution of the aerial attack of 12 September 1999 and the actions of the pilots who participated in that attack.'

[218] Ibid, 139. [219] *Nachova and Others* 93.

[220] *Esmukhambetov and Others v Russia* 76; *Benzer and Others v Turkey* 89; *Hassan v the United Kingdom* 76, 77, and 100.

[221] See among others *McCann and Others* and *Isayeva, Yusupova and Bazayeva v Russia.*

of awareness of the requirement to use alternatives to the use of lethal force in the first instance, and no knowledge of the human rights requirements of Article 2. In *McCann*, for example, while the soldier's cards that provided the guidelines for the use of lethal force complied with Article 2, the circumstances in Gibraltar in which they were interpreted by the SAS soldiers and, it was inferred by the Court, the training that had been provided led to the SAS soldiers immediately resorting to the use of lethal force. In order to comply with Article 2, the training provided to armed forces personnel with respect to the use of lethal force must consist of two distinct phases. First, initial general training must provide armed forces personnel with sufficient knowledge to correctly interpret the use of force cards. Second, task-specific training must be provided and give due regard to the requirements of Article 2 measured against the environment within which the armed forces personnel will operate. The provision of both the limbs of training can only be made possible by robust military doctrine that underpins and informs the actions of armed forces. As such, the Court has considered the content of such doctrine to be a relevant factor in determining whether there has been a violation of a state's positive obligation to protect the right to life.[222]

1.10.4 Conduct of a military operation

As a corollary to the requirement to plan a military operation in order to minimize recourse to lethal force to the greatest extent possible, military operations must be conducted in a commensurate way. For example, in *Isayeva, Yusupova and Bazayeva* the failure to employ a forward air controller to positively identify legitimate targets for the aircraft was considered by the Court to be a significant failing that directly contributed to a loss of life in contravention of Article 2.[223] Equally, the UK government was criticized for the inadequate planning of the operation using SAS soldiers in *McCann*,[224] as was the Turkish government in *Benzer*.[225] In the first instance, the conduct of a military operation must be undertaken with a requirement to employ alternatives to lethal force wherever possible and to 'take all feasible precautions in the choice of means and methods of a security operation mounted against an opposing group with a view to avoiding and, in any event, minimizing incidental loss of civilian life'.[226] If recourse to lethal force is justified with respect to Article 2, and there is no viable alternative, then all feasible methods must be employed to minimize the loss of life.[227] Crucially, military operations must also be conducted in accordance with requirements for the use of force to be 'absolutely

[222] *Isayeva v Russia* 199.

[223] Ibid, 188. See also *McCann and Others; Andronicou and Constantinou; Hugh Jordan v the United Kingdom*, Application no 24746/95 (ECtHR, 4 May 2001); and, *mutatis mutandis, Yaşa v Turkey*, 100 and *Makaratzis v Greece*.

[224] *Isayeva v Russia* 212. [225] Ibid, 180.

[226] *Ergi v Turkey*, Application no 23818/06 (ECtHR, 28 July 1998) 79.

[227] Ibid, para 171 and, inter alia, *Güleç, Nachova and Others; McCann and Others*; and *Andronicou and Constantinou, Khashiyev and Akayeva v Russia*, Application nos 57942/00 and 57945/00 (ECtHR, 24 February 2005) 159.

necessary' for the achievement of legitimate purposes as defined in sub-paragraphs a–c of Article 2 ECHR and 'strictly proportionate' to the achievement of permitted aims.[228]

1.10.4.1 'Absolute necessity'—ECtHR analysis in armed conflict

Analysis of the Chechen cases before the ECtHR reveals a willingness on the part of the Court to broadly interpret the term 'absolute necessity' within the context of a non-international armed conflict.[229] The Court has been prepared to accept the theoretical notion that 'the use of force may have been justified ... for achieving the declared purpose',[230] which in this case was to 'regain control over the Republic and to suppress the illegal armed insurgency'.[231] As such, in the first stage of the analysis, the Court recognized that the use of force is justified in the circumstances. The Court also accepted that force can include 'the deployment of army units equipped with combat weapons, including military aviation and artillery'.[232] While not explicitly stated by the Court, 'use of force' is clearly a reference to the use of lethal force. Having established that the use of lethal force is justified in the 'exceptional' circumstances, the Court then, as a second stage in its analysis, considered the issue of proportionality.

1.10.4.2 'Proportionality'—ECtHR analysis in armed conflict

A consistent theme throughout the 'Chechen' cases echoed in the judgments of the Court when considering Turkish military action against the PKK was that the states' action in response to the recognized threat was wholly disproportionate. Notwithstanding the Court's acceptance that some harm to civilians may be inevitable in enunciating that 'the operation was conducted in such a way as to avoid *or minimize* [my emphasis], to the greatest extent possible, harm to civilians',[233] a strict proportionality assessment has been applied. As a consequence, the use of, inter alia, unguided missiles and bombs, heavy artillery, and other indiscriminate weapons in highly populated areas has constituted gross violations of Article 2.[234] Ultimately, the threshold for the use of lethal force in a non-international armed conflict where there may be a loss of civilian life is high, and has been interpreted to reflect the protection afforded civilians in Common Article 3 of the Geneva Conventions and Additional Protocol II.

[228] The tests have been referred to consistently by both the Commission and Court in, inter alia, *Wolfgram v Germany*, *McCann v the United Kingdom*, *Andronicou and Constantinou v Cyprus*, *Güleç*, and *Nachova and Others*.

[229] The Court's approach can be typified by its judgment in *Isayeva v Russia* 180: 'The Court accepts that the situation that existed in Chechnya at the relevant time called for exceptional measures by the State in order to regain control over the Republic and to suppress the illegal armed insurgency. Given the context of the conflict in Chechnya at the relevant time, those measures could presumably include the deployment of army units equipped with combat weapons, including military aviation and artillery.'

[230] Ibid, 181. [231] Ibid, 180. [232] Ibid, 180. [233] Ibid, 183.

[234] Ibid, 179–201.

1.11 Death in Military Custody and Article 2

Where, in the course of an armed conflict, armed forces detain individuals in custody, they have an obligation to protect the detainees' right to life. The obligation has been considered by the Court thus: 'national authorities are responsible for the well-being of persons in custody and ... states bear the burden of providing a plausible explanation for any injuries, deaths and disappearances which occur in custody.'[235] The Court in *Hassan* considered that for the purposes of an assessment of ECHR obligations, 'custody' amounts to the time when an individual is 'within the physical power and control of the United Kingdom soldiers and therefore fell within the United Kingdom jurisdiction under the principles outlined in paragraph 136 of *Al-Skeini*'.[236] In this case, Tarek Hassan 'remained in the custody of armed military personnel and under the authority and control of the United Kingdom until the moment he was let off the bus that took him from the camp'.[237] Significantly, the point at which an individual is captured—in the case of Tarek Hassan, in Umm Qasr, Basrah, Iraq—amounts to custody for the purposes of Article 2.[238] The Court has yet to consider a situation where an individual is captured in circumstances that present a significant threat to life, for example an ongoing firefight in a non-international armed conflict. In such circumstances, it is likely that the Court will require that states 'take all feasible precautions' to ensure the life of the detainee is protected. This would include ensuring the detainee is moved to a place of safety as soon as circumstances on the ground permit.

[235] *Selmouni v France* [GC], Application no 25803/94 (ECtHR, 1999) 87; *Salman v Turkey* [GC], Application no 21986/93 (ECtHR, 2000) 99; *Tanış and Others v Turkey*, Application no 65899/01 (ECtHR, 2005) 160; *Er and Others v Turkey*, Application no 23016/04 (ECtHR, 31 July 2012) 66; *Meryem Çelik and Others v Turkey*, Application no 3598/03 (ECtHR, 16 April 2013) 48.

[236] *Hassan v the United Kingdom*, 76.

[237] Ibid, 79.

[238] Ibid, 76.

2

Procedural Right to Life Obligations

2.1 The Procedural Element of the Right to Life in Armed Conflict

The text of Article 2 does not include a procedural element to the right to life; rather, it simply establishes the substantive positive obligation on states and provides for permissible deprivations of the right. Initially the Commission[1] and latterly the Court[2] have determined that, when read in conjunction with a state's general obligations in Article 1, there must be an effective official investigation where an individual is killed in order to 'safeguard' the right to life. The Court has considered the requirement for a general procedural duty thus: 'the general legal prohibition of arbitrary killing by agents of the state would be ineffective in practice if there existed no procedure for reviewing the lawfulness of the use of lethal force by state authorities.'[3] It adds that 'the essential purpose of such an investigation is to secure the effective implementation of the domestic laws safeguarding the right to life and, in those cases involving state agents or bodies, to ensure their accountability for deaths occurring under their responsibility'.[4] With respect to the accountability of armed forces as agents of the state, the Court has developed detailed requirements in order to comply with the procedural element of the right to life.

2.1.1 The nature of procedural right to life obligations

When considering the litigation in the ECtHR following alleged right to life violations by armed forces in Iraq,[5] one might be forgiven for assuming that procedural right to life obligations can be pursued independently of a substantive breach. This, however, is not the case. While the duty to investigate a death that may involve a breach of a state's substantive right to life obligations by a state agent is not part of the substantive duty, it *is* dependent upon it.[6] It has been described as an 'ancillary or

[1] The European Commission on Human Rights, *The Taylor, Crampton, Gibson and King Families v the United Kingdom*, Application no 23412/94, 30 August 1994, 79-A DR (1994) 127–37.

[2] Most recently, the Court in *Jaloud v the Netherlands*, Application no 47708/08 (ECtHR, 20 November 2014) 186, referred at length to the principles established in *Al-Skeini and Others v the United Kingdom*, Application no 55721/07 (ECtHR, 7 July 2011).

[3] *Al-Skeini and Others v the United Kingdom* 163.

[4] Ibid, 163.

[5] See, for example, *Al-Skeini and Others*, 3 and 151; *Hassan v United Kingdom*, Application no 29750/09 (16 September 2004) 3; *Jaloud v the Netherlands*, Application no 47708/08 (20 November 2014) 3.

[6] *Al-Saadoon and Others v Secretary of State for Defence* [2015] EWHC 715 282.

adjectival duty implied from Article 2 read in conjunction with Article 1';[7] it is 'parasitic upon the existence of the substantive right, and cannot exist independently'.[8]

A procedural duty can only arise where there is 'reason to believe that there has been, or may have been, a violation of the substantive right'.[9] This threshold test does not establish a particularly high bar and has been described by the UK House of Lords as making an 'arguable case'[10] or providing 'grounds for suspicion'[11] that a violation of the substantive obligation has occurred. In *Al-Saadoon*, Leggatt J did not consider there to be any 'subtle differences' between the two tests and thought they were essentially 'expressing the same test'.[12] Analysis of ECtHR judgments reveals an approach not dissimilar to the threshold test developed in the UK courts.

In *Jaloud*, for example, a vehicle checkpoint in Iraq was fired upon by occupants of a car at around 2.12 am on 21 April 2004. Approximately thirty minutes later a car approached the checkpoint at speed, hit several barrels that had been set out to form the checkpoint, yet continued to advance. At this point a Royal Netherlands Army Lieutenant and Iraq Civil Defence Corps personnel opened fire, killing the applicant's son. Given the circumstances pertaining at the time, this could certainly be considered legitimate self-defence, yet as a death had occurred it was necessary to conduct an investigation that complied with the procedural element of Article 2. In *Al-Skeini*, the first, second, third, fourth, and fifth applicants' relatives were allegedly killed by UK armed forces whilst they conducted patrols in Basra, Iraq. In respect of the cases involving the first to fourth applicants the UK soldiers contended that they were acting within their rules of engagement, and this was accepted by their commanding officers, who did not investigate the matter further. It follows therefore that in such circumstances, despite it being at least arguable that the soldiers acted lawfully, an Article 2-compliant investigation is required.

2.1.2 Applicability of the procedural element of the right to life in armed conflict

The Court has consistently determined that a state's procedural obligations continue to apply in 'difficult security conditions, including armed conflict'.[13] This has

[7] Ibid, 182.

[8] As per Lord Bingham in *R (Gentle) v Prime Minister* [2008] AC 1356 6. See also *Jordan v United Kingdom*, Application no 24746/95 (ECtHR, 4 May 2001) 105; *Edwards v United Kingdom*, Application no 46477/99 (ECtHR, 14 June 2002) 69; *McKerr v United Kingdom*, Application no 28883/95 (ECtHR, 4 April 2000) 18–22.

[9] *Al-Saadoon and Others* 282; *R (Middleton) v West Somerset Coroner* [2004] 2 AC 182, 3; *R (Smith) v Oxfordshire Assistant Deputy Coroner* [2011] 1 AC 1 84, 97, 150, and 202.

[10] *R (Gentle) v Prime Minister* [2008] UKHL 20, 6: 'Thus to make good their procedural right to the enquiry they seek the appellants must show, as they accept, at least an arguable case that the substantive right arises on the facts of these cases. Unless they can do that, their claim must fail.'

[11] *R (Smith) v Oxfordshire Assistant Deputy Coroner* 84: 'The obligation to hold an article 2 investigation is triggered by circumstances that give ground for suspicion that the State may have breached a substantive obligation imposed by article 2.'

[12] *Al-Saadoon and Others* 282.

[13] *Jaloud v the Netherlands* 163. Other examples include *Güleç v Turkey*, Application no 21593/93 (ECtHR, 27 July 1998) 81; *Ergi v Turkey*, Application no 23818/94 (ECtHR, 28 July 1998) 79 and 82; *Ahmet Özkan and Others v Turkey*, Application no 21689/93 (ECtHR, 6 April 2004) 85–90, 309–20,

included, inter alia, cases concerning the situation in Northern Cyprus following the commencement of military operations by Turkey in July/August 1974,[14] the conflict between Turkish security forces and the PKK,[15] the conflict in Chechnya,[16] the war in Bosnia and Herzegovina,[17] and international military operations in Iraq,[18] as well as interstate cases concerning the Georgia–Russia and Ukraine–Russia armed conflicts.

2.1.3 The purpose of an investigation

Once aware of a potential violation of Article 2, a state must act of its own volition and with 'promptness and reasonable expedition'[19] to commence, conduct, and complete an investigation into the incident. A failure to act may constitute a violation. The Court has considered that the 'essential purpose of such an investigation is to secure the effective implementation of the domestic laws safeguarding the right to life and, in those cases involving state agents or bodies, to ensure their accountability for deaths occurring under their responsibility'.[20] In order to be effective, an investigation must be independent, be empowered to secure and preserve evidence and prevent collusion, establish a cause of death, be sufficient to inform a judicial finding as to whether the force used was or was not justified in the circumstances[21]

and 326–30; *Isayeva v Russia*, Application no 57950/00 (ECtHR, 24 February 2005) 180 and 210; *Kanlıbaş v Turkey*, Application no 32444/96 (ECtHR, 27 July 1998) 39–51.

[14] *Cyprus v Turkey*, Application no 25781/94, 10 May 2001; *Varnava and Others v Turkey*, Application nos 16064/90, 16065/90, 16066/90, 16068/90, 16069/90, 16070/90, 16071/90, 16072/90, and 160/73/90 (ECtHR, 18 September 2009); *Andreou v Turkey*, Application no 45653/99 (ECtHR, 27 October 2009); *Charalambous and Others v Turkey*, Application no 46744/07 (ECtHR, 3 April 2012); *Emin and Others v Cyprus*, Application no 59623/08 (ECtHR, 3 April 2012).

[15] The European Court of Human Rights has delivered around 280 judgments finding violations of the Convention which took place against the background of the fight against terrorism in the 1990s, in particular in connection with the conflict between Turkish security forces and the PKK, an illegal party. The Court found numerous violations of the Convention on account of:

- deaths of the applicants' next-of-kin as a result of excessive use of force by members of security forces;—failure to protect the right of life of the applicants' next-of-kin;—death and/or disappearance of the applicants' next-of-kin;
- ill-treatment;—destruction of property and—lack of effective domestic remedies into the applicants' complaints.

Taken from ECtHR Statistics and Factsheet, November 2014.

[16] To date the European Court of Human Rights has delivered more than 230 judgments finding violations of the Convention in connection with the armed conflict in the Chechen Republic of the Russian Federation. More than 350 cases are pending. About 60 per cent of the applications concern enforced disappearances; other issues include killing and injuries to civilians, destruction of homes and property, indiscriminate use of force, use of landmines, illegal detention, torture, and inhuman conditions of detention (ECtHR Statistics and Factsheet, November 2014).

[17] For example, see *Palić v Bosnia and Herzegovina*, Application no 4704/04 (ECtHR, 15 February 2011).

[18] For example, see *Al-Skeini and Others v the United Kingdom; Pritchard v the United Kingdom*, Application no 1573/11 (ECtHR, 18 March 2014) (strike-out decision); *Hassan v the United Kingdom; Jaloud v the Netherlands*.

[19] *Al-Skeini and Others v the United Kingdom* 167.

[20] Ibid.

[21] See, inter alia and *mutatis mutandis, Edwards v the United Kingdom*, 16 December 1992, 36; *Rowe and Davis v the United Kingdom* [GC], Application no 28901/95, 60; *I.J.L. and Others v the United*

(within the context of armed conflict this must involve a consideration of the lawfulness of the extant rules of engagement/self-defence card in use at the time),[22] and finally, be able to identify and punish those responsible. This by definition requires a fair judicial or quasi-judicial process that in turn complies with Article 6, ECHR.

2.1.3.1 Expeditious investigation

There is an 'implicit requirement of promptness and reasonable expedition'[23] in an investigation of an alleged violation of the right to life.[24] The Court in *Edwards*[25] summarized the position thus:

> it is crucial in cases of deaths in contentious situations for the investigation to be prompt. The passage of time will inevitably erode the amount and quality of the evidence available and the appearance of a lack of diligence will cast doubt on the good faith of the investigative efforts, as well as drag out the ordeal for the members of the family.[26]

The Court has interpreted Article 35(1) with considerable latitude in relation to cases involving an alleged violation of the right to life in circumstances of armed conflict, has recognized the exigencies of the situation, and the requirement to exhaust domestic remedies. Equally, the requirement to bring a case to the Court within six months of the final determination in the domestic courts has been flexibly interpreted. In a similar vein, the Court has recognized that 'concrete constraints ... may cause an investigation to be delayed'.[27] This does not, however, exonerate a state of its obligations under Article 2.

The Court has been extremely critical of investigations that have not been handled expeditiously. In *Bazorkina* the Court considered a delay of one year and four months in commencing an investigation and four years in interviewing the main protagonists thus:

> these delays alone compromised the effectiveness of the investigation and could not but have had a negative impact on the prospects of arriving at the truth. While accepting that some explanation for these delays can be found in the exceptional circumstances that have prevailed in Chechnya and to which the Government refer, the Court finds that in the present case they clearly exceeded any acceptable limitations on efficiency that could be tolerated in dealing with such a serious crime.[28]

Kingdom, Application nos 29522/95, 30056/96, and 30574/96, 112; *Dowsett v the United Kingdom*, Application no 39482/98, 41.

[22] *Jaloud v the Netherlands*, 201.

[23] *Yaşa v Turkey*, Application no 63/1997/847/1054 (ECtHR, 2 September 1998) 102–04, and *Mahmut Kaya v Turkey*, Application no 22535/93 (ECtHR, 28 March 2000) 106–07. This is considered 'essential by the court in maintaining public confidence in the maintenance of the rule of law and in preventing any appearance of collusion in or tolerance of unlawful acts': *Esmukhambetov and Others v Russia* 117.

[24] See also *Shanaghan v the United Kingdom*, Application no 37714/94 (ECtHR, 4 May 2001) 120 with respect to a delay in commencing an investigation.

[25] *Edwards v the United Kingdom* [2002] EHRR 487.

[26] Ibid, 86.

[27] *Bazorkina v Russia* 121.

[28] Ibid.

In such circumstances, the delay in commencing and conducting an investigation may of itself lead to a violation of the procedural element of Article 2. In *Bazorkina* the Court made only passing reference to other failings on the part of the state that constitute a violation of the procedural element of Article 2. The main focus and *ratio decidendi* is manifestly the delay in commencing and conducting the investigation.[29]

2.1.3.2 Cooperation of the state

In assessing a violation of the procedural element of Article 2, the Court has consistently stressed the requirement that governments cooperate fully with both the initial domestic investigation and subsequent court proceedings.[30] Not only is the cooperation of states an essential element of the right of individual petition as required by Article 34,[31] but a failure to effectively discharge their obligations pursuant to Article 34 in respect of the procedural element of Article 2 may 'reflect negatively on the level of compliance by a respondent state with its obligations under Article 38 (1) (a) of the Convention'.[32] The cooperation of states is particularly important when investigating an alleged violation of Article 2, as the government often exclusively holds crucial information required to assist with the investigation. A failure to disclose such information can result in an incomplete investigation and therefore a violation of the procedural element of Article 2.[33] The Court is cognizant, however, of the requirement to safeguard militarily sensitive information that has a nexus to national security. In *McCann* the Court considered that, notwithstanding the non-disclosure of certain information,[34] the inquest proceedings as an investigative

[29] Ibid 121–25.

[30] *Tanrikulu v Turkey*, Application no 23763/94 (ECtHR, 8 July 1999) 70.

[31] ECHR, Article 34, Individual Petition: 'The Court may receive applications from any person, nongovernmental organisation or group of individuals claiming to be the victim of a violation by one of the High Contracting Parties of the rights set forth in the Convention or the Protocols thereto. The High Contracting Parties undertake not to hinder in any way the effective exercise of this right.'

[32] *Timurtaş v Turkey*, Application no 23531/94 (ECtHR, 13 June 2000) 66 and 70.

[33] For example, ibid, 66 and 70; *Khashiyev v Russia*, Application nos 57942/00 and 57945/00 Judgment (ECtHR, 24 February 2005) 137.

[34] *McCann v the United Kingdom*, Application no 18984/91 (ECtHR, 27 September 1995) 104:

> Prior to the inquest, three certificates to the effect that certain information should not, in the public interest, be disclosed, were issued by the Secretary of State for the Home Department, the Secretary of State for Defence and the Deputy Governor of Gibraltar, dated respectively 26 August, 30 August and 2 September 1988. These stated that the public interest required that the following categories of information be protected from disclosure:
>
> 1. In the case of the seven military witnesses, the objection was to the disclosure of any information or documents which would reveal:
>   (i) their identity;
>   (ii) the identity, location, chains of command, method of operation and the capabilities of the units with which the soldiers were serving on 6 March 1988;
>   (iii) the nature of their specialist training or equipment;
>   (iv) the nature of any previous operational activities of the soldiers, or of any units with which any of them might at any time have served;
>   (v) in the case of Soldier G (the ammunition technical officer), any defence intelligence information, activities or operations (and the sources of intelligence), including

mechanism constituted a 'thorough, impartial and careful examination of the circumstances of the killings'[35] and therefore did not amount to a violation of Article 2(1).[36]

The judgment in *McCann* must, however, be contrasted with the Chechen body of cases, in which the Court has been critical of the Russian government not only in respect of the delay in investigative proceedings but also in relation to its unwillingness to disclose vital information.[37] Moreover, there appears to be a greater willingness on the part of certain states, for example the United Kingdom[38] and the Netherlands,[39] to disclose military information during the course of an investigation. Ultimately, however, a distinction can be drawn between the special forces operations in *McCann* and regular army operations in *Al-Skeini* and *Jaloud*. In the former, the Court is more likely to endorse its approach in *McCann* and recognize the requirement to safeguard operationally sensitive information that would undermine the future effectiveness of special forces and, in turn, the ability of a state to effectively counter terrorist activity.

2.1.3.3 An effective investigation defined

States must devote significant resources to the investigation of alleged violations of Article 2 that occur during armed conflict in order to comply with the requirement that 'all reasonable steps must be taken to ensure that an effective, independent investigation is conducted'.[40] This will include ensuring that states: secure the evidence concerning the incident, including, *inter alia*, physical evidence;[41] documentary evidence[42] and eyewitness testimony[43] (this includes ensuring that there is no possibility of collusion between witnesses);[44] forensic evidence;[45] and, where appropriate, an autopsy[46] which provides a complete and accurate record of injury and an objective analysis of clinical findings, including the cause of death.[47] It is evident

those on the basis of which his assessments were made and details of security forces counter-measures capabilities, including methods of operation, specialist training and equipment.

2. In the case of Security Service witnesses, the objection was to the disclosure of information which would reveal:
   (a) the identities of members of the Security Service, and details of their deployment, training and equipment;
   (b) all sources of intelligence information;
   (c) all details of the activities and operations of the Security Service.

35 Ibid, 163. 36 Ibid, 164.

37 *Esmukhambetov and Others v Russia*, Application no 23445/03 (ECtHR, 29 March 2011) 119.

38 *Al-Skeini and Others v the United Kingdom* 168–77.

39 *Jaloud v the Netherlands* 157–226.

40 By way of illustrative example see *Kaya v Turkey* 86–92; *Ergi v Turkey* 82–85; *Tanrıkulu v Turkey* 101–10; *Khashiyev and Akayeva v Russia* 156–66; *Isayeva* 215–24; *Musayev and Others v Russia* 158–65; *Jaloud v the Netherlands* 164.

41 *Jaloud v the Netherlands* 227. 42 Ibid. 43 *Tanrikulu v Turkey* 109.

44 *Jaloud v the Netherlands* 227. 45 *Gül and Others v Turkey* 89.

46 *Salman v Turkey* 106 and *Jaloud v the Netherlands* 227.

47 *Esmukhambetov and Others v Russia* 116.

that there are certain resource implications[48] in conducting such an investigation and complying with the procedural requirement set by the Court. The impact that this may have on the conduct of military operations will be considered in Chapter 4.

2.1.3.4 Circumstances on the ground during military operations

The Court has made reference to the difficulties inherent in conducting an investigation during armed conflict.[49] This is not only in relation to a potentially volatile security situation on the ground, but also in relation to tracing and interviewing witnesses, a lack of experts to conduct certain tasks such as autopsies and ballistics assessments, and the potential for linguistic and cultural misunderstandings.[50] Consequently, the Court has stated that 'in circumstances such as these ... the procedural duty under Article 2 must be applied realistically, to take account of specific problems faced by investigators'.[51]

Analysis of the judgments in, inter alia, *Al-Skeini* and *Jaloud* reveal that despite this assertion, in practice the Court has afforded very little latitude in this respect. In *Al-Skeini*, for example, the failure to interview Iraq nationals who witnessed the events, despite the difficulties inherent in doing so, was considered to be a significant failing.[52] Similar criticisms were made in *Jaloud* in respect of the failure to interview Iraq Civil Defence Corps personnel who witnessed the shooting at the checkpoint.[53] It would appear, therefore, that there are significant obligations on states to comply with the procedural element of Article 2, despite the conditions on the ground in which they may be operating. The position of the Court is summarized thus:

> neither the prevalence of violent armed clashes nor the high incidence of fatalities can displace the obligation under Article 2 to ensure that an effective, independent investigation is conducted into the deaths arising out of clashes involving the security forces, the more so in cases ... where the circumstances are in many respects unclear.[54]

As a consequence, states must plan and resource their armed forces sufficiently to comply with this requirement.

2.1.4 Independence of the investigation

In order to comply with the procedural element of Article 2, an investigation into an alleged violation must have hierarchical, institutional, and practical independence.[55] Given the inherently hierarchical nature of the armed forces,

[48] As an illustrative example this will include suitably qualified investigators; financial and administrative support; force protection, to enable interviews to be conducted in potentially hostile areas; logistic, communication, and air support; the use of interpreters; and the potential cooperation of the host government.

[49] For example, *Al-Skeini and Others v the United Kingdom* 161–68; *Jaloud v the Netherlands* 226.

[50] *Al-Skeini and Others v the United Kingdom* 168.

[51] Ibid.

[52] Ibid, 170–71.

[53] *Jaloud v the Netherlands* 103.

[54] *Ahmet Özkan and Others v Turkey* 302.

[55] *Al-Skeini and Others v the United Kingdom* 168; *Jaloud v the Netherlands* 164.

this requirement presents a challenge to states in ensuring the necessary independence, particularly when operating in the unstable environment of an armed conflict.

2.1.4.1 Hierarchical independence

In *Al-Skeini* the Court considered that 'if any investigation into acts allegedly committed by British soldiers was to be effective, it was particularly important that the investigating authority was, and were seen to be, operationally independent of the military chain of command'.[56] The Court did not limit its analysis to the investigations but considered the entire quasi-judicial and judicial process, including the scope of the courts martial into the soldiers alleged to have been responsible for the death of the fifth applicant's son.

In analysing the deaths caused by UK soldiers in *Al-Skeini*, the investigations fell into three categories. The investigations into the shooting of the first, second, and third applicant's relatives were limited to taking statements from the soldiers concerned and were neither independently conducted nor scrutinized.[57] They remained entirely within the military chain of command and as such did not comply with the procedural requirements of Article 2. The Court's assessment that there was no 'hierarchical independence' was not challenged by the British government. The second category involved investigations into the deaths of the fourth applicant's brother and the fifth applicant's son conducted by the Royal Military Police Special Investigations Branch (SIB). These investigations did not comply with the procedural element of Article 2 in that the SIB were not, at the relevant time, operationally independent from the military chain of command.[58] In fact, all SIB reports into deaths were sent to the commanding officer of the unit within which the soldiers concerned served, who had unfettered authority to discontinue the proceedings. There was not, therefore, immediate recourse from the SIB to an independent prosecutorial body. Further, the SIB could not 'decide for itself'[59] when to commence and cease an investigation. As a consequence of, inter alia, this lack of hierarchical independence, the Court considered that the investigations into the deaths of the fourth and fifth applicants' relatives did not comply with the procedural requirements of Article 2. The third category involved the death of Mr Baha Mousa, which was subject to a full public inquiry. This investigation complied with the procedural element of Article 2.

The lack of hierarchical independence identified by the Court in *Al-Skeini*, in which it placed its judgments in *Ramsahai*,[60] *Hugh Jordan*,[61] and *McKerr*[62] within the context of an armed conflict, can be contrasted with its judgment in *Jaloud*.

[56] *Al-Skeini and Others v the United Kingdom* 169. [57] Ibid, 171. [58] Ibid, 171.

[59] Ibid, 171, citing Brooke LJ.

[60] *Ramsahai and Others v the Netherlands*, Application no 52391/99 (ECtHR, 31 July 2007) 337.

[61] *Hugh Jordan v the United Kingdom* 120. [62] *McKerr v the United Kingdom* 128.

Significantly, the investigators in *Jaloud* had unfettered recourse to the Office of the Public Prosecutor, an independent prosecutorial body.

2.1.4.2 *Institutional independence*

The issue of institutional independence concerns the ability, or otherwise, of state bodies to act independently without interference. Within the context of the armed forces it is possible for the requirement of institutional independence to be satisfied subject to the following conditions. First, those under investigation and those being investigated must not come from the same unit[63] or be in the same chain of command.[64] Second, the investigation reports must be considered by an independent reviewing or prosecutorial body.[65] And finally, the investigative body must not be subject to interference, both in practice and due to the procedural hierarchical structure, from the military chain of command.[66]

2.1.4.3 *Practical independence*

In contrast to the procedural failings identified in *Al-Skeini*, in *Jaloud* the mere fact that the Royal Netherlands Military Constabulary unit charged with conducting the investigation lived in close proximity to the soldiers they were investigating was not considered to contravene the procedural element of Article 2. What was crucial in the view of the Court was the nature of the relationship between those conducting the investigation and those under investigation,[67] namely that there was no personal or professional nexus between the individuals concerned. This approach further refines the judgment in *Shanaghan*,[68] in which a violation of the procedural element of Article 2 was found where the police officer responsible for both the investigation and those under investigation was the Chief Constable of the Royal Ulster Constabulary.

2.1.5 Rules of engagement and self-defence

In order to make a determination as to whether or not the lethal use of force was lawful, an investigation must be able to interpret the extant rules of engagement under which the soldier was operating and the extent to which the concept of self-defence justifies the use of lethal force. This will require an analysis of the justification advanced for opening fire. If the soldier opened fire pursuant to the extant rules of engagement, then the analysis must occur in two stages. First, did the rules of engagement authorize the use of offensive force at the material time? Second, did the soldier act in accordance with the extant rules of engagement given the situation they faced? If the soldier acted in self-defence then a determination must occur based upon the analysis provided at 1.4.2.

[63] *Ramsahai and Others v the Netherlands* 337.
[64] *Al-Skeini and Others v the United Kingdom* 173.
[65] Ibid, 172.
[66] Ibid.
[67] *Ramsahai and Others v the Netherlands* 337.
[68] *Shanaghan v the United Kingdom* 104.

2.1.6 Punishment of those directly responsible for the death

The identification and punishment of the state agent(s) responsible for a violation of Article 2 is an integral element of the investigatory process,[69] but is not always sufficient to comply with the procedural element of Article 2.[70] Within a military context, the punishment of those responsible for a violation of Article 2 is dependent upon a military justice system that complies with Article 6, ECHR and is considered in Chapter 4.

In respect of fully complying with a state's Article 2 obligations, it is particularly significant that the court martial in respect of the death of the fifth applicant's son in *Al-Skeini* did not comply with the procedural element of Article 2. This is because the Court considered that the court martial did not determine the 'broader issues of state responsibility for the death, including the instructions, training and supervision given to soldiers undertaking tasks such as this in the aftermath of the invasion'.[71] Noting that this is not the purpose of a court martial, it would appear that an independent *non-judicial* inquiry would be required where there are systemic failures on the part of the state to comply with the procedural element of Article 2 in respect of non-operational[72] deaths during armed conflict.

2.1.7 Article 34 ECHR and victim status

The Court has not placed an unduly onerous burden upon states to disclose every detail of an investigation to the deceased's next of kin or respond to their every request.[73] The Court has, however, stated unequivocally that 'in all cases, the next of kin of the victim must be involved in the procedure to the extent necessary to safeguard his or her legitimate interests'.[74] It has been critical of states and drawn adverse inferences[75] where no disclosure has been forthcoming.[76] In respect of military operations where disclosure of information to the next of kin may compromise national security, the Court has not considered it a breach of the procedural element of Article 2.[77]

Where an investigation or judicial process has not complied with the procedural element of Article 2, the Court has determined that the applicant can still be considered to have victim status pursuant to Article 34.[78] As a consequence, the state will

[69] See, inter alia and *mutatis mutandis, Edwards v the United Kingdom*, 16 December 1992, 36; *Rowe and Davis v the United Kingdom* [GC], Application no 28901/95, 60; *I.J.L. and Others v the United Kingdom*, Application nos 29522/95, 30056/96, and 30574/96, 112; *Dowsett v the United Kingdom*, Application no 39482/98, 41. Within an armed conflict context see *Al-Skeini and Others v the United Kingdom* 175 and *Jaloud v the Netherlands* 224.

[70] *Al-Skeini and Others v the United Kingdom* 175.

[71] Ibid, 174.

[72] The term 'non-operational' defines those deaths either that do not involve enemy combatants or where a soldier has acted beyond their rules of engagement or self-defence. This will be considered in Chapter 4.

[73] *Ramsahai and Others v the Netherlands* 349–50; *Jaloud v the Netherlands* 221–25.

[74] *Shanahgan v the United Kingdom* 91–92 and *Esmukhambetov and Others v Russia* 118.

[75] *Esmukhambetov and Others v Russia* 120.

[76] Ibid, 119.

[77] *McCann v the United Kingdom* 104.

[78] In respect of the fifth applicant in *Al-Skeini and Others v the United Kingdom* 175.

not be considered to have discharged its Article 2 obligations until the outstanding issues identified by the Court have been satisfactorily resolved.

2.1.8 Public accountability

The requirement that a state is held responsible and publically accountable for the unlawful actions of its agents is considered by the Court to be an essential tenet of the rule of law,[79] and, in turn, necessary in order to respect, protect, and fulfil its human rights obligations. The Court has further stressed that accountability must exist in 'practice as well as theory',[80] clearly placing an emphasis on the requirement, where necessary, to publicly disseminate the finding of investigations into alleged violations of Article 2. With exceptions being made for national security caveats, this applies equally to investigations involving the armed forces, in terms of the investigation itself, dissemination of the report, and any judicial proceedings that may follow. It is therefore axiomatic that the judicial proceedings not only comply with the requirements of Article 6, ECHR, but are also held in public.

2.1.9 The effect of financial settlement

Where there has been financial settlement of a civil claim and an admission of liability on behalf of the state, the Court can still find a violation of the procedural element of Article 2 if it considers that there has not been a full and independent investigation into an alleged unlawful killing by a state agent.[81] Conversely, however, where a friendly settlement is reached and the Court considers that 'the settlement is based on respect for human rights as defined in the Convention and its Protocols',[82] it has been prepared to strike out[83] the proceedings in accordance with Article 39, ECHR. In *Prichard*, the Court considered that this requirement was satisfied by the production of an investigation and learning account into the death of Dewi Pritchard, a Territorial Army soldier killed while serving in Iraq, that was subsequently briefed to his family by a representative of the UK Ministry of Defence.

2.1.10 The requirement to provide appropriate training

A natural corollary to a state's substantive right to life obligations is the procedural requirement to ensure state agents tasked with the use of lethal force receive appropriate training. The Human Rights Committee[84] has stressed the need for law enforcement personnel to 'undergo appropriate training'[85] in order to comply with the state's right to life obligations.[86] The requirement to receive appropriate

[79] *Esmukhambetov and Others v Russia* 118.
[80] Ibid.
[81] *Al-Skeini and Others v the United Kingdom* 175.
[82] *Pritchard v the United Kingdom*, Application no 1573/11 (ECtHR, 18 March 2014).
[83] Article 37, ECHR.
[84] Concluding Observations: *Central African Republic (2006)* 12.
[85] Concluding Observations: *Kenya (2012)* 11.
[86] Concluding Observations: *Central African Republic (2006)* 12.

training would apply equally to armed forces personnel acting in a law enforcement capacity. Moreover, it comports with the requirement in international humanitarian law that parties to a conflict (international and non-international) must provide training in international humanitarian law.[87] As the ICRC Customary International Law Study notes, '[t]he obligation of States to provide instruction on international humanitarian law to their armed forces has been recalled on numerous occasions by the UN Security Council, UN General Assembly and UN Commission on Human Rights',[88] indicating a degree of convergence between international humanitarian law and human rights law on the requirement to provide training in the use of lethal force. Naturally, the content of the training differs between international humanitarian law and human rights law and will be considered further in Chapter 4.

2.2 The Procedural Element of Article 6

In addition to an assessment of the substantive element of Article 6(1), the Human Rights Committee have also considered the procedural element of Article 6, namely ensuring the enforcement and investigation of alleged violations of the provision. In draft General Comment 36, the Human Rights Committee considered that

> An important element of the protection afforded to the right to life by the Covenant is the obligation to investigate and prosecute allegations of deprivation of life by State authorities[89] or by private individuals and entities,[90] including allegations of excessive use of lethal force.[91]

The obligation to respect the procedural element of the right to life

> arises both from the general duty to ensure the rights recognized in the Covenant, which is articulated in article 2, paragraph 1, when read in conjunction with Article 6, and from the duty to provide an effective remedy to victims of human rights violations[92] and their families,[93] which is articulated in article 2, paragraph 3 of the Covenant, when read in conjunction with article 6, paragraph 1.[94]

[87] First Geneva Convention, Article 47; Second Geneva Convention, Article 48; Third Geneva Convention, Article 127; Fourth Geneva Convention, Article 144; Additional Protocol I, Article 83 (adopted by consensus); Additional Protocol II, Article 19 (adopted by consensus); Hague Convention for the Protection of Cultural Property, Article 25; Second Protocol to the Hague Convention on the Protection of Cultural Property, Article 30; Convention on Certain Conventional Weapons, Article 6.

[88] ICRC Customary International Humanitarian Law Study, Rule 142, 'Instruction in International Humanitarian Law within Armed Forces'.

[89] See, eg, Communication No 888/99, *Telitsin v Russian Federation*, Views adopted on 29 March 2004, 7.6.

[90] Concluding Observations: *Yemen (2012)*, 24.

[91] Human Rights Committee, Draft General Comment 36, 29.

[92] Human Rights Committee, General Comment 31, 15 and 18. See also Communication no 1619/07, *Pestano v Philippines*, Views adopted on 23 March 2010, 7.2; Communication no 1458/2006, *Gonzalez v Argentina*, Views adopted on 17 March 2001, 9.4; Concluding Observations: *Jamaica (2011)*, 16. Cf *Calvelli and Ciglio v Italy* (ECtHR, 17 January 2002) 51 (civil proceedings may be appropriate in some medical negligence cases).

[93] Concluding Observations: *Israel (2010)* 12.

[94] Human Rights Committee, Draft General Comment 36, 29.

An investigation into an alleged right to life violation must be: independent;[95] impartial;[96] prompt;[97] thorough;[98] effective;[99] credible;[100] and transparent;[101] and, in the event that a violation is found, a remedy must be provided that would include adequate measures of compensation, rehabilitation and satisfaction, including guarantees for non-repetition.[102] The investigation should also, if the circumstances necessitate and allow, include a rigorous autopsy of the victim's body.[103]

The Human Rights Committee has effectively established a 'reverse-burden'[104] approach when states have not cooperated at all with the communication process or have failed to provide comprehensive information following substantiated allegations of a breach of Article 6. In other words, the committee will assume a breach absent any explanation from the state party. In the case of *Eduardo Bleier*,[105] the Committee concluded:

> In cases where the author has submitted to the Committee allegations supported by substantial witness testimony, as in this case, and where further clarification of the case depends on information exclusively in the hands of the State party, the Committee may consider such allegations as substantiated in the absence of satisfactory evidence and explanations to the contrary submitted by the State party.[106]

And further,

> the failure of the State party to address in substance the serious allegations brought against it and corroborated by unrefuted information, cannot but lead to the conclusion that Eduardo Bleier is either still detained, incommunicado, by the Uruguayan authorities or has died while in custody at the hands of the Uruguayan authorities ... there are serious reasons to believe that the ultimate violation of article 6 has been perpetrated by the Uruguayan authorities.[107]

It is submitted therefore that the Human Rights Committee has established a rigorous framework to regulate the procedural element of the right to life that places a significant onus on states to investigate alleged violations and prosecute offenders.[108]

95 Concluding Observations: *Cameroon (2010)* 15.

96 Concluding Observations: *Bolivia (2013)* 15.

97 See, eg, Communication no 1556/2007, *Novakovic v Serbia*, Views adopted on 21 Oct 2010, 7.3; Concluding Observations: *Russia (2009)* 14.

98 Concluding Observations: *Mauritania (2013)* 13.

99 Concluding Observations: *UK (2015)* 8.

100 Concluding Observations: *Israel (2010)* 9.

101 Concluding Observations: *UK (2015)* 8.

102 Communication no R11/45, *Suarez de Guerrero v Colombia*, Views adopted on 31 March 1982, 15.

103 See Principles on the Effective Prevention and Investigation of Extra-Legal, Arbitrary and Summary Executions, ESC res 1989/65, annex, 12–14, UN Doc E/1989/89 (1989); *Kawas-Fernández v Honduras*, Judgment of the I/A CHR of 3 April 2009, 102.

104 *Bleier v Uruguay*, Communication no 30/1978. 'With regard to the burden of proof, this cannot rest alone on the author of the communication, especially considering that the author and the State party do not always have equal access to the evidence and that frequently the State party alone has access to relevant information. It is implicit in article 4 (2) of the Optional Protocol that the State party has the duty to investigate in good faith all allegations of violation of the Covenant made against it and its authorities, especially when such allegations are corroborated by evidence submitted by the author of the communication, and to furnish to the Committee the information available to it.'

105 Ibid, 13.3. 106 Ibid, 13.3. 107 Ibid, 14.

108 This is encapsulated in Human Rights Committee, Draft General Comment 36, 29–31.

2.3 Conclusion—The Relationship between Article 6, ICCPR and Article 2, ECHR

In *Streletz, Kessler and Krenz v Germany*[109] the Court considered 'that in the course of the development of that protection the relevant conventions and other instruments have constantly affirmed the pre-eminence of the right to life'.[110] It further noted that 'the convergence of the above-mentioned instruments is significant: it indicates that the right to life is an inalienable attribute of human beings and forms the supreme value in the hierarchy of human rights'.[111] At their inception the scope of the provisions establishing the right to life in the ECHR and ICCPR were inextricably linked, since both had the UDHR as a common foundation and early drafts of Article 6 served as a blueprint for Article 2, ECHR.[112] There are many similarities between the provisions in both general themes and specific detail.

Article 6, ICCPR and Article 2, ECHR both contain a positive obligation on states to protect the right to life through enforcement mechanisms in domestic legislation. This includes independent procedures to investigate and prosecute alleged violations of the right to life. Similarly, they both contain a negative obligation on states to ensure that state agents do not 'arbitrarily' deprive individuals of their right to life. It is on this point that the wording of the provisions diverges, but it is contended that in both meaning and interpretation they are fundamentally the same.

In drafting Article 2, ECHR the committee rejected the use of the term 'arbitrary' found in early drafts of Article 6, ICCPR,[113] and in the provision itself, in favour of a comprehensive and exhaustive declaration of permissible deprivations. In interpreting[114] Article 2, however, the Court has specifically referred to Article 6, ICCPR;[115] made reference to Human Rights Committee General Comment No. 6, paragraph 3;[116] and used the term 'arbitrary deprivation' when considering the scope and meaning of the right to life.[117] It has also referred to recognized international standards for the use of lethal force in law enforcement.[118]

In terms of scope, notwithstanding the differences in the content of the provisions, Article 2, ECHR and Article 6, ICCPR share many common features, such as to make them, to a large extent, compatible and mutually reinforcing. First, both

[109] *Streletz, Kessler and Krenz v Germany*, Application nos 34044/96, 35532/97, and 44801/98 (ECtHR, 22 March 2001).

[110] Ibid, 92. [111] Ibid, 94.

[112] CK Boyle, 'The Concept of Arbitrary Deprivation of Life' in BG Ramcharan (ed), *The Right to Life in International Law* (Martinus Nijhoff 1989) 228–29.

[113] Ibid, 228.

[114] The specific applicability of Article 2, ECHR and Article 6, ICCPR across the range of armed conflict activities, including the applicability and effect of derogations, will be considered in Chapters 4 and 6.

[115] *Streletz, Kessler and Krenz v Germany* 92. [116] *Makaratzis v Greece* 29 and 58.

[117] For example see *Nachova and Others v Bulgaria* 97 and 99; *Makaratzis v Greece* 29; and *Esmukhambetov and Others v Russia* 118.

[118] The United Nations Basic Principles on the Use of Force and Firearms by Law Enforcement Officials were referred to in, among other cases, *Nachova and Others v Bulgaria* 71 and 76 and *Makaratzis v Greece* 30.

instruments allow for situations where deprivation of life may be justified, but these circumstances must be narrowly interpreted.[119] Second, the use of force that may result in the deprivation of life must be 'absolutely necessary' and 'strictly proportionate' to either achieve one of the purposes in Article 2(2), ECHR[120] or not be considered 'arbitrary' within the definition of Article 6, ICCPR;[121] additionally, where possible, a warning[122] or opportunity to surrender[123] must be given. Third, operations that may involve the deliberate use of lethal force must be carefully planned and controlled in order to minimize the potential for loss of life.[124] And finally, states are required to secure the right to life in two ways: they must establish an 'appropriate legal and administrative framework defining the limited circumstances in which [state agents] may use force and firearms, in the light of the relevant international standards'[125] and 'the national law must secure a system of adequate and effective safeguards against arbitrariness and abuse of force'.[126] Equally, in terms of procedure, both the HRC and ECtHR have been willing to consider cases where it is apparent that states have either not conducted a satisfactory investigation or a significant period of time has elapsed from the time of the alleged violation, notwithstanding the requirement for applicants to exhaust domestic remedies.[127]

Despite there being similarities between the right to life provisions in the ICCPR and in the ECHR, a fundamental difference remains when the provisions are considered within the context of armed conflict. It is submitted that due to the use of the term 'arbitrarily deprived . . . of life', Article 6, ICCPR is more easily reconciled with an analysis of right to life obligations interpreted with reference to the applicable international humanitarian law than is Article 2, ECHR. The prescriptive nature of the exceptions to the right to life in Article 2(2) make it more difficult—although not impossible—to interpret, on a strict reading of the convention text, a state's right to life obligations with reference to international humanitarian law. This analysis, and a comparison of the terms 'necessity' and 'proportionality' in human rights law and international humanitarian law, will be considered in more detail in Chapter 4.

[119] UNHRC, *Suarez de Guerrero v Colombia* (1982) 13.1; *Esmukhambetov and Others v Russia* 138.

[120] As an illustrative example see *Esmukhambetov and Others v Russia* 138.

[121] As illustrative examples see *Suarez de Guerrero v Colombia* (1982) 13.1; *Baboeram et al v Suriname* (1985) 14.3.

[122] *Esmukhambetov and Others v Russia* 149.

[123] *Suarez de Guerrero v Colombia* (1982) 13.2.

[124] *McCann v the United Kingdom* 146–50; *Andronicou and Constantinou* 171; *Oğur v Turkey* 78; *Suarez de Guerrero v Colombia* (1982) 13.1–13.3; *Baboeram et al v Suriname* (1985) 14.3.

[125] *Nachova and Others v Bulgaria* 96; *Makaratzis v Greece* 57–59. *Suarez de Guerrero v Colombia* (1982) 13.3 specifically states: 'Inasmuch as the police action was made justifiable as a matter of Colombian law by Legislative Decree No. 0070 of 20 January 1978, the right to life was not adequately protected by the law of Colombia as required by article 6 (1).'

[126] *Makaratzis v Greece* 58; *Suarez de Guerrero v Colombia* (1982) 13.3.

[127] *Suarez de Guerrero v Colombia* (1982) 8.1–8.2; *Aksoy v Turkey* 51–52; *Akdivar and Others v Turkey* 1210; *Isayeva v Russia* 144.

PART II

APPLICATION OF THE RIGHT TO LIFE IN ARMED CONFLICT

3

The Extraterritorial Application of International Human Rights Law

3.1 Introduction

When conducting military operations beyond their borders, *potential* accountability under international human rights law exists wherever a state agent acts and thereby is alleged to have violated a human rights obligation of the state responsible for the acts of the state agent.[1] The accountability of the state will be determined by the extent to which the relevant international human rights law provisions are applicable to the situation in which the state agent is acting, or failing to act. An assessment of the applicability of a state's human rights obligations is required to determine, first, if right to life obligations are relevant to the military activities being undertaken,[2] and second, the actual scope of the obligation—or, put another way, the extent to which it applies. Only then can an assessment be made in respect of any alleged violation, noting, however, the applicability and effect of other bodies of international law.[3] The ECHR[4] and the International Covenant on Civil and Political Rights (ICCPR)[5] only apply to acts or omissions within the jurisdiction of the state. It is therefore necessary to consider the issue of jurisdiction as an essential prerequisite in determining a state's right to life obligations during armed conflict.

[1] See Sarah Joseph, 'Scope of Obligations' in Daniel Moeckli, Sangeeta Shah, and Sandesh Sivakumaran (eds), *International Human Rights Law* (Oxford University Press 2010) 160.

[2] The ECtHR has termed this the 'factual context': see *Jaloud v the Netherlands*, Application no 47708/08 (ECtHR, 20 November 2014) 140.

[3] The relationship between international human rights law and international humanitarian law will be considered in Chapter 4.

[4] Article 1, ECHR: 'The High Contracting Parties shall secure to everyone within their jurisdiction the rights and freedoms defined in Section I of this Convention.'

[5] Article 2(1), ICCPR: 'Each State Party to the present Covenant undertakes to respect and to ensure to all individuals within its territory and subject to its jurisdiction the rights recognized in the present Covenant.'

3.2 Jurisdiction in International Human Rights Law

In the ECHR and ICCPR the term jurisdiction refers to the jurisdiction of the state[6] and not the supranational judicial[7] or quasi-judicial body.[8] It is axiomatic therefore that the state must exercise jurisdiction in order to be held responsible for any acts or omissions of state agents that give rise to an alleged violation of the relevant human rights instrument.[9] When armed forces operate in the territory of another state, this requires an examination of the extent to which human rights treaties have extraterritorial effect. Jurisdiction acts as a 'threshold criterion'[10] in that, in order for a state to be held responsible for alleged violations of an international human rights law instrument, it must first exercise 'jurisdiction'.[11] Despite the European Court of Human Rights (ECtHR) making assertions to the contrary,[12] several commentators have argued that as a consequence, the function of jurisdiction in human rights law is different to that in international law.[13] In international law, jurisdiction is the legal authority to regulate the conduct of persons vested in a state.[14] This

[6] See Noam Lubell, *Extraterritorial Use of Force against Non-State Actors* (Oxford University Press 2010) 232–35 and Marko Milanovic, *Extraterritorial Application of Human Rights Treaties: Law, Principles and Policy* (Oxford University Press 2011) 8. For examples, see Article 1, European Convention on Human Rights—'The High Contracting parties shall secured to everyone within their jurisdiction the rights and freedoms defined in Section I of this Convention'; Article 2(1), International Covenant on Civil and Political Rights—'each state party to the present Covenant undertakes to respect and to ensure to all individuals within its territory and subject to its jurisdiction the rights recognised in the present Covenant'; Article 1, American Convention on Human Rights—'The States Parties to this Convention undertake to respect the rights and freedoms recognized herein and to ensure to all persons subject to their jurisdiction the free and full exercise of those rights and freedoms'; and Article 2(1), Convention against Torture and Other Cruel, Inhuman or Degrading Treatment or Punishment—'each state party shall take effective legislative, administrative, judicial or other measures to prevent acts of torture in any territory under its jurisdiction'.

[7] For example, the European Court of Human Rights, African Court of Human and Peoples' Rights, and Inter-American Court of Human Rights.

[8] For example, the Human Rights Committee and Committee against Torture.

[9] *Al-Skeini v the United Kingdom*, Application no 55721/07 (ECtHR, 7 July 2011) 130: 'The exercise of jurisdiction is a necessary condition for a Contracting State to be able to be held responsible for acts or omissions imputable to it which give rise to an allegation of the infringement of rights and freedoms set forth in the Convention.'

[10] Ibid.

[11] Sandy Ghandhi, 'Al-Skeini and the Extra-Territorial Application of the European Convention on Human Rights' in Andrew Burrows, David Johnston QC, and Reinhard Zimmerman, *Judge and Jurist: Essays in Memory of Lord Rodger of Earlsferry* (Oxford University Press 2013) 577.

[12] *Ilaşcu and Others v Moldova and Russia*, Application no 48787/99 (ECtHR, 8 July 2000) 311: 'The Court refers to its case-law to the effect that the concept of 'jurisdiction' for the purposes of Article 1 of the Convention must be considered to *reflect the term's meaning in public international law*.'

[13] Samantha Besson, 'The Extraterritoriality of the European Convention on Human Rights: Why Human Rights Depend on Jurisdiction and What Jurisdiction Amounts To' (2012) *LJIL* 870; Milanovic, *Extraterritorial Application of Human Rights Treaties* 19.

[14] AV Lowe and C Staker, 'Jurisdiction', in Malcolm Evans, *International Law* (3rd edn, (Oxford University Press 2010) 313; Michael Akehurst, 'Jurisdiction in International Law' *BYIL* (1975) 46 145–257; Alexander Orakhelashvili, 'The Concept of International Judicial Jurisdiction: A Reappraisal', *Law & Practice of Int Courts & Trib* (2003) 3(Fall) 501–50; and Milanovic, *Extraterritorial Application of Human Rights Treaties* 51 all argue that there is no universal definition of jurisdiction generally and with respect to human rights treaties specifically, but for different reasons. Akehurst draws a distinction between the jurisdiction of a court and the jurisdiction of a state and contends that, with respect to the

concept concerns the ability to 'make, apply and enforce rules'.[15] Put another way, it 'concerns essentially the extent of each state's right to regulate conduct or the consequences of events'.[16] Jurisdiction in international law is not therefore concerned with 'defining state jurisdiction in the first place'.[17] While there is general agreement among commentators on the nature of jurisdiction in human rights law, that is to say vis-à-vis international law, there is little agreement on what the elements of jurisdiction in human rights law are,[18] or, put another way, what the constitutive elements of jurisdiction are.[19]

In considering the issue of the extraterritorial application of the ECHR to military activities in Northern Cyprus, Iraq, NATO bombings in Belgrade, and law enforcement operations at sea, the ECtHR has broadly established two types or models of jurisdiction—territorial and personal—and also introduced the notion of jurisdiction arising where armed forces exercise some or all of the 'public powers' of the state within which they operate. What remains unclear, however, is the exact nature of these types or models of jurisdiction and how they interact with each other and the concept of attribution. The purpose of this chapter is therefore threefold: first, with reference to the ECHR, to analyse the nature of the geographical and personal models of jurisdiction and the notion of 'public powers', and how these models interact with reference to the activities of armed forces; second, to assess the extent of the extraterritorial application of the ICCPR; and finally, to assess the significance of the related notion of attribution of armed forces' actions to states or international organizations. Ultimately, a determination must also be made as to when individuals are within the jurisdiction of the state for the purposes of right to life obligations when armed forces operate overseas.

3.2.1 ECHR Article 1

Article 1 of the ECHR provides: 'The High Contracting Parties shall secure to everyone within their jurisdiction the rights and freedoms defined in Section 1 of this Convention.'

ECHR, the jurisdiction has its foundation in the jurisdiction of the state. Orakhelashvili further contends that there is no universal definition of jurisdiction within public international law, and therefore the ECtHR's reference to it as the benchmark for its analysis of jurisdiction is misplaced. Milanovic goes further and suggests that within a human rights context generally, and with reference to the ECHR especially, all that is meant by 'jurisdiction' is simply the exercise of power.

[15] Lowe and Staker, 'Jurisdiction' 313.

[16] RY Jennings and AD Watts (eds), *Oppenheim's International Law—Volume 1, Peace* (Oxford University Press 9th edn, London 1992) 456.

[17] Samantha Besson, 'The Extraterritoriality of the European Convention on Human Rights' 870.

[18] Ibid; Milanovic, *Extraterritorial Application of Human Rights Treaties* 8, 27, 32, 34, 39–41; R Lawson, 'Really Out of Sight? Issues of Jurisdiction and Control in Situations of Armed Conflict under the ECHR' in Antoine Buyse (ed), *Margins of Conflict: The ECHR and Transitions to and from Armed Conflict* (Intersentia 2011) 57; Max Schaefer, 'Al-Skeini and the Elusive Parameters of Extraterritorial Jurisdiction' (2011) 5 *EHRLR* 579.

[19] Samantha Besson, 'The Extraterritoriality of the European Convention on Human Rights' 872.

As a point of departure in the assessment of the extraterritorial jurisdiction of the ECHR, the Court asserted that jurisdiction is 'essentially territorial'.[20] It further asserted that only in 'exceptional cases'[21] jurisdiction will be regarded as extraterritorial, since the ECHR is essentially a regional treaty that applies within the 'legal space' or *espace juridique*[22] of the contracting states. Subsequent judgments of the Court support the notion that the ECHR is *essentially* territorial, but it is doubtful that it can be said that the circumstances in which it is applied extraterritorially can now be considered truly 'exceptional'. Moreover, any assertion that it applies only within the 'legal space' of the contracting states is simply not consistent with the Court's approach over the past decade.[23]

The Court has found that the ECHR applies extraterritorially as a consequence of, inter alia, Turkish military and governmental activity in Northern Cyprus;[24] Russian influence in Transdnistria;[25] French,[26] Italian[27] and Turkish[28] military and security forces acting outside of their states; and UK[29] and Dutch[30] military activity in Iraq. The Court's willingness to establish jurisdiction in these cases, particularly *Issa*,[31] cannot be compatible with the ECHR applying only within the 'legal space' of the contracting state.[32] Furthermore, it demonstrates a willingness to apply the Convention across a broad canvas of factual situations in which the level of overall control of both individuals and territory by state agents varies considerably. This, in part, has been made possible by the Court's willingness to 'divide and tailor' rights depending on the circumstances by which a state exercises jurisdiction.[33]

[20] *Banković and Others v Belgium and 16 Other Contracting States*, Application no 52207/99. Admissibility (ECtHR, 12 December 2001) 59–63.

[21] Ibid. [22] Ibid, 80.

[23] *Al-Skeini v the United Kingdom* 137; Anna Cowan, 'A New Watershed: Re-Evaluating Banković in Light of Al-Skeini' (2012) (1)1 *CJICL* 219; David Goddard, 'Applying the European Convention on Human Rights to the Use of Physical Force: Al-Saadoon' (2015) 91 *Intl L Stud* 402, at 412.

[24] *Cyprus v Turkey*, Application no 25781/94 (ECtHR, 10 May 2001); *Andreas Manitaras and Others v Turkey*, Application no 54591/00 (ECtHR, 3 June 2008).

[25] *Ilaşcu and Others v Moldova and Russia*, Application no 48787/99 (ECtHR, 8 July 2004); *Ivanţoc and Others v Moldova and Russia*, Application no 23687/05 (ECtHR, 15 November 2011).

[26] *Ilich Sanchez Ramirez v France*, Application no 28780/95 (EComHR, 24 June 1996); *Medvedyev and Others v France*, Application no 3394/03 (ECtHR, 23 March 2010).

[27] *Hirsi Jamaa and Others v Italy*, Application no 27785 (ECtHR, 23 February 2012).

[28] *Pad and Others v Turkey*, Application no 60167/00 (ECtHR, 28 June 2007); *Issa and Others v Turkey*, Application no 31821/96 (ECtHR, 16 November 2004).

[29] *Al-Jedda v the United Kingdom*, Application no 27021/08 (ECtHR, 7 July 2011); *Al-Skeini v the United Kingdom; Hassan v the United Kingdom*, Application no 29750/09 (ECtHR, 16 September 2014).

[30] *Jaloud v the Netherlands*, Application no 47708/08 (ECtHR, 20 November 2014).

[31] On the facts in *Issa*, the Court could not conclude that the Turkish armed forces were responsible for the deaths of Iraqi shepherds in Iraqi territory near the Turkish border. Nonetheless, in respect of jurisdiction arising as a consequence of control over individuals, the Court considered that 'a State may also be held accountable for violation of the Convention rights and freedoms of persons who are in the territory of another State but who are found to be under the former State's authority and control through its agents operating—whether lawfully or unlawfully—in the latter State ... Accountability in such situations stems from the fact that Article 1 of the Convention cannot be interpreted so as to allow a State party to perpetrate violations of the Convention on the territory of another State, which it could not perpetrate on its own territory' (para 71).

[32] See Leggatt J citing Lord Hope in *Al-Saadoon and Others v Secretary of State for Defence* [2015] EWHC 715 (Admin) 59.

[33] *Al-Skeini and others v the United Kingdom* 137.

3.2.2 Dividing and tailoring human rights

The ECtHR has stated that

> whenever the State, through its agents, exercises control and authority over an individual, and thus jurisdiction, the state is under an obligation under Article 1 to secure to that individual the rights and freedoms under Section 1 of the Convention that are relevant to the situation of that individual. In this sense, therefore, the Convention rights can be 'divided and tailored'.[34]

The Court did not elaborate further, although the judgment in *Al-Skeini* marks a significant departure from the previous approach of the Court, which considered that the positive obligation in Article 1, ECHR 'to secure the rights and freedoms defined in ... this Convention' could not be 'divided and tailored'.[35] Not only does the judgment in *Al-Skeini* mark a departure from the previous approach of the Court in respect of the scope of human rights protections, but when read in conjunction with subsequent judgments[36] it illustrates a willingness on the part of the Court to interpret a state's human rights obligations in light of the situation on the ground during armed conflict and with reference to other applicable bodies of international law[37] that may modify the applicability of human rights provisions.

In respect of 'dividing' Convention rights, the term 'relevant to the situation of that individual' must be considered within the context of the nature of armed forces activity existing at the time. The Court has expressly stated[38] that states are not always under an obligation to afford an individual the entire panoply of human rights protections. Specifically, therefore, a state can 'divide' the corpus of human rights protections and recognize and afford only certain rights. The extent to which a state can afford and protect certain rights will be a function of the 'situation on the ground' and a state's capability to act and to accord the specific human right. This point will apply especially to a state's positive[39] human rights obligations, namely, the requirement for a state to take action to secure the enjoyment of a right, but also to a state's negative human rights obligations, namely, an obligation on the state to refrain from an action that would violate a human rights protection.

In respect of 'tailoring' specific human rights, this refers both to adapting particular rights to the situation under consideration and to the degree of application of

[34] Ibid.

[35] *Banković and Others v Belgium and 16 Other Contracting States*, Application no 52207/99 (ECtHR, 12 December 2001) 75.

[36] *Jaloud v the Netherlands*, 226 and *Hassan v the United Kingdom*, Application no 29750/09, 16 September 2014, 77.

[37] *Hassan v the United Kingdom* 107.

[38] Ibid, 37.

[39] The relevant test is set out in *Osman v the United Kingdom* 116: 'positive obligations flowing from Article 2 should be interpreted in a way which does not impose an impossible or disproportionate burden on the authorities ... Where there is an allegation that the authorities have violated their positive obligation to protect the right to life ... it must be established to the [Court's] satisfaction that the authorities knew or ought to have known at the time of the existence of a real and immediate risk to the life of an identified individual or individuals from the criminal acts of a third party and that they failed to take measures within the scope of their powers which, judged reasonably, might have been expected to avoid that risk.'

those rights. By way of illustration, the Court has recognized the difficulties inherent in fully complying with the procedural element of Article 2 in times of armed conflict[40] and, as such, has interpreted states' obligations in light of these. A volatile situation on the ground may therefore prevent a full investigation into the death of a civilian if, for example, it proves impossible to identify and interview witnesses or to secure the body for post-mortem examination. Similarly, the Court has also recognized both conflicting 'priorities'[41] (of states) and the 'resource implications'[42] of recognizing human rights, and has concluded that, in certain circumstances, 'obligations be interpreted in such a way as [not] to impose an impossible or disproportionate burden'.[43]

Recent judgments of the Court[44] demonstrate a willingness not only to adapt human rights obligations to the circumstances faced by armed forces operating overseas, but also to recognize the difficulties inherent in operating in a complex legal and operational environment. The extent of a state's human rights obligations, and therefore the requirement to recognize both positive and negative human rights, can only be determined by an examination of the situation within which armed forces operate, in concert with an assessment of degree of control exercised by the state over the act or omission said to constitute a violation.

3.3 Categories of Extraterritorial Application of Human Rights Laws

Armed conflicts can be dynamic, volatile, and unpredictable or, conversely, following a period of frenetic activity, settled and relatively peaceful, with only sporadic violent activity. Equally, within an area of responsibility, the situation on the ground can be vastly different depending on both geographical and temporal factors. In order to determine a state's human rights obligations it is therefore necessary to conduct an assessment of the applicable circumstances on the ground at any given time. For example, during the armed conflict in Afghanistan the nature of the conflict changed dramatically over time and depending upon geographical area. The vast majority of fighting took place in the south and east of the country and, by comparison, the conditions in the north and west were relatively benign.

The nature of armed forces activity can therefore be usefully classified as a consideration of the human rights obligations of states in the following circumstances: in a state's own territory; in a stable and settled 'occupation'; where a state exercises 'decisive influence'; where there is 'localized control'; and when state agents exercise 'physical power and control over a person'—and, within this context, in dynamic

[40] *Jaloud v the Netherlands* 226.

[41] *Ilaşcu and Others v Moldova and Russia*, Application no 48787/99 (ECtHR, 8 July 2000) 332.

[42] Ibid.

[43] *Özgür Gündem v Turkey*, Application no 23144/93 43 and *Ilaşcu and Others v Moldova and Russia* 332.

[44] *Al-Skeini and Others v the United Kingdom* 137; *Jaloud v the Netherlands*, 226; *Hassan v the United Kingdom* 77 and 107.

situations, for example while manning checkpoints, patrolling, or targeting combatants. It is important to note, however, that these categories, with the exception of operating in a state's own territory, are not mutually exclusive and there can be significant overlap between them. Moreover, within any overall area of responsibility, different circumstances may exist in different locations at different times.

3.3.1 State's own territory

When military operations are conducted within the state's own territory, as a matter of jurisdiction, the entire corpus of human rights instruments to which the state is a party are applicable.[45] Naturally, the scope of such obligations will be subject to the interaction of international human rights law with other applicable bodies of law, principally international humanitarian law. A state's human rights obligations may, however, be modified where the state loses control of an area of territory that hitherto had been subject to their control and remains within their internationally recognized borders.[46]

3.3.2 Stable and settled occupation

Occupation within the context of international human rights law is taken to mean the stable and settled control of territory rather than the specific meaning attributable to 'occupation' in international humanitarian law.[47] Further, for the purposes of a jurisdictional analysis of human rights provisions occupation includes control by the 'occupying' state of public authorities within the territory.[48] The Court has repeatedly asserted that the status of 'occupying power' within the meaning of Article 42 of the Hague Regulations, or the lack of it, is not per se determinative.[49] As a consequence, an assessment of jurisdiction is determined more by the actions of the state agents rather than as a consequence of the international humanitarian law notion of 'occupation' being ascribed to the actions of the state. That is not to say, however, that when a state is an occupying power under international humanitarian law, human rights law obligations cannot exist. Rather, it has been persuasively argued that they can,[50] but the method in which the obligations arise is not solely a consequence of an international humanitarian law assessment.

In a situation of stable and settled 'occupation' where a state's armed forces have 'effective overall control'[51] of the territory, in jurisdictional terms the

[45] *Ilaşcu and Others v Moldova and Russia* 312 and *Assanidze v Georgia*, Application no 71503/01 (ECtHR, 8 April 2004) 139.

[46] *Ilaşcu and Others v Moldova and Russia* 331.

[47] Hague Convention IV (1907), Annex on the Laws and Customs of War on Land, Section III; Geneva Convention IV, Section III and Common Article 2, Additional Protocol I (1977).

[48] *Cyprus v Turkey*, Application no 25781/94 (ECtHR, 10 May 2001) 77.

[49] *Jaloud v the Netherlands* 142.

[50] See Eyal Benvenisti, *The International Law of Occupation* (Oxford University Press, 2nd edn, 2012) 14–15; Noam Lubell, 'Human Rights in Military Occupation' (2012) 94(885) *IRRC* 337; International Committee of the Red Cross, Expert Meeting on the Law of Occupation and Other Forms of the Administration of Territory (2012) Geneva 117–19.

[51] *Cyprus v Turkey* 77 and *Loizidou v Turkey*, Application no 15318/89 (ECtHR, 18 December 1996) 56.

'occupied' territory is akin to a state's own territory.[52] Consequently, human rights provisions cannot be divided and tailored and the entire corpus of relevant human rights instruments is applicable.[53] This, by definition, includes positive and negative right to life obligations. Where circumstances of stable and settled occupation have arisen, the Court has found violations across the spectrum of human rights protections.[54] Cognizant of this, states must ensure sufficient resources are available in order to ensure compliance with their positive and negative human rights obligations in circumstances of stable and settled occupation.

3.3.3 Decisive influence

Decisive influence is considered to represent a situation in which a state, through political, economic, and financial support[55]—often in concert with the use of armed forces—exercises control over the public authorities that in turn control territory in another state.[56] This is not therefore simply a calculation based upon the number of troops in a specific geographical area and the size of the civilian population living therein. In his dissenting opinion in *Ilaşcu*, Judge Kovler, with some incredulity, contrasted the situations in Northern Cyprus and the Transdnistrian region of Moldova based on an analysis of numerical military presence and function.[57] This analysis, however, failed to sufficiently recognize the more subtle influence to be asserted through political, economic, and financial support that can, in turn, establish jurisdiction.

In order to satisfy the 'decisive influence' test there must be a 'continuous and uninterrupted link of responsibility'[58] for human rights violations on the part of the 'influencing' state. The applicability of specific human rights provisions is determined by the extent to which the 'influencing' state controls the activities in the territory where the alleged violation has occurred. In circumstances where this

[52] *Loizidou v Turkey* 56.

[53] *Cyprus v Turkey* 77: 'Having effective overall control over northern Cyprus, its responsibility cannot be confined to the acts of its own soldiers or officials in northern Cyprus but must also be engaged by virtue of the acts of the local administration which survives by virtue of Turkish military and other support. It follows that, in terms of Article 1 of the Convention, Turkey's "jurisdiction" must be considered to extend to securing the entire range of substantive rights set out in the Convention and those additional Protocols which she has ratified, and that violations of those rights are imputable to Turkey.' *Al-Skeini* 136.

[54] In respect of the Turkish occupation of Northern Cyprus, the ECtHR have found, inter alia, violations of Articles 2, 3, 5, 8, 9, 10, and 13, ECHR (*Cyprus v Turkey*) and violations of Protocol 1 to the ECHR (eg see *Cyprus v Turkey* and *Loizidou v Turkey*).

[55] *Ilaşcu and Others v Moldova and Russia* 392.

[56] Ibid, 314–16, 393.

[57] Ibid. Dissenting opinion of Judge Anatoly Kovler: 'I learned during my initial military training that the term "active duty" presupposes control of roads and railways, surveillance of strategic points (telegraph/telephone posts), and control of stations, airports, frontiers, etc. Even without being a military strategist, anyone can compare the two situations: in one case 30,000 troops in a small territory inhabited by between 120,000 and 150,000 people, and in the other 2,500 officers and other ranks in a territory of 4,163 km^2 with an 852 km-long border and a population of more than 750,000!'

[58] Ibid, 393.

influence is considered to be significant, there will be correspondingly high obligations on the 'influencing' state.[59] This has included the 'influencing' state being required to satisfy its positive and negative human rights obligations in respect of the right to life.[60]

Conversely, a situation can arise where a state does not have authority over specific regions within its territory due to the military, financial, economic, or political involvement of another state, yet 'still has a positive obligation under Article 1 of the Convention to take the diplomatic, economic, judicial or other measures that it is in its power to take and are in accordance with international law to secure to the applicants the rights guaranteed by the Convention'.[61] In such circumstances, the positive human rights obligations on the state are 'interpreted in such a way as [not] to impose an impossible or disproportionate burden'.[62] Notwithstanding that the scope of a state's human rights obligations is limited[63] in such circumstances, violations have been found in respect of the prohibition on torture.[64]

Where a state exercises decisive influence in the territory of another state, then responsibility for violations of both positive and negative human rights obligations exists. Human rights obligations can, however, be divided and tailored, and therefore an assessment must be made to determine the applicable rights. Once established, a state must take all measures deemed reasonable in the circumstances to satisfy these obligations.[65]

3.3.4 Localized control over territory

Where armed forces of a state conduct military operations in the territory of another state, they can be considered to have temporarily exercised effective overall control over a specific 'portion of territory'.[66] As a consequence, those persons within that 'portion of territory' at the time during which the armed forces exercised effective overall control can come within the jurisdiction of the armed forces' state. In turn, therefore, the state can have certain human rights obligations, exercised through the armed forces, during the relevant period.

A distinction must be made between circumstances in which a state exercises 'effective overall control' of an area for a significant period of time evinced by, for example, the presence of a large number of troops, constant patrols, and checkpoints,[67] and circumstances in which a relatively small number of troops conduct a discrete and relatively small mission in the territory of another state. The notion of

[59] In *Ilaşcu and Others v Moldova and Russia*, the Russian state was held responsible for violations of Articles 3 and 5 and a failure to discharge its obligations under Article 34. In *Ivanţoc and Others v Moldova and Russia*, Application no 23687/05 (ECtHR, 15 November 2011), the Russian state was held responsible for violations of Articles 3, 5, 8, and 13.

[60] *Ilaşcu and Others v Moldova and Russia* 494.

[61] Ibid, 331.

[62] *Özgür Gündem v Turkey* 43 and *Ilaşcu and Others v Moldova and Russia* 332.

[63] *Ilaşcu and Others v Moldova and Russia* 333.

[64] Ibid, 494.

[65] Ibid, 352 and 494.

[66] *Issa and Others v Turkey*, Application no 31821/96 (ECtHR, 3 March 2005) 74.

[67] *Cyprus v Turkey* 76 and *Loizidou v Turkey* 52.

localized control of territory is principally concerned with the latter scenario, and raises two main questions. First, what amounts to localized control of territory? Second, in the event that this is determined, what human rights obligations do armed forces personnel, acting as state agents, have for the period during which they exercise localized control of territory?

Localized control of territory will occur when armed forces personnel operate in the territory of another state in sufficient numbers and with sufficient support to potentially adversely affect the human rights of the citizens of that state. These operations are usually of a limited temporal as well as geographical nature. Notwithstanding, for the duration of the operation, state agents are expected to respect relevant human rights to the extent to which they control the act or omission said to constitute a violation. The extent to which they are expected to protect persons from the risk of a violation will depend on the degree of control exercised over the act or omission said to constitute a violation. In such circumstances the state agents would not be expected to be obliged to guarantee the entire panoply of a state's human rights obligations. As such, it is axiomatic that in these circumstances, human rights obligations can be divided and tailored.

3.3.5 Temporary control of territory and a jurisdictional nexus

A question of fundamental significance for a military commander is whether temporary control of an area is sufficient to create a jurisdictional nexus such that citizens in a non-contracting state are afforded *some* ECHR protections. While the Court in *Al-Skeini* was silent on this matter, an indication of the likely approach to be taken by the Court when confronted by such a question can be found in *Issa*:[68]

> The Court does not exclude the possibility that, as a consequence of this military action, the respondent State could be considered to have exercised, *temporarily*, effective overall control of a particular portion of the territory of northern Iraq. Accordingly, if there is a sufficient factual basis for holding that, at the relevant time, the victims were within that specific area, it would follow logically that they were within the jurisdiction of Turkey.[69]

Notwithstanding that any assessment of 'effective overall control' is a complex and imprecise art, a compelling argument can be constructed to support the view that the temporary presence of small number of troops from a contacting state can exercise temporary control over a 'particular portion of territory' in a non-contracting state sufficient to create ECHR obligations upon the contracting state. First, it can be seen from *Ilaşcu* that large numbers of troops are not necessary to create a jurisdictional nexus. Second, as an illustration, consider a raid to capture alleged terrorists in a non-contracting state. The ability and military capability of the troops must be a significant factor. In other words, if the troops on the ground were extremely well-armed, well-trained, and supported by significant ISTAR[70]

[68] *Issa v Turkey* (Merits) (31821/96). [69] Ibid, 74 (emphasis added).

[70] ISTAR is an acronym used in military terminology to mean intelligence, surveillance, target acquisition, and reconnaissance.

and constant air assets, then it is likely that, in a military sense, they could dominate the immediate territory they occupy, assuming that there were not significant numbers of well-armed and well-organized opposing forces. This domination of the immediate territory they occupy in a military sense must then translate to 'effective control' in the legal sense, as the troops would exercise significant control over personnel within that territory—not least of all have control over whether or not they live or die. This is therefore a clear and direct jurisdictional link to Article 2, ECHR. Third, the troops in this circumstance are state agents performing an executive function on behalf of the contracting state, and finally, it is not necessary to consider further evidence of governmental control such as in *Ilaşcu*,[71] given the temporary nature of the action.

3.3.6 Article 56, ECHR and the 'effective control' principle

Article 56[72] of the ECHR makes explicit provision for contracting states to extend the application of the ECHR to territories for whose international relations it is responsible. The Court has, however, unequivocally stated that the 'effective control' principle in no way limits the operation of Article 56.[73] Similarly, it can be asserted that the 'public powers' principle interacts with Article 56 in exactly the same way as the 'effective control' principle. In other words, the 'effective control' principle does not replace the system of declarations under Article 56 of the ECHR that enable states to extend the application of the Convention to territories for whose international relations they are responsible.

[71] *Ilaşcu and Others v Moldova and Russia* 333.

[72] Article 56:
Territorial application

1. Any State may at the time of its ratification or at any time thereafter declare by notification addressed to the Secretary General of the Council of Europe that the present Convention shall, subject to paragraph 4 of this Article, extend to all or any of the territories for whose international relations it is responsible.
2. The Convention shall extend to the territory or territories named in the notification as from the thirtieth day after the receipt of this notification by the Secretary General of the Council of Europe.
3. The provisions of this Convention shall be applied in such territories with due regard, however, to local requirements.
4. Any State which has made a declaration in accordance with paragraph 1 of this Article may at any time thereafter declare on behalf of one or more of the territories to which the declaration relates that it accepts the competence of the Court to receive applications from individuals, non-governmental organisations or groups of individuals as provided by Article 34 of the Convention.

[73] *Al-Skeini and Others v the United Kingdom* 140: 'The "effective control" principle of jurisdiction set out above does not replace the system of declarations under Article 56 of the Convention (formerly Article 63) which the States decided, when drafting the Convention, to apply to territories overseas for whose international relations they were responsible. Article 56 § 1 provides a mechanism whereby any State may decide to extend the application of the Convention, "with due regard ... to local requirements," to all or any of the territories for whose international relations it is responsible. The existence of this mechanism, which was included in the Convention for historical reasons, cannot be interpreted in present conditions as limiting the scope of the term "jurisdiction" in Article 1.'

3.3.7 Limitations of the territorial model

Any analysis of extraterritorial jurisdiction arising based upon the control of territory by armed forces is subject to a number of limitations. First, the Court has not been consistent in elucidating criteria that indicate a sufficient military presence to establish the requisite level of control. A crude calculation based upon the number of troops in a certain geographic area is insufficient.[74] Second, as jurisdiction can only arise through the control of territory in circumstances where the armed forces can guarantee 'the entire range of substantive rights set out in the convention',[75] the threshold is consequently set extremely high. The fact that a state is in occupation of another state does not necessarily establish extraterritorial jurisdiction based on the control of territory.[76] As a practical matter, therefore, this militates against the establishment of jurisdiction on this basis, particularly given that the range of rights which armed forces can afford and protect could, depending upon the nature of the armed conflict or occupation, be extremely limited. Finally, what amounts to territory is ill-defined in the jurisprudence and lends itself to a consideration of jurisdiction arising over an ever decreasing physical area of territory.[77] Taken to its logical conclusion, control over an ever decreasing area of territory will ultimately merge into the personal model of jurisdiction where control is exercised directly over individuals. This can in turn create confusion over how jurisdiction arises in such circumstances and, as a consequence, what rights ought to be guaranteed. It is therefore necessary to consider the notion of jurisdiction arising as a consequence of control over individuals in order to better understand the relationship between the two models.

3.4 Personal Jurisdiction—'State Agent Authority and Effective Control'

The ECtHR judgment in *Al-Skeini* comprehensively reconsidered the notion of state agent authority and effective control or 'personal' jurisdiction. The judgment in *Al-Skeini* cannot, however, be seen as an entirely definitive proclamation of the ECtHR's view on the extraterritorial application of the ECHR, nor does it provide all the answers to questions concerning the applicability of the right to life in armed conflict. It is necessary first to consider the Court's judgment in *Banković* to see what, if any, residual reasoning remains when it is considered in light of subsequent judgments in, inter alia, *Issa, Öcalan, Al-Saadoon, Medvedyev, Al-Skeini, Hassan*, and

[74] *Al-Skeini v the United Kingdom* 139. [75] Ibid, 138.

[76] See *Jaloud v the Netherlands* 142: 'the status of "occupying power" within the meaning of Article 42 of the Hague Regulations, or lack of it, is not *per se* determinative. Although it found that concept relevant in *Al-Skeini* and in *Al-Jedda v the United Kingdom*, the Court did not need to have recourse to it in finding that the responsibility of Turkey was engaged in respect of events in northern Cyprus (see, *inter alia, Loizidou v Turkey* and *Cyprus v Turkey*), or that of Russia in respect of the situation in Moldovan territory east of the Dniester.'

[77] For example, the physical area of the checkpoint in *Jaloud* could, potentially, be viewed as territory that the Netherlands army officer had control over.

Jaloud, and whether there exists any scope to apply any of the principles enunciated in *Banković* to the use of force by armed forces overseas.

In *Banković*, the Court rejected the applicant's argument that jurisdiction could be based upon effective control over an individual.[78] They reasoned that, first, the 'applicants' submission is tantamount to arguing that anyone adversely affected by an act imputable to a Contracting State, wherever in the world that act may have been committed or its consequences felt, is thereby brought within the jurisdiction of that State for the purpose of Article 1 of the Convention',[79] and this proposition could not be supported given its broad scope. Second, 'the rights and freedoms defined in section 1 of this convention' cannot be 'divided and tailored in accordance with the particular circumstances of the extra-territorial act in question'.[80] The Court contended that the situation was therefore binary, in that an individual either came within the jurisdiction of the state and was afforded all the ECHR rights or they did not. Finally, the Court in *Banković* narrowly defined the applicable scope of the ECHR as existing within the 'legal space'[81] of the contracting states and stated:

> The Convention was not designed to be applied throughout the world, even in respect of the conduct of Contracting States. Accordingly, the desirability of avoiding a gap or vacuum in human rights' protection has so far been relied on by the Court in favour of establishing jurisdiction only when the territory in question was one that, but for the specific circumstances, would normally be covered by the Convention.[82]

Within the context of *Banković*, the Court considered that no 'specific circumstances' existed that precluded the application of the ECHR where it would otherwise have applied in respect of the Federal Republic of Yugoslavia. Ultimately, what emerges from *Banković* is a narrow territorial conception of jurisdiction in which a state can only exercise jurisdiction in the territory of another state 'through the effective control of the relevant territory and its inhabitants abroad as a consequence of military occupation or through the consent, invitation or acquiescence of the Government of that territory, exercises all or some of the public powers normally to be exercised by that Government'. By defining jurisdiction in such narrow terms, the Court was subject to considerable,[83] albeit not universal,[84] criticism for failing to properly consider the notion of jurisdiction as defined in its previous case law. This narrow focus is gradually broadened in subsequent judgments to reflect the universal nature of human rights. Moreover, notwithstanding that the personal model of jurisdiction is rejected by the Court in *Banković*, it emerges in subsequent judgments and crystallizes to form the basis of a more expansive interpretation of the scope of Article 1.

In *Issa*, the Court restated its view that jurisdiction can arise where a state exercises control of territory in another state. Significantly, however, it went further, directly contradicting its previous view in *Banković* in respect of the regional scope of the

[78] *Bankovic v Belgium* 75. [79] Ibid. [80] Ibid. [81] Ibid, 80. [82] Ibid.

[83] Ralph Wilde, 'Triggering State Obligations Extraterritorially: The Spatial Test in Certain Human Rights Treaties' (2007) 40(2) *Isr Law Rev* 503; Marko Milanovic, 'From Compromise to Principle: Clarifying the Concept of State Jurisdiction in Human Rights Treaties' (2008) 8 *HRLR* 441.

[84] Matthew Happold, 'Bankovic v. Belgium and the Territorial Scope of the European Convention on Human Rights' (2003) 3(1) *HRLR* 90.

ECHR by stating: 'the concept of "jurisdiction" within the meaning of Article 1 of the Convention is not necessarily restricted to the national territory of the High Contracting Parties ... [and] cannot be interpreted so as to allow a State party to perpetrate violations of the Convention on the territory of another State, which it could not perpetrate on its own territory'.[85] This restatement accords with the view of Besson in that the notion of jurisdiction contains an element of 'normative guidance' in addition to 'effective power' and 'overall control',[86] the normative dimension being vested in the universal nature of human rights as opposed to any narrow regional conception.

The judgment in *Issa* was followed by the case of *Öcalan*, in which the Court stated:

> it is common ground that, directly after being handed over to the Turkish officials by the Kenyan officials, the applicant was effectively under Turkish authority and therefore within the 'jurisdiction' of that State for the purposes of Article 1 of the Convention, even though in this instance Turkey exercised its authority outside its territory. It is true that the applicant was physically forced to return to Turkey by Turkish officials and was under their authority and control following his arrest and return to Turkey.[87]

It is difficult to interpret the phrase 'their [Turkish officials'] authority and control' as amounting to anything other than an acceptance by the Court of a personal model of jurisdiction, in that Mr Öcalan was under the physical authority and control of Turkish state agents. Moreover, the Court specifically accepted that the actions of Turkish state agents occurred outside Turkish territory, and no reference is made to Turkish state agents exercising effective control of Kenyan territory.

In *Medvedyev*, the Court held that jurisdiction arose where French commandos (state agents) raided a merchant vessel (the *Winner*) in international waters and assumed control of the vessel: 'France having exercised full and exclusive control over the *Winner* and its crew, at least *de facto*, from the time of its interception, in a continuous and uninterrupted manner until they were tried in France, the applicants were effectively within France's jurisdiction for the purposes of Article 1 of the Convention.'[88] The Court does not elaborate further on the exact nature of jurisdiction, yet it would appear to be a function of the control over individuals exerted by the French commandos. It is difficult to envisage how a vessel in international waters could be considered akin to territory to enable jurisdiction to arise on a territorial basis as set out in the Cyprus line of cases or expressed in *Banković*.

In *Al-Skeini*, the ECtHR articulated its position in respect of a personal model of jurisdiction and identified three 'principles'[89] where Article 1 would extend to the actions of state agents absent any control of territory. First, the Court contended that 'it is clear that the acts of diplomatic and consular agents, who are present on foreign territory in accordance with provisions of international law, may amount to

[85] *Issa and Others v Turkey* 68 and 71.
[86] Samantha Besson, 'The Extraterritoriality of the European Convention on Human Rights' 872.
[87] *Öcalan v Turkey*, Application no 46221/99 (ECtHR, 12 May 2005) 91.
[88] *Medvedyev and Others v France*, Application no 3394/03 (ECtHR 29 Mar 2010) 67.
[89] *Al-Skeini v the United Kingdom* 133–36.

an exercise of jurisdiction when these agents exert authority and control over others'.[90] Second, the Court stated that jurisdiction can arise where 'through the consent, invitation or acquiescence of the Government of that territory, it exercises all or some of the public powers normally to be exercised by that Government'.[91] The Court defined 'public powers' as 'executive or judicial functions'[92] and concluded by stating the significance of attribution thus: 'the Contracting State may be responsible for breaches of the Convention thereby incurred, as long as the acts in question are attributable to it rather than to the territorial State.'[93] Finally, the Court asserted that jurisdiction can arise where state agents use force outside of their territory. The specific examples cited related to circumstances where 'an individual is taken into the custody of state agents abroad';[94] however, the Court stressed that it did 'not consider that jurisdiction in the above cases arose solely from the control exercised by the Contracting State over the buildings, aircraft or ship in which the individuals were held. What is decisive in such cases is the exercise of physical power and control over the person in question'.[95]

The first principle, concerning the actions of diplomatic and consular agents, is uncontroversial. The second principle, concerning circumstances where jurisdiction arises 'through the consent, invitation or acquiescence of the Government of that territory, [such that the armed forces in that territory] ... exercise all or some of the public powers normally to be exercised by that Government'[96] is, however, problematic. Jurisdiction can arise in circumstances where a state acts without the 'consent, invitation or acquiescence' of the government of the territorial state. This can be seen in respect of the UK military action in Iraq that was considered by UK courts in *Al-Saadoon*[97] and *Smith*.[98] In these cases, the UK could not exercise public powers 'through the consent, invitation or acquiescence of the Government of that territory' as there was no government in Iraq at the material time. It would therefore appear that jurisdiction, in respect of this principle, is not determined by the existence and subsequent actions of the government (or non-existence of a government) in the territorial state, but rather by a factual determination of whether state agents are exercising 'authority and control' over individuals and the state is exercising 'some or all of the public powers normally exercised by the government'. The crucial question that subsequently must be addressed, however, is whether jurisdiction can arise in circumstances where state agents are exercising 'authority and control' over individuals and the state is not exercising 'some or all of the public powers normally exercised by the government'. The third principle outlined in *Al-Skeini*, the Court's subsequent judgments in *Hassan* and *Jaloud*, and the approach of the Divisional Court in *Al-Saadoon* can all assist in addressing this issue.

In *Al-Skeini*, the Court appeared to envisage a situation where jurisdiction could arise in the context of individuals being within the custody of state agents in the following terms: 'what is decisive in such cases is the exercise of physical power

[90] Ibid, 134. [91] Ibid, 135. [92] Ibid. [93] Ibid. [94] Ibid, 136.
[95] Ibid. [96] *Al-Skeini v the United Kingdom* 135.
[97] *Al-Saadoon and Others v Secretary of State for Defence* [2015] EWHC 715 (Admin) at 73.
[98] *Smith v Ministry of Defence* [2014] AC 52 40.

and control over the person in question.'[99] In support of this proposal, the Court cited four cases: *Öcalan v Turkey*, *Issa and Others v Turkey*, *Al-Saadoon and Mufdhi v the United Kingdom*, and *Medvedyev and Others v France*, in all of which control had been exercised by state agents. Yet the Court did not raise the issue of the state exercising 'some or all of the public powers normally exercised by governments'. In *Öcalan*, Turkish state agents took physical control of Mr Öcalan from Kenyan authorities in Kenya. In *Issa and Others*, the Court indicated that, had it been established that Turkish forces had taken control of the applicants' relatives in Northern Iraq and, while they were under such control, moved them to a nearby cave and executed them, then the deceased would have come within the jurisdiction of Turkey. In *Al-Saadoon and Mufdhi*, the Court held that the UK exercised jurisdiction over two Iraqi nationals held in a UK-controlled military prison on the basis that the UK exercised 'total and exclusive control' over the prisons and individuals therein. In *Medvedyev and Others*, jurisdiction arose as a consequence of the 'French agents' full and exclusive control over a ship and its crew'. With the exception of *Al-Saadoon and Mufdhi*, it would appear that the factual circumstances in each of these cases would not afford an interpretation of jurisdiction that required a nexus between the exercise of 'some or all of the public powers normally exercised by governments' and 'physical power and control over individuals'. The question of jurisdiction in *Al-Skeini* was ultimately established on the basis of the UK exercising 'some of the public powers normally to be exercised by a sovereign government', specifically 'authority and responsibility for the maintenance of security in south-east Iraq', which in turn facilitated 'security operations in Basra' that enabled the exercise of 'authority and control over individuals killed in the course of such security operations, so as to establish a jurisdictional link between the deceased and the United Kingdom for the purposes of Article 1 of the Convention'.[100] Notwithstanding, it is submitted that the Court contemplated a situation in which jurisdiction over individuals could arise absent the exercise of 'public powers'.[101] Support for this proposition can also be found in the Court's approach to jurisdiction in *Isaak v Turkey*[102] and *Andreou v Turkey*.[103] In *Isaak*, a demonstrator, Anastassios Isaak, was killed by Turkish forces in the neutral UN buffer zone in Cyprus. The Court did not consider this territory to be under Turkish control; rather, that jurisdiction arose as the demonstrator was 'under the authority and/or effective control'[104] of Turkey through the actions of its agents. Similarly, in *Andreou*, the Court held:

> even though the applicant had sustained her injuries in territory over which Turkey exercised no control, the opening of fire on the crowd from close range, which was the direct and immediate cause of those injuries, had been such that the applicant should be regarded as 'within [the] jurisdiction' of Turkey within the meaning of Article 1 of the Convention.[105]

[99] Ibid, 136. [100] Ibid, 149. [101] Ibid, 136.
[102] *Isaak v Turkey*, Application no 44587/98 (ECtHR, 28 September 2006) 553.
[103] *Andreou v Turkey*, Application no 45653/99 (ECtHR, 3 June 2008) 25.
[104] *Isaak v Turkey*, Application no 44587/98 (ECtHR, 2008) 553.
[105] *Andreou v Turkey*, Application no 45653/99 (ECtHR, 3 June 2008) 25.

It would appear, therefore, that right to life obligations can arise in circumstances where there is neither control of territory nor the exercise of public powers. Put another way, obligations can arise based upon the actions of state agents constituting a personal model of jurisdiction. This theme has been developed, after *Al-Skeini*, by the Court in respect of armed conflict and occupation in Iraq.

In *Hassan*, where the alleged ECHR violations occurred during the 'active hostilities' phase of the armed conflict in Iraq, the Court established jurisdiction as a consequence of Mr Hassan, following his capture by British troops, having been 'within the physical power and control of the United Kingdom soldiers and therefore ... within United Kingdom jurisdiction'.[106] Three points would indicate that the Court, although without explicit mention, acknowledged that the UK was not exercising any 'public powers' at the material time. First, the relevant paragraph of *Al-Skeini* cited to justify the establishment of jurisdiction, or the cases referenced therein, does not mention or require the exercise of 'public powers' by the state. Second, the activities undertaken by UK armed forces in Iraq at the material time are not representative of the exercising of 'executive or judicial functions' either generally or specifically in relation to their conduct towards Mr Tarek Hassan. His detention was part of a military operation to detain his brother, a general in the Al-Quds Army—the army of the Ba'ath Party and accepted as such by the Court.[107] Equally, UK armed forces were still participating in the 'active hostilities' phase of the armed conflict. Finally, the Court considered that

> Tarek Hassan fell within the jurisdiction of the United Kingdom from the moment of his capture by United Kingdom troops, at Umm Qasr on 23 April 2003, until his release from the bus that took him from Camp Bucca to the drop-off point, most probably Umm Qasr on 2 May 2003.[108]

In this respect, they widened the scope of the exercise of control over individuals from that enunciated in *Al-Saadoon and Mufdhi*[109] to encompass circumstances beyond incarceration in a detention facility, including capture and transportation by, and under the control of, state agents. This approach was continued in *Jaloud*.[110]

As it had done in *Hassan*, the Court in *Jaloud* citied significant sections of its judgment in *Al-Skeini* verbatim. In applying its reasoning in *Al-Skeini* to the facts of *Jaloud* it found that jurisdiction, on the part of the Netherlands government, could arise where a Royal Netherlands Army Officer commanded and supervised a military checkpoint in Iraq. The exercise of jurisdiction appears to be limited to 'asserting authority and control over persons passing through the checkpoint'.[111] While there is a reference to the Netherlands exercising jurisdiction 'within the limits of the Stabilization Force Iraq (SFIR) mission',[112] the Court does not make a specific reference to the exercise of public powers and appears to consider that jurisdiction arises solely as a function of the authority and control that can be asserted over

[106] *Hassan v the United Kingdom* 76. [107] Ibid, 53–54. [108] Ibid, 80.

[109] *Al-Saadoon and Mufdhi v the United Kingdom*, Application no 61498/08 (ECtHR, 2 March 2010) 86–89.

[110] *Jaloud v the Netherlands.* [111] Ibid, 152. [112] Ibid.

individuals who pass through the checkpoint. In this sense it recognizes a personal model of jurisdiction in which the relevant consideration is not the limited territorial footprint of the checkpoint, but rather the extent to which those manning the checkpoint can assert 'authority and control' over those passing through. The Court does not explore what form this authority and control can take, but it is submitted that it must include circumstances where personnel manning the checkpoint open fire and kill those passing through. As checkpoints can be mobile and ad hoc, it follows that a natural development of this analysis must include circumstances in which armed forces personnel exercise authority and control in associated circumstances pursuant to their duties. In terms of the exercise of authority and control, it is difficult to distinguish a situation in which a foot patrol stopped and questioned an individual from that of a temporary checkpoint. Equally, it is difficult to meaningfully differentiate between a situation where jurisdiction arises following the capture of an individual who is subsequently killed by state agents and a situation in which an individual is killed by state agents without being captured. These issues have been addressed by the Supreme Court and Divisional Court in the '*Susan Smith* case'[113] and *Al-Saadoon*[114] respectively.

The Supreme Court in *Susan Smith*, relying upon the Grand Chamber judgment in *Al-Skeini*, held that the ECHR could have extraterritorial effect in certain circumstances. Lord Hope considered that 'extraterritorial jurisdiction can exist wherever a state through its agents exercises authority and control over an individual'.[115] This in turn was founded on the justifiable presumption that the state has authority and control over its armed forces.[116] As a consequence, the members of a state's armed forces are brought within the jurisdiction of Article 1. Given that the UK armed forces are subject to considerable political oversight and regulation through both the military justice system and, when conducting operations overseas, the rules of engagement process, Lord Hope's assertion is entirely consistent with the actual authority and control exercised by the state. Of course, such an analysis must also be predicated upon the ability to 'divide and tailor' Convention rights as asserted by the ECtHR in *Al-Skeini*.[117] Lord Hope elucidated the issue thus: 'The concept of dividing and tailoring goes hand in hand with the principle that extraterritorial jurisdiction can exist wherever a state through its agents exercises authority and control over an individual.'[118]

The Divisional Court in *Al-Saadoon* adopted this general approach proposed by Lord Hope and sought to disaggregate the notion of the exercise of 'public powers' cited in *Al-Skeini* from jurisdiction arising solely on the basis of a state agent's control over an individual. As a first step, Leggatt J asserted, correctly, that jurisdiction is not to be equated with the legal basis or legitimacy of a state's actions.[119] The adoption of such an approach would lead to an 'absurd'[120] situation in which human

[113] *Smith v Ministry of Defence.*
[114] *Al-Saadoon and Others v Secretary of State for Defence* [2015] EWHC 715 (Admin).
[115] *Smith v Ministry of Defence* 49. [116] Ibid.
[117] *Al-Skeini v the United Kingdom* 137. [118] *Smith v Ministry of Defence* 49.
[119] *Al-Saadoon and Others v Secretary of State for Defence* 100. [120] Ibid.

rights obligations would only arise in circumstances where a state acted pursuant to a recognized legal mandate. This rationale can apply equally to the actions of armed forces personnel that go beyond their rules of engagement or contravene the military justice code. It would be equally 'absurd' if responsibility for human rights violations on the part of a state could not arise if a soldier had acted unlawfully by, for example, committing murder. Despite the fact that in such circumstances the cause of action ought to be resolved through the domestic courts, a residual right of appeal to the ECHR ought to exist in order to afford a degree of human rights protection. On a similar theme, Leggatt J then argued that it would be 'illogical if the Convention applied when state agents shoot and kill an individual on territory over which they do not exercise control when the state agents purport to act as policemen but not if they simply assassinate the individual'.[121] There is considerable force to this argument that finds support in the ECtHR's approach in, inter alia, *Al-Skeini* and *Öcalan* and leads to the proposition that 'The fact that state agents are purporting to exercise powers normally exercised by a sovereign government of the territory when they detain, or kill, an individual may make sense as a sufficient condition but not as a necessary condition of the exercise of jurisdiction by the state over that individual'.[122]

Ultimately, Leggatt J concludes, 'whenever and wherever a state which is a contracting party to the Convention purports to exercise legal authority or uses physical force, it must do so in a way that does not violate Convention rights'.[123] Implicit in this analysis is a recognition that defining jurisdiction in such broad terms could lead to a series of practical difficulties in both peacekeeping operations and armed conflict. Such concerns are predicated on the applicable human rights obligations applying directly, without, for example, a state entering a derogation pursuant to Article 15, ECHR or the impact of international humanitarian law mitigating the effect of the human rights obligations as has been accepted by the ECtHR in, for example, *Hassan*.[124]

3.5 Jurisdiction and the Exercise of 'Public Powers'

The Court in *Al-Skeini* did not consider that jurisdiction arose as a consequence of UK armed forces exercising control over territory or individuals in Iraq. Rather, they considered that jurisdiction arose as a consequence of the UK having 'assumed in Iraq the exercise of some of the public powers normally to be exercised by a sovereign government'.[125] The public powers took the form of 'authority and responsibility for the maintenance of security in south-east Iraq'.[126] This included UK armed forces conducting 'patrols, arrests, anti-terrorist operations, policing of civil demonstrations, protection of essential utilities and infrastructure and protecting police stations'.[127] The concept of public powers was, however, defined more

[121] Ibid. [122] Ibid. [123] Ibid, 106.
[124] *Hassan v the United Kingdom* 108–11. [125] *Al-Skeini v the United Kingdom*, 149.
[126] Ibid. [127] Ibid, 147.

broadly by the Court to include the exercise of 'executive or judicial functions on the territory of another State'[128] provided that the 'acts in question are attributable to it rather than to the territorial State'.[129] What exactly amounts to the exercise of 'public powers' remains unclear[130] and was not clarified by the Court's subsequent judgments in *Hassan* and *Jaloud*, as jurisdiction was established on a different basis. It can be asserted, however, that, first, in order to exercise 'public powers', the state does not have to control territory. The exercise of 'public powers' would appear to be a mechanism by which state agents assume control over individuals, not territory. Of the six fatalities in *Al-Skeini*, five occurred during UK security operations in Iraq; the remaining fatality (that of the third applicant's wife) occurred during an exchange of fire between UK armed forces and an unknown gunman. The Court implicitly accepted that the presence of 5,000 UK troops in 96,000 square kilometres of Multinational Division Iraq (South East) in which there lived 2.75 million people was insufficient to control territory in a manner akin to Turkish armed forces in Northern Cyprus.[131] Second, where jurisdiction arises on the basis of state agents exercising control over individuals as a function of the state exercising some public powers, Convention rights can be divided and tailored.[132] As a matter of logic this has some force, as it could not be said that the UK could afford all ECHR rights in Iraq at the time the human rights violations by UK armed forces in *Al-Skeini* occurred. Finally, as the Court's assessment of extraterritorial jurisdiction arising as a consequence of the exercise of 'public powers' has not been overruled or explicitly contradicted in subsequent judgments, it must remain as a principle by which states can assume ECHR obligations during armed conflict and occupation. That said, the exercise of 'public powers' ultimately manifests itself in state agents acting or failing to act in a way that violates the rights of individuals. In that sense there is a nexus to, and control over, the fate of individuals, and therefore the notion of public powers and the personal model of jurisdiction are inextricably linked. Lord Justice Lloyd Jones' approach to the test cases in *Al-Saadoon*,[133] in which he analyses the actions of UK armed forces in Iraq with respect to the 'public powers' exception, attempts to disassociate 'public powers' from control of individuals. In all but one of these test cases, however, he asserts that any determination of whether or not jurisdiction would arise based

[128] Ibid, 135. [129] Ibid.

[130] Samantha Miko, 'Al-Skeini v. United Kingdom and Extraterritorial Jurisdiction under the European Convention of Human Rights' (2013) 35 *BC Intl & Comp L Rev* 63 at 76–77; Milanovic, *Extraterritorial Application of Human Rights Treaties* (Oxford University Press 2011) 129–31.

[131] In addition, the situation at the time was unstable, as reflected in the Aitken Report: 'United Kingdom military records show that, as at 30 June 2004, there had been approximately 178 demonstrations and 1,050 violent attacks against Coalition forces in Multinational Division (South East) since 1 May 2003. The violent attacks consisted of five anti-aircraft attacks, 12 grenade attacks, 101 attacks using improvised explosive devices, 52 attempted attacks using improvised explosive devices, 145 mortar attacks, 147 rocket propelled grenade attacks, 535 shootings and 53 others. The same records show that, between May 2003 and March 2004, 49 Iraqis were known to have been killed in incidents in which British troops used force.' *The Aitken Report—An Investigation into Cases of Deliberate Abuse and Unlawful Killing in Iraq in 2003 and 2004*, 25 January 2008, quoted in *Al-Skeini*, 22.

[132] *Al-Skeini v the United Kingdom* 137.

[133] *Al-Saadoon and Others v The Secretary of State for Defence* 75–97.

upon the 'control of the individual' exception would require further investigation of the facts.[134] Ultimately, therefore, it can be asserted that the exercise of 'public powers' by state agents can create a jurisdictional nexus to the state, but exactly how this concept relates to state agents' exercise of control over individuals remains opaque and underexplored by the courts.

3.6 Jurisdiction and Positive and Negative Right to Life Obligations

In *Susan Smith*, Lord Hope stated:

> The concept of dividing and tailoring goes hand in hand with the principle that extraterritorial jurisdiction can exist wherever a state through its agents exercises authority and control over an individual. The court need not now concern itself with the question whether the state is in a position to guarantee Convention rights to that individual other than those it is said to have breached.[135]

In part Lord Hope's analysis is correct in recognizing that Convention rights can be divided and tailored, but his assertion that a state's obligations only extend to 'convention rights ... it is said to have breached' is open to question. Such an approach tends to place undue emphasis on a 'negative' obligation not to breach an applicable Convention right, but fails to recognize a state's positive obligation to protect an individual's rights. This issue highlights the requirement to assess the situation in which the state agents operate within the context of the right to life obligations in armed conflict.

Once it is accepted that right to life obligations can arise in armed conflict, it is necessary to understand the context within which state agents must guarantee these rights. For example, and as the Divisional Court recognizes in *Al-Saadoon*, when an individual is in custody during an armed conflict, 'the state may not only have a negative obligation under article 2 not to kill unlawfully but an obligation in certain circumstances to take positive measures to protect the person's life'.[136] Certain commentators argue that this illustrates one of the difficulties in attempting to establish useful and non-arbitrary criteria upon which to establish jurisdiction based upon a personal model. Absent any non-arbitrary criteria, Milanovic contends that the personal model simply collapses.[137] This view can be challenged. Far from being dependent upon non-arbitrary criteria, a situation in which jurisdiction arises as a consequence of the use of force by state agents against individuals in another state appears to be both easily understood and supported by ECtHR and domestic jurisprudence. It is not, however, the entire story, and does not account for situations in which positive human rights obligations arise, for example, in respect of those held in the custody of armed forces. Within the context of armed conflict and with reference to positive right to life obligations, state agents would be

134 Ibid. 135 *Smith v Ministry of Defence* 49.

136 *Al-Saadoon and Others v Secretary of State for Defence* 48.

137 Milanovic, *Extraterritorial Application of Human Rights Treaties* 207–08.

required to protect such a right to the extent that is reasonably practicable given the circumstances pertaining at the material time. It is submitted that this would not be inconsistent with existing international humanitarian law obligations pursuant to the Geneva Conventions and Additional Protocols. Nor would this be in contravention of existing ECtHR jurisprudence established in *Al-Skeini* and restated in *Hassan* and *Jaloud*, in that 'whenever the State, through its agents, exercises control and authority over an individual, and thus jurisdiction, the State is under an obligation under Article 1 to secure to that individual the rights and freedoms under Section I of the Convention that are relevant to the situation of that individual'.[138] In respect of custody, the protections that armed forces personnel can afford a PoW/detainee/internee will be determined by the circumstances pertaining at the time. It is unlikely that the same positive obligations would exist in respect of battlefield capture during a firefight in an international armed conflict vis-à-vis detention in a permanent secure detention facility during a military occupation. This issue is addressed in Chapter 4.

3.7 Article 1, ECHR and Attribution

It has been persuasively argued[139] that, in certain circumstances, before the question of jurisdiction can be addressed by the ECtHR it is necessary to consider the independent question of whether the wrongful act complained of is attributable[140] to the contracting state.[141] Only if this is answered in the affirmative can the further question 'does this wrongful act amount to a violation of a human rights treaty?'[142] be addressed. When considering the actions of members of armed forces operating in the territory, airspace, or territorial seas of a non-contracting state, as a matter of logic, this approach has considerable merit. In *Al-Skeini*,[143] for example, the UK could not have exercised 'public powers' in the Al-Basrah region of Iraq and therefore had jurisdiction over the citizens in that area without the presence of troops on the ground. The same could be said of Turkish troops in Northern Cyprus[144] or Russian troops in the Transdniestrian territory of Moldova.[145] It is therefore contended that, as a first step in the process of determining whether or not there has been a violation of the ECHR, the physical presence of armed forces personnel in the geographical area in question at the material time must be established. In terms of attribution, any alleged human rights violations that take place in the national

[138] *Al-Skeini v the United Kingdom* 137.

[139] Milanovic, *Extraterritorial Application of Human Rights Treaties* 41–53; 'Jurisdiction, Attribution and Responsibility in Jaloud'.

[140] Attribution of conduct has been described by Milanovic as 'a question of whether the acts or omissions of a living, breathing human being (or group of human beings) should *in law* be regarded as the conduct of a state, a constructed, abstract entity, which (just like a corporation in domestic law) can in reality only act through living, breathing human beings': Ibid.

[141] Ibid. [142] Ibid. [143] *Al-Skeini v the United Kingdom*.

[144] *Loizidou v Turkey (Merits)* (40/1993/435/514) and *Solomou and Others v Turkey*, Application no 36832/97 (ECtHR, 24 June 2008).

[145] *Ilaşcu and Others v Moldova and Russia* and *Catan and Others v Moldova and Russia*.

airspace or internal waters or territorial seas[146] of a non-contracting state require the same consideration as within the territory of the state. For this reason, in order to attribute any acts to the contracting state, the presence of air force personnel or naval personnel in these areas must also be determined. Naturally, the separate question of whether actions of the state agent/s are attributable to the state, another state, or a supranational body such as the UN or NATO may also have to be addressed.

3.7.1 Conduct attributable to a supranational body

In the jurisprudence of the ECtHR, the issue of the attribution of armed forces personnel's conduct has received inconsistent treatment. This was most notable in the case of *Behrami and Saramati*,[147] where it was held that the actions of NATO-led peacekeepers in Kosovo were attributable to the United Nations as the international body that authorized their presence in the country and not either NATO or the contracting state from which they originated. Moreover, as the UN is not a contracting party to the ECHR, it could not exercise jurisdiction over acts attributed to it. This decision was severely criticized.[148] In *Al-Jedda*[149] the Court revisited this issue, distinguished the factual scenario from *Behrami and Saramati*, and therefore concluded that the acts of soldiers in the Multi-National Force (Iraq) were attributable to the troop-contributing nations and not the UN, as the organization 'did not ... assume any degree of control over either the force or any other of the executive functions of the Coalition Provisional Authority'.[150] Rather, the US and UK, 'through the Coalition Provisional Authority which they had established at the start of the occupation, continued to exercise the powers of government in Iraq'.[151] While the Court is clearly at significant pains to distinguish *Behrami and Saramati* from *Al-Jedda* on a factual basis,[152] the more compelling argument is that *Behrami and Saramati* was wrongly decided, and such a justification for denying admissibility will not be revisited by the Court again. In *Al-Jedda*, the Court laid down a clear marker regarding the approach to be taken in resolving any apparent conflict between UN Security Council Resolutions and the conduct of the Court thus: 'in the event of any ambiguity in the terms of a Security Council Resolution, the Court must therefore choose the interpretation which is most in harmony with the requirements of the Convention and which avoids any conflict of obligations.'[153] The key messages that states ought to take away from *Al-Jedda* is that as a starting and compelling presumption, the conduct of troops in a non-contracting state is attributable to the 'sending' state and not any other supranational body. This includes any unlawful conduct by armed forces.[154] In addition, the UN Security Council, in the opinion of the ECtHR,

[146] RR Churchill and AV Lowe, *The Law of the Sea* (3rd edn, Juris Publishing 1999), at 66 and 71, give the definitive legal definition of internal water and the territorial seas. As a matter of law, the jurisdiction of the state extends to these areas. The same is true of super-adjacent airspace.

[147] *Behrami and Saramati v France and Others* (Admissibility) (71412/01).

[148] Marco Milanovic and Tatjana Papic, 'As Bad as It Gets: The European Court of Human Rights' Behrami and Saramati Decision and General International Law', *ICLQ* (2009) 267 267–300.

[149] *Al-Jedda v the United Kingdom*, 83. [150] Ibid, 80. [151] Ibid.

[152] Ibid, 84. [153] Ibid, 102. [154] *Ilaşcu and Others v Moldova and Russia* 384–90.

ought to be cognizant of its obligations in respect of fundamental human rights when authorizing military actions pursuant to the UN Charter and not authorize any action inconsistent with them.[155]

3.7.2 Conduct attributable to another state

In *Jaloud*, the Netherlands argued that, at the material time, its armed forces contingent in Iraq had 'been under the operational control of the commander of the Multinational Division (South East), an officer of the United Kingdom'.[156] As such, the actions of the Netherlands officer were attributable to the US and UK as the 'occupying powers' in Iraq pursuant to UN Security Resolution 1482, or, alternatively, the UK alone as the 'lead nation' in south-eastern Iraq. The Court rejected this submission for a number of reasons. First, the fact that a country or countries were occupying powers pursuant to Article 42 of the Hague Regulations was not determinative of their jurisdiction under Article 1, ECHR.[157] Second, executing an order given by an officer from another state, in this case the UK, did not divest the Netherlands of its Convention obligations.[158] Finally, the Netherlands government exercised full command over its troops in Iraq, was responsible for providing security in the immediate geographical area in which the shooting at the checkpoint took place, and established the rules of engagement to which its troops were to adhere. The rules of engagement regulated when, where, and how the troops could use lethal force.[159] The fact that the Netherlands exercised full command of its troops *and* that they were responsible for providing security in the area in which the shooting at the checkpoint took place is significant. Sari suggests that as a consequence of *Jaloud*, 'full command constitutes a sufficient link between the state and its armed forces as to preserve the national character of their activities'.[160] While this is a supportable position, it cannot be based solely on the judgment in *Jaloud*, as it fails to recognize the fundamental significance of the Dutch troops' role in providing security at the checkpoint.

In *Behrami and Saramati*, as in *Jaloud*, the state retained full command over its troops, yet the finding in terms of attribution was the opposite. The judgment in *Jaloud* is, therefore, most convincingly read as a significant departure from *Behrami and Saramati*. Moreover, it would appear to leave little room for the Court to invoke an analysis based on the reasoning in *Behrami and Saramati* in the future, as states very rarely, if at all, relinquish all control of their armed forces to another state.

In respect of attribution, therefore, what emerges is, potentially, a three-part test. First, if attribution is disputed, then the Court must establish that the armed forces of the state were present in the area where the alleged violations occurred at the

[155] Ibid. [156] *Jaloud v the Netherlands* 115.

[157] The Court found the concept relevant in *Al-Skeini* and *Al-Jedda*, but not in *Loizidou, Cyprus v Turkey, Catan*, and *Ilaşcu.*

[158] *Jaloud v the Netherlands*, 143. [159] Ibid, 146–47.

[160] Aurel Sari, 'Jaloud v Netherlands—New Direction in Extraterritorial Military Operations', *EJIL:Talk!* blogpost, <http://www.ejiltalk.org/jaloud-v-netherlands-new-directions-in-extra-territorial-military-operations/> (accessed 19 December 2015).

material time. Second, once the presence of armed forces is determined, the Court must establish that the conduct of the state agents is attributable to the state and not a supranational organization or another state. Finally, the actual acts or omissions of the state agents are attributable to the state. In *Jaloud*, for example, the first question does not arise, but it has in other cases, particularly in respect of Turkish armed forces' activity against Kurds in Northern Iraq.[161] The second question in *Jaloud* is addressed by the Court, invoking Article 6 of the ILC's Articles on State Responsibility, in the following terms: 'the Court cannot find that the Netherlands troops were placed "at the disposal" of any foreign power, whether it be Iraq or the United Kingdom or any other power, or that they were "under the exclusive direction or control" of any other State.'[162] As Milanovic correctly asserts, the third question then becomes 'obvious and trivial',[163] but nonetheless necessary, in that the Netherlands remained responsible for the conduct of an investigation following the death at the checkpoint that complied with its procedural Article 2 obligations.

3.8 The Extraterritorial Application of the ICCPR

There is no consensus on the extraterritorial application of the ICCPR during armed conflict, with states, courts, commentators, and human rights bodies advancing at times irreconcilable positions.[164] Three principal objections to the extraterritorial application of the Covenant have arisen. The first is founded on a legal interpretative analysis of the jurisdiction and derogation clauses within the Covenant;[165] the second focuses on the perceived adverse impact on states' willingness to use military force overseas if bound by such provisions;[166] and the third considers the absence of any state practice to support extraterritorial application.[167] On the other hand, those in favour of a more expansive interpretation of the ICCPR's jurisdictional clause offer a different legal interpretation of the relevant provision and contend, inter alia, that the universality of human rights must ensure that states cannot potentially violate human rights overseas in a way that would be prohibited within their own territory.[168]

[161] *Issa and Others v Turkey*, Application no 31821/96 (ECtHR, 16 November 2004) 81.

[162] *Jaloud v the Netherlands* 151.

[163] Sari, 'Jaloud v Netherlands—New Direction in Extraterritorial Military Operations'.

[164] For a consideration of the issues concerned, see Manfred Nowak, *United Nations Covenant on Civil and Political Rights CCPR Commentary* (2nd edn, Engel 2005); Karen Costa, *The Extraterritorial Application of Selected Human Rights Treaties* (Martinus Nijhoff 2014); Martin Scheinin, 'Extraterritorial Effect of the International Covenant on Civil and Political Rights' in Fons Coomans and Menno T Kamminga (eds), *Extraterritorial Application of Human Rights Treaties* (Intersentia 2004) 73-82; Dominic McGoldrick, 'Extraterritorial Application of the International Covenant on Civil and Political Rights' in Fons Coomans and Menno T Kamminga (eds), *Extraterritorial Application of Human Rights Treaties* (Intersentia 2004) 73–82.

[165] Michael J Dennis and Andre M Surena, 'Application of the International Covenant on Civil and Political Rights in Times of Armed Conflict and Military Occupation: The Gap between Legal Theory and State Practice' (2008) 6 *EHRLR* 724–27.

[166] Ibid, 724–25. [167] Ibid, 715–17.

[168] Marko Milanovic, *Extraterritorial Application of Human Rights Treaties: Law, Principles and Policy* (Oxford University Press 2011) 226; Ralph Wilde, 'Legal "Black Hole"? Extraterritorial State Action

We turn first to the interpretative argument. At the request of the United States delegation,[169] the sub-clause 'within its territory' was included within Article 2(1), ICCPR such that it read: 'Each State Party to the present Covenant undertakes to respect and to ensure to all individuals within its territory *and* subject to its jurisdiction the rights recognized in the present Covenant.'[170] This has led some states,[171] including the United States,[172] and certain commentators[173] to favour a literal reading and interpret the provision conjunctively to require that individuals are both 'within its territory' and 'subject to its jurisdiction' for the ICCPR to afford them protections.[174] This approach is problematic for a number of reasons.

First, on its face, Article 2(1) is not unambiguous and affords two differing interpretations. As the United States submits, the requirements of 'within its territory' and 'subject to its jurisdiction' can be read conjunctively. Equally, however, they could be read disjunctively as alternatives. As Professor Koh contends, the concepts are not coterminous.[175] Jurisdiction can arise outside a state's physical territory, for example, in an embassy, on a military base overseas, or upon a flagged-state vessel on the high seas. Conversely, individuals within the physical territory of the United States may not be within its jurisdiction—examples would include foreign diplomats and consuls working in their nation's embassy or consulate.[176]

Second, noting these alternative possible interpretations and recognizing the requirements of Articles 31 and 32 of the Vienna Convention on the Law of Treaties[177] that requires, inter alia, that treaty provisions are interpreted 'in the

and International Treaty Law on Civil and Political Rights' (2005) 26 *Michigan J Int Law* 791; *Lopez Burgos v Uruguay*, Communication no 52/1979, 12.3, UN Doc CCPR/C/13/D/52/1979 (1981).

[169] Nowak, *UN Covenant on Civil and Political Rights* 30–34.

[170] ICCPR, Article 2(1) [emphasis added].

[171] Human Rights Committee, *Fourth Periodic Report—Israel*, UN Doc CCPR/C/ISR/4/ (12 December 2013) 48: 'Moreover, in line with basic principles of treaty interpretation, Israel believes that the Convention, which is territorially bound, does not apply, nor was it intended to apply, to areas beyond a state's national territory'; *Human Rights Committee, Second Periodic Report—Israel*, UN Doc CCPR/C/ISR/2001/2 (4 December 2001) 8.

[172] One-Year Follow-Up Response of the United States of America to Priority Recommendations of the Human Rights Committee on Its Fourth Periodic Report on Implementation of the International Covenant on Civil and Political Rights, Permanent Mission of the United States of America, Geneva, 31 March 2015. In response to recommendation 21 in respect of detainees at Guantanamo Bay, para 24 stated: 'We preface this response by recalling the longstanding position of the United States that obligations under the Covenant apply only with respect to individuals who are both with the territory of a State Party and within its jurisdiction.' See also Human Rights Committee, *Third Periodic Report—United States*, UN Doc CCPR/C/USA/3 (26 November 2005) 130: 'The United States recalls its longstanding position ... that the obligations assumed by the United States under the Covenant apply only within the territory of the United States.'

[173] Michael J Dennis and Andre M Surena, 'Application of the International Covenant on Civil and Political Rights in Times of Armed Conflict and Military Occupation: The Gap between Legal Theory and State Practice' (2008) 6 *Eur Hum Rts L Rev* 726–27; Michael J Dennis, 'Application of Human Rights Treaties Extraterritorially in Times of Armed Conflict and Military Occupation' (2005) 99(1) *Am J Int Law* 123–24.

[174] Human Rights Committee, *Third Periodic Report—United States*, UN Doc CCPR/C/USA/3 (26 November 2005), Annex I.

[175] Memorandum Opinion on the Geographic Scope of the International Covenant on Civil and Political Rights, Office of the Legal Adviser, United States Department of State, October 19, 2010, p 7.

[176] Ibid.

[177] Vienna Convention on the Law of Treaties, 23 May 1969, 1155 UNTS 331, 8 ILM 679.

context' of the treaty and 'in light of [the treaty's] object and purpose', it can be asserted that Article 2(1) would not seek to unnecessarily limit the universal scope of human rights. By doing so it would place the ICCPR in conflict with the aim and purpose of both the United Nations Charter and the Universal Declaration of Human Rights that extol 'universal respect for, and observance of, human rights and freedoms'.[178] Equally, such an interpretation would create an internal incoherence within the ICCPR, in that Article 5(1) states:

> Nothing in the present Covenant may be interpreted as implying for any State, group or person any right to engage in any activity or perform any act aimed at the destruction of any of the rights and freedoms recognized herein or at their limitation to a greater extent than is provided for in the present Covenant.

This incoherence has been recognized by the Human Rights Committee, who considered that

> Article 2 (1) of the Covenant places an obligation upon a State party to respect and to ensure rights 'to all individuals within its territory and subject to its jurisdiction', but it does not imply that the State party concerned cannot be held accountable for violations of rights under the Covenant which its agents commit upon the territory of another State, whether with the acquiescence of the Government of that State or in opposition to it. According to article 5 (1) … it would be unconscionable to so interpret the responsibility under article 2 of the Covenant as to permit a State party to perpetrate violations of the Covenant on the territory of another State, which violations it could not perpetrate on its own territory.[179]

Furthermore, Professor Tomuschat considers that to interpret the words 'within its territory' as applying only to the physical territory of the state would lead to 'utterly absurd results' in that it would allow states an 'unfettered' power to attack their citizens living abroad.[180] This presumably would include the use of lethal force against these individuals. In addition to the internal incoherence between Article 2(1) and Article 5(1), Professor Koh highlights the inconsistency with Article 12(1),[181] in that the territorial clause contained therein is superfluous and redundant if a conjunctive interpretation of Article 2(1) is preferred.[182] A similar incoherence arises in respect of Article 1 of the First Optional Protocol to the ICCPR, which contains no 'territorial' requirement and reads:

> A State Party to the Covenant that becomes a Party to the present Protocol recognizes the competence of the Committee to receive and consider communications from individuals

[178] Charter of the United Nations, Article 56 (26 June 1945); Universal Declaration of Human Rights, GA Res 217 (III) A, UN Doc A/RES/217/(III) 10 December 1948.

[179] *Lopez Burgos v Uruguay*, Saldias de Lopez (on behalf of Lopez Burgos) v Uruguay, Merits, Communication no 52/1979, UN Doc CCPR/C/13/D/52/1979, IHRL 2796 (UNHRC 1981), 29 July 1981, Human Rights Committee [UNHRC].

[180] Ibid, Appendix. See also Nowak, *United Nations Covenant*, 43: 'an expressly literal reading would … lead to often absurd results.'

[181] ICCPR, Article 12(1): 'Everyone lawfully within the territory of a State shall, within that territory, have the right to liberty of movement and freedom to choose his residence.'

[182] Memorandum Opinion on the Geographic Scope of the International Covenant on Civil and Political Rights, Office of the Legal Adviser, United States Department of State, 19 October 2010, 11.

subject to its jurisdiction who claim to be victims of a violation by that State Party of any of the rights set forth in the Covenant.[183]

Therefore, on a strict reading of Article 1, First Optional Protocol to the ICCPR, it would appear that the competence of the Committee in respect of the Optional Protocol arises without the requirement for the alleged violation to occur within the territory of the state party. Again, a conjunctive interpretation of Article 2(1), ICCPR would result in an unusual jurisdictional discrepancy between the ICCPR and its First Optional Protocol.

Third, the Human Rights Committee in its General Comments, in its concluding observations on states parties' reports, and in responses to communications has preferred an expansive and disjunctive interpretation of Article 2(1). In General Comment 31, it considered that

States Parties are required by article 2, paragraph 1, to respect and to ensure the Covenant rights to all persons who may be within their territory and to all persons subject to their jurisdiction. This means that a State party must respect and ensure the rights laid down in the Covenant to anyone within the power or effective control of that State Party, even if not situated within the territory of the State Party.[184]

The Human Rights Committee then considered the applicability of the ICCPR to situations of armed conflict as follows: 'the Covenant applies also in situations of armed conflict to which the rules of international humanitarian law are applicable ... both spheres of law are complementary, not mutually exclusive.'[185] With respect to the right to life, this approach is reinforced by the Human Rights Committee in its draft General Comment 36,[186] and therefore by necessity requires the extraterritorial application of the ICCPR beyond the state's own territory in order to apply to armed conflict outside a state's territory.

[183] International Covenant on Civil and Political Rights, First Optional Protocol, Article 1, 19 December 1966, 999 UNTS 302, GA Res 2200A (XXI), 21 UN GAOR Supp (No 16) at 59, UN Doc A/6316.

[184] Human Rights Committee, General Comment 31, Nature of the General Legal Obligation on States Parties to the Covenant, UN Doc CCPR/C/21/Rev.1/Add.13 (2004) 10.

[185] Ibid, 11.

[186] Human Rights Committee, Draft General Comment 36, Article 6: Right to life CCPR/C/GC/R.36/Rev.2, 63: 'article 6 continues to apply also in situations of armed conflict to which the rules of international humanitarian law are applicable. While rules of international humanitarian law may be relevant for the interpretation and application of article 6, both spheres of law are complementary, not mutually exclusive. Uses of lethal force authorized and regulated by and complying with international humanitarian law are, in principle, not arbitrary. By contrast, practices inconsistent with international humanitarian law, entailing a real risk to the lives of civilians and persons hors de combat, including the targeting of civilians and civilian objects, failure to apply adequate measures of precaution to prevent collateral death of civilians, and the use of human shields, violate article 6 of the Covenant. Furthermore, State parties should, subject to compelling security considerations, disclose the criteria for attacking with lethal force individuals or objects whose targeting is excepted to result in deprivation of life, including the legal basis for specific attacks, the process of identification of military targets and combatants or persons taking a direct part in hostilities, the circumstances in which relevant means and methods of warfare have been used, and whether less lethal alternatives for attaining the same military objective were considered.'

Finally, in the '*Wall* case',[187] the International Court of Justice (ICJ) considered the requirements in Article 2(1) to apply disjunctively.[188] Having examined the *travaux préparatoires*[189] and the 'constant practice'[190] and approach of the Human Rights Committee to this issue in *Lopez Burgos v Uruguay, Lilian Celiberti v Uruguay, Montero v Uruguay* and its concluding observations on Israel, the ICJ stated: 'In conclusion, the Court considers that the International Covenant on Civil and Political Rights is applicable in respect of acts done by a State in the exercise of its jurisdiction outside its own territory.'[191] This position was reaffirmed in the '*Congo* case', where the ICJ stated that 'international human rights instruments are applicable in "respect of acts done by a State in the exercise of its jurisdiction outside its own territory," particularly in occupied territories.'[192]

Despite the views of the Human Rights Committee and the ICJ, states' approaches to the extraterritorial application of the ICCPR during armed conflict vastly differ. The United States has steadfastly maintained a position that the ICCPR does not have extraterritorial effect,[193] save in circumstances where the 'State Party controls [territory] as a governmental authority'.[194] Israel, on the other hand, asserts that the Covenant does not apply beyond the state's national territory.[195] Other states, including Belgium,[196]

[187] *Legal Consequences of the Construction of a Wall in the Occupied Palestinian Territory*, International Court of Justice, Advisory Opinion of 9 July 2004 [2004] ICJ Reports.

[188] Ibid, 108–11.

[189] See the discussion of the preliminary draft in the Commission on Human Rights, ElCN.4lSR.194, 46; United Nations, *Official Record of the General Assembly, Tenth Session, Annexes,* Al2929, Part II, Chap V, para 4 (1955).

[190] *Legal Consequences of the Construction of a Wall in the Occupied Palestinian Territory*, International Court of Justice, Advisory Opinion of 9 July 2004 [2004] ICJ Reports.

[191] Ibid, 111.

[192] *Case Concerning Armed Activities on the Territory of the Congo (Democratic Republic of the Congo v. Uganda)*, Judgment 2005 ICJ Reports 168 (19 December 2005) 243, citing *Legal Consequences of the Construction of a Wall in the Occupied Palestinian Territory*, at 178–81.

[193] One-Year Follow-Up Response of the United States of America to Priority Recommendations of the Human Rights Committee on Its Fourth Periodic Report on Implementation of the International Covenant on Civil and Political Rights, Permanent Mission of the United States of America, Geneva (31 March 2015); Human Rights Committee, *Third Periodic Report—United States*, UN Doc CCPR/C/USA/3 (26 November 2005) 24: 'We preface this response by recalling the longstanding position of the United States that obligations under the Covenant apply only with respect to individuals who are both within the territory of a State Party and within its jurisdiction.'

[194] One-Year Follow-Up Response of the United States of America to Recommendations of the Committee against Torture on Its Combined Third to Fifth Periodic Reports on Implementation of the Convention Against Torture and Other Cruel, Inhuman, or Degrading Treatment or Punishment (27 November 2015) 5.

[195] Human Rights Committee, *Fourth Periodic Report—Israel*, UN Doc CCPR/C/ISR/4 (12 December 2013) 48: 'Moreover, in line with basic principles of treaty interpretation, Israel believes that the Convention, which is territorially bound, does not apply, nor was it intended to apply, to areas beyond a state's national territory'; Human Rights Committee, *Second Periodic Report—Israel*, UN Doc CCPR/C/ISR/2001/2 (4 December 2001) 8.

[196] Human Rights Committee, Consideration of Reports Submitted by States Parties under Article 40 of the Covenant: Fifth Periodic Report: Belgium, 15, UN Doc CCPR/C/BEL/5 (17 July 2009): 'when members of such armed forces are deployed abroad, as for example in the context of peacekeeping or peace enforcement operations, Belgium ensures that all persons who come under its jurisdiction enjoy the rights recognized in the International Covenant on Civil and Political Rights.'

France,[197] Italy,[198] Poland,[199] Sweden,[200] and Switzerland[201] take the contrary position and assert that the ICCPR does, as a matter of principle, have extraterritorial effect. To illustrate with just two examples: in its written communication in the '*Wall* case', France considered that:

> The construction of the wall appears to infringe other rules of international humanitarian law or human rights rules binding on Israel ... the two bodies of rules apply in the present case and are mutually complementary. Thus, violations of one or the other resulting from the construction of the wall should be examined together.[202]

And Switzerland submitted that:

> Switzerland considers that in a situation of armed conflict, the special, complementary and parallel character of protective norms, especially the norms of international humanitarian and human rights law, are particularly important.[203]

By definition, therefore, if human rights law is 'particularly important' during armed conflict, it must have extraterritorial effect given the likelihood, or possibility, of an armed conflict occurring in the territory of another state.

Australia, Germany, the United Kingdom, and the Netherlands, among others, have taken a more nuanced view of the extraterritorial application of the ICCPR. Australia accepted in principle that there 'may be exceptional circumstances in which the rights and freedoms set out under the Covenant may be relevant beyond the territory of a State party'.[204] It considered that the obligations in the ICCPR are 'essentially territorial'[205] in nature, but recognized and accepted the Human Rights Committee's view expressed in General Comment 31 insofar as the state may have obligations pursuant to the ICCPR in discrete circumstances. In its view, the only circumstances in which Australia would be required to afford all the rights of the Covenant extraterritorially would be where it was 'exercising all of the powers normally exercised by the sovereign State',[206] such as an 'occupation, consensual

[197] Legal Consequences of the Construction of a Wall in the Occupied Palestinian Territory Written Statement of the French Republic, 30 January 2004, 39.

[198] Human Rights Committee, Concluding Observations on Italy, UN Doc CCPR/C/ITA/CO/5 (24 April 2006) 3.

[199] Human Rights Committee, Concluding Observations on Poland, UN Doc CCPR/CO/82/POL (2 December 2004) 3.

[200] 'The Embassy of Sweden presents its compliments to the International Court of Justice and, with reference to the letter of 19 December 2003 from the Court's Registrar to the Ambassador of Sweden to the Netherlands concerning the request for an advisory opinion by the United Nations and its Member States, has the honour to submit the enclosed reply': 30 January 2004, 8.

[201] Written statement addressed to the International Court of Justice by the Swiss Confederation pursuant to the Order of the Court of 19 December 2003, 33.

[202] Legal Consequences of the Construction of a Wall in the Occupied Palestinian Territory, Written Statement of the French Republic, 30 January 2004, 39.

[203] Written statement addressed to the International Court of Justice by the Swiss Confederation pursuant to the Order of the Court of 19 December 2003, 33.

[204] Human Rights Committee, Replies to the List of Issues (CCPR/C/AUS/Q/5) to be taken up in connection with the considerations of the Fifth Periodic Report of the Government of Australia (CCPR/C/AUS/5), 16–18, UN Doc CCPR/C/AUS/Q/5/Add.1 (5 February 2009).

[205] Ibid, 17. [206] Ibid, 18.

deployment or UN mandated mission'.[207] Ultimately, as Professor Koh asserts, Australia takes the position that the extent to which the ICCPR applies extraterritorially is determined by the 'degree of authority and control that a State party exercises in certain circumstances'.[208] Germany, in response to criticism by the Human Rights Committee in its Fifth Periodic Report concerning the country's failure to take 'a position regarding the applicability of the Covenant to persons subject to its jurisdiction in situations where its troops or police forces operate abroad',[209] responded by stating: 'wherever ... armed forces are deployed abroad ... Germany ensures to all persons that they will be granted the rights recognized in the Covenant, insofar as they are subject to its jurisdiction.'[210] While this statement would appear to acknowledge the potential for the existence of ICCPR obligations extraterritorially, *when* Germany considers these obligations may arise is far from clear.

The UK has only accepted that the ICCPR applies extraterritorially during armed conflict in very limited circumstances, specifically when a person is 'taken into custody by UK forces and held in military detention facilities outside of the UK'.[211] It has been critical of what it considers to be the Human Rights Committee's lack of specificity in defining what is meant by 'within the power or effective control of the forces of the State party acting outside its territory'.[212] This approach reflects the position taken by the UK government in respect of its litigation strategy in *Al-Skeini* and *Hassan* and would appear to consider that ICCPR obligations arise only when an individual is in a military detention facility, not within the control of UK armed forces outside of this. This understanding does not, however, reflect the view of the ECtHR in *Hassan* and *Jaloud* and the Divisional Court in *Serdar Mohammed* and *Al-Saadoon*. Moreover, it also falls short of the more expansive view of jurisdiction elucidated by the Human Rights Committee in General Comment 31. In a similar vein, the Netherlands considers the ICCPR to have extraterritorial effect in circumstances where state agents have 'full and effective' control of individuals or territory, albeit that they considered that this threshold was not met—contrary to the view of the Human Rights Committee[213]—in respect of Dutch 'blue helmets' in Srebrenica.[214]

[207] Ibid.

[208] Memorandum Opinion on the Geographic Scope of the International Covenant on Civil and Political Rights, Office of the Legal Adviser, United States Department of State, 19 October 2010, 38.

[209] Human Rights Committee, Concluding Observations on Germany, UN Doc CCPR/CO/80/DEU (4 May 2004), 11.

[210] Human Rights Committee, Comments by the Government of Germany on the Concluding Observations on Germany, 3 UN Doc CCPR/CO/80/DEU/Add.1 (11 April 2005).

[211] Human Rights Committee, Information Received from the United Kingdom on the Implementation of the Concluding Observations of the Human Rights Committee, UN Doc. CCPR/C/GBR/CO/6/Add 1 (3 November 2009) 24.

[212] Human Rights Committee, Consideration of Reports Submitted by States Parties under Article 40 of the Covenant: Sixth Periodic Report: United Kingdom of Great Britain and Northern Ireland, UN Doc CCPR/C/GBR/6 (18 May 2007) 59.

[213] Human Rights Committee, Concluding Observations on the Netherlands, UN Doc CCPR/CO/72/NET (27 August 2001) 4–5.

[214] Human Rights Committee, Replies of the Government of the Netherlands to the concerns expressed by the Human Rights Committee in its Concluding Observations on the Netherlands, UN Doc CCPR/CO/72/NET/Add.1 (29 April 2003).

What emerges from a consideration of states' responses to the question of the extraterritorial application of the ICCPR during armed conflict is, at best, a diverse range of opinions. The full spectrum of views is offered, from Israel's stance on its non-applicability, through its limited application—a position favoured by, among others, the UK and Australia—to the belief of its general applicability supported by, for example, France and Belgium. The position of the United States is interesting in that it continues to assert 'that obligations under the Covenant apply only with respect to individuals who are both within the territory of a State Party and within its jurisdiction'[215] while at the same time recognizing, in respect of the Convention against Torture, that

> although the law of armed conflict is the controlling body of law with respect to the conduct of hostilities and the protection of war victims, a time of war does not suspend the operation of the Convention [against Torture], which continues to apply even when a State is engaged in armed conflict.[216]

The US has not adopted the same view in respect of the ICCPR, yet it would appear that—as a matter of strict logic—at least in respect of Article 7, the same approach ought to be taken.

What can be said in support of Israel's position is that the extraterritorial application of the ICCPR in times of armed conflict is far from generally accepted. Equally, little support can be found for the United States' assertion that states would be unwilling to intervene in armed conflicts overseas if they considered themselves subject to the jurisdiction of the ICCPR. The continued presence until 2014 of numerous nations' armed forces in the International Security Assistance Force (ISAF) mission in Afghanistan, and the limited intervention of French, Belgian, Netherlands, and German armed forces in the fight against Islamic State in Iraq, would appear to suggest that they are willing to contribute armed forces in such circumstances. Of all positions adopted by states, the non-applicability stance taken by the United States and Israel is the least convincing.[217] Considering the language of the treaty in the context of human rights generally, the object and purpose of the ICCPR and its other provisions would favour a disjunctive

[215] One-Year Follow-Up Response of the United States of America to Priority Recommendations of the Human Rights Committee on Its Fourth Periodic Report on Implementation of the International Covenant on Civil and Political Rights, Permanent Mission of the United States of America, Geneva, 31 March 2015; Human Rights Committee, *Third Periodic Report—United States*, UN Doc CCPR/C/USA/3 (26 November 2005) 24.

[216] One-Year Follow-Up Response of the United States of America to Recommendations of the Committee Against Torture on its Combined Third to Fifth Periodic Reports on Implementation of the Convention Against Torture and Other Cruel, Inhuman, or Degrading Treatment or Punishment (27 November 2015) 6.

[217] Beth Van Schaack, 'The United States' Position on the Extraterritorial Application of Human Rights Obligations: Now is the Time for Change' (2014) 90(20) *Intl L Stud* 61–65; Memorandum Opinion on the Geographic Scope of the International Covenant on Civil and Political Rights, Office of the Legal Adviser, United States Department of State, 19 October 2010, 55; Nigel Rodley, 'The Extra-Territorial Reach and Applicability in Armed Conflict of the International Covenant on Civil and Political Rights: A Rejoinder to Dennis and Surena' (2009) 5 *EHRLR* 628–36.

interpretation of the jurisdiction clause at Article 2(1). The views of the Human Rights Committee, the International Court of Justice, and a significant number of states would also support such an approach. That said, the exact nature and contours of the extraterritorial jurisdiction of the ICCPR during armed conflict remain unclear. Arguably the most persuasive interpretation would be that favoured by Professor Koh, in which 'a state is obligated to respect rights under its control in circumstances in which the State exercises authority or effective control over a particular person or context without regards to territory'[218] and there are 'positive obligations on a state to ensure rights ... for individuals who are both within the territory and subject to the jurisdiction of the State party'.[219] In other words, obligations arise on the basis of a personal model of jurisdiction where armed forces operate in the territory of another state. Such an approach is certainly consistent with the recent judgments of the ECtHR and Divisional Court, although it has been criticized by certain commentators.[220] It may, however, be problematic in that extraterritorial jurisdiction in respect of the ECHR can arise in circumstances other than just control over individuals. For example, ECHR jurisdiction could be established based on the 'control of territory' by armed forces, yet in exactly the same factual circumstances jurisdiction in respect of the ICCPR may not arise due to insufficient control over individuals. This could result in coalition armed forces partners from ECHR contracting and non-contracting states being subject to different legal obligations. In practice, however, this is typical during any multinational military operation, in which national laws and caveats can play a significant role in the range of operations that various nations' armed forces can undertake.[221]

While no state has specifically addressed the issue, their willingness to accept that, as a matter of jurisdiction, the ICCPR applies to the activities of their armed forces operating in the territory of another state may be a consequence of this being simply the first stage in any analysis of their obligations. In other words, once the applicability of the ICCPR is established, then the interaction of human rights law and international humanitarian law must be addressed. This subsequent analysis may reveal that any human rights obligations are modified to reflect the state's existing international humanitarian law obligations and therefore, in any practical sense, limit the effect of the ICCPR. This issue will be addressed in respect of the right to life in Chapter 4.

[218] Memorandum Opinion on the Geographic Scope of the International Covenant on Civil and Political Rights, p 55.

[219] Ibid, 56.

[220] Marko Milanovic, 'Some Thoughts on the Serdar Mohammed Appeals Judgment', *EJIL:Talk!* blogpost at <http://www.ejiltalk.org/some-thoughts-on-the-serdar-mohammed-appeals-judgment/> (accessed 26 November 2015).

[221] For example, armed forces from various nations have differing interpretations of individual and collective self-defence or the meaning of the term 'hostile intent' in rules of engagement terms. Equally, national constitutions can place restrictions on how armed forces are employed overseas. For example, both Germany and Japan have been subject to such limitations.

3.9 Jurisdiction and Royal Naval Warships and Royal Air Force Aircraft

In circumstances where armed forces take control of a civilian vessel, irrespective of its flag state, Milanovic[222] makes a compelling case for ECHR jurisdiction arising on the basis of the state agents exercising authority and control over the individuals in the vessel. In his opinion, jurisdiction does not arise because the state agents control the vessel itself. This situation can, however, be distinguished in respect of jurisdiction arising in a Royal Navy warship or Royal Air Force aircraft. The question of jurisdiction with respect to warships and military aircraft is an extremely straightforward matter, as they are considered to be a sovereign entity of the UK.[223] As a matter of law, therefore, the ECHR applies to all those civilian personnel who are on board. When considering the exercise of control, while it is recognized that the Court in *Al-Skeini* made clear that the decisive factor is control of an individual, not a ship, 'the Court does not consider that jurisdiction in the above cases arose solely from the control exercised by the state over the buildings, aircraft or ship in which the individuals were held.'[224] In warships and military aircraft the military personnel exercise exclusive control over the vessel or aircraft and therefore, by definition, all those personnel on board. In other words, once an individual from a non-contracting state sets foot on board a warship or military aircraft, they are afforded all the rights and protections of the ECHR. In *Hirsi Jamaa and Others v Italy*[225] the Court supported this position when it held that when Somali and Eritrean migrants were taken on board vessels of the Italian armed forces, they came under the exclusive jurisdiction of the flag state for the following reasons:

> The Court observes that in the instant case the events took place entirely on board ships of the Italian armed forces, the crews of which were composed exclusively of Italian military personnel. In the Court's opinion, in the period between boarding the ships of the Italian armed forces and being handed over to the Libyan authorities, the applicants were under the continuous and exclusive de jure and de facto control of the Italian authorities.[226]

In *Medvedyev and Others v France*[227] the Court held that when French troops seized control of a Cambodian-registered vessel, placed the crew under French military guard, and took control of navigation, the French authorities exercised 'full and effective control'[228] over the vessel and its crew. States' ability to exercise control over individuals on board ships is markedly easier than on land, notwithstanding the contradiction between the position taken by the Court in *Al-Skeini* when contrasted with *Medvedyev* and *Hirsi Jamaa*. The more persuasive position is that when a ship or aircraft is under the 'effective control' of a state through the presence of 'state

[222] Milanovic, *Extraterritorial Application of Human Rights Treaties*, 163–67.

[223] This is stated at <http://www.royalnavy.mod.uk/About-the-Royal-Navy/~/media/Files/Navy-PDFs/About-the-Royal-Navy/Future%20Navy%20Vision.pdf>.

[224] *Al-Skeini v the United Kingdom* 136.

[225] *Hirsi Jamaa and Others v Italy*.

[226] Ibid, 81.

[227] *Medvedyev and Others v France*.

[228] Ibid, 67.

agent' military personnel on board, the state exercises exclusive jurisdiction in these circumstances by virtue of having exclusive control of the ship or aircraft.

3.10 Conclusion

While the exact circumstances in which the ECHR and ICCPR apply extraterritorially are still keenly debated and far from settled, some conclusions can be drawn. Despite the protestations of certain states, it can be said that both instruments are capable of having extraterritorial effect and create obligations for armed forces operating overseas. With respect to the ECHR, these obligations can arise in circumstances where armed forces exercise control over territory and/or individuals or exercise certain 'public powers' normally undertaken by the state within which they operate. The rights to be guaranteed can be 'divided and tailored' according to the manner in which the control is exercised, namely, over territory, over individuals, or through the exercise of public powers. With respect to the ICCPR, a compelling proposition is that jurisdiction can arise in circumstances where 'the State exercises authority or effective control over a particular person or context without regards to territory'.[229] This approach does, however, create a distinction between how jurisdiction arises in the ECHR and the ICCPR. This situation can be resolved by understanding jurisdiction as arising in circumstances where a state agent/s exercise control over individuals, and not necessarily by the control of territory or by exercising 'public powers'.

Notwithstanding recent judgments that appear to indicate that jurisdiction can arise where armed forces have the power to kill individuals, it can be argued that some residual reasoning from *Banković* remains due to the ECtHR's unwillingness to directly and explicit depart from this judgment. Additionally, in *Al-Saadoon*,[230] when determining the existence of jurisdiction in the test cases, Lord Justice Lloyd Jones uses the 'public powers' exception to assess the extent to which actions of UK armed forces in Iraq fall within the jurisdiction of the UK in preference to an analysis based upon control over individuals. Ultimately, this means that where there is the application of lethal force absent any exercise of 'public powers' or control of territory, then, it could be asserted, there may be no jurisdiction.[231] This lack of clarity is unsatisfactory, clashes with the concept of exercising control over individuals, and ought to be resolved. The Divisional Court in *Al-Saadoon* proposed a solution when it concluded that 'whenever and wherever a state which is a contracting party to the Convention purports to exercise legal authority or uses physical force, it must do so in way that does not violate Convention rights'.[232] While not without difficulty, and having been modified by the Court of Appeal in the same case,[233] this approach

[229] Memorandum Opinion on the Geographic Scope of the International Covenant on Civil and Political Rights 55.

[230] *Al-Saadoon and Others v The Secretary of State for Defence* 106.

[231] Marco Milanovic, 'Al-Skeini and Al-Jedda in Strasbourg' (2012) 23 *Eu J Int Law* 126, at 139.

[232] *Al-Saadoon and Others v Secretary of State for Defence* 106.

[233] Ibid, 73.

would, however, provide a clear basis upon which states could then assess their human rights obligations during armed conflict. The fact that jurisdiction is established in such a manner does not necessarily create onerous obligations for states that would adversely affect armed forces' ability to achieve their military objectives. Once jurisdiction is established, the next step is to examine how international humanitarian law may modify a state's right to life obligations during armed conflict.

4

How the Right to Life Applies during Armed Conflict

4.1 Introduction

In order to address the issue of how the right to life applies during armed conflict and the extent to which the UK can ensure compliance with its substantive and procedural right to life obligations, this chapter will consider a number of interrelated issues. First, the relationship between international humanitarian law and human rights law in armed conflict must be analysed. To begin this analysis, the limitations and unsuitability of general theories to explain this relationship will be considered. An analysis of the legal framework governing the use of lethal force in international and non-international armed conflict then follows. It is, however, recognized that the law in this area is far from settled in respect of, inter alia, who is considered a member of an organized armed group, what constitutes a continuous combat function, and what amounts to a direct participation in hostilities.[1] Second, the relationship between international humanitarian law and human rights law in respect of the procedural right to life is assessed. Third, the methods used by UK armed forces to regulate the use of lethal force during armed conflict and investigate deaths are considered against the applicable legal framework. Finally, as part of the above analysis, an assessment of the extent to which the UK can comply with its substantive and procedural right to life obligations is made in two respects: first, where the UK's right to life obligations are determined in light of the applicable international humanitarian law; second, recognizing the uncertainty in this area of law, with reference only to human rights law.

4.2 The Relationship between International Humanitarian Law and Human Rights Law in Armed Conflict

Human rights law is applicable, ***potentially*** in a modified way, during international and non-international armed conflict where international humanitarian law

[1] To illustrate, compare Jean-Marie Henckaerts and Louise Doswald-Beck, *ICRC Study on Customary International Humanitarian Law* (Cambridge University Press 2009) 11–19 and Sandesh Sivakumaran, *The Law of Non-International Armed Conflict* (Oxford University Press 2012), 359–72.

applies.[2] A determination of the extent to which human rights law applies during armed conflict is of pivotal importance not only to ensure that states comply with their human rights law obligations, but also to determine the role and significance of international humanitarian law. If human rights law applies without modification during armed conflict, as it does in peacetime, then this would leave little scope for international humanitarian law. The UN Human Rights Committee,[3] the International Committee of the Red Cross (ICRC),[4] the International Court of Justice (ICJ),[5] and the European Court of Human Rights (ECtHR)[6] have all

[2] This issue has received considerable attention and a range of views have been offered to analyse the relationship between international humanitarian law and human rights law during armed conflict. See, among others, Daniel Bethlehem, 'The Relationship between International Humanitarian Law and International Human Rights Law in Situations of Armed Conflict' (2013) *CJICL* 2(2) 180–95; Oona A Hathaway, Rebecca Crootof, Philip Levitz, Haley Nix, William Perdue, Chelsea Purvis, and Julia Spiegel, 'Which Law Governs during Armed Conflict? The Relationship between International Humanitarian Law and Human Rights Law' (2012) 96(6) *Minnesota L Rev* 1883–1943; Orna Ben-Naftali, *International Humanitarian Law and International Human Rights Law* (Oxford University Press 2011); Erika de Wet and Jann Kleffner (eds) *Convergence and Conflicts of Human Rights and International Humanitarian Law in Military Operations* (PULP 2014); Marko Milanovic, 'A Norm Conflict Perspective on the Relationship between International Humanitarian Law and Human Rights Law' (2009) 14(3) *JC&SL* 459–83; Françoise J Hampson, 'The Relationship between International Humanitarian Law and Human Rights Law from the Perspective of a Human Rights Treaty Body' (2008) 90(871) *IRRC* 549–72; Paul Eden and Matthew Happold, 'Symposium: The Relationship between International Humanitarian Law and International Human Rights Law' (2009) 14(3) *JC&SL* 441–47; Bill Bowring, 'Fragmentation, Lex Specialis and the Tensions in the Jurisprudence of the European Court of Human Rights' (2009) 14(3) *JC&SL* 485–98; Iain Scobbie, 'Principle or Pragmatics? The Relationship between Human Rights Law and the Law of Armed Conflict' (2009) 14(3) *JC&SL* 449–57; Alexander Orakhelashvili, 'The Interaction between Human Rights and Humanitarian Law: Fragmentation, Conflict, Parallelism, or Convergence?' (2008) 19(1) *EJIL* 161–82; Martti Koskenniemi, 'Fragmentation of International Law: Difficulties Arising from the Diversification and Expansion of International Law, Report of the Study Group of the International Law Commission', UN Doc A/CN.4/L.682, 13 April 2006; Report of the International Law Commission (ILC), Fifty-sixth session, UN Doc A/59/10; Theodor Meron, 'The Humanization of Humanitarian Law' (2000) 94 *AJIL*, 239–78; Christine Byron, 'A Blurring of the Boundaries: The Application of Inter-National Humanitarian Law by Human Rights Bodies' (2007) 47 *Va J Intl L*, 839–48; UN Sub-Commission on the Promotion and Protection of Human Rights, Working Paper by Ms Hampson and Mr Salama on the Relationship between Human Rights Law and International Humanitarian Law, 9-37, UN Doc E/CN.4/Sub.2/2005/14, 21 June 2015; William Abresch, 'A Human Rights Law of Internal Armed Conflict: The European Court of Human Rights in Chechnya' (2005) 16 *EJIL* 741.

[3] Human Rights Committee, General Comment No 31 (Article 2) on the Nature of the General Legal Obligations Imposed on States Parties to the Covenant, UN Doc E/CCPR/C/21/Rev.1/Add.3 (26 May 2004), 11; Human Rights Committee, draft General Comment no 36.

[4] The ICRC position is set out unequivocally at <https://www.icrc.org/eng/war-and-law/ihl-other-legal-regimes/ihl-human-rights/overview-ihl-and-human-rights.htm>/.

[5] *Legality of the Threat or Use of Nuclear Weapons*, Advisory Opinion, 1996 ICJ 226 at 25; *The Legal Consequences of the Construction of a Wall in the Occupied Palestinian Territory* International Court of Justice, 9 July 2004; *Case Concerning Armed Activity on the Territory of the Congo* (Democratic Republic of the Congo v Uganda), International Court of Justice Judgment of 19 December 2005.

[6] The ECtHR, for example, has applied the ECHR in, inter alia, the following armed conflicts: Cyprus (as illustrative examples, see *Cyprus v Turkey*, Application no 25781/94 (ECtHR, 10 May 2001) 77; *Loizidou v Turkey*, Application no 15318/89 (ECtHR, 18 December 1996) 56; *Andreou v Turkey*, Application no 45653/99 (ECtHR, 3 June 2008) 25; Moldova (an illustrative example is *Ilaşcu and Others v Moldova and Russia*, para 332); Chechnya (as illustrative examples, see *Isayeva, Yusupova and Bazayeva v Russia*, Application nos 57947/00, 57948/00, and 57949/00 (ECtHR, 24 February 2005) 178 and *Esmukhambetov and Others v Russia*, Application no 23445 (ECtHR, 29 March 2011) 76; Georgia (*Georgia v Russia* (I), Application no 13255/07 (ECtHR, 3 July 20 14) 159 and 163; and Iraq (as illustrative examples, see *Al-Skeini and Others v the United Kingdom*, Application no 55721/

asserted that human rights law does apply during armed conflict, albeit that the extent to which this is the case remains open to question. Most recently, in respect of the right to life, the Human Rights Committee considered that 'the use of lethal force in military operations is *primarily* regulated by ... international humanitarian law'.[7] The use of the term *primarily* would appear to suggest that, in the view of the Human Rights Committee, human rights law has a role to play during armed conflict.

A state's substantive right to life obligations and their relationship with the international humanitarian law regulation of the use of lethal force in armed conflict will therefore be examined.[8] The requirement to conduct an investigation following the use of lethal force in armed conflict, as established in international humanitarian law, must also be considered alongside a state's procedural right to life obligations. As human rights law and international humanitarian law approach the issue of the use of lethal force from fundamentally different positions, it is particularly important to examine any differences. Only when the nature of this relationship has been determined can rules of engagement be issued and training undertaken to ensure that armed forces personnel comply with their state's right to life obligations.

To date, the focus of commentators has, for the most part, been on the de jure application[9] of human rights law in armed conflict, as well as the general conceptual interplay between the two bodies of law.[10] In order to establish the effect of recognizing the right to life during armed conflict it is necessary to closely examine the relationship between international humanitarian law and international human rights law with reference to the use of lethal force by armed forces. An analysis of the classification of armed conflicts is beyond the scope of this study;[11] however, for the purposes of an assessment of the right to life of those affected by the actions of armed forces, the criteria indicating the existence of an international or non-international armed conflict will be considered to be satisfied.

07 (ECtHR, 7 July 2011), *Jaloud v the Netherlands*, Application no 47708/08 (ECtHR, 20 November 2014), and *Hassan v the United Kingdom*, Application no 29750/09 (ECtHR, 16 September 2014).

[7] Human Rights Committee, draft General Comment 36, 13.

[8] Gloria Gaggioli and Robert Kolb, 'A Right to Life in Armed Conflicts? The Contribution of the European Court of Human Rights' (2007) *Israel YB Hum Rts* 115 at 138; Andrea Gioia, 'The Role of the European Court of Human Rights in Monitoring Compliance with Humanitarian Law in Armed Conflict' in Orna Ben-Naftali (ed), *International Humanitarian Law and International Human Rights Law* (Oxford University Press 2011) at 225–26; Stefan Oeter, 'Collateral Damages—Military Necessity and the Right to Life', in Christian Tomuschat, Evelyne Lagrange, and Stefan Oeter (eds), *The Right to Life* (Koninklijke Brill 2011) 167–93; Vera Gowlland-Debbas, 'The Right to Life and the Relationship between Human Rights and Humanitarian Law' in Christian Tomuschat, Evelyne Lagrange, and Stefan Oeter (ed), *The Right to Life* (Koninklijke Brill 2011) 123–50.

[9] Examples include Gerd Oberleitner, *Human Rights in Armed Conflict: Law, Practice, Policy* (Cambridge University Press 2015); J Klefner, J 'Human Rights and International Humanitarian Law: General Issues' in T Gill and D Fleck (eds) *The Handbook of the International Law of Military Operations* (Oxford University Press 2010) 51–77.

[10] See Bethlehem, 'The Relationship between International Humanitarian Law and International Human Rights Law in Situations of Armed Conflict'.

[11] This issue is considered at length in Elizabeth Wilmshurst (ed), *International Law and the Classification of Armed Conflicts* (Oxford University Press 2012).

4.2.1 The use of lethal force in armed conflict—differences between human rights law and international humanitarian law

Human rights law and international humanitarian law approach the issue of the use of lethal force during armed conflict from a fundamentally different standpoint. The most significant difference is that international humanitarian law generally allows individuals to be lethally targeted based upon their status, irrespective of their conduct, whereas human rights law permits the use of lethal force, or exceptions to the right to life, based exclusively on the conduct of individuals. If international humanitarian law is applied then armed forces or armed groups may be attacked at any time and under any circumstances, except when their intention to surrender has been accepted or when *hors de combat*.[12] Article 2, ECHR, on the other hand, only allows an exception to the right to life 'in defence of any person from unlawful violence; in order to effect a lawful arrest or to prevent the escape of a person lawfully detained and in action lawfully taken for the purpose of quelling a riot or insurrection' or where a derogation has been entered pursuant to Article 15(2) in 'respect of death resulting from lawful acts of war'. Article 6, ICCPR is less prescriptive and merely requires that individuals are not killed 'arbitrarily'. Given these differences, numerous attempts have been made to explain the relationship between the two bodies of law during armed conflict.

4.2.1.1 The limitations of a general theoretical analysis

In attempting to analyse the general relationship between human rights law and international humanitarian law during armed conflict, broadly speaking, three theoretical methods of interpretation have emerged.[13] Each method suffers from limitations and cannot be applied universally to all circumstances in armed conflict as a panacea to resolve norm conflict.[14] The first method asserts that international humanitarian law is the *lex specialis* in times of armed conflict and therefore entirely displaces human rights law, leaving no scope for the application of human rights law in armed conflict in any circumstances. A general *lex specialis* approach has been largely abandoned[15] within academic circles and no longer finds unequivocal support among states.[16] It can be said, however, that where there is no conflict between

[12] Yves Sandoz, Christophe Swinarski, and Bruno Zimmerman (eds), *Commentary on the Additional Protocols of 8 June 1977 to the Geneva Conventions of 12 August 1949* (Nijhoff 1987) 4789.

[13] Hathaway et al, 'Which Law Governs during Armed Conflict?'

[14] Marko Milanovic, 'A Norm Conflict Perspective on the Relationship between International Humanitarian Law and Human Rights Law' (2009) *JC&SL* 14(3) 459–83.

[15] Very few commentators assert there is no place for human rights law in armed conflict, but examples can be found: see Geoffrey Corn, 'Mixing Apples and Hand Grenades: The Logical Limit of Applying Human Rights Norms to Armed Conflicts' (2010) 1(1) *IHLS* 52–94.

[16] Fourth Periodic Report of the United States of America to the United Nations Committee on Human Rights Concerning the International Covenant on Civil and Political Rights (30 December 2011), 506: 'With respect to the application of the Covenant and the international law of armed conflict (also referred to as international humanitarian law or "IHL"), the United States has not taken the position that the Covenant does not apply "in time of war." Indeed, a time of war does not suspend the operation of the Covenant to matters within its scope of application.'

the two bodies of law in respect of specific and discrete norms, then a *lex specialis* approach ought not to be controversial. Equally, it may be that the principle of *lex specialis* can operate in reverse in discrete circumstances where human rights law is the *lex specialis* that regulates certain conduct absent any applicable rules in international humanitarian law.

The second approach aims to clarify the norm in each body of law by reference to the other body of law. Such an approach would, for example, lend itself to an analysis of the definition of torture. It would not, however, greatly assist in determining the regulation of the use of lethal force in armed conflict. The third approach seeks to avoid norm conflict by distorting the meaning of the norm in one body of law to align it with the definition in another. Again, a norm conflict approach would not lend itself to general application as, on the face of it, this would result in certain human rights provisions being distorted to such an extent as to make them meaningless. Equally, a norm conflict approach would not lend itself to an analysis of the use of lethal force in targeting given the irreconcilable differences between the meaning of necessity and proportionality in each body of law, if strictly interpreted.[17]

To briefly recap, in human rights law, the use of lethal force must be 'absolutely necessary' and 'proportionate' in pursuance of a legitimate aim. With respect to the ECHR, what amounts to a legitimate aim is set out at Article 2(2). Article 6, ICCPR is less prescriptive, stating that 'no one shall be arbitrarily deprived of his life'. Proportionality must therefore first be considered with reference to the achievement of the legitimate aim; second, the measures taken to achieve the legitimate aim must be necessary and no more than necessary; finally, there must be a reasonable balance of proportionality between the effects caused by the measure and the harm sought to be countered.

In international humanitarian law, the notions of 'military necessity' and 'proportionality' are interpreted differently. In international humanitarian law, military necessity

> permits a state engaged in an armed conflict to use only that degree and kind of force, not otherwise prohibited by the law of armed conflict, that is required in order to achieve the legitimate purpose of the conflict, namely the complete or partial submission of the enemy at the earliest possible moment with the minimum expenditure of life and resources.[18]

Military necessity contains four elements[19] that seek to regulate the use of lethal force. It is measured against the legitimate purpose of the armed conflict, namely the

[17] Milanovic, 'A Norm Conflict Perspective on the Relationship between International Humanitarian Law and Human Rights Law'.

[18] UK Manual on the Law of Armed Conflict, 2.2.

[19] UK Manual on the Law of Armed Conflict, 2.2 states:

1. The force used can be and is being controlled;
2. since military necessity permits the use of force only if it is 'not otherwise prohibited by the law of armed conflict', necessity cannot excuse a departure from that law;
3. the use of force in ways which are not otherwise prohibited is legitimate if it is necessary to achieve, as quickly as possible, the complete or partial submission of the enemy;
4. conversely, the use of force which is not necessary is unlawful, since it involves wanton killing or destruction.

defeat of the enemy. The requirement not to be 'arbitrarily deprived of life' in Article 6, ICCPR could be reconciled with military necessity in international humanitarian law on the basis that the use of lethal force is not arbitrary, but regulated by well-established rules governing armed conflict. With reference to Article 2(2), ECHR, such an analysis is more problematic, given its prescriptive nature, as 'the defeat of the enemy' is clearly not listed. On a strict interpretation, therefore, it is difficult to envisage how Article 2(2) could be reconciled with the definition of 'military necessity' in international humanitarian law.

The principle of proportionality in international humanitarian law 'requires that the losses resulting from a military action should not be excessive in relation to the expected military advantage'.[20] The definition is further refined in Article 51(5)(b), Additional Protocol I: it is '[A]n attack which may be expected to cause incidental loss of civilian life, injury to civilians, damage to civilian objects, or a combination thereof, which would be excessive in relation to the concrete and direct military advantage anticipated' and incorporates precautions in attack.[21] It is also considered to be an integral part of customary international humanitarian law applicable to both international and non-international armed conflict, and defined thus: 'Launching an attack which may be expected to cause incidental loss of civilian life, injury to civilians, damage to civilian objects, or a combination thereof, which would be excessive in relation to the concrete and direct military advantage anticipated, is prohibited.'[22]

Noting that the principle of proportionality is applicable equally to international and non-international armed conflict, it follows that civilian casualties are permissible in non-international armed conflict where they are not considered to be excessive in relation to the 'concrete and direct military advantage anticipated'. What is considered to amount to excessive casualties is not a qualitative or quantitative assessment, but rather is determined as a fact-specific exercise in relation to the anticipated military advantage. It therefore is generally accepted that large numbers of civilian casualties would not, in all circumstances, offend against the principle of proportionality under international humanitarian law.

It is submitted that the notion of 'proportionality' in international humanitarian law and human rights law can in practice, to an extent, be reconciled. Clearly, the legitimate aim against which a proportionality assessment is being measured is different in the two bodies of law. The 'proportionality' analysis undertaken by the ECtHR in the 'Chechen cases', for example, found violations of the right to life that, in the context of an armed conflict, would have equally violated the principles of international humanitarian law. This general theoretical analysis must, however, be explored further.

In order to identify the applicable legal framework in respect of the use of lethal force and the right to life in armed conflict, it is necessary to examine a series of issues in turn. It is first necessary to consider the evolving approaches of the ICJ and ECtHR to the question of the relationship between human rights law and

[20] UK Manual on the Law of Armed Conflict, 2.6.
[21] AP I, Art 57(2)(a)(iii) and (b).
[22] ICRC Study on Customary International Humanitarian Law, Rule 14.

international humanitarian law. Once determined, the Court's reasoning can be examined in respect of international and non-international armed conflict and a state's substantive and procedural right to life obligations.

4.2.1.2 The International Court of Justice

The ICJ has considered the relationship between human rights law and international humanitarian law in two advisory opinions and one contentious case. The issue was first considered in an advisory opinion on *The Legality or Threat of Use of Nuclear Weapons.*[23] The ICJ recognized that the right not to be *arbitrarily* deprived of one's life is applicable during armed conflict; however, what amounts to an arbitrary deprivation of life can only be determined by reference to the applicable international humanitarian law. The ICJ, therefore, advocated a modified *lex specialis* approach in that they recognized human rights law could apply during armed conflict but noted:

> [t]hus whether a particular loss of life, through the use of a certain weapon in warfare, is to be considered an arbitrary deprivation of life contrary to Article 6 of the Covenant can only be decided by reference to the law applicable in armed conflict and not deduced from the terms of the Covenant itself.[24]

Such an approach has some force when the wording of Article 6, ICCPR is considered. Unlike Article 2, ECHR, Article 6, ICCPR does not exhaustively set out the exceptions to the right to life, but rather, at 6(1), states that 'No one shall be arbitrarily deprived of his life', without any further qualification or amplification that would be directly relevant in armed conflict. Absent any further directly applicable guidance within the text of Article 6, and recognizing that a derogation under Article 4, ICCPR is not applicable to the right to life,[25] it can be understood why the ICJ originally adopted the approach they did.

In a subsequent advisory opinion on *The Legal Consequences of the Construction of a Wall in the Occupied Palestinian Territory,*[26] the ICJ sought to further elaborate on the relationship between human rights law and international humanitarian law during armed conflict. The ICJ stated:

> As regards the relationship between international humanitarian law and human rights law, there are thus three possible situations: some rights may be exclusively matters of international humanitarian law; others may be exclusively matters of human rights law; yet others may be matters of both these branches of international law. In order to answer the question put to it, the Court will have to take into consideration both these branches of international law, namely human rights law and, as *lex specialis*, international humanitarian law.[27]

[23] *The Legality or Threat of Use of Nuclear Weapons*, International Court of Justice (8 July 1996) 226.
[24] Ibid, 25.
[25] ICCPR, Article 4(2)—No derogation from articles 6, 7, 8 (paragraphs I and 2), 11, 15, 16, and 18 may be made under this provision.
[26] *The Legal Consequences of the Construction of a Wall in the Occupied Palestinian Territory*, International Court of Justice, 9 July 2004, ICJ GC No 131 [2004], ICJ Rep 136, (2004) ILM 1009, ICGJ 203 (ICJ 2004), 9 July 2004.
[27] Ibid, 106.

This statement further reinforces the assertion that there is no general model that can be applicable to all circumstances during armed conflict to resolve a situation where norm conflict arises between human rights law and international humanitarian law. It also indicates the primacy of international humanitarian law during armed conflict. In the *Case concerning Armed Activity on the Territory of the Congo* (Democratic Republic of the Congo v Uganda),[28] the ICJ was required to apply the principles outlined in the two advisory opinions to the use of lethal force during armed conflict. The result was less than satisfactory. While the ICJ did find that Uganda were responsible for violations of human rights law and international humanitarian law in areas of territory that it both did (Ituri) and did not (Democratic Republic of Congo) occupy, the ICJ did not explicitly explain how the violations arose.[29] It is therefore unclear whether a violation of Article 6, ICCPR had been found on the basis of a violation of international humanitarian law or whether this determination had been reached independently under human rights law, or by some combination of human rights law and international humanitarian law.

Nonetheless, recognizing that the ICJ only considered the relationship between the two bodies of law during international armed conflict, it is submitted that certain principles can be ascertained. First, it is not possible to identify a 'universal model' that explains the relationship between international humanitarian law and human rights law during armed conflict. Rather, the relationship between the two bodies of law will be determined by the circumstances under consideration and not the nature of the conflict itself. Second, the fact that international humanitarian law is applicable to a certain set of circumstances does not prevent a human rights body from exercising jurisdiction. Third, human rights law may be directly applicable in circumstances where international humanitarian law is silent. These principles do not, however, provide the complete picture. Questions remain, particularly in respect of the relationship between international humanitarian law and human rights law in a non-international armed conflict. An examination of ECtHR jurisprudence can assist in providing some answers.

4.2.1.3 The European Court of Human Rights

The ECtHR has recognized the requirement to interpret the ECHR in harmony with other rules of international law, including international humanitarian law:

> Turning to the criterion contained in Article 31 § 3(c) of the Vienna Convention, the Court has made it clear on many occasions that the Convention must be interpreted in harmony with other rules of international law of which it forms part. This applies no less to international humanitarian law.[30]

[28] *Case Concerning Armed Activity on the Territory of the Congo* (Democratic Republic of the Congo v Uganda), International Court of Justice Judgment of 19 December 2005.

[29] Ibid, 216–20.

[30] See, inter alia, *Al Adsani v United Kingdom*, Application no 35763/97 (ECtHR, 21 November 2001) 55; *Hassan v United Kingdom*, Application no 29750/09 (ECtHR, 6 September 2014) 77 and 102.

The Court has also indicated a willingness to adopt such an approach specifically in respect of Article 2:

> The Court has already held that Article 2 of the Convention should be interpreted in so far as possible in light of the general principles of international law, including the rules of international humanitarian law which play an indispensable and universally-accepted role in mitigating the savagery and inhumanity of armed conflict.[31]

Without specifically referring to international humanitarian law, the Court has been willing to apply Article 2 with some flexibility when states resort to the use of lethal force, in the spirit of the prior assertion. Evidence of this can be found in the 'Chechen cases' thus:

> given the context of the *conflict* in Chechnya at the relevant time, the Court will assume . . . that the military reasonably considered that there was an attack or a risk of attack from illegal insurgents, and that the air strike was a legitimate response to that attack. [my emphasis][32]

> the situation that existed in Chechnya at the relevant time called for exceptional measures by the State in order to regain control over the Republic and to suppress the *illegal armed insurgency*. Given the context of the conflict in Chechnya at the relevant time, those measures could presumably include the deployment of army units equipped with combat weapons, including military aviation and artillery. The presence of a very large group of armed fighters in Katyr-Yurt, and their active resistance to the *law-enforcement* bodies, which are not disputed by the parties, may have justified use of lethal force by the agents of the State, thus bringing the situation within paragraph 2 of Article 2. [my emphasis][33]

Despite interpreting Article 2 with some degree of flexibility in the 'Chechen cases', it must be noted that the Court analysed the use of lethal force 'outside wartime'[34] and against a 'normal legal background'.[35] The Court therefore found a violation of Article 2 on the basis that Russia had failed to exercise a sufficient 'degree of caution',[36] given the weapons it used in a heavily populated area. Nonetheless, it is submitted that the use of such weapons by Russian forces in a heavily populated area, within the context of an international or non-international armed conflict, would have equally violated international humanitarian law principles. As a consequence, if international humanitarian law had been used as the legal framework to analyse the use of lethal force and interpret the state's right to life obligations, a violation would have been found on this basis.

In *Hassan*, the Court held that in situations of international armed conflict, the ECHR continued to apply. It therefore interpreted the UK's human rights law

[31] *Hassan v United Kingdom*, 102 citing *Varnava and Others v Turkey* [GC], Application nos 16064/90, 16065/90, 16066/90, 16068/90, 16069/90, 16070/90, 16071/90, 16072/90, and 16073/90 (ECtHR, 18 September 2009) 185.

[32] *Isayeva, Yusupova and Basayeva v Russia*, Application no 57947-9/00 (ECtHR, 24 February 2005) 181.

[33] *Isayeva v Russia*, Application no 57950/00 (ECtHR, 24 February 2005) 180.

[34] Ibid, 191. [35] Ibid. [36] Ibid.

obligations (Article 5) in line with international humanitarian law. The Divisional Court in *Al-Saadoon* expanded upon this reasoning thus:

> the same approach must in principle apply to article 2. Thus where the armed forces of a state kill someone in the course of an armed conflict the killing will be lawful provided it is consistent with IHL even if it results from use of force which is not absolutely necessary to achieve any of the purposes set out in sub-paragraphs (a) to (c) of article 2.[37]

The Divisional Court also advocated a position in which courts recognize their lack of jurisdictional competence regarding decisions taken on the battlefield and apply a wide margin of appreciation. It is submitted, however, that the issue of the applicability of international humanitarian law regulating the use of lethal force during non-international armed conflict may require closer examination than the Divisional Court in *Al-Saadoon* appeared to suggest. In *Hassan*, the Court stated:

> It can only be in cases of *international armed conflict*, where the taking of prisoners of war and the detention of civilians who pose a threat to security are *accepted features of international humanitarian law*, that Article 5 could be interpreted as permitting the exercise of such broad powers. [my emphasis][38]

This may indicate that human rights law obligations can only be interpreted by reference to international humanitarian law where such actions are an 'accepted feature' of that specific type of armed conflict. In other words, if the action of the state that led to an alleged human rights law violation was not an 'accepted feature' of non-international armed conflict, then international humanitarian law would not be applicable. It is therefore necessary to consider the relationship between human rights law and international humanitarian law in respect of international and non-international armed conflict separately in order to determine if a different approach is required to each.

A further potential difficulty also arises that must be addressed. In adopting an approach that interprets right to life obligations in armed conflict in line with international humanitarian law principles, there is a potential risk of a violation of treaty interpretation pursuant to the Vienna Convention on the Law of Treaties in respect of the potential redundancy of the Article 15, ECHR derogation clause.

4.2.2 The relationship between international humanitarian law and human rights law in international armed conflict—the use of lethal force

During international armed conflict it can be convincingly asserted that, while a state has substantive right to life obligations, the use of lethal force is regulated by international humanitarian law principles. Support for this proposition can be found in the advisory opinions and relevant cases of the ICJ, ECtHR judgments, domestic jurisprudence, and academic opinion.

37 *Al-Saadoon and Others v Secretary of State for Defence* [2016] EWCA 811, 111.
38 *Hassan v United Kingdom* 104.

In their *amicus curiae* submission in *Hassan*, Hampson and Lubell[39] provide a comprehensive analysis[40] of the relationship between international humanitarian law and human rights law in which they make the following assertions:

> first, that the applicability of international humanitarian law [does] not displace the jurisdiction of a human rights body. That resulted from the finding that human rights law remained applicable in all circumstances. Secondly, where international humanitarian law [is] applicable, a human rights body [has] two choices. Either it [has] to apply human rights law through the lens of international humanitarian law or it [has] to blend human rights law and international humanitarian law together. That was the only possible interpretation of certain matters being the province of both bodies of rules, whilst others were regulated by international humanitarian law.[41]

They further contend that the 'criteria that will affect the interplay'[42] between international humanitarian law and human rights law will include (but not be limited to): the status of the individuals concerned; the proximity of hostilities; the control the military has over the situation; the means used in the operation; and whether the state has relied upon international humanitarian law or entered a derogation.[43] Finally, as a general proposition, they contend that where the use of force is regulated by international humanitarian law, a human rights violation can only occur where there has been a violation of international humanitarian law.[44]

Turning first to Article 6, ICCPR, it is submitted that, as only an 'arbitrary' deprivation of life is prohibited, any use of lethal force authorized and properly conducted in accordance with the relevant principles of international humanitarian law could not be considered arbitrary and therefore would not contravene Article 6. Clear support for such an approach can be found in the ICJ advisory opinions[45] and the *Case concerning Armed Activity on the Territory of the Congo*. The analysis in respect of Article 2, ECHR is not as straightforward, but yields the same result. To briefly recap, Article 2(2), ECHR states:

> Deprivation of life shall not be regarded as inflicted in contravention of this article when it results from the use of force which is no more than absolutely necessary:
> a. in defence of any person from unlawful violence;
> b. in order to effect a lawful arrest or to prevent the escape of a person lawfully detained;
> c. in action lawfully taken for the purpose of quelling a riot or insurrection.

39 Ibid, 91–5.

40 Based upon *Legality of the Threat or Use of Nuclear Weapons*, Advisory Opinion; *The Legal Consequences of the Construction of a Wall in the Occupied Palestinian Territory*, Advisory Opinion; and *Case Concerning Armed Activity on the Territory of the Congo* (Democratic Republic of the Congo v Uganda).

41 *Amicus curiae* brief in *Hassan*, 93.

42 *Amicus curiae* brief in *Hassan*, 27.

43 The effect of derogations will be considered in Chapter 6.

44 *Amicus curiae* brief in *Hassan*, 26.

45 *Legality of the Threat or Use of Nuclear Weapons*, Advisory Opinion, 1996 ICJ 226 at 25, *The Legal Consequences of the Construction of a Wall in the Occupied Palestinian Territory*, International Court of Justice, 9 July 2004.

A strict interpretation of this provision, recognizing its applicability during international armed conflict, would inevitably mean that any use of lethal force, except as permitted in the preceding quotation, would result in a contravention of Article 2. It is, however, possible to adopt a more permissive interpretation of Article 2 that allows for a consideration of international humanitarian law norms in respect of the use of lethal force. The proposition advanced by Hampson and Lubell,[46] asserting that in such circumstances a human rights violation could only occur where there [has] been a violation of international humanitarian law, addresses this issue directly. It also finds support, inter alia, in the judgments of the ECtHR in *Varnava* and *Hassan* and the Divisional Court in *Al-Saadoon*. In *Hassan* the Court cited the judgment in *Varnava* in asserting that 'Article 2 of the Convention should be interpreted in so far as possible in light of the general principles of international law, including the rules of international humanitarian law which play an indispensable and universally-accepted role in mitigating the savagery and inhumanity of armed conflict.'[47] This principle was also adopted, albeit *obiter*, by Leggatt J in *Al-Saadoon*.[48] Ultimately, therefore, during international armed conflict a compelling case can be advanced that the use of lethal force by states is regulated by recourse to international humanitarian law norms. This would result in there being no violation of a state's substantive right to life obligations where the applicable international humanitarian law principles for the use of lethal force were adhered to. It must be accepted, however, that this approach goes beyond what a strict reading of Article 2(2) permits; yet the Court does appear willing to accept such an analysis.

4.2.3 The relationship between international humanitarian law and human rights law in non-international armed conflict—the use of lethal force

The conclusions reached in respect of the relationship between international humanitarian law and human rights law concerning the use of lethal force during international armed conflict cannot be simply transposed into non-international armed conflict. A number of potential differences exist that must be addressed. First, there remains considerable debate concerning when individuals may be targeted in non-international armed conflict.[49] This lack of specificity may present difficulties in identifying the applicable international humanitarian law to be considered when interpreting a state's right to life obligations. Second, the legal framework applicable to low-intensity conflicts that just meet the Common Article 3 threshold remains keenly debated and could preclude the applicability of international humanitarian law. Third, the scope of Article 2(2) ECHR must be assessed to determine if the use of lethal force to 'quell . . . an insurrection' during a non-international armed conflict amounts to a 'blanket' exception to the right to life, absent any further regulation of

[46] *Amicus curiae* brief in *Hassan*, 26. [47] *Hassan v the United Kingdom* 91–5.

[48] *Al-Saadoon and Others* 111.

[49] See Sivakumaran, *The Law of Non-International Armed Conflict*, 372 in respect of what constitutes membership of an armed group.

the use of lethal force. Finally, following the judgment in *Hassan* and with respect to non-international armed conflict, where a state has not entered a derogation to Article 2, the extent to which the Court may permit a reliance on international humanitarian law must be considered.

4.2.3.1 Targeting in non-international armed conflict

To briefly recap, in *Hassan*, the Court noted:

> It can only be in cases of *international armed conflict*, where the taking of prisoners of war and the detention of civilians who pose a threat to security are accepted features of international humanitarian law, that Article 5 could be interpreted as permitting the exercise of such broad powers. [my emphasis][50]

This statement could be read as limiting the applicability of international humanitarian law to interpreting human rights law in circumstances where specific provisions are 'accepted features' of international humanitarian law. If so, this could present certain difficulties where the international humanitarian law applicable to non-international armed conflicts is not clearly defined. This could be said to arise in respect of the use of lethal force in non-international armed conflict. To illustrate, Sivakumaran notes that

> civilians benefit from various protections, including not being made the object of attack. Civilians who take a direct part in hostilities on an ad hoc basis fall outside the scope of these protections for such time as they take a direct part in hostilities. When they cease to take such part, their protections resume. Members of the state armed forces and of the military wing of the non-state armed group ... do not benefit from the protections afforded to civilians and may be targeted at any time, although this may be queried as a matter of *lex ferenda*.[51]

It follows that if uncertainty exists in respect of when individuals may be lethally targeted during non-international armed conflict pursuant to international humanitarian law, then it may not be possible to interpret a state's right to life obligations with reference to this international humanitarian law norm. To illustrate, Sivakumaran highlights an area of uncertainty in respect of the membership of armed groups in non-international armed conflict thus—'the ICRC Guidance unreasonably narrows the notion of membership in the military wing of an armed group'[52]—before proposing an alternative and convincing formulation.[53] It is submitted, however, that such a lack of clarity is not fatal to interpreting right to life obligations in light of the applicable international humanitarian law. By taking a cautious and restrictive view of when individuals may be targeted in non-international armed conflict as a matter of policy, through narrowly defined rules of engagement, a state could resolve any ambiguity in the definition of membership of the military wing of an armed group. For example, during the International Security Assistance Force (ISAF)

[50] *Hassan v the United Kingdom* 104.
[51] Sivakumaran, *The Law of Non-International Armed Conflict*, 372.
[52] Ibid, 360.
[53] Ibid.

mission in Afghanistan, a narrow interpretation of 'military wing of an armed group' was adopted, albeit for different purposes, namely affording maximum protection to civilians. Nonetheless, this demonstrates that such an approach is possible. Alternatively, states could clearly define their understanding of the applicable international humanitarian law norms in respect of lethal targeting and analyse their human rights law obligations in light of these. This would involve states clearly articulating what amounted to, for example, membership of an armed group, or what activities amounted to direct participation in hostilities. In practice this should happen in any event, in order to give soldiers the requisite guidance to enable them to open fire.

4.2.3.2 Low-intensity non-international armed conflict

Droege[54] has advanced the argument that whether international humanitarian law or human rights law applies to a specific situation will be determined by whether the 'conduct of hostilities' or 'law enforcement' paradigm is applicable. If this analysis is accepted, a member of a non-state armed group merely sitting in a café and taking no direct part in hostilities during a non-international armed conflict in an area of territory entirely controlled by the state could not be lethally targeted. The analysis advanced by Droege is problematic for three reasons. First, it may necessitate the application of a constantly changing legal framework throughout a non-international armed conflict depending upon the intensity of fighting in different geographical areas at different times. Second, it significantly qualifies the ICJ *lex specialis* view enunciated in its *Nuclear Weapons* and *the Wall* advisory opinions and its judgment in *Uganda v DRC* by asserting that even though there may be an armed conflict, international humanitarian law is not an appropriate legal framework. Finally, it may create practical difficulties insofar as the applicable legal framework is determined not by the nature of the armed conflict, but by the level of hostilities, which can be fluid and change rapidly. This, if Droege's analysis is accepted, would require a potentially constantly evolving legal framework to regulate the use of lethal force. Ultimately, therefore, it may be preferable for states or a supranational body to determine the nature of an armed conflict. Once made, this proclamation can then be used to determine the applicable legal framework. Absent this determination, it is submitted that states ought to proceed on the basis that affords maximum protection to civilians, and rules of engagement must be drafted accordingly.

4.2.3.3 The use of lethal force to quell an insurrection during non-international armed conflict

The use of lethal force to quell an insurrection during non-international armed conflict has been advanced as a possible interpretative mechanism to further elucidate

[54] Cordula Droege, 'The Interplay between International Humanitarian Law and International Human Rights Law in Situations of Armed Conflict' (2007) 40(2) Israel L Rev 310–55; 'Elective Affinities? Human Rights and Humanitarian Law' (2008) 90(871) IRRC 501–48.

the relationship between international humanitarian law and human rights law. Aughey and Sari[55] seek to justify the use of lethal force by armed forces in a non-international armed conflict and reconcile human rights law and international humanitarian law by reference to Article 2(2), ECHR. They consider the exception to the right to life contained in Article 2(2), ECHR in the following terms:

> Once the violence reaches the requisite level of intensity and organization, the rules of the law of armed conflict in NIAC become applicable to the situation. There is no reason why the use of lethal force for the purposes of quelling the insurrection should suddenly cease to be a legitimate aim. On the contrary, since the applicability of the law of armed conflict is triggered by an escalation of the level of violence, there is every reason to believe that the use of lethal force is now more, rather than less, necessary from the perspective of Article 2(2).[56]

They further cite the decision in *Tadić*[57] to create a nexus to the applicable customary *jus in bello* rules once the hostilities have reached a sufficient level of intensity:

> According to the Tribunal, customary rules analogous to those applicable in international armed conflict have developed to govern NIACs in such areas as the protection of civilians from hostilities and the prohibition of certain means and methods of warfare. Indeed, convergence extends to targeting.[58]

Ultimately, they conclude that it is inconceivable that the drafters of Common Article 3 and Additional Protocol II intended to treat everyone in a non-international armed conflict as a civilian and could not foresee status-based targeting. Any such proposition, they contend, would render the principle of distinction meaningless in a non-international armed conflict.[59] In effect, they seek to justify the use of lethal force in a non-international armed conflict not in terms of modifying Article 2 in light of the relevant international humanitarian law principles, but rather as an exception to the right to life contained within Article 2(2) on the basis of the requirement to 'quell … an insurrection'. It must be noted, however, that such an approach still presents difficulties in determining exactly who may be lethally targeted and when.

4.2.4 The relationship between international humanitarian law and human rights law—the requirement to investigate the loss of life during armed conflict

In the case of substantive right to life obligations, the corresponding principles governing the use of lethal force under international humanitarian law are well

[55] Sean Aughey and Aurel Sari, 'Targeting and Detention in Non-International Armed Conflict: Serdar Mohammed and the Limits of Human Rights Convergence' (2015) 91 *Intl L Stud* 60.

[56] Ibid, 90–91.

[57] *Prosecutor v Tadić*, Case No IT-94-1-AR72, Decision on Defence Motion for Interlocutory Appeal on Jurisdiction, 31, 33 (International Criminal Tribunal for the former Yugoslavia, 2 October 1995).

[58] Sean Aughey and Aurel Sari, 'Targeting and Detention in Non-International Armed Conflict: Serdar Mohammed and the Limits of Human Rights Convergence' (2015) 91 *Intl L Stud* 100.

[59] Ibid.

established and understood. The same cannot be said of procedural right to life obligations and the corresponding requirement to investigate loss of life in international humanitarian law. The Geneva Conventions,[60] Additional Protocol I (AP I),[61] and the Rome Statute require states to investigate and prosecute grave breaches of international humanitarian law and 'war crimes'. They also place obligations on military commanders of 'armed forces under their command and other persons under their control, to prevent and, where necessary, to suppress and to report to competent authorities breaches'[62] of the Geneva Conventions and AP I. The Turkel Commission,[63] citing the Rome Statute,[64] also persuasively argued that these obligations apply equally during non-international armed conflict. Nonetheless, these obligations of international humanitarian law would not encompass all procedural violations of the right to life during armed conflict that have been considered by the ECtHR in cases such as *Jaloud*. Moreover, individual violations of international humanitarian law could occur in respect of the use of lethal force that would fall short of being considered crimes against humanity[65] or war crimes,[66] given the relatively high threshold required to establish a violation.[67] As a consequence, international human rights bodies are more likely to be required to consider alleged violations of a state's procedural right to life obligations during armed conflict. An obligation on states to fully investigate *all* loss of life during armed conflict would, however, create a potentially unachievable burden. It is therefore important to determine the circumstances in which an independent investigation *must* be conducted.

The right to life's procedural requirement to investigate certain losses of life does not apply equally during armed conflict and in peacetime. The ECtHR has recognized that the nature of armed conflict 'may compel the use of less effective measures of investigation or cause an investigation to be delayed'.[68] The Court has not, however, gone as far as to determine that during armed conflict there is no requirement to investigate alleged violations of the right to life. Rather, it has regularly required states to do this, albeit potentially in a modified way.[69] A two-stage process exists. First, a state must determine if an investigation is required following a death

[60] See, inter alia, GCI Article 52, GCII Article 53, GCIII Articles 121, 132, GCIV Articles 131, 146, 147

[61] API, Article 87. [62] Ibid. [63] The 'Turkel Commission', Second Report, 27.

[64] Ibid, 6. [65] Rome Statute, Article 7. [66] Rome Statute, Article 8.

[67] Rome Statute, Article 7(1): 'For the purpose of this Statute, "crime against humanity" means any of the following acts when committed as part of a *widespread or systematic attack* directed against any civilian population, with knowledge of the attack:

(a) Murder;
(b) Extermination.'

Rome Statute, Article 8(2)(a): '*Grave breaches* of the Geneva Conventions of 12 August 1949, namely, any of the following acts against persons or property protected under the provisions of the relevant Geneva Convention:

(i) Wilful killing.'

[my emphasis].

[68] *Al-Skeini v the United Kingdom* 164.

[69] For example, see *Kerimova and Others v Russia*, Application nos 17170/04, 20792/04, 22448/04, 5681/05, and 5684/05, (ECtHR, 3 May 2011); *Al-Skeini v the United Kingdom*; *Jaloud v the Netherlands*.

attributable to the state's armed forces. Second, if an investigation is required, recognizing the circumstances present at the time, a state must determine how it must be conducted to ensure compliance with its procedural right to life obligations.

In addressing the first question, a potential middle ground that would not create an unduly onerous burden on states, but would still allow them to comply with their right to life obligations, would be to require an investigation where there are allegations of violations of the applicable law regulating the use of force resulting in loss of life. Turning to the second question, the mechanics of how the investigation is initiated and conducted are far from straightforward, although not insurmountable. In order to facilitate such investigations a method of reporting alleged violations must be available, and records of the use of lethal force must be kept by armed forces. Additionally, there would be a need for a sufficient number of independent investigators to be available to conduct the investigation. The specific detail concerning the conduct of an investigation pursuant to a state's procedural right to life obligations have been addressed in Chapter 2.

4.3 Applying Substantive Right to Life Principles to the Activities of UK Armed Forces

Prior to a stage-by-stage analysis of land, maritime, air, and special forces operations in respect of the substantive right to life obligations of the UK, the preliminary and overarching issues of planning of operations, command and control, and rules of engagement must be considered.

4.3.1 Planning of operations

In international humanitarian law, military operations in armed conflict must be planned in order to, inter alia, minimize civilian casualties. The UK manual on the law of armed conflict, drawing heavily on Additional Protocol I,[70] considers the situation thus [my emphasis]:

(1) those who *plan* or decide upon an attack shall:

   (a) do everything feasible to verify that the objectives to be attacked are neither civilians nor civilian objects and are not subject to special protection but are military objectives ... and that it is not prohibited ... to attack them;

   (b) take all feasible precautions in the choice of means and methods of attack with a view to avoiding, and in any event to minimizing, incidental loss of civilian life, injury to civilians and damage to civilian objects;

   (c) refrain from deciding to launch any attack which may be expected to cause incidental loss of civilian life, injury to civilians, damage to civilian

[70] Article 57(1)(2)(3), AP I.

> objects, or a combination thereof, which would be excessive in relation to the concrete and direct military advantage anticipated [the *rule of proportionality*].

The requirement for sufficient planning in human rights law[71] requires the protection of civilians in much the same way as the international humanitarian law provision. Similarly, it is concerned with the planning of a specific mission, attack, or operation and not the overall campaign plan. To that end, both international humanitarian law and human rights law require the military planning to involve, at a minimum, an assessment of the number of civilians in the area of the proposed attack; consideration of the evacuation of civilians if required and sufficient time to effect this; and an analysis of the effect of the proposed weaponry, including, specifically, the damage radius.[72] Once this planning is complete, a proportionality assessment can be made. The specific details of the targeting process reveal, prima facie, the irreconcilable difference between international humanitarian law and human rights law in respect of the notions of absolutely necessary/necessity and proportionality. It is submitted, however, that the planning process required by international humanitarian law and human rights law in respect of the use of lethal force is comparable.

In UK military doctrine, a general consideration of the planning process is contained in Joint Doctrine Publication 1-00, Campaigning (3rd Edition) (JDP 1-00) and Joint Doctrine Publication 5-00, Campaign Planning (2nd Edition, Change 1) (JDP 5-00). Specific detail is contained in Joint Doctrine Publication 3-00, Campaign Execution (3rd Edition) (JDP 5-00). In JDP 3-00, Chapter 3 establishes the doctrinal position in respect of 'Joint Action'. This includes the specific element of armed conflict that involves the loss of life and therefore creates international humanitarian and human rights law obligations, namely, joint fires.[73]

In turn, in accordance with UK military doctrine, the use of joint fires is regulated via rules of engagement[74] and a targeting directive[75] delivered and regulated through an effective command and control structure. In order to determine if there is a sufficiently robust system to control the use of lethal force in armed conflict within UK doctrine, it is therefore necessary to consider these respective elements.

4.3.2 Command and control

Command and control in multinational operations[76] is complex, and consequently can lead to confusion in respect of delineation of responsibility.[77] This is particularly acute in terms of ascribing responsibility and accountability for the use of

[71] For example see *Isayeva v Russia* 181. [72] Ibid, 179–201.

[73] Joint fires is defined as 'The deliberate use of physical, or virtual, means to achieve, primarily, physical effects'—JDP 3-00, 307.

[74] JDP 3-00, 327. [75] JDP 3-00, 3B10(d).

[76] Appendix 1 (JDP 3-00, Appendix 1C1) is an illustrative example of some of the differences between US and NATO command and control terminology.

[77] Appendix 2 (JDP 3-00, Annex 1C) is an illustrative example of command and control terminology.

lethal force.[78] The problem is twofold and concerns both differences in terminology between coalition partners and complex command and control structures.[79] Such complexity can be exacerbated yet further when more than one mission is occurring in the same territory. Within the territory of Afghanistan, for example, the NATO ISAF mission and the US Operation Enduring Freedom mission (OEF) occurred simultaneously, and, in an added layer of complexity, certain ISAF nations could, in extremis, assist US OEF forces.

In respect of terminology, the following extract from JDP 3-00[80] illustrates an element of the difficulties:

1 *Full Command.* Authority and responsibility of a commander to issue orders to subordinates. It covers every aspect of military operations.

2 *Operational Command.* Authority granted to a commander to assign missions or tasks to subordinate commanders, to deploy units, to reassign forces, and to retain or delegate OPCON/TACON as necessary. It does not include responsibility for administration and exists only within national services. The term command, as used internationally, implies a lesser degree of authority than when used in a purely national sense. No NATO or coalition commander has Full Command over forces assigned to him since, in assigning forces to NATO, nations will delegate only OPCOM or OPCON.

3 *Operational Control.* Authority delegated to a commander to direct forces assigned so that he may accomplish specific missions or tasks, usually limited by function, time or location; to deploy units concerned, and to retain or assign TACON of those units. It does not include authority to assign separate employment of components of the units concerned nor does it include administrative or logistic control.

4 *Tactical Command.* Authority delegated to a commander to assign tasks to forces under his command for the accomplishment of the mission assigned by higher authority.

5 *Tactical Control.* The detailed direction and control of movements or manoeuvres necessary to accomplish missions or tasks.

A commander who was delegated any of these elements of command and control would, subject to the necessary rules of engagement delegations, be authorized to use lethal force in offensive, as opposed to defensive, actions in both international and non-international armed conflict. The crucial issue, however, is recognizing the requirement to disaggregate authority and responsibility in command and control. Within the context of NATO- and UN-authorized and controlled military operations, the UK government, and therefore UK military commanders, will always

[78] This is illustrated by the Netherlands government's pleadings in *Jaloud v the Netherlands* that were rejected by the Court: at 143.

[79] Appendix 3 (JDP 3-00, Annex 1D) is an illustrative example of a typical command and control structure.

[80] JDP 3-00, Annex 1C, part b).

retain full command over their deployed forces, notwithstanding that elements of the forces may come under the operational command, operational control, tactical command, or tactical control of officers from other nations in respect of missions involving the use of lethal force. This distinction is of crucial significance within a human rights law context as the UK cannot therefore divest itself of its human rights obligations in respect of the actions of its deployed armed forces by reference to the forces being under the operational command or operational control of another state.[81] The issue of the UK government's ability to divest its human rights obligations by virtue of contributing forces to a UN-mandated[82] or NATO-sponsored mission will be considered at 4.9.

4.3.3 Rules of engagement

In UK military doctrine, the use of lethal force is regulated by rules of engagement, tactical and targeting directives, and self-defence cards held by individual armed forces personnel. Rules of engagement can be considered as 'being issued by competent authorities and assist in the delineation of the circumstances and limitations within which military forces may be employed to achieve their objectives'. They also 'provide authorisation for and/or limits on, among other things the use of force, the position and posturing of forces, and the employment of certain specific capabilities'.[83] While the use of rules of engagement must recognize and reflect the tenets of international humanitarian and human rights law, if applicable, they also reflect the political dimension of armed conflict and allow the government to place further limitations on the use of lethal force, beyond that required by law. In practice, control of and limitations on the use of lethal force are achieved by holding the authorization to use certain methods of lethal force at a specific level within the military hierarchy or government. In circumstances where loss of life would be particularly politically sensitive, albeit not unlawful, authorization for the use of offensive lethal force can be held at ministerial or prime ministerial level. For example, the authorization for lethal drone strikes against UK citizens Reyaad Khan and Ruhul Amin in Syria on 21 August 2015 was given by the Secretary of State for Defence.[84] Authorization at ministerial level is typically required where large numbers of civilian casualties would be politically unacceptable. To illustrate, a specific rule may read: 'attack on declared hostile forces and other military objectives, that result in predicted civilian casualties of greater than 20, within the Regional Command (South West) Area of Responsibility, Afghanistan, is permitted.' If the authority to use this rule were to be held at ministerial level, then clearly this would place significant restrictions on the use of lethal force in 'Regional Command (South West) Area of Responsibility,

[81] *Jaloud v the Netherlands* 143.

[82] *Behrami v France*, Application no 71412/01 (ECtHR, 2 May 2007), *Saramati v France, Germany and Norway*, Application no 78166/01 (ECtHR, 2 May 2007).

[83] International Institute of Humanitarian Law, *Rules of Engagement Handbook*, Sanremo, November 2009.

[84] <http://www.theguardian.com/world/2015/sep/07/drone-british-citizens-syria-uk-david-cameron> [accessed 16 September 2015].

Afghanistan.' It is, however, worthy of note that rules of engagement never place restrictions on the use of lethal force in armed forces personnel's individual or unit self-defence.

In practice, states often enter caveats into multinational rules of engagement profiles to reflect both national law and the political dimension of the role of a nation's armed forces in any armed conflict. Alternatively, the rules of engagement under which a nation's armed forces operate in a multinational operation remain, at all times, the state's national rules of engagement, and do not use the multinational rules of engagement profile.[85] Ultimately, a state must ensure that either the use of the multinational rules of engagement profile, if adopted, or the national rules of engagement profile ensure compliance with their substantive right to life obligations. This is achieved by the state first understanding its right to life obligations given the nature and location of the operation, and thereafter considering the extent to which adherence to the tenets of international humanitarian law can comply with this requirement. This can only be achieved by a thorough analysis of the situations in which the armed forces are operating and the guidance provided, in the form of rules of engagement as well as targeting and tactical directives that have been issued.

4.3.4 Tactical directives

Tactical directives are used by military commanders to promulgate their guidance and intentions in respect of how a military operation will be conducted. Tactical directives are not law, although, within the UK military justice system, disregarding a tactical directive may amount to a contravention of an order and therefore amount to a military disciplinary offence.[86] In the NATO ISAF mission in Afghanistan, tactical directives referenced human rights generally[87] and have reflected both the substantive[88] and

[85] *Jaloud v the Netherlands* 147. [86] s 12, Armed Forces Act 2006.

[87] Commander International Security Assistance Force, Afghanistan, Tactical Directive 30 November 2011: '*Respect for Human Rights*. A significant component of our campaign is championing the respect for human rights and supporting GIRoA's development of institutional protections of every citizen's human rights in accordance with LOAC, international law, and the laws of Afghanistan. ISAF will support and encourage the Government of the Islamic Republic of Afghanistan to hold those responsible accountable for their actions. These actions are vital in building the Afghan population's confidence and trust' [original emphasis].

[88] Commander International Security Assistance Force, Afghanistan, Tactical Directive 30 November 2011: '*Commander's Intent. My intent is to eliminate ISAF-caused civilian casualties across Afghanistan, and minimize civilian casualties throughout the area of operations by reducing their exposure to insurgent operations. I am equally determined that my direction in no way compromises the inherent right of every individual and unit to employ appropriate measures in self-defense.*

Direction.
In order to achieve my intent:

- Presume that:
  - o every Afghan is a civilian until otherwise apparent;
  - o all compounds are civilian structures until otherwise apparent;
  - o in every location where there is evidence of human habitation, civilians are present until otherwise apparent' [original emphasis].

procedural[89] elements of the right to life specifically. Naturally, these tactical directives must be read within the context of that NATO ISAF operation in which minimizing or eliminating civilian casualties was of the utmost significance. They aptly illustrate the relationship between international humanitarian law, rules of engagement, tactical directives, and targeting as follows:

> Finally, we must be consistent in our application of this directive, the rules of engagement and the Law of Armed Conflict (LOAC). I expect all commanders to conduct regular reinforcement training in the application and employment of force, guided by Rules of Engagement (ROE), LOAC and the intent of this Directive. I also insist that all planning and execution of operations account for our obligations to employ force consistent with the principles of military necessity, proportionality, distinction and humanity in accordance with LOAC.[90]

Tactical directives must reflect the international humanitarian law and human rights law obligations of states to the extent required by the situation. UK military doctrine contained within joint defence publications is silent on human rights obligations during military operations. In theory, however, this failing can be rectified via rules of engagement and tactical and targeting directives. Tactical directives issued by ISAF and agreed by the UK demonstrate this: the use of lethal force was so closely regulated that it would comply with human rights law absent any reference to international humanitarian law, as civilian casualties were deemed unacceptable.[91]

4.4 The Relationship between Individual Self-Defence in Armed Conflict and the Right to Life

The UK interpretation of the rules of individual self-defence of UK armed forces personnel in armed conflict is contained within Card A.[92] Similar interpretations

[89] Commander International Security Assistance Force, Afghanistan, Tactical Directive 30 November 2011: 'In order to achieve my intent: Investigate every allegation of civilian casualties.'

[90] Commander International Security Assistance Force, Afghanistan, Tactical Directive 30 November 2011.

[91] An ISAF Tactical Directive can be found at <http://www.nato.int/isaf/docu/official_texts/Tactical_Directive_090706.pdf> [accessed 3 May 2015].

[92] Card A—Joint Service Publication 398 (2013 Edition):

> *Guidance on the opening fire in self defence for service personnel authorised to carry arms and ammunition on duty*
>
> General guidance
>
> 1. In all situations you are to use no more force than absolutely necessary.
>   Firearms must only be used as a last resort.
>   Protection of human life
> 2. You may only open fire against a person if he/she is committing or about to commit an act likely to endanger human life and there is no other way to prevent the danger.
> 3. When guarding property you must not use lethal force other than for the protection of human life.
>   Warnings
> 4. A warning must be given before opening fire unless:

can be found in the cards of soldiers involved in multinational operations.[93] In situations of armed conflict where armed forces personnel use lethal force in accordance with their self-defence cards, even where their honestly held belief that their life or the life of someone else was in danger proves to be mistaken, a breach of the state's right to life obligation will not occur. The approach taken by the ECtHR in, inter alia, *McCann*,[94] *McKerr*,[95] and *Kelly*[96] can, *mutatis mutandis*, be transposed into a situation of armed conflict to reflect the exigencies of the situation as well as Article 2(2)(a), ECHR and Article 6, ICCPR. The use of lethal force in self-defence is specifically referenced in Article 2(2), ECHR and would not be considered an arbitrary use of lethal force for the purposes of Article 6, ICCPR.

The issue becomes more opaque in respect of the use of lethal force in self-defence during armed conflict seeking to defend property. The guidance to commanders and troops during Operation Telic II in Iraq from 2003 onwards was drafted exclusively with reference to international humanitarian law and is represented thus:

a. To do this would increase the risk of death or grave injury to you or any other persons other than the attacker;
   Or
b. You or others in the immediate vicinity are under armed attack.

5. Warnings may be in the form of a challenge. If challenging you are to shout:
   Navy, Army, air force, stop or I fire or words to that effect
   Opening fire
6. If you have to open fire you are to:
   a. Fire only aimed shots;
      And
   b. Fire no more rounds than are necessary;
      And
   c. Take all reasonable precautions not to injure anyone other than your target.

[93] The relevant section from the Stabilisation Force in Iraq Soldier's Card (24 July 2003) reads:

AIMED FIRE

You may open aimed fire if you yourself, own troops or persons under your protection are threatened with violence that may cause serious bodily harm or death and there are no other ways to prevent this.

Here are some examples:

you may fire at a person who is firing or aiming his weapon at you, at own troops or persons under your protection;

you may fire at a person who is placing explosives or incendiary devices or throwing them or preparing to throw them at you, at own troops or persons under your protection;

you may fire at a person who is deliberately driving a car into you, own troops or persons under your protection.

MINIMUM FORCE

If you have to open fire, you must:

fire only aimed shots;

fire no more shots than is necessary; and

cease firing as soon as the situation allows.

It is forbidden to use deliberate force against civilians, unless this is necessary for self-defence.

[94] *McCann and Others v the United Kingdom*, Application no 18984/91 (ECtHR, 27 September 1995).

[95] *McKerr v the United Kingdom*, Application no 28883/95 (ECtHR, 4 April 2000).

[96] *Kelly and Others v the United Kingdom*, Application no 30094/96 (ECtHR, 4 May 2001).

SELF-DEFENCE

The use of strictly necessary force, including force that may cause death or serious bodily harm (*deadly force*) and involving the use of permitted weapons, is permitted:

(a) to defend yourself;
(b) to prevent the theft or destruction of property belonging to Stabilization Force in Iraq (SFIR) that are essential for the execution of the mission.[97]

When this guidance is analysed with respect to the right to life, potential difficulties arise where civilians are stealing property that cannot be used for lethal purposes, and that belongs to coalition forces, in circumstances that do not amount to a riot or insurrection (Article 2(2)(c), ECHR).

Analysing the above scenario with respect to international humanitarian law and human rights law reveals a marked contrast between the two. A strict reading of the guidance set out above would suggest that the use of lethal force is authorized if the equipment is mission-critical, yet in such circumstances it is extremely unlikely that the civilians, by dint of such behaviour, would become targetable in international humanitarian law. The only justification for the use of lethal force pursuant to international humanitarian law would be that the theft or destruction of mission-essential equipment amounts to direct participation in hostilities.[98] Such action by civilians would satisfy the threefold requirement articulated by the ICRC thus:

> Acts amounting to direct participation in hostilities must meet three cumulative requirements: (1) a threshold regarding the harm likely to result from the act, (2) a relationship of direct causation between the act and the expected harm, and (3) a belligerent nexus between the act and the hostilities conducted between the parties to an armed conflict.[99]

It could therefore be convincingly asserted that civilians stealing mission-essential equipment during a non-international armed conflict could be lethally targeted pursuant to international humanitarian law. Analysing the same scenario with reference to human rights law would not, however, lead to the same conclusion.

The theft or destruction of mission-essential equipment during a non-international armed conflict when interpreted with reference to human rights law would not constitute unlawful violence for the purposes of Article 2(2)(a), ECHR.[100] Ultimately, therefore, in order to comply with their right to life obligations, states must ensure that in any recourse to the use of lethal force in defence of property, a nexus to protection from unlawful violence exists. Alternatively, the destruction of property must constitute a riot or insurrection, with the concomitant nexus to imminent loss of life.

In respect of the use of lethal force in defence of property, it is asserted that international humanitarian law and human rights law cannot be reconciled and a state's

[97] Stabilisation Force in Iraq—Commander's *aide-mémoire*, 24 July 2003.

[98] The ICRC *Interpretive Guidance on the Notion of Direct Participation in Hostilities under International Humanitarian Law* (ICRC, 2009), notes DPH will include 'Military harm may be caused, for example, by . . . damaging military objects'.

[99] Ibid.

[100] See, *mutatis mutandis, Putintseva v Russia*, Application no 33498/04 (ECtHR, 10 May 2012), *Nachova and Others v Bulgaria* and *Perisan v Turkey*, Application no 12336/03, (ECtHR, 20 May 2010).

right to life obligations in armed conflict must be interpreted with reference to international humanitarian law. In order to avoid norm conflict, a state must therefore clearly articulate in its rules of engagement the scope of the use of lethal force with reference to the defence of mission-essential property.[101]

4.5 Stage by Stage Analysis—Conduct of Battlefield Operations—Planning, Control, and Execution

4.5.1 Targeting

Substantive right to life considerations are most likely to arise during armed conflict when armed forces target individuals. In UK doctrine, targeting is defined as 'the process of selecting targets and matching the appropriate response to them, taking account of operational requirements and capabilities'.[102] A target is defined as 'the object of a particular action, for example a geographic area, a complex, and installation, a force, equipment, an individual, a group or a system, planned for capture, exploitation, neutralisation or destruction by military forces'.[103] Doctrinally, targeting falls into two general categories of target—deliberate and dynamic[104]—and one specific type of target, namely, time-sensitive targets. Deliberate targets are those that are known to exist in an operational area and are within the deliberate targeting cycle. They are further sub-divided into two categories: scheduled and on-call targets. Scheduled targets, as the name suggests, are those targets where actions are planned to be taken at a specific time. On-call targets are known targets where a strike time has not been specified. Dynamic targets are those targets that have been identified too late to be included in the deliberate targeting cycle; therefore, striking of these targets is unscheduled. Dynamic targets have two further sub-classifications: anticipated[105] and unanticipated.[106] UK and NATO doctrine also makes reference to time-sensitive targets as a specific group of targets in addition to the two general classes. Time-sensitive targets are defined as 'those targets requiring immediate response because they pose (or will soon pose) a danger to friendly operations or are highly lucrative, fleeting targets of opportunity'.[107] Examples of time-sensitive targets include mobile rocket launchers, mobile high-threat surface-to-air missile systems, mobile command and control vehicles, naval vessels which pose

[101] See, *mutatis mutandis*, *Soare and Others v Romania*, Application no 24329/02 (ECtHR, 22 February 2011); *Gorovenky and Bugara v Ukraine*, Application nos 36146/05 and 42418/05 (12 January 2012); *Nachova and Others v Bulgaria; McCann and Others v the United Kingdom*.

[102] Allied Joint Publication 3-9 (AJP 3-9), S1.

[103] Allied Administrative Publication 6—NATO Glossary of Terms and Definitions.

[104] AJP 3-9, 0106.

[105] Anticipated targets are known to exist in an operational area but are not detected, located, or selected for action in sufficient time to be included in the deliberate targeting cycle: AJP 3-9, 0106 (b) (1).

[106] Unanticipated targets are unknown or not expected to exist in an operational area but, when detected or located, meet criteria specific to operational objectives: AJP 3-9, 0106 (b) (2).

[107] AJP 3-9, 0107.

a threat and demand immediate action to neutralize, loaded transporters, erector launchers, and deployed theatre ballistic missiles.[108]

The targeting process applies equally in international and non-international armed conflict and must comply with the international humanitarian law principles of distinction, proportionality, military necessity, and humanity. These are well documented and considered in UK military doctrine,[109] and a proportionality assessment is analysed in detail through the collateral damage-estimate process.[110] There is, however, no reference to human rights law in targeting doctrine. It is asserted that human rights obligations arise in respect of the planning, control, and execution of the targeting process in order to comply with a state's right to life obligations.[111] As Hampson and Lubell[112] contend, it is likely that a violation of human rights law will only occur in respect of targeting where there has been a violation of international humanitarian law. It is nonetheless still necessary to examine the doctrinal targeting process to assess whether the procedures to ensure compliance with international humanitarian law are sufficiently robust.

4.5.1.1 The targeting process—NATO and UK doctrine

In UK and NATO doctrine, the targeting process occurs at the strategic[113] and operational levels.[114] The overall process is commonly known as the joint[115] targeting cycle and is a six-phase process.[116] In international humanitarian law terms this occurs after the necessary *jus ad bellum* considerations, and the regulation of targeting involves the *jus in bello* of international humanitarian law.

4.5.1.2 Strategic targeting

In any NATO military operation, the North Atlantic Council (NAC) defines the military mission and issues an initiating directive through the NATO military committee to the military strategic commander(s) (SC). In theory, this directive should provide objectives and guidance that are clear and comprehensive, and define rules of engagement and other limitations.[117] Upon receipt, the military strategic commander will develop target sets.[118] These target sets are then passed through the

[108] AJP 3-9, 0501. [109] AJP 3-9, 0112–0114. [110] AJP 3-9, 0114–0119.

[111] *Esmukhambetov and Others v Russia* 138; *Isayeva, Yusupova and Bazayeva v Russia; Isayeva v Russia* 180–82.

[112] *Amicus curiae* brief in *Hassan*, 26. [113] AJP 3-9, Chapter 3.

[114] AJP 3-9, Chapter 4.

[115] In this context 'joint' simply denotes that land, maritime, air, and special forces elements can be used.

[116] AJP 3-9, 0201. The land targeting cycle (AJP 3.9.2) is composed of five phases and reference will be made to any significant difference where appropriate.

[117] AJP 3-9, 0302.

[118] Target sets include command, control, communication, computers, and intelligence (C4I); weapons of mass destruction; ground forces and facilities; air forces and airfields; air defence; naval forces and ports; space forces; ballistic missiles; electric power; petroleum industry; industry; transportation/lines of communication; military supply and storage; military leadership; political leadership; economic leadership; media: Annex A, AJP 3-9.

military committee for approval by the NAC.[119] Significantly, these target sets may include the criteria for time-sensitive targets and include a no-strike list that identifies legitimate military targets that, for military or political reasons, must not be struck under any circumstances. In UK doctrine this process involves strategic military direction from the government, through senior military commanders, to the operational commander, in the form of a targeting directive. Phase 1 of the joint targeting cycle is conducted at the strategic level, while phases 2 to 6 are conducted at the operational level.

4.5.1.3 The joint targeting cycle

Phase 1 consists of guidance provided by the NATO NAC and UK government and senior military personnel to the joint force commander (JFC).[120] In UK doctrine, this will be in the form of a targeting directive[121] that typically consists of strategic direction in the form of the overall military objective and the authority to use lethal force. It will also specify the level at which discrete missions are to be approved. This is typically determined by the number of expected casualties based upon collateral damage estimates—taking into account both combatants and non-combatants—where the higher the number of projected casualties, the more senior the approving military officer or government minister must be. For example, approval to sink the Argentine ship the *General Belgrano* during the Falklands conflict was given by the Prime Minister.

4.5.1.4 Operational targeting

In phase 2 of the targeting cycle, potential targets are developed, validated, nominated, and prioritized.[122] Target development involves an 'analysis of the adversary to determine the best targets to engage in order to achieve the Joint Force Commander's objectives'.[123] The extent to which this phase of targeting complies with international humanitarian law and human rights law obligations is dependent on a thorough validation of the targets that have been developed. Such validation requires a critical analysis of the approved target sets and the quality of military intelligence. The accuracy and reliability of the intelligence information must be carefully scrutinized irrespective of its source, and this must be done on at least two occasions: first, when the target sets are being developed; second, before the target is struck. For example, up-to-date intelligence is essential to identify the use of specific buildings that may historically have been within the control of opposing forces, to ensure that they are legitimate targets. In a dynamic armed conflict buildings often change use or have multiple uses. Immediately prior to any strike taking place, an

[119] This process is in accordance with NATO's Operational Planning System, MC 133/3.

[120] The Joint Force Commander is the military officer with overall responsibility for the conduct of the military element of an operation.

[121] Targeting directives are not referred to in NATO doctrine.

[122] AJP 3-9, 0203.

[123] AJP 3-9, 0203(a).

accurate assessment of the likely civilian casualties must also be undertaken to ensure compliance with international humanitarian law and international human rights law principles. The nomination and prioritization of targets is a largely administrative process that involves selecting and ordering proposed targets to best achieve the joint force commander's guidance and comply with a state's legal obligations.

In phase 3 a capability analysis is undertaken, in which limited military resources in terms of, inter alia, troops, aircraft, ships, and weapons are matched to targets whose elimination is likely to result in a military advantage. This involves a thorough assessment of the most appropriate means of striking a target given its location, military significance, and probability of civilian casualties. The means of striking a target can range from special forces operations, through the use of precision weapons, to the use of unguided ordnance from air or sea. Inherent in the capability assessment process is a thorough assessment of the mitigation required in order to minimize, as far as possible, the adverse effects of targeting, namely, the impact on civilians. There is no legal requirement to use the most accurate weapon system in every case, but only to ensure that the result does not offend against the principles of international humanitarian law and human rights law.[124]

Phases 4 and 5 are linked[125] and involve the planning and execution of the targeting engagements. In multinational operations this will involve the use of a joint targeting coordination board.

4.5.1.5 Joint targeting coordination board

The role of the joint targeting coordination board is to 'review target information, develop targeting guidance, establish targeting priorities and prepare and refine targeting lists for approval by the joint force commander'.[126] The board includes representatives from the land, air, maritime, and special forces component commanders; targeting experts in terms of weaponeer, battle-damage assessment, and intelligence experts; a political adviser; and, significantly, a legal adviser.[127] The legal adviser must ensure that their role is satisfied in accordance with AP I, Article 82 and that the striking of any proposed targets conforms to international humanitarian and human rights law principles.

Phase 6 is an assessment phase in which the effectiveness of the target engagement is determined.[128] Assessment occurs at the strategic level in which the progress towards the overall military objective is considered, and also at the tactical level where the effectiveness of each individual engagement is determined. Tactical-level assessment is commonly known as combat assessment and consists of three interrelated components:[129] battle-damage assessment, weapons effectiveness assessment,

[124] *Esmukhambetov and Others v Russia* 76 and 138.

[125] Specifically, phase 4 is titled 'force planning and assignment' and phase 5 'mission planning and force execution'. To all intents and purposes, however, these phases involve the planning and execution of the mission.

[126] AJP 3-9, 0413.

[127] AP I, Article 82.

[128] AJP 3-9, 0208.

[129] AJP 3-9, 0208 (b) (c).

and future targeting or re-engagement recommendation. Battle-damage assessment considers the extent to which the target was destroyed. This applies equally to objects and individuals. It is common that a human target is injured during an attack, and the nature and severity of the injuries may determine the extent to which they can continue to contribute to the effectiveness of the opposition forces. Battle-damage assessment also considers the number of civilian casualties. A weapons effectiveness assessment determines if the weapon performed in the expected manner both in terms of striking the intended target and in the nature of detonation. A combination of battle-damage assessment and weapons effectiveness assessment will inform the decision whether or not to re-engage the target.

4.5.1.6 The role of military intelligence in targeting

When the targeting process is used in practice, the extent to which it complies with international humanitarian law and human rights law is determined to a large extent by the quality of information provided by military intelligence. The military intelligence function in armed conflict 'locates, identifies and analyses potential targets and target systems in order to identify their value to an adversary and expose their vulnerabilities. This information is then used to allocate relative importance to targets, or target elements, in support of operational decisions and the target prioritisation process.'[130] Put bluntly, if the military intelligence information in respect of, for example, a potential human target, the role of a building, the activities of suspected insurgents, or the number of civilians in the vicinity of a proposed target is known to be flawed, then the resulting death and destruction will constitute a violation of international humanitarian law or human rights law. It is vital therefore that the legal adviser objectively and critically assesses the quality of the intelligence information. This is usually undertaken in accordance with a strict protocol that considers the relevance, reliability, and credibility of sources.

4.5.1.7 Targeting in practice—UK compliance with its right to life obligations

In NATO and UK doctrine the targeting process is detailed and comprehensive, and recognizes the requirement to consult a legal adviser and adhere to the principles of international humanitarian law. It does not reference or recognize human rights law, yet it is submitted that if the doctrine is strictly adhered to, there would be no substantive violation of the right to life with reference to Article 2, ECHR and Article 6, ICCPR law for two reasons. First, adopting the principle that in times of international and non-international armed conflict, a violation of human rights law can only occur where there is a violation of international humanitarian law,[131] it is submitted that UK targeting doctrine is sufficiently robust to prevent such a violation. Second, supposing this principle were abandoned, it is

[130] AJP 3-9, 0425 and AJP 2.1.

[131] *Hassan v the United Kingdom* 102–04.

contended that in light of the ECtHR judgments in, inter alia, *Esmukhambetov, Isayeva, Yusupova and Bazayeva*, and *Isayeva*, notwithstanding the Court's unwillingness to use the term 'non-international armed conflict', it clearly recognized a situation where the use of lethal force by a state's armed forces was necessary[132] and, by implication, the death of legitimate targets[133] would not contravene a state's right to life obligations.[134] If civilian casualties resulted from a military operation in armed conflict this would not, in all circumstances, amount to a violation of the right to life so long as the mission was planned, controlled, and executed with sufficient care to minimize casualties. It is accepted, however, that while the result may not be different if an international humanitarian law or human rights analysis is applied, there is a significant difference if a discrete approach is applied to the targeting process. If international humanitarian law exclusively determines the targeting processes then, while every effort will be made to minimize civilian casualties, this will be subject to a permissive proportionality assessment in respect of perceived military advantage to be achieved. If human rights law were to exclusively determine the approach taken to targeting, then, while civilian casualties may be permissible, the jurisprudence of the ECtHR would suggest a far stricter 'proportionality' assessment.[135] Ultimately, given the strict proportionality assessment that is presently applied in practice by the UK and NATO, it is contended that their targeting doctrine, if strictly adhered to, does not contravene a state's right to life obligations.

In a conventional international armed conflict (state(s) v state(s)), the targeting process is relatively straightforward, as armed forces tend to comply with the requirement to distinguish themselves from civilians.[136] In non-international armed conflict and circumstances where a state intervenes on behalf of a non-state actor against a state, thereby transforming a non-international armed conflict into an

[132] *Isayeva v Russia* 180–82.

[133] In international armed conflict it is uncontroversial to assert that individuals may be targeted on the basis of status alone: see Yoram Dinstein, *The Conduct of Hostilities under the Law of International Armed Conflict* (Cambridge University Press 2010) at chapter 5. In non-international armed conflict the position is more controversial. A compelling analysis of the categories of persons that can be legitimately targeted during a NIAC is presented in S Sivakumaran, *The Law of Non-International Armed Conflict* (Oxford University Press 2012) at 2.6. It includes 'members of the military wing of the armed group, be they *de jure* or *de facto* members, may be targeted, it is submitted at any time, regardless of whether or not they are taking a direct part in hostilities at the time at which they are targeted' and 'persons for such time as they take a direct part in hostilities'.

[134] Gaggioli and Kolb, 'A Right to Life in Armed Conflicts? The Contribution of the European Court of Human Rights' (2007) *Israel YB Hum Rts* 115 at 138; Andrea Gioia, 'The Role of the European Court of Human Rights in Monitoring Compliance with Humanitarian Law in Armed Conflict' in Orna Ben-Naftali, *International Humanitarian Law and International Human Rights Law* (Oxford University Press 2011) at 225–6.

[135] *Esmukhambetov and Others v Russia* 138; *Isayeva, Yusupova and Bazayeva v Russia; Isayeva v Russia* 180–2.

[136] AP I, Article 44(3) and HR, Article 1; GC III, Article 4A(2). Four conditions are laid down. These are:

a. being commanded by a person responsible for his subordinates;
b. having a fixed distinctive sign recognizable at a distance;
c. carrying arms openly;
d. conducting their operations in accordance with the laws and customs of war.

international armed conflict, however, certain practical difficulties can arise. These relate to the changing status of individuals who play a limited role in hostilities, what amounts to direct participation in hostilities, and the legitimacy of targeting known insurgents when they are not participating in hostilities.

Experience in recent non-international armed conflicts has shown that insurgents have modified their tactics to limit the involvement of any one individual in activities that may make them a legitimate target. This relates to both the activity itself and the time during which they are doing it. To illustrate with reference to the recent armed conflict in Afghanistan, the planting of an improvised explosive device (IED) would typically occur over three nights. On the first night, an individual would dig a hole on a track in an area where ISAF troops were known to patrol. On the second night, a different individual would place wires, a battery, and an improvised pressure sensor in the hole and loosely cover them. On the third night, a different individual would assemble the wires, battery, pressure sensor, and explosive charge they were carrying and cover them, thereby creating an improvised explosive device. The extent to which each of these individuals can be targeted requires careful analysis, not only in relation to this discrete activity, but also regarding the patterns of behaviour of the individuals concerned over a period of time, in order to assess the level of their direct participation in hostilities. If there existed no intelligence information to determine that the individuals concerned had performed the same function in the past, then, according to ISAF rules of engagement, only the individual acting on the third night would be a legitimate target for the time during which they were assembling the IED. Recognizing the notion of direct participation in hostilities in international humanitarian law,[137] it is arguable that the individuals on both the second and the third night could be lethally targeted. The actions occurring on the second night could be said to demonstrate a sufficiently close causal relation between the act and the resulting harm from the IED. They can be distinguished from the following example cited by the ICRC, which contends that this does not amount to direct participation in hostilities on the basis that the actions are only part of the planting of the IED:

> the assembly and storing of an improvised explosive device (IED) in a workshop, or the purchase or smuggling of its components, may be connected with the resulting harm through an uninterrupted causal chain of events, but, unlike the planting and detonation of that device, do not cause that harm directly.[138]

If this same example were analysed with exclusive reference to human rights law, then it is submitted that only the individual on the third night could potentially be a legitimate target, on the basis of the imminent nature of the threat to life once the IED had been constructed and covered. Lethal force could be used pre-emptively to prevent loss of life, but it is extremely unlikely that this concept could be extended

[137] ICRC, *Interpretive Guidance on the Notion of Direct Participation in Hostilities under International Humanitarian Law* (ICRC, 2009) part 2.

[138] Ibid.

to justify targeting the individual on the second night, on the basis that their actions in isolation would be incapable of causing loss of life.

The example of an IED being planted over three nights during the armed conflict in Afghanistan illustrates two points. First, when the scenario is analysed with reference to international humanitarian law and human rights law, the individuals that can be lethally targeted differ, with international humanitarian law being more permissive. The two bodies of law cannot be reconciled, and it is therefore submitted that a state's right to life obligations in these circumstances must be interpreted with reference to the applicable international humanitarian law. Second, the restrictive nature of rules of engagement can in reality restrict the application of international humanitarian law, such that the actions of armed forces during non-international armed conflict would comply with the state's right to life obligations if they were directly applicable.

4.5.1.8 Time-sensitive targeting

Time-sensitive targeting presents legal and practical difficulties. By their nature, time-sensitive targets must be attacked within a finite window of opportunity and are usually 'high-value individuals' from opposing forces. As such, the usual rigorous targeting process must be compressed, and authority to attack time-sensitive targets delegated to low-level commanders.[139] This delegation must occur during the planning phase of an operation and must establish the criteria for what amounts to a time-sensitive target. During the execution of an attack on a time-sensitive target, particular care must be taken in applying a proportionality assessment to ensure that the expected loss of civilian life is not disproportionate to the anticipated military advantage achieved.

In international and non-international armed conflict, time-sensitive targeting of an individual would comply with international humanitarian law if the following conditions were met: the target was a legitimate military target, as considered at 4.5.1.8, and a thorough proportionality assessment had been undertaken to ensure that any anticipated loss of civilian life was not disproportionate to the concrete and definite military[140] advantage predicted. While doctrinally and in practice the time-sensitive targeting procedure requires decisions to be made quickly, this is not at the expense of a thorough analysis of the intelligence information to ensure that the relevant criteria pursuant to international humanitarian law permitting the use of lethal force are complied with. During the latter part of the ISAF mission in Afghanistan, the acceptable civilian casualty rate for time-sensitive targets was set at an extremely low level[141] and therefore placed a significant burden on intelligence analysts, commanders, and legal advisers to ensure that no civilian casualties would ensue from a strike at a time-sensitive target.

[139] AJP 3-9, 0502. [140] AP I, 51(5)(b).
[141] Evidence of this can be found in ISAF Tactical Directives: see <http://www.nato.int/isaf/docu/official_texts/Tactical_Directive_090706.pdf> [accessed 3 May 2015].

4.5.1.9 Right to life in land targeting

In UK military doctrine, land targeting[142] is regulated by modified procedures to reflect the nature of the environment.[143] Rather than the six-stage process in the joint targeting cycle, the land-targeting cycle consists of five phases or functions: decide, detect, track, deliver, and assess.[144] The process again relies heavily on the quality of intelligence input to ensure that the targets are legitimate, and is supported by a robust protocol to ensure that international humanitarian law obligations are complied with. To illustrate, the 'decide' function consists of six elements[145] to ensure that the target is legitimate and the proposed method of attack is designed to minimize collateral damage. These include identifying target areas and types, establishing the accuracy of proposed weapon systems, verifying the intelligence information, establishing battle-damage assessment criteria, and collating all relevant information into an attack-guidance matrix.

The 'detect' and 'track' phases in land targeting ought to allow sufficient time for the legitimacy of the target to be verified and the likelihood of civilian casualties to be assessed. In the 'deliver' function, the most appropriate weapon system available at the time will be used to attack the target. Finally, battle-damage assessment and munitions-effectiveness analysis will be conducted to assess the effect of the attack and recommendations will be made to the military commander in respect of re-attack options if required. The battle-damage assessment process can also serve an additional purpose by providing a record of the attack (if conducted by aircraft or drone) that may be used in any subsequent investigation if an allegation of unlawful use of force is made.

If strictly adhered to, the land-targeting process in UK military doctrine provides a robust framework for the identification and engagement of targets. While human rights law is not referenced in the doctrinal publications, a thorough analysis of international humanitarian law obligations is required during the land targeting process. As such, given the detailed nature of the planning process it is unlikely that right to life obligations, if interpreted to reflect international humanitarian law obligations, would be violated if the procedure is fully adhered to and the intelligence information accurate. Where an alleged violation of the right to life was made, the battle-damage assessment information would contribute to an initial investigation and would perhaps be a first step in complying with a state's procedural right to life obligations.

4.5.1.10 Recording of decisions in targeting

States have been criticized when targets have been attacked and information regarding the planning and execution of the attack has either not been disclosed to the Court or does not exist.[146] Therefore, in order to comply with their procedural right

[142] Land targeting is defined as the engagement of targets on the land from the land, sea, or air, most typically from the air: AJP 3-9-3, Land Targeting.

[143] AJP 3-9-3, Land Targeting. [144] AJP 3-9-3, figure 4-1. [145] AJP 3-9-3, 0404.

[146] For example, see *Isayeva v Russia* 182–3, 196.

to life obligations, it is vital that a state must be able to demonstrate that it has an auditable record of decisions made in respect of targeting. This applies equally to the joint targeting process, land targeting, and the engagement of time-sensitive targets. Within UK doctrine, the records of targeting decisions made by commanders are signed and retained. Similarly, if available, footage from aircraft, drones, and 'eyes in the sky'[147] is retained and analysed. In NATO ISAF Afghanistan, for example, targeting decisions were recorded formally in writing and signed by both the targeting commander empowered to authorize the strike and the legal adviser.

4.5.2 Land operations

In addition to the joint targeting cycle and land targeting, land operations in international and non-international armed conflict doctrinally consist of tactical offensive, defensive, stabilizing, and enabling actions.[148] While in practice these activities cannot be neatly compartmentalized and can be conducted simultaneously, it is necessary to examine each in turn in order to determine the extent to which each action may create right to life obligations.

4.5.2.1 Tactical offensive actions

Tactical offensive actions are concerned with the use of lethal force against an adversary and have the following general characteristics: 'surprise and shock; the seizure and retention of the initiative; agility, by which fleeting opportunities are taken; and superior tempo, through which the intensity and sequence of activities is maintained to keep the adversary off balance.'[149] They are further classified into ten discrete offensive activities,[150]each of which involves recourse to the use of lethal force.

[147] 'Eyes in the sky' are typically barrage balloons tethered to the ground with remote-controlled infra-red cameras attached, or remotely operated airships.

[148] Army Doctrine Publication—Operations, 0821–833. [149] Ibid, 0823.

[150]

1. Deliberate attacks to defeat the adversary, with an emphasis on massing fighting power at the expense of time. Hasty attacks to defeat the adversary, trading mass for time, in order to seize fleeting opportunities. Counter-attacks and spoiling attacks to defeat or disrupt an adversary made vulnerable by his own offensive action. Spoiling attacks have the more limited aim of disruption.
2. Raid. A raid is launched as a swift penetration of hostile territory to secure information, confuse the adversary, seize a high value individual or target, or to destroy physical positions. Raids end with a planned withdrawal upon completion of the assigned mission.
3. Exploitation. Exploitation as a Tactical Action is characterised by a rapid advance against lessening resistance. The purpose is both physical and psychological. Physically, the aim is to retain the initiative by preventing an opponent from reorganising his defence or conducting an orderly withdrawal. The psychological effect of exploitation is to create confusion and apprehension throughout the adversary's command, reducing his, or its, capacity to react. This may be decisive in itself.
4. Pursuit. The role of a pursuit is to catch or cut off a hostile force attempting to escape or an absconding individual, with the aim of defeating or perhaps destroying it or him. It should develop from a successful exploitation and commence when the target is demoralised and beginning to disintegrate under pressure. A pursuit may target an adversary seeking to escape from his own initiated ambush. In this case, rapidly following up into his depth in order to cut off his extraction would be vital.

In armed conflict, these activities are regulated by UK armed forces through the use of rules of engagement and self-defence cards. In turn, the rules of engagement conform to international humanitarian law principles and all armed forces personnel are trained to instinctively recognize and respect them. Right to life obligations are not, however, specifically recognized or introduced into training in respect of tactical offensive operations.

In respect of international and non-international armed conflict, it is contended that tactical offensive actions do not violate the UK's right to life, provided that the armed forces personnel comply fully with the principles of international humanitarian law and those targeted during tactical offensive actions are legitimate targets. As previously submitted, in respect of the offensive use of lethal force during armed conflict, the substantive right to life obligations of states pursuant to Article 2, ECHR and Article 6, ICCPR can be interpreted to reflect the principles of international humanitarian law.[151] With reference to the ECHR, this applies irrespective of whether the UK has entered a derogation to Article 2.[152] Naturally, where a member of the armed forces violates the principles of international humanitarian law that also amount to a violation of the right to life, the UK would be liable for the actions of that individual. For example, if an insurgent is wounded by UK armed forces during an 'overseas' non-international armed conflict, they must be afforded the protections of Common Article 3 and Articles 4 and 7, AP II. If they are subsequently executed by a member of the UK armed forces then not only would international humanitarian law principles be violated but the UK's right to life obligations would also be violated and, under UK criminal and military law, an offence of murder would have been committed. This situation occurred in respect of the actions of Sergeant Blackman of the Royal Marines in Helmand Province, Afghanistan, who was subsequently convicted of murder, reduced to manslaughter on appeal to the Courts Martial Appeal Court.

5. Feint. The purpose of a feint is to distract an adversary force by seeking combat or contact with it.
6. Demonstration. The role of a demonstration is to distract an adversary's attention without seeking contact. Both feints and demonstrations can contribute to fixing, and should be designed to have psychological as well as physical effects.
7. Reconnaissance in Force. Reconnaissance in force is used to induce an adversary to disclose the location, size, strength, disposition or the intention of his force by making him respond to offensive action.
8. Ambush. The purpose of an ambush is to inflict damage on the adversary while denying him an opportunity to counter-attack, principally through surprise, in an action concentrated in space and time.
9. Breakout of Encircled Forces. A breakout leads to an encircled force taking offensive action to link up with a main force. The breakout should attempt to surprise the encircling adversary, so there is considerable advantage in attempting to break out at the earliest opportunity, before the encirclement solidifies.
10. Infiltration. An infiltration is penetration using stealth, entering an adversary's physical or virtual space without being detected, probably to gain understanding or to execute another offensive action.

[151] *Varnava and Others v Turkey* 185.

[152] *Hassan v the United Kingdom* 103.

4.5.2.2 *Tactical defensive actions*

Tactical defensive actions are not concerned with the use of offensive lethal force; rather, they are 'intended to protect the force and to provide the right conditions for offensive actions'.[153] By definition, they are responding to a threat, or actual use, of lethal force. As such, irrespective of the context within which they occur, they come within the 'self-defence' ambit of Article 2(2)(a), ECHR, and any death resulting from such actions would not be considered arbitrary for the purposes of Article 6, ICCPR. An examination of the extent to which the use of lethal force in armed conflict violates Article 2, ECHR and Article 6, ICCPR is not required in respect of tactical defensive actions.

4.5.2.3 *Stabilizing actions*

Stabilizing actions are not concerned with the offensive use of lethal force, but rather with creating an environment to provide security and stability during armed conflict through the use of troops.[154] Any use of lethal force would be undertaken in individual or unit self-defence, and therefore the right to life considerations set out above in respect of tactical defensive actions apply equally.

4.5.2.4 *Enabling actions*

Enabling actions are those actions that precede or support tactical offensive actions and typically involve the movement of troops and reconnaissance. In much the same way as stabilizing actions, any use of lethal force would be in individual or unit self-defence and, therefore, the right to life considerations set out in respect of tactical defensive actions would again apply.

4.6 Right to Life Obligations during Detention in Armed Conflict

In international armed conflict, the protections afforded prisoners of war in international humanitarian law are comprehensive[155] and compatible with a state's right to life obligations. Similarly, the treatment of internees in international humanitarian law[156] is comprehensive and recognizes right to life obligations in respect of both the treatment of internees and the location of internment facilities.

In non-international armed conflict, states have right to life obligations where individuals are captured and subsequently detained by armed forces. Once captured, a state assumes right to life obligations in respect of the detainee as follows:

153 Army Doctrine Publication—Operations, 0826. 154 Ibid, 0831.
155 Articles 4(A), 5, 12, 19 GC III. Article 41(3), AP I.
156 Articles 21, 118, GC III, Articles 42, 43, 78, 133(1), 132(2), GC IV.

detained persons are in a vulnerable position and the authorities are under a duty to protect them. Consequently, where an individual is taken into police custody[157] in good health and is found to be injured on release, it is incumbent on the State to provide a plausible explanation of how those injuries were caused.[158] The obligation on the authorities to account for the treatment of a detained individual is particularly stringent where that individual dies or disappears thereafter.[159]

The ECtHR has further considered that

> where the events in issue lie wholly, or in large part, within the exclusive knowledge of the authorities, as in the case of persons within their control in detention, strong presumptions of fact will arise in respect of injuries and death occurring during that detention. Indeed, the burden of proof may be regarded as resting on the authorities to provide a satisfactory and convincing explanation.[160]

The Court judgments and right to life violations found in *Orhan, Avşar, Salman, Çakıcı, Ertak*, and *Timurtaş* occurred against the background of government military operations against the PKK in Turkey. As such, it is contended that there are significant right to life obligations on states during non-international armed conflict within their own territory. It is further contended that these obligations apply equally when conducting a non-international armed conflict overseas where both the domestic courts[161] and ECtHR[162] have recognized the applicability of Article 2, ECHR.

In both international and non-international armed conflict, the specific right to life obligations afforded detainees or internees during their period of confinement cease when the detainees or internees are released.[163] A state may, however, have wider right to life obligations to the population generally, including released internees and detainees, dependent upon the circumstances at the time—for example, if the state is an occupying power.[164]

4.7 Maritime Operations

In international and non-international armed conflict, UK military operations in the maritime environment are governed by rules of engagement and the principles

[157] Given the constabulary function that can be undertaken by armed forces through the military police it is contended that 'police custody' also includes being detained by armed forces personnel in a secure military compound.

[158] *Avşar v Turkey*, Application no 25657/94 (ECtHR, 10 July 2001) 391.

[159] *Orhan v Turkey*, Application no 25656/94 (ECtHR, 16 November 2002) 326.

[160] *Salman v Turkey*, Application no 21986/93, 100; *Çakıcı v Turkey*, Application no 23657/94, 85; *Ertak v Turkey*, Application no 20764/92, 32; *Timurtaş v Turkey*, Application no 23531/94, 82.

[161] *Serdar Mohammed v Ministry of Defence* [2014] EWHC 1369 (QB) 419–24; *R (Maya Evans) v Secretary of State for Defence* [2010] EWHC 1445 (Admin) 17; *Al-Saadoon and Others v Secretary of State for Defence* [2015] EWHC 715 294.

[162] *Hassan v the United Kingdom* 76.

[163] Article 118, GC III, Articles 132(1), 132(2), GC IV. *Hassan v the United Kingdom* 111.

[164] *Al-Skeini v the United Kingdom; Al-Saadoon and Others v Secretary of State for Defence.*

of self-defence. As discussed at 4.3.3, the rules of engagement incorporate the tenets of, and cannot authorize the use of lethal force that contravenes, international humanitarian law.

4.7.1 The use of lethal force in the maritime environment

The use of lethal force in the maritime environment is multifaceted and can include, inter alia, naval gunfire support and precision weapons[165] to strike land targets, the engagement of aircraft with surface-to-air missiles, the engagement of ships with surface-to-surface missiles, and the engagement of submarines with torpedoes. In each case, however, human rights law and substantive right to life considerations are not explicitly incorporated into the planning and authorization of the use of lethal force process.[166] This does not, however, inexorably lead to a violation of a state's right to life obligations. When lethal force is used from, or in, the maritime environment, as it is for the land and air environments, it is either in response to a perceived threat or as an offensive action. With respect to the use of lethal force in legitimate self-defence, this would come within the ambit of Article 2(2)(a), ECHR, and any death resulting from such actions would not be considered arbitrary for the purposes of Article 6, ICCPR. Any use of offensive lethal force would conform to a variation of the joint targeting cycle[167] in which the rules of engagement, intelligence information, and collateral damage estimates would be independently assessed by a legal adviser. The legal adviser would assess the proposed actions against the requirements of international humanitarian law commensurate with the situation under consideration. It is contended, therefore, that the procedural safeguards in place prior to the use of offensive lethal force in the maritime environment would comply with the substantive element of the right to life if adhered to correctly.

4.7.2 Visit, search, and diversion of vessels in armed conflict

Where armed forces visit and search[168] merchant vessels in armed conflict, right to life obligations may arise. Depending upon the length of the visit and the nature of the search, the state, through those personnel conducting the search, may have an obligation to ensure right to life protections of the civilian crew. Right to life obligations will arise where the armed forces personnel assume control of the navigation and safety of the vessel[169] or have crew members under armed guard in a certain area of the ship.[170] In general terms, the longer the visit and search, the more likely the state is to assume right to life obligations in respect of the crew. This is due to the

[165] For example, Tomahawk Land Attack Missiles (TLAM).

[166] AJP 3-9, 0203.

[167] With the exception of TLAM engagements that are conducted through the joint targeting cycle.

[168] Para 118 of the *Sanremo Manual on the International Law Applicable to Armed Conflicts at Sea* (Cambridge University Press 1995) specifies the circumstances in which visit and search of merchant vessels is permissible.

[169] *Medvedyev and Others v France*, Application no 3394/03 (ECtHR, 29 March 2010); *Hirsi Jamaa and Others v Italy*, Application no 27765/09 (ECtHR, 23 February 2012).

[170] See, *mutatis mutandis, Al-Saadoon and Others v Secretary of State for Defence*.

increased likelihood that, given the passage of time, the armed forces personnel are, de facto, in control of the vessel.

Where a merchant vessel is diverted with armed forces personnel in control of navigation and safety of the vessel, then the state will assume substantive right to life obligations. If the merchant vessel is diverted while being escorted by a warship, with the civilian crew in control and no military personnel on board, right to life obligations would arise only to the extent that the warship commander would have to choose a route that did not, as far as is practicable, endanger the crew of the merchant vessel.

4.7.3 Capture of vessels in armed conflict

In the event that vessels are captured[171] during international and non-international armed conflict, right to life obligations in respect of the crews will arise. In an international armed conflict, where the crews are military personnel they will be afforded prisoner of war status[172] irrespective of the vessel on which they are found,[173] and treated accordingly. Prisoner of war protections will also be afforded to civilians who are on board captured military vessels.[174] Where civilian vessels are captured then all personnel on board will be subject to the jurisdiction of the state exercising power over them[175] and, as such, the state would assume substantive right to life obligations in respect of those on board. In a situation of armed conflict this would include ensuring, as far as is practicable, the safety of the vessel from attack. In non-international armed conflict, any personnel on board a captured vessel, irrespective of their status, would come within the jurisdiction of the state exercising power over them, and therefore substantive right to life obligations would again arise.

4.7.4 Right to life obligations in respect of the wounded, sick, and shipwrecked at sea

In respect of the treatment of the wounded, sick, and shipwrecked members of armed forces at sea in international armed conflict, the provisions of GC II and AP I (Part II), if properly adhered to, comply with the right to life obligations in Article 2, ECHR and Article 6, ICCPR. In respect of non-international armed conflict, AP II (Part III) complies with the same requirement.

[171] Paras 135 and 136 of the *Sanremo Manual* classify the vessels that can be captured and those exempt from capture in accordance with treaty law and customary international law.

[172] Ibid, 165.1.

[173] Ibid, 165.1 and Article 47 of the London Declaration Concerning the Laws of Naval Warfare of 1909 state that 'Any individual embodied in the armed forces of the enemy who is found on board in neutral merchant vessel may be made a prisoner of war even though there be no grounds for the capture of the vessel.'

[174] Ibid, 165.2, GCIII Article 4A(4).

[175] Ibid, 161 and *Medvedyev and Others v France* and *Hirsi Jamaa and Others v Italy*.

4.8 Air Operations—Including Drone Operations

4.8.1 Attacks against aircraft

In international and non-international armed conflict, attacks on aircraft are regulated by rules of engagement and self-defence principles. In turn, the rules of engagement reflect international humanitarian law principles in that medical aircraft,[176] aircraft granted safe conduct by agreement between the parties to the conflict, and civil airliners[177] are exempt from attack. In order to qualify for the aforementioned protections, aircraft must conform to strict criteria in terms of their function.[178] In the event of any doubt as to the role or function of an aircraft, it must be presumed to be innocent and not making any effective contribution to military action.[179] If such an aircraft were attacked there would be a violation of both international humanitarian law and the state's right to life obligations.

4.8.2 Diversion and capture of civil aircraft

In the event that civil aircraft are diverted or captured, the state ordering such action would assume jurisdiction[180] over the aircraft and, therefore, right to life obligations in respect of the civilians on board. The state would be required to protect the right to life of those on board in accordance with their Article 2, ECHR obligations irrespective of the nature of the armed conflict.

4.8.3 Engagement of land targets from the air

In UK military doctrine, the use of lethal force from the air is regulated by the joint targeting process. In recent armed conflicts, a significant number of targets have been prosecuted from the air.[181] This can take the form of guided and unguided weapons delivered from manned aircraft and drones. Irrespective of the method of delivering the weapons, the targeting process is the same. In respect of jurisdiction, however, it is contended that the position taken by the ECtHR in *Banković*[182] in respect of the right to life obligations of states during air attack has been undermined by

[176] Para 53 *Sanremo Manual*, based on 1923 Hague Rules of Aerial Warfare, Article 36, GC I, Article 39, GC II, Article 22, GC IV, Articles 24–31, AP I, Article 11, AP II.

[177] 1984 Protocol to the Chicago Convention, Article 3: 'the contracting States recognise that every State must refrain from resorting to the use of weapons against civil aircraft in flight and that, in case of interception, the lives of persons on board and the safety of the aircraft must not be endangered. This provision shall not be interpreted as modifying in any way Rights and obligations of states as set forth in the Charter of United Nations.'

[178] Paras 54–57, *Sanremo Manual*.

[179] Para 58, *Sanremo Manual*.

[180] Ibid, 161 and, *mutatis mutandis, Medvedyev and Others v France* and *Hirsi Jamaa and Others v Italy*.

[181] In 2003, of nearly 20,000 targets engaged during combat operations in Iraq, more than 15,000 were primarily prosecuted by air power—AP 3000, British Air and Space Power Doctrine, 51.

[182] *Banković and Others v Belgium and Others* 82.

subsequent judgments of the same Court, notwithstanding the Court's unwillingness to explicitly depart from it.[183] As such, it is likely that states do have both substantive and procedural right to life obligations in such circumstances.[184] Naturally, this extends to the use of drones when used to deliver lethal effects.

4.8.4 The use of drones in air operations

Once it has been determined that a state has jurisdiction in respect of the use of drones, the supplementary question is: which area of law regulates their use when delivering lethal weapons? There is significant support for the view that the use of drones is regulated by international humanitarian law when used in armed conflict.[185] While right to life obligations will exist, they will be interpreted in light of a state's international humanitarian law obligations. The rigorous targeting process used by the UK, if adhered to correctly, complies with the state's international humanitarian law obligations in respect of the use of lethal force[186] and therefore with substantive right to life obligations in respect of drone operations.

4.9 Multinational Operations and the Application of the Right to Life

Multinational military operations bring an added level of complexity to issues of ensuring ECHR compliance. Ultimately, whenever armed forces personnel from 'ECHR states' operate with armed forces of 'non-ECHR states', it is imperative that they adhere to their own national rules of engagement and self-defence cards. This is due to differing national interpretations of self-defence and notions of 'hostile act' and 'hostile intent' that may justify the use of pre-emptive lethal force in circumstances that would not comply with Article 2, ECHR. The most often cited example is the US military definition of hostile intent[187] that includes using lethal force to defend property. If taken by UK armed forces personnel during, for example,

[183] *Al Skeini and Others v the United Kingdom; Hassan v the United Kingdom.*

[184] UN General Assembly, Report of the Special Rapporteur on extrajudicial, summary and arbitrary executions, 13 September 2013, 48.

[185] Ibid, 40 and Human Rights Committee, Concluding Observations on the fourth periodic report of the United States of America, CCPR/C/USA/CO/4. 23 April 2014, 9 also reference IHL principles used in lethal targeting.

[186] For a discussion of this issue see 4.5.1.

[187] Hostile Intent—US Department of Defense definition (JP 3-01):

> The threat of imminent use of force by a foreign force, terrorist(s), or organization against the United States and US national interests, US forces and, in certain circumstances, US nationals, their property, US commercial assets, and other designated non-US forces, foreign nationals, and their property. When hostile intent is present, the right exists to use proportional force, including armed force, in self-defense by all necessary means available to deter or neutralize the potential attacker or, if necessary, to destroy the threat. A determination that hostile intent exists and requires the use of proportional force in self-defense must be based on evidence that an attack is imminent. Evidence necessary to determine hostile intent will vary depending on the state of international and regional political tension, military preparations, intelligence, and indications and warning information.

military occupation, without a sufficient nexus to an imminent threat to life, such action would contravene UK self-defence rules of engagement and, in turn, Article 2, ECHR.

4.10 UK Procedures and Investigations and the Procedural Element of the Right to Life—Action Following a Death in Armed Conflict

In international and non-international armed conflict, UK armed forces have recourse to numerous methods to determine the legitimacy of the use of lethal force that has resulted in the death of a combatant, civilian, or member of the UK armed forces. The extent to which such investigations comply with the procedural element of Article 2, ECHR and Article 6, ICCPR have been, and can be, scrutinized by domestic courts,[188] the ECtHR,[189] and the Human Rights Committee.[190] It is not merely the quality of discrete investigations that has been considered by the courts and Human Rights Committee, but also the institutional framework within which the investigations are commenced, conducted, and reviewed, and the recommendations adopted and enforced.

In order to assess the extent to which the UK complies with its procedural right to life obligations, it is necessary to first consider the overarching framework and circumstances in which investigations are used. Second, the type of investigation must be assessed against the criteria identified in Chapter 2. Third, the relationship between types of investigation must be considered to determine if failings in a specific type of investigation can be rectified or addressed elsewhere in the overall process of review by armed forces or independent bodies. Finally, in the event that an investigation results in a prosecution, the independence of the prosecutorial process must be considered in order to demonstrate 'accountability in practice as well as in theory', as required by the ECtHR.[191]

The UK has a complex and multilayered investigatory process following a death during armed conflict, which begins with a serious incident report.

4.10.1 Serious incident report

In international and non-international armed conflict, a serious incident report is the first assessment of all shooting incidents[192] involving UK armed forces that result in a fatality.[193] This report is a mandatory requirement and consists of a very

[188] *Smith and Others (FC) (Appellants) v The Ministry of Defence (Respondent)* [2013] UKSC 41.

[189] *Al-Skeini and Others v the United Kingdom* 161–77.

[190] Human Rights Committee, Seventh Periodic Report on the United Kingdom, CCPR/C/GBR/7, 29 April 2013, 562–66.

[191] *Al-Skeini and Others v the United Kingdom* 167.

[192] A 'shooting incident' includes all situations where a death is suspected.

[193] Written evidence to the House of Commons Defence Select Committee from the Ministry of Defence in respect of operations in Afghanistan, <http://www.publications.parliament.uk/pa/cm201012/cmselect/cmdfence/554/554we02.htm> 19 [accessed 6 April 2015].

brief statement of the facts as they perceive them from the military unit involved in the incident. The report is forwarded to the unit operations room in the first instance, and then up through the chain of command until it reaches the commander of the battlegroup. No investigation is undertaken at this stage, but a decision in respect of an investigation must be made, which, once it is submitted, brings the process within the ambit of the procedural element of Article 2, ECHR and Article 6, ICCPR.

Having received the serious incident report, the commander of the battlegroup will have to decide upon one of three possible courses of action, namely:

1. If only positively identified enemy forces have been killed or injured and there is no suggestion of any breach of the Laws of International Armed Conflict (LOAC) or Rules of Engagement (ROE) then no further action will be necessary.
2. If civilians may have been killed or injured although there is no indication that LOAC/ROE have been breached a Shooting Incident Review (SIR) should be initiated.
3. If it appears there *may* have been a breach of the ROE or LOAC or a friendly fire incident[194] or any other circumstances deemed appropriate then the incident is reported to the Service police. [my emphasis][195]

Taken in isolation, this procedure is beset with legal, procedural, and practical difficulties. First, it encounters an immediate problem with reference to the requirement for 'a lack of hierarchical or institutional connection but also a practical independence'[196] in the investigatory mechanism and therefore, by definition, in the decision-making process.

To illustrate, and with reference to UK military operations in Afghanistan, the commanding officer of a 'unit involved in an incident' would be, for example, a lieutenant colonel[197] in command of 42 Commando Royal Marines.[198] The lieutenant colonel would report directly to the brigadier in command of 3 Commando Brigade, Royal Marines, who also would act as the commander of Task Force Helmand. The

[194] Friendly fire is an attack by a military force on friendly forces while attempting to attack the enemy, either by misidentifying the target as hostile, or due to errors or inaccuracy. Fire not intended to attack the enemy, such as negligent discharge and deliberate firing on one's own troops for disciplinary reasons, is not called friendly fire. Nor is unintentional harm to non-combatants or structures, which is sometimes referred to as *collateral damage*. Geoffrey Regan, *Backfire: A History of Friendly Fire from Ancient Warfare to the Present Day* (Robson Books, 2002); Robert E Rasmussen Commander, USN, *The Wrong Target: The Problem of Mistargeting Resulting in Fratricide and Civilian Casualties*, Joint Forces Staff College Joint Advanced Warfighting School Publication (2007).

[195] Defence Committee—Written Evidence, Operations in Afghanistan, para 19.3 of the Report, 6 July 2011: <http://www.publications.parliament.uk/pa/cm201012/cmselect/cmdfence/554/554we02.htm> (accessed 7 November 2017).

[196] *Al-Skeini and Others v the United Kingdom* 167.

[197] NATO rank designation—OF4.

[198] 42 Commando Royal Marines is a battalion consisting of approximately 650 Royal Marine Commandos. Further information can be found at <http://www.royalnavy.mod.uk/our-organisation/the-fighting-arms/royal-marines/3-commando-brigade/42-commando> (accessed 3 May 2015).

brigadier[199] of 3 Commando Brigade[200] would not only give legally enforceable orders to the lieutenant colonel in command of 42 Commando in respect of the conduct of military operations in Afghanistan, but is also their reporting officer for the purposes of advancement and promotion. It is clear therefore that in such circumstances there is no hierarchical, institutional, or practical independence, in the sense that the decision-maker (brigadier, battlegroup commander) is in the same chain of command as the group of individuals providing the information. That said, however, the range of options available to the decision-maker is very limited, and in essence they are simply being asked to determine whether the account given by the troops responsible for the use of lethal force is truthful. In practice, the version of events provided by soldiers can be corroborated or contradicted by locals who witnessed the incident, or, in the case of air strikes, by video footage from the aircraft or drone. The threshold for commencing the next stage of the investigatory process is very low, namely, that 'civilians *may* have been killed or injured'. Therefore, absent a definitive proclamation from the troops in question, or if there is any doubt at all, it is likely a shooting incident review will be conducted. This is the second stage in the process.

Second, there is no specific requirement for the battlegroup commander to take independent legal advice prior to making a decision in respect of a serious incident report. As such, irrespective of the decision made, the process could be improved by recourse to an analysis of the relevant international humanitarian law principles and rules of engagement carried out by an independent legal adviser. This independent oversight would go a considerable way to countering any allegations of institutional bias or impropriety.

Finally, the decision of the battlegroup commander is not subject to review in the event that they choose option 1 above, to take no further action. Procedurally, therefore, the decision-making process in response to a serious incident report is open to abuse. What emerges is that, notwithstanding the low threshold to continue with further investigation following a serious incident report, the process—taken in isolation, and if no further action is taken—is unlikely to comply with the procedural requirements of Article 2, ECHR and Article 6, ICCPR.

4.10.2 Shooting incident review

Shooting incident reviews are used by UK armed forces in international and non-international armed conflict following the death or injury of any person, and follow the recommendation of the battlegroup commander upon their review of the serious incident report. A shooting incident is defined as

> an incident where shots or munitions employed or controlled by UK forces are known, or believed, to have resulted in the death or injury of any person. This includes all types of

[199] NATO rank designation—OF6.

[200] 3 Commando Brigade Royal Marines consists of eight battalions. Further information can be found at <http://www.royalnavy.mod.uk/our-organisation/the-fighting-arms/royal-marines#3-commando-brigade> (accessed 3 May 2015).

munitions: land-based, air-delivered, direct or indirect.[201] It does not include non-kinetic events, death or injury due to aircraft accidents, or damage to property following delivery of munitions.[202]

A shooting incident review is conducted by an officer of at least the rank of army captain[203] who was not directly involved in the incident,[204] but who typically comes from the unit responsible for the use of lethal force. The purpose of a shooting incident review is to determine if an incident requires further investigation by the military police. The officer conducting the shooting incident review is empowered to take statements from those involved in the incident and review all other evidence in relation to it. The review should be completed within forty-eight hours.

Once a shooting incident review is complete, it is provided to the commanding officer of the unit involved in the incident, who has three alternative courses of action:

'a. If the shooting incident review discloses, or the Commanding Officer otherwise becomes aware of, an allegation or circumstances that would indicate to a reasonable person that a schedule 2 offence[205] has been committed or he becomes aware of circumstances that meet a prescribed description,[206] he must ensure the military police are made aware as soon as practicable.

[201] The difference between direct and indirect fire is simply that with direct fire it is possible to see the munitions land and with indirect fire this is not possible.

[202] Defence Committee—Written Evidence, Operations in Afghanistan, 19.3.

[203] NATO rank designation—OF2.

[204] Defence Committee—Written Evidence, Operations in Afghanistan, 19.3.

[205] 'Schedule 2 offence' refers to Schedule 2 of the Armed Forces Act 2006, which considers the most serious criminal matters. These include, inter alia, murder, manslaughter, an offence under section 1 of the Geneva Conventions Act 1957 (*c.* 52) (grave breaches of conventions) and an offence under section 51 or 52 of the International Criminal Court Act 2001 (*c.* 17) (genocide, crimes against humanity, war crimes, etc).

Any allegations in respect of these offences involving any military personnel must be referred to the military police for investigation. See <http://www.legislation.gov.uk/ukpga/2006/52/schedule/2> for the most up-to-date list.

[206] Prescribed description refers to an allegation of an offence committed in prescribed circumstances, thus:

> OFFENCES COMMITTED IN 'PRESCRIBED CIRCUMSTANCES' (REGULATIONS 5, 6, 7 AND 8 OF THE ARMED FORCES (PART 5 OF THE ARMED FORCES ACT 2006) REGULATIONS 2009 Referral of case following investigation by service or civilian police
>
> 14. For the purposes of section 116(2)(b) AFA 06, the following are prescribed circumstances—
>
> (a) the evidence referred to in section 116(2)(b) AFA 06 is evidence that a person subject to service law has been the victim of—
>
> (i) a course of conduct by a person subject to service law, involving on at least two occasions an assault in which that individual participated as a principal offender or as a secondary party; or
>
> (ii) an offence under section 42 AFA 06 as respects which the corresponding offence under the law of England and Wales is the offence under section 4 of the protection from Harassment Act 1997, committed by a person subject to service law;
>
> (b) the evidence referred to in section 116(2)(b) AFA 06 is evidence that an assault causing serious injury was inflicted on a person subject to service law by a person of superior rank or rate while the assailant was otherwise carrying out his duties;
>
> (c) the evidence referred to in section 116(2)(b) AFA 06 is evidence—

b. Where the shooting incident review discloses an alleged military offence which falls outside the scope of sub-paragraph a above, the Commanding Officer has discretion in the matter of reporting such an offence to the military police. The Commanding Officer may decide to conduct a unit investigation.
c. Where a Commanding Officer believes that a military police investigation is not required (because there are no grounds to suspect that a criminal act, or breach of rules of engagement, has or may have been committed by a military person) he may decide that the matter is not reported to the military police.'[207]

The process that the commanding officer must follow is clear. Sections 113 and 114, Armed Forces Act 2006 referencing schedule 2, Armed Forces Act 2006; section 1, Geneva Conventions Act 1957; and sections 51 and 52, International Criminal Court Act 2001 stipulate that in any circumstances where conduct resulting in the unlawful loss of life is alleged, the military police must be made aware of the circumstances. Taken in isolation, therefore, if the commanding officer chose option (a) in the extract above and referred the matter to the military police to investigate, this would elevate the process to the next level and would not in itself contravene the procedural element of Article 2, ECHR or Article 6, ICCPR. The investigation would therefore remain 'live' and under consideration by the military police.

If the commanding officer considers that an investigation by the military police is not necessary, then this recommendation (option (c) above) must be made to their senior officer. The commanding officer cannot make a final determination on the requirement not to commence a military police investigation. The senior officer—in Afghanistan, for example, a brigadier (Commander Task Force Helmand)—must in turn consult a legal adviser and a senior military police officer before making a final decision in respect of the requirement to conduct a military police investigation. This process creates a circumstance in which the commanding officer can initiate a unit investigation (option b above) and there is no requirement to have this decision endorsed by a senior officer. A unit investigation is conducted within the unit,[208] using unit resources, and not by the military police. The extent to which a unit investigation complies with the procedural element of Article 2, ECHR and Article 6, ICCPR is considered at 4.10.3.

(i) that a person ('A') participated (as a principal offender or as a secondary party) in the inflicting of serious injury on a relevant person in a relevant place;
(ii) that A was under a duty to safeguard a relevant person ('B') while B was in a relevant place and that A failed to prevent an assault inflicting serious injury on B in that place; or
(iii) that A was under a duty to safeguard a person ('B') while B was in a relevant place and that A failed to prevent B's death being caused while B was in that place;

(d) the evidence referred to in section 116(2)(b) AFA 06 is evidence that the death of a person was caused (directly or indirectly), or contributed to, by the misconduct of a person subject to service law or a civilian subject to service discipline, and that the misconduct occurred while the deceased was being held in a relevant place while in service custody.

[207] Defence Committee—Written Evidence, Operations in Afghanistan, 19.3.

[208] For example, 42 Commando Royal Marines.

4.10.2.1 Advisers in the shooting incident review process

If, following a shooting incident review, the senior officer (for example, a brigadier who was the Commander Task Force Helmand) receives a recommendation not to initiate an investigation then he or she must, in accordance with UK doctrine, consult a legal adviser and a senior military police officer. The legal adviser and senior military police officer will both be regular armed forces personnel and of a rank subordinate to the senior officer empowered to make a decision in respect of any further investigation following a shooting incident review.

4.10.2.2 The role of the senior military police officer in the shooting incident review process

The senior military police officer is completely independent of the chain of command and therefore, while subordinate in rank to the senior officer, does not receive orders from them. Moreover, in the event that information is revealed to the military police officer during the shooting incident review process that discloses a potentially serious criminal offence, the military police are under a duty to investigate.[209] The mandated presence of the military police officer provides an additional safeguard that contributes to the independence of the process, but does not guarantee it.

4.10.2.3 The role of the legal adviser in the shooting incident review process

The legal adviser does not enjoy the same hierarchical and practical independence as the senior military police officer in the shooting incident review process. Therefore, while they can advise the senior officer on the legal elements of the shooting incident review process, their presence does not, in isolation, provide the necessary procedural safeguards to ensure compliance with the procedural element of the right to life.

4.10.2.4 The decision in the shooting incident review process

Ultimately, the decision to commence a formal military police investigation following a shooting incident review rests solely with the senior officer. They are not bound to take the advice of the legal or military police advisers. The mandated presence of the hierarchically and practically independent military police officer does not, therefore, provide the necessary safeguards in the process to ensure compliance with the procedural element of the right to life,[210] as the decision to commence a military police investigation is not vested in the police, but in the military chain of command.[211]

[209] Armed Forces Act 2006, s 116.

[210] *Ramsahai and Others v the Netherlands* 337; *Al-Skeini and Others v the United Kingdom* 167; *Jaloud v the Netherlands* 190.

[211] Written evidence to the House of Commons Defence Select Committee from the Ministry of Defence in respect of operations in Afghanistan, para 19.

As early as 2005, the independence of the decision-making and investigatory procedures used by UK armed forces in Iraq was heavily criticized by Brooke LJ[212] in the Court of Appeal in *Al-Skeini*, and subsequently by the ECtHR[213] in the same case. Yet, notwithstanding this criticism, the process of decision-making with regard to initiating an investigation following the loss of life in Afghanistan suffered from the same flaws and fundamental lack of independence. In short, UK doctrine in respect of this process is inadequate and requires updating.

4.10.2.5 Measures to ensure the independence of the shooting incident review process

The measures required to ensure that the shooting incident review process complies with the procedural element of the right to life are beguilingly simple in theory, yet may present some organizational and cultural difficulties in implementation. To address the criticisms of the courts and ensure a compliant procedure, the UK armed forces would simply have to remove the military chain of command from the shooting incident review process and vest the decision in an independent, albeit uniformed, military police officer, advised by a military legal adviser who is also independent of the military chain of command.

To date, UK military commanders have taken a central role in the overall coordination of all military campaigns, and this has included the instigation of investigations following allegations of misconduct on the part of troops. The rationale behind this policy is that military commanders are responsible for the maintenance of discipline and morale, both vital commodities in armed conflict. Culturally, divesting a military commander of an element of their responsibility may be controversial, yet it is necessary to ensure compliance with the state's procedural right to life obligations.

4.10.3 Unit investigations

A unit investigation may be initiated by a commanding officer following a shooting incident review. This could occur in circumstances where there had been a civilian death but the commanding officer had assessed that the rules of engagement had not been contravened[214] and an offence pursuant to Schedule 2,[215] Armed Forces Act

[212] *R. (on the application of Al-Skeini and Others) v Secretary of State for Defence*, [2005] EWCA Civ 1609, [2005] All ER (D) 337 (Dec) at 140: 'if international standards are to be observed, the task of investigating incidents in which a human life is taken by British forces must be completely taken away from the military chain of command and vested in the [Royal Military Police]. It contains the requisite independence so long as it *is free to decide for itself when to start and when to cease an investigation*, and so long as it reports in the first instance to the [Army Prosecuting Authority] and is not to the military chain of command' [my emphasis].

[213] *Al-Skeini and Others v the United Kingdom* 172: 'It was generally for the Commanding Officer of the unit involved in the incident to decide whether the Special Investigations Branch [of the Royal Military Police] should be called in. If the Special Investigations Branch decided on its own initiative to commence an investigation, this investigation could be closed down at the request of the military chain of command.'

[214] Written evidence to the House of Commons Defence Select Committee from the Ministry of Defence in respect of operations in Afghanistan, 19.5.

[215] Schedule 2, Armed Forces Act 2006 offences include murder and manslaughter.

2006 or committed in prescribed circumstances[216] had not occurred. As previously discussed, this decision is made based upon particularly scant information given the considerable limitations of the shooting incident review process and, as such, has concomitant failings in respect of the procedural element of the right to life. Notwithstanding these limitations, it is necessary to consider the specific nature of unit investigations in order to determine the extent to which they may comply with the procedural element of the right to life.

4.10.3.1 Unit investigations defined

Within the context of armed conflict, a unit investigation can be initiated by a commanding officer where, owing to operational circumstances, it is not possible to conduct a military police investigation.[217] This could include following a civilian death caused by a member of the commanding officer's unit. The unit investigation is conducted by an officer, or senior non-commissioned officer, from the commanding officer's unit. The officer or senior non-commissioned officer charged with conducting the unit investigation will not be a military police officer. Brief guidance is provided on how to conduct the investigation[218] and covers the following areas: witness evidence, medical evidence, identification, interviews, and the rights of a suspect. The investigators do not have any power to compel individuals to cooperate with the investigations, and unit investigations do not comply with the evidential requirements of the Police and Criminal Evidence Act 1984.[219] It is not mandated that those conducting the unit investigation consult legal advisers, the military police, or specialist experts such as forensic teams during the course of the investigation.

4.10.3.2 Hierarchical, institutional, and practical independence of unit investigations

Unit investigations do not have any hierarchical, institutional, or practical independence for the following reasons: the decision to commence and end an investigation is made solely by a Commanding Officer without recourse to any independent authority;[220] no review procedure exists;[221] the investigation is conducted by an officer or senior non-commissioned officer from within the unit and therefore is not independent of the chain of command; the decision to bring a charge or refer the matter for trial by court martial is determined solely by the commanding officer;[222]

[216] 'Prescribed circumstances' refer to a discrete set of factors contained within the Armed Forces Act 2006 that require a case is sent from the investigating police force directly to the Director of Service Prosecutions. These include allegations of repeated physical or sexual assault, harassment, or bullying.

[217] Annex F to Volume 1 Chapter 6 Joint Service Publication 830, 2.

[218] Annex F to Volume 1 Chapter 6 Joint Service Publication 830.

[219] Police and Criminal Evidence Act 1984, Part VIII and s 113.

[220] Joint Service Publication 830, 1-6-16, 32. [221] Ibid, 1-6-16, 37.

[222] Ibid, 1-6-16, 36.

there is no mandated requirement to seek guidance or advice from any independent authority;[223] the investigation is not conducted by trained military police officers and therefore the likelihood of them having the requisite skills and training to properly secure evidence involved in the incident, including, inter alia, eyewitness testimony, forensic evidence, and an accurate determination of the cause of death are extremely low; it is not mandated that the next of kin of a civilian victim are consulted. The investigations are held within the unit and are not open to public consultation or scrutiny.

On any construction, unit investigations do not comply with the procedural element of Article 2, ECHR or Article 6, ICCPR; however, they can still, according to extant doctrine, be used by UK commanding officers following the death of a civilian during armed conflict. The option for commanding officers to conduct unit investigations following a shooting incident review ought to be removed entirely, thus preventing the possibility of a non-compliant investigation being conducted that would subsequently be criticized by the ECtHR. A more robust procedure is required in terms of both the options available to commanding officers following a shooting incident review and the quality of the investigatory function designed to determine the cause of a civilian death. It is therefore necessary to consider the extent to which a formal military police investigation following the death of a civilian during armed conflict can comply with the procedural element of the right to life.

4.10.4 UK military police investigations

At the outset, it is necessary to distinguish between, on one hand, the circumstances in which, through the procedural failings in the shooting incident review process identified at 4.10.2.4, a military police investigation is not initiated at all, and on the other, a consideration of the compliance of a military police investigation with the procedural element of the right to life once it has been initiated. The following analysis will assess the degree of compliance with the procedural element of the right to life once a military police investigation has commenced, in respect of both the conduct of the investigation and the procedural framework governing its regulation and subsequent use.

4.10.4.1 Procedural framework governing UK military police investigations

Both the context within which UK military police investigations have been terminated and prosecuted in the military justice system and the conduct of the investigations themselves have been subject to significant criticism.[224] The events under consideration in *Al-Skeini* did, however, occur prior to the introduction of the Armed Forces Act 2006,[225] which, inter alia, redefined the relationship between the military chain of command and the military police in respect of commanding

[223] Ibid, 1-6-16, 35. [224] *Al-Skeini and Others v the United Kingdom* 168–77.

[225] The Armed Forces Act 2006 can be found at <http://www.legislation.gov.uk/ukpga/2006/52/contents>.

officers' powers to terminate investigations and decide not to refer them for prosecution within the military justice system. Where a military police investigation concludes that there is sufficient evidence to support a charge of murder, manslaughter, or any offence pursuant to section 1, Geneva Conventions Act 1957 and sections 51 and 52, International Criminal Court Act 2001 against any member of the armed forces, then the military chain of command cannot terminate the military police investigation or prevent the case being forwarded to the independent Service Prosecuting Authority for consideration of trial by court martial.[226] This legislative change addresses a significant procedural failing identified by the ECtHR in *Al-Skeini*,[227] such that

> if the special investigation branch decided on its own initiative to commence an investigation, this investigation could be closed at the request of the military chain of command . . . on conclusion of a special investigation branch investigation, the report was sent to the commanding officer, who was responsible for deciding whether or not the case should be referred to the army prosecuting authority[228] . . . the fact that the special investigation branch was not free to decide when to start and cease an investigation and did not report in the first instance to the army prosecuting authority rather than to the military chain of command, meant that it could not be seen as sufficiently independent from the soldiers implicated in events.[229]

While this legislative change addresses a procedural failing in the administration of investigations, wider chain of command and independence issues must also be considered.

4.10.4.2 Independence of the military police investigators

Within the context of military operations, numerous chains of command can run simultaneously in respect of, for example, functional[230] and operational[231] command of individuals, the issuing of orders, assessment and reporting, disciplinary conduct, administration, and the award of minor administrative action.[232] In order to ensure sufficient independence of the investigatory function, military police officers must not be subject to any oversight or influence from the military chain of command. This would mean that the military police investigating an alleged offence only take orders from senior military police officers within a functionally separate and

[226] Armed Forces Act 2006, s 116–18.

[227] *Al-Skeini and Others v the United Kingdom* 172.

[228] The Army Prosecuting Authority has been replaced by the Service Prosecuting Authority as a consequence of the Armed Forces Act 2006.

[229] *Al-Skeini and Others v the United Kingdom* 172.

[230] Functional command refers to the administrative command of armed forces personnel in respect of ensuring they are paid, their welfare is taken care of, they are fed, etc.

[231] Operational command refers to the issuing of orders in respect of the conduct of a military operation. Examples are instructions on patrolling routes or for an attack on the enemy.

[232] Minor administrative action is regulated via Joint Service Publication 833 and is action taken to rehabilitate, censure, or initiate sanctions to correct professional or personal failings of armed forces personnel in respect of minor transgressions of rules and regulations. This can include formal and informal interview, extra work and drill, or being returned to unit due to unsatisfactory performance in an operational theatre or on a training course.

discrete chain of command, and not operational military commanders. Similarly, it would be necessary to ensure that the military police officers' performance was assessed and reported upon within this framework and that senior military police officers had the power to administer minor administrative action sanctions, as well as to initiate disciplinary action against their subordinate military police officers. In Afghanistan, for example, these criteria were not entirely satisfied, as military police officers were subject to the administration and control of the military chain of command and not that of the military police for the purposes of disciplinary conduct and minor administrative action.[233] Significantly, however, military police officers did not receive orders from the military chain of command in respect of the conduct of their investigatory duties. Equally, the military chain of command did not have any input into police officers' performance reports that were used to inform future promotion decisions. On balance, therefore, it is likely that the military police officers were sufficiently independent to comply with this discrete aspect of the procedural element of the right to life. The circumstances of the armed conflict in Afghanistan cannot be seen as representative of all UK military operations overseas, however, and it is important that the requirements set out above are recognized by the UK armed forces and incorporated into both doctrine and standard operating procedures, to ensure compliance with the state's procedural right to life obligations.

4.10.4.3 Promptness and expedition of investigations

The ECtHR has been willing to accept that the exigencies of armed conflict can have an adverse impact upon both the promptness with which an investigation is commenced and the efficiency with which it is conducted, without necessarily contravening a state's procedural right to life obligations.[234] The test applied is whether 'all reasonable steps' are taken to ensure that an effective, independent investigation is conducted into alleged breaches of the right to life.[235] Naturally, the UK armed forces do not have an inexhaustible cadre of suitably trained and qualified military police officers. There are, however, at present circa 2,500 royal military police,[236] 1,200 Royal Air Force police,[237] 280 Royal Navy police, and 1,962 Ministry of Defence police,[238] a significant number of whom could be deployed on operations in an investigatory role. While the overall numbers will not represent those who could be deployable on operations overseas, a conservative estimate would be 10 per cent of the overall cadre providing a deployable military police force of in excess of

[233] Written evidence to the House of Commons Defence Select Committee from the Ministry of Defence in respect of operations in Afghanistan, 19.5.

[234] *Bazorkina v Russia* 121.

[235] *Kaya v Turkey* 86–92; *Ergi v Turkey* 82–85; *Tanrıkulu v Turkey* 101–10; *Khashiyev and Akayeva v Russia* 156–66; *Isayeva v Russia* 215–24; *Musayev and Others v Russia* 158–65; *Al-Skeini and Others v the United Kingdom* 164.

[236] Data at <http://www.army.mod.uk/agc/provost/23207.aspx> (accessed 9 April 2015).

[237] Data at <http://www.rafpa.com/RAFP%20Factsheet%20Jan12.pdf> (accessed 9 April 2015).

[238] Data at <https://www.gov.uk/government/uploads/system/uploads/attachment_data/file/380044/20141121_MDP_Recruitment_Patterns_Redacted.pdf> (accessed 9 April 2015).

500 personnel. Strictly in terms of numbers, as presently configured, the UK could provide sufficient investigators to independently review alleged right to life violations, given the nature and size of campaigns to which they contribute forces.

By way of illustration, overall numbers of armed forces personnel in Afghanistan did not exceed 10,500, of which fewer than 3,500 were troops deployed outside of main military bases. It would be incumbent upon the government and the armed forces to have the capacity to deploy sufficient numbers of investigators in future armed conflicts as a first step in being able to comply with their procedural right to life obligations. It must also be borne in mind that the vast majority of lethal targeting conducted by UK armed forces in recent armed conflicts in Afghanistan, Iraq (2003–11), Libya, Syria, and Northern Iraq has been from the air, and therefore video footage can be reviewed as part of the investigatory process, considerably increasing the efficiency of the process.

If sufficient numbers of investigators are available, the extent to which an investigation during armed conflict can be completed efficiently will be determined to a large extent by the security situation in the area in which the alleged violation occurred. It is axiomatic that in benign conditions, the requirement to complete an investigation capable of a determination of whether the force used was or was not justified in the circumstances, as well as identification and punishment of those responsible, will be significantly higher than during a volatile and dangerous situation.[239] As the obligation on states is one of means and not result, it is therefore necessary, within the bounds of what is operationally safe, to deploy force protection soldiers to ensure the investigators can acquire sufficient evidence. The UK has armed forces personnel specifically trained in force protection and all military police deployed to areas of armed conflict are armed and trained, at the very least, in the use of lethal force in self-defence.

In terms of means available to assist investigators, UK armed forces operating in Afghanistan typically had access to forensic specialists; medical, ballistics, and cultural experts; and interpreters. It is contended that, in future military operations, overseas access to such experts must be an integral part of the planning process in order to comply with procedural right to life obligations. While the ECtHR has repeatedly asserted that the 'procedural duty under Article 2 must be interpreted realistically, to take account of specific problems faced by the investigators',[240] in its judgments it has applied a high and exacting standard in terms of the conduct of the investigation. This is most aptly illustrated with reference to the requirement for, and standard of, the autopsy of the deceased in *Jaloud*.[241]

4.10.4.4 The standard of autopsy

Despite the Netherlands government arguing that the autopsy in *Jaloud* was as effective as it could be given the circumstances at the time, the ECtHR rejected this

[239] *Al-Skeini and Others v the United Kingdom* 165.
[240] For example, *Al-Skeini and Others v the United Kingdom* 165; *Jaloud v the Netherlands* 186.
[241] *Jaloud v the Netherlands* 212–16.

assertion and imposed a particularly high standard. The Court effectively mandated that the autopsy ought to be conducted by a pathologist from a coalition power[242] (the Netherlands did not have such a facility) and should contain photographs.[243] As such, and as noted by Judges Casadevall, Berro-Lefevre, Šikuta, Hirvelä, López Guerra, Sajó, and Silvis in their joint concurring opinion,[244] this does not, implicitly, realistically apply the Court's own direction in *Al-Skeini*[245] and referred to in *Jaloud*, and it explicitly presents difficulties in demonstrating the legal basis for claiming control over the body, escalating tensions and provoking confrontation. In respect of the conduct of the autopsy in *Jaloud*, the judges conclude: 'Is this not an example of concrete constraints which may compel the use of less effective measures of investigation?'[246]

The extent to which a failure to conduct a thorough autopsy would, taken in isolation, render the entire investigation flawed to the degree that it constituted a violation of the state's procedural duty would depend upon whether it was necessary to definitively determine the cause of death. In cases where the UK accepts causing the death, the issue becomes, first, not how the death was caused but rather whether the soldier acted within their rules of engagement, and second, whether the rules of engagement were in accordance with the applicable international humanitarian law. To this extent, the evidential value of an autopsy is limited. Ultimately, however, in the planning of military operations overseas, the ability to conduct a thorough autopsy should be accommodated. The requirement to conduct an autopsy is not, however, specifically recognized in UK military medical doctrine.[247]

4.10.4.5 Powers of military investigators

The powers of UK military police are identical to those of civilian police officers, and military investigations are governed by the Police and Criminal Evidence Act 1984.[248] As such, the military police have sufficient powers to conduct an effective investigation into an alleged violation of the right to life. Without adequate specialist training, however, the mere existence of the statutory power to conduct an investigation is meaningless. In the UK Royal Military Police the basic training package lasts thirty-five weeks.[249] Those responsible for leading an investigation following an allegation of a violation of the right to life would be members of the Special Investigation Branch, who receive specialist accredited training in serious crime and

[242] Ibid, 215. [243] Ibid, 214.

[244] *Jaloud v the Netherlands*, Joint Concurring Opinion of Judges Casadevall, Berro-Lefevre, Šikuta, Hirvelä, López Guerra, Sajó and Silvis, 6.

[245] *Al-Skeini and Others v the United Kingdom* 168.

[246] *Jaloud v the Netherlands*, Joint Concurring Opinion of Judges Casadevall, Berro-Lefevre, Šikuta, Hirvelä, López Guerra, Sajó and Silvis, 6.

[247] Joint Doctrine Publication 4-03, Joint Medical Doctrine.

[248] Police and Criminal Evidence Act 1984 s 113. Armed Forces Act 2006, Part 3

[249] Information provided at <http://www.army.mod.uk/documents/general/proRmpRecruitment.pdf> (accessed 9 April 2015).

crime scene investigation.[250] In theory, therefore, the powers and training of those UK military police officers responsible for investigating alleged violations of the right to life are sufficient to comply with the procedural element of the right to life.

In respect of the right to life, the only area of potential difficulty would arise when an allegation of murder or manslaughter was made against a member of the military police. Following the judgment in *Ali Zaki Mousa (No 1)*,[251] the allegation would have to be investigated by Special Investigation Branch officers from another branch of the armed forces in order to maintain the requisite levels of independence.

4.10.5 Public scrutiny of military police investigation reports

A military investigation forms an integral part of the wider military justice system and, where a case is tried by court martial, this is conducted in public and only subject to *in camera* proceedings where it is necessary or expedient to do so.[252] The police investigation report will not be generally available to the public, but redacted elements may be given to the next of kin, and where criminal conduct or that requiring disciplinary action is alleged it will be reviewed and assessed by the independent Service Prosecuting Authority with a view to the prosecution of those involved.[253] As the requirement for public scrutiny of military investigation reports is not absolute,[254] it is unlikely that the non-disclosure of a military police investigation report is, in isolation, sufficient to contravene the procedural element of the right to life where the report has been reviewed by an independent prosecutorial body such as the UK Service Prosecuting Authority. There is an additional safeguard to further guarantee independence, in that the Service Prosecuting Authority's decision not to prosecute can be subject to judicial review by the Divisional Court. The criteria for an application for judicial review are numerous; however, it is typically used in this context where a prosecutorial body fails to follow its own guidelines.[255]

4.10.6 Involvement of victim's next of kin in military police criminal investigations

The involvement of the victim's next of kin is not an absolute requirement, but they must be 'involved in the procedure to the extent necessary to safeguard his or her legitimate interests'.[256] Where there has been an allegation of murder or manslaughter committed by a member of the UK armed forces, the victim's next of kin

[250] Information provided at <https://www.army.mod.uk/rolefinder/role/193/military-police-detective> (accessed 9 April 2015).

[251] *R (on the application of Ali Zaki Mousa) v Secretary of State for Defence and Equality and Human Rights Commission* [2011] EWCA Civ 1334 36–38.

[252] Armed Forces (Court Martial) Rules 2009 rule 153(1).

[253] The wider military justice system will be considered at 4.13.

[254] *Al-Skeini and Others v the United Kingdom* 167.

[255] *R v DPP, ex parte C* [1995] 1 Cr App R 136.

[256] *Ahmet Özkan and Others v Turkey* 311–14; *Isayeva v Russia* 211–14; *Al-Skeini and Others v the United Kingdom* 167; *Güleç v Turkey* 82; *Oğur v Turkey* 92; *McKerr v the United Kingdom* 148.

are treated in accordance with the code of practice on services to be provided by the armed forces to victims of crime.[257] While as a matter of strict policy the code does not apply during military operations overseas, wherever possible the 'spirit of the code'[258] should apply. The code also covers circumstances where the action of the member of the armed forces 'led, or was intended or likely to lead to the person's death or to cause physical or mental injury to the victim',[259] therefore bringing an alleged violation of the right to life within the ambit of the code.

The Service Prosecuting Authority is bound by the code of practice and therefore required to provide information on the decision to prosecute an alleged perpetrator and, once initiated, the progress of the case. In practice, where there is a prosecution in these circumstances, the next of kin are informed of the progress of the case. This has occurred, inter alia, during the court martial proceedings[260] against Cpl Donald Payne and others in relation to the death of Mr Baha Mousa.

It is not necessary to import the entire panoply of rights and duties contained in the victim's code in order to comply with the requirement to involve the victim's next of kin in the proceedings to the extent necessary to safeguard their legitimate interests—not least of all because it could involve, if applied strictly, civilians who provide counselling services, for example, being required to deploy overseas and provide their services in a dangerous, volatile, and hostile environment. Rather, a diluted version of the code in which the next of kin are kept informed of the progress of any investigation through a military liaison officer, as the UK armed forces presently do, would, it is submitted, comply with the requirement to involve the victim's next of kin in the investigation.

It is likely that, in terms of providing sufficient means to conduct an independent and impartial investigation, the UK has the resources available to comply with the procedural requirements of the right to life. The extent to which they are utilized would be dependent upon establishing robust doctrine and standard operating procedures.

4.10.7 Service inquiry

In the event of death or serious injury to any person while in the custody[261] of UK armed forces, a statutory requirement exists to convene a service inquiry.[262] This

[257] This can be found at <https://www.gov.uk/government/uploads/system/uploads/attachment_data/file/190877/jsp839.pdf> (accessed 9 April 2015).

[258] Joint Service Publication 839, Code of practice on services to be provided by the Armed Forces to victims of crime, 4.4.

[259] Ibid, 4.2(b).

[260] The following charges were brought in those proceedings: Cpl Donald Payne—manslaughter, inhumane treatment of persons, perverting the course of justice; L/Cpl Wayne Crowcroft—inhumane treatment of persons; Pte Darren Fallon—inhumane treatment of persons; Sgt Kelvin Stacey—actual bodily harm, alternatively assault; Warrant Officer Mark Davies—negligently performing a duty; Maj Michael Peebles—negligently performing a duty; Col Jorge Mendonca—negligently performing a duty.

[261] What is meant by custody, control of a person, and the limits of jurisdiction is considered in Chapter 3.

[262] Armed Forces Act 2006, s 343, Armed Forces (Service Inquiries) Regulations 2008, regulation 4 (1) (b).

requirement extends to operational theatres.[263] A service inquiry can run independently of any military police criminal investigation. It is therefore necessary to assess the extent to which a service inquiry can comply with the procedural element of the right to life both in isolation and as part of a wider investigatory process.

4.10.7.1 Hierarchical, practical, and institutional independence of the service inquiry

Service inquiries lack any degree of hierarchical, practical, or institutional independence. The decision to initiate a service inquiry, while regulated by statute, is taken by a military officer in the chain of command of those involved in the death.[264] The service inquiry is conducted by members of the armed forces, who, unlike military police officers, are not independent of the chain of command.[265] The final service inquiry report is reviewed by senior officers, and can be amended prior to publication.[266]

Notwithstanding these significant limitations, other elements of the service inquiry process provide those conducting the investigation with wide-ranging authority to fully investigate the circumstances surrounding, for example, a death in military custody, and make recommendations as to referral for criminal investigation or closing down detention facilities. The powers of those conducting a service inquiry are derived from statute[267] and include the power to require that evidence is given on oath, the power to compel the attendance of witnesses through the issue of a summons by a judge advocate,[268] and the ability to secure the entitlement that the affected person(s) are present during the service inquiry process.[269] Furthermore, service inquiries are allocated significant financial resources,[270] have access to legal advice, and can commission reports from any independent expert in order to determine the cause of death. This can include access to independent medical and forensic experts.

4.10.7.2 Public scrutiny of the service inquiry report

Redacted versions of high-profile service inquiry reports that remove the names of those involved in the incident are published by the UK government on the internet[271] and are available for widespread public scrutiny. Other service inquiry reports

[263] Joint Service Publication 832, Guide to Service Inquiries, 120(a) (b).

[264] The Armed Forces (Service Inquiries) Regulations 2008—Regulation 3(1), 3(2), JSP 832, 2.4: 'The convening authority will normally be in the chain of command of the ship/unit/establishment or the personnel involved in the matter to be investigated.'

[265] JSP 832, 2.13, The Armed Forces (Service Inquiries) Regulations 2008—Regulation 6.

[266] The Armed Forces (Service Inquiries) Regulations 2008—Regulation 19(1).

[267] Armed Forces Act 2006, s 343, The Armed Forces (Service Inquiries) Regulations 2008.

[268] The Armed Forces (Service Inquiries) Regulations 2008—Regulation 13.

[269] The Armed Forces (Service Inquiries) Regulations 2008—Regulation 18.

[270] JSP 832, 2.44: 'An inquiry should not be constrained on the grounds of cost'.

[271] Examples of service inquiries can be found at <https://www.gov.uk/government/collections/service-inquiry-si>.

are available through the UK freedom of information process.[272] To this extent, service inquiries undoubtedly comply with the discrete element of an effective investigation as defined by the ECtHR.[273]

4.10.7.3 Involvement of next of kin in the service inquiry process

A positive aspect of the service inquiry process is the ability for the next of kin to be involved.[274] To this extent, service inquiries comply with this discrete element of an effective investigation as required by the ECtHR.[275]

4.10.7.4 Compliance of the service inquiry process with the procedural element of the right to life

It is clear that service inquiries are not, and do not purport to be, fully compliant with the procedural element of the right to life.[276] Notwithstanding, with some modification enabling independence from the military chain of command, they would be an effective way of complying with the investigatory element of a state's procedural right to life obligations. Due to the information they adduce not being admissible in criminal proceedings, they would not contribute towards the 'punishment [in a criminal sense] of any alleged perpetrator'.[277] Ultimately, therefore, in their present form they are of limited value in ensuring that a state fully complies with its procedural right to life obligations.

4.11 UK Military Justice System

In *Al-Skeini*, the ECtHR restated the requirement that 'any investigation must be effective in the sense that it is capable of leading to a determination of whether the force used was or was not justified in the circumstances and to the identification and *punishment* of those responsible' [my emphasis].[278] When members of the UK

[272] JSP 832, 7.8: 'under the terms of the Freedom of Information Act, every public authority must "adopt and maintain" a Publication Scheme setting out the classes of information it already publishes or intends to publish proactively. Publication Schemes must be kept under review and in deciding what to publish the Act requires authorities to "have regard to the public interest" in the information they hold. Every Publication Scheme must be approved by the Information Commissioner, and the addition of new classes of information is therefore notified to the Commissioner's office to confirm the commitment.' Service inquiry reports are deemed to come within this publication scheme.

[273] *Ahmet Özkan and Others v Turkey* 311–14; *Isayeva v Russia* 211–14; *Al-Skeini and Others v the United Kingdom* 167; *Güleç v Turkey* 82; *Oğur v Turkey* 92; *McKerr v the United Kingdom* 148.

[274] The Armed Forces (Service Inquiries) Regulations 2008—Regulation 17(2).

[275] *Ahmet Özkan and Others v Turkey* 311–14, *Isayeva v Russia* 211–14; *Al-Skeini and Others v the United Kingdom* 167; *Güleç v Turkey* 82; *Oğur v Turkey* 92; *McKerr v the United Kingdom* 148.

[276] JSP 832, Appendix 1, para 1(b): 'It does not replace a Coroner's Inquest and is not, and does not purport to be, a tribunal that is compliant with Article 2 of the European Convention on Human Rights.'

[277] *Hugh Jordan v the United Kingdom* 141.

[278] *Al-Skeini and Others v the United Kingdom* 166.

armed forces operate overseas, the available methods of punishment come either through the military disciplinary or administrative processes. The disciplinary process is governed by the Armed Forces Act 2006 and culminates in trial by court martial. The administrative process is governed by the principles of employment law and regulated by tri-service[279] policy. Where a violation of the right to life is alleged that amounted to murder, in that there was no justification for the killing under international humanitarian law, the matter would fall within the disciplinary sphere and ultimately be tried by court martial. The extent to which the court martial system and appellate structure comply with the procedural element of Article 2 has been examined within this context by the ECtHR[280] and must be considered here.

The decision on whether or not to prosecute an allegation of murder committed during armed conflict is made by the Director of Service Prosecutions[281] at the Service Prosecuting Authority. In the past, the commanding officer of the individual against whom serious allegations[282] had been made had the discretion not to forward the case for prosecution if they considered it was not necessary to do so. This obvious failing was criticized by the ECtHR[283] and rectified by the Armed Forces Act 2006.[284] In respect of serious allegations, the case cannot be considered by the commanding officer and will be referred directly from the service or civilian police investigating the allegation to the Director of Service Prosecutions in all circumstances.[285]

The Service Prosecuting Authority was established in response to the cumulative effect of a number of criticisms of the ECtHR, due to the lack of independence and impartiality in the UK military justice system.[286] As such, its senior prosecutor and director is an experienced civilian lawyer who is entirely independent of the military chain of command and accountable only to the Attorney General for the conduct of cases. The Director of Service Prosecutions has wide-ranging statutory powers to bring charges independent of the military chain of command and can act with complete autonomy.[287] A decision not to prosecute a case is subject to judicial review by the Divisional Court and, as a consequence, a further independent safeguard exists. It is therefore likely that once a case arrives at the Service Prosecuting Authority there is a sufficient degree of independence in the prosecutorial decision-making process not to contravene the procedural element of Article 2. This independence was confirmed by the domestic courts in *Ali Zaki Mousa (No 1)*.[288] Following a decision to prosecute a case, it enters the military justice system.

279 Tri-service refers to the Royal Navy (including Royal Marines), Army, and Royal Air Force.

280 *Jaloud v the Netherlands* 195–96.

281 The current Director of Service Prosecutions at the time of writing is Andrew Cayley QC.

282 Serious allegations are defined and listed in Schedule 2 of the Armed Forces Act 2006.

283 *Findlay v the United Kingdom*, Application no 39685/98 (ECtHR, 3 March 1997).

284 ss 113–18, Armed Forces Act 2006.

285 s 116(2)(a), Armed Forces Act 2006.

286 *Findlay v United Kingdom* [1997] 24 EHRR 221; *Martin v United Kingdom* [2007] 44 EHRR 31; *Grieves v United Kingdom* [2004], Application no 57067/00, para 69.

287 ss 121, 122, 125, 126, Armed Forces Act 2006.

288 *R (on the application of Ali Zaki Mousa) v Secretary of State for Defence and Equality and Human Rights Commission* [2010] EWHC 3304 (Admin), 67.

The military justice system consists of first instance trial by court martial, then appeal to the Court Martial Appeal Court,[289] thereafter to the Supreme Court, and ultimately, on ECHR matters, to the ECtHR. In *Jaloud*,[290] the ECtHR made an assessment of the independence of the Netherlands Military Chamber of the Court of Appeal due to the presence of one military member on its three-person panel. It concluded that because the military member was not subject to 'military authority and discipline' their functional independence and impartiality were the same as a civilian judge's, and therefore they were sufficiently independent for the purposes of Article 2, ECHR.[291] In other circumstances,[292] however, the ECtHR

> has found that . . . courts do not fulfill the requirement of independence imposed by Article 6, ECHR of the Convention, due to the presence of a military judge whose participation gives rise to legitimate fears that the court may be unduly influenced by considerations which had nothing to do with the nature of the case.[293]

Notwithstanding the reference to Article 6, ECHR above, it is contended that for the purposes of an assessment of the independence in respect of the procedural element of Article 2, ECHR, the analysis is the same as that of the ECtHR in *Jaloud*[294] with specific reference to the requirement of 'functional independence and impartiality'. As such, the independence and impartiality of the UK court martial must be considered.

In respect of the UK court martial system, the panel deciding upon guilt or innocence consists entirely of military officers, with a civilian judge advocate presiding.[295] The independence and impartiality of this system in respect of the composition of the court martial has been challenged unsuccessfully on Article 6, ECHR grounds, namely that the court martial members were all military officers and therefore could not be independent of the military chain of command.[296] The ECtHR considered that the military officers were sufficiently independent of the chain of command due to the clear directions given to them by the judge advocate in respect of their oath and deliberations, the possibility of a prosecution for perverting the course of justice under the common law for any officer using their superior rank to unduly influence another court martial member, and the fact that the court martial members could not be reported upon for their decision in a court martial.[297] Given the further safeguards inherent in the Court Martial Appeal Court, which consists of three civilian Court of Appeal or High Court judges, has no military representatives, and can hear cases on procedural or substantive grounds, it is likely that this element of the military justice system complies with the procedural element of the right to life as considered in *Jaloud*.

[289] The Court Martial Appeal Court sits in the Royal Courts of Justice and is akin to the Criminal Division of the Court of Appeal. It can hear appeals from court martial on conviction or sentence.

[290] *Jaloud v the Netherlands* 195–96.

[291] Ibid, 196.

[292] *Incal v Turkey*, judgment of 9 June 1998, *Reports* 1998-IV, 1571–73, §§ 65–73.

[293] *Akkoç v Turkey*, Application nos 22947/93 and 22948/93 (10 October 2000) 90.

[294] *Jaloud v the Netherlands* 195–96.

[295] s 155(1)(a) AFA 06 in response to the ECtHR judgment in *Grieves v United Kingdom*, 69.

[296] *Cooper v the United Kingdom* [2003] Application no 48843/99, 119–26.

[297] See also Lord Bingham in *R v Boyd* 18 July 2002 [2002] UKHL 31, 15.

Where a future challenge based upon Article 2, ECHR may be successful is not in the composition of the court martial, but rather in the voting regulations they adopt.

In the court martial system the determination of guilt or innocence is on a simple majority basis of the voting members, namely the military officers present.[298] In cases of murder this would be either five[299] or, more likely, seven[300] officers. This is compared to the UK civilian court system, where, in the Crown Court of England and Wales, the jury of twelve members is required at the outset to reach a unanimous verdict.[301] If this is not possible, after a minimum of two hours[302] the judge may issue a majority verdict direction that must be complied with.[303] When this is given, the verdict of the jury need not be unanimous if, in a case where there are not fewer than eleven jurors, ten of them agree on the verdict,[304] or, in a case where there are ten jurors, nine of them agree on the verdict.[305] As a consequence this creates a high threshold upon which to establish guilt. Recognizing that the offence under consideration at a court martial or in the Crown Court would be exactly the same, namely murder, the unfairness is immediately apparent, in that the threshold at which a member of the armed forces could be acquitted in the court martial is significantly lower. This issue has been considered by the Court of Appeal,[306] which held that, based on the ECtHR judgments[307] in which the Court considered the court martial system to be incompatible with Article 6 on alternative grounds,[308] the fact that it made no comment *obiter* on the issue of the voting regime does not conclusively determine that this element of the process is compatible with Article 6.[309]

[298] s 160 Armed Forces Act 06:

(1) Subject to the following provisions of this section, the finding of the Court Martial on a charge, and any sentence passed by it, must be determined by a majority of the votes of the members of the court.
(2) The Judge Advocate is not entitled to vote on the finding.
(3) In the case of inequality of votes on the finding the court must acquit the defendant.
(4) In the case of inequality of votes on sentence, the Judge Advocate has a casting vote.

[299] s 155(2)(a) Armed Forces Act 06 and Armed Forces (Court Martial) Rules 2009 rule 29 —this includes serious offences as listed in schedule 2 Armed Forces Act 06 and offences for which the defendant, if found guilty, would be sentenced to at least seven years imprisonment.

[300] s 155(2)(a) Armed Forces Act 06 and Armed Forces (Court Martial) Rules 2009 rule 30.

[301] s 17 Juries Act 1974 and Practice Direction (Criminal Proceedings: Consolidation), IV.46.1 [2000] 1 WLR 2870.

[302] s 17(4) Juries Act 1974. In practice, the minimum period is two hours and ten minutes: Judicial Studies Board, Crown Court Bench Book, March 2010, p 388.

[303] *R v Georgiou*, 53 Cr AR 428, CA; *R v Barry*, 61 Cr AR 172.

[304] s 17(1)(a) Juries Act 1974. [305] s 17(1)(b) Juries Act 1974.

[306] *R v Twaite* [2010] EWCA Crim 2973, 24–29; *Blackman v Secretary of State for Defence* [2014] EWCA Crim 1029, 18–24.

[307] *Martin v United Kingdom; Findlay v United Kingdom*.

[308] In *Martin v United Kingdom* the court concluded that 'the composition, structure and procedure of the applicant's court-martial were in themselves sufficient to raise in him a legitimate fear as to its lack of independence and impartiality'. In *Findlay v United Kingdom* the appointment of members and composition of the court violated Article 6 due to the influence that could be brought to bear by the senior officer and the fact that the members of the court martial were within the same chain of command.

[309] *R v Twaite* 26.

Recalling the ECtHR's judgments in *Bryan*[310] and *Pullar*,[311] the independence and impartiality of a tribunal must be both objectively and subjectively justifiable.[312] If litigated within the context of Article 2, ECHR, the composition of the court martial combined with the relative ease with which fellow members of the armed forces may arrive at a not guilty verdict, conceivably due to having a degree of sympathy with the defendant given the demanding circumstances within which the murder took place, could result in a lack of subjective independence. It is equally significant that this issue could not be resolved by way of appeal to the Court Martial Appeal Court, as the person alleging the violation of Article 2 is entitled to a first instance tribunal, not an appellate structure that complies with the requirements of Article 2.[313] This lack of subjective independence could be easily resolved by trying matters that involve an allegation of murder committed by members of the armed forces during armed conflict in the Crown Court. At present, it is arguable that the court martial system would not comply fully with the procedural element of Article 2 as considered and elucidated in *Jaloud*. Moreover, the fact that a court martial has been conducted with regard to, for example, a death in custody during armed conflict does not necessarily comply with the procedural element of Article 2. Those considered responsible for the death of Mr Baha Mousa while in UK armed forces custody in Iraq were tried by court martial,[314] yet a public inquiry was convened that examined, inter alia, the court martial proceedings.

4.12 Public Inquiry

The UK government has ordered public inquiries, under the Inquiries Act 2005, on two occasions in respect of the activities of UK armed forces during Operation Telic II in Iraq that took place from 2003 onwards. The inquiries relate directly to alleged violations of the substantive and procedural elements of the right to life.

On 14 May 2008, the Secretary of State for Defence appointed a retired judge, Sir William Gage, to conduct a public inquiry into the death of Mr Baha Mousa, who died on 14 September 2003 while in the custody of UK armed forces. The terms of reference for the inquiry were as follows:

> To investigate and report on the circumstances surrounding the death of Baha Mousa and the treatment of those detained with him, taking account of the investigations which have already taken place, in particular where responsibility lay for approving the practice of conditioning

[310] *Bryan v the United Kingdom*, judgment of 22 November 1995, Series A no 335-A, p 15, 37.

[311] *Pullar v the United Kingdom*, judgment of 10 June 1996, Reports 1996-III, p 792, 30.

[312] See also, *mutatis mutandis, Sramek v Austria*, judgment of 22 October 1984, Series A no 84, p 20, 42 and, *mutatis mutandis, Van de Hurk v the Netherlands*, judgment of 19 April 1994, Series A no 288, p 16, 45.

[313] See, *mutatis mutandis, De Cubber v Belgium*, judgment of 26 October 1984, Series A no 86, pp 16–18, 31–32.

[314] *R v Donald Payne and Others*, unreported, 2008.

detainees by any members of the 1st Battalion, The Queen's Lancashire Regiment in Iraq in 2003, and to make recommendations.[315]

The report was published on 8 September 2011, ran to three volumes, and made seventy-three recommendations. It considered in detail issues relating to international humanitarian law and right to life obligations including government policy and higher-level doctrine, training provided to those handling detainees, military commands and orders in respect of the treatment of detainees, soldiers' cards regulating the use of force, and interrogation techniques, tactics, and procedures. In *Al-Skeini*, the ECtHR recognized that a full public inquiry into the death of Mr Baha Mousa complied with the UK government's procedural obligations under Article 2.[316]

A requirement for a second public inquiry was conceded by the Secretary of State for Defence during proceedings in the Divisional Court[317] in respect of further allegations—brought by relatives of Mr Hamid Al-Sweady—of mistreatment or unlawful killing by UK armed forces in Iraq. This public inquiry was established on 29 November 2009, conducted by Sir Thayne Forbes, and the report was published on 17 December 2014. The terms of reference for the inquiry were as follows:

> To investigate and report on the allegations made by the claimants in the Al-Sweady judicial review proceedings against British soldiers of (1) unlawful killing at Camp Abu Naji on 14 and 15 May 2004, and (2) the ill-treatment of five Iraqi nationals detained at Camp Abu Naji and subsequently at the divisional temporary detention facility at Shaibah Logistics Base between 14 May and 23 September 2004, taking account of the investigations which have already taken place, and to make recommendations.[318]

Sir Thayne Forbes rejected most of the allegations made. He did, however, inter alia, make specific recommendations in respect of the shooting incident review policy in the following terms:

> A Shooting Incident Policy should be drafted which is achievable in practice in Theatre, which is compliant with Article 2 of the ECHR and which enables the ascertainment of the relevant facts leading up to, during and consequent upon the Shooting Incident by an independent body such as the Royal Military Police within a time limited but reasonable period after the Shooting Incident.[319]

The UK policy for shooting incident review and the associated procedures are considered at 4.10.2. The public inquiry report also made a specific recommendation in relation to the training of armed forces personnel to enable the UK to comply with its right to life obligations: not only must the training (in the lawful use of

[315] Terms of reference are at <http://webarchive.nationalarchives.gov.uk/20120215203912/http://www.bahamousainquiry.org/index.htm>.

[316] *Al-Skeini and Others v the United Kingdom* 176.

[317] *R (Al-Sweady) v Secretary of State for Defence* [2009] EWHC 2387 (Admin).

[318] Terms of reference are at <http://webarchive.nationalarchives.gov.uk/20150115114702/http:/www.alsweadyinquiry.org/> (accessed 3 May 2015).

[319] The report of the Al Sweady Public Inquiry, Appendix 7, recommendation 4, 1115 <http://webarchive.nationalarchives.gov.uk/20150115114702/http://www.alsweadyinquiry.org/linkedfiles/alsweadyinquiry/theal-sweadyinquiryreport-volume2part2.pdf> (accessed 3 May 2015).

lethal force in armed conflict pursuant to the state's international humanitarian law obligations) take place, but it must be well documented and recorded in order to establish an auditable trial in the event of future litigation. The report recommended thus: 'All training material should be dated, appropriately retained and archived in such a way that it can easily be established when the training material was composed, when it came into force and the period during which it remained in force.'[320] Notwithstanding the judgment in *Al-Skeini* that determined a public inquiry complies with the procedural element of Article 2,[321] taken in isolation, a contradiction arises within the case. At paragraph 166 in *Al-Skeini* the ECtHR restated the requirement that 'any investigation must be effective in the sense that it is capable of leading to a determination of whether the force used was or was not justified in the circumstances and to the identification and ***punishment*** of those responsible' [my emphasis].[322] A public inquiry does not, however, have any power to make any determination in respect of any person's criminal or civil liability.[323] In order to punish an individual or individuals that were prima facie liable as state agents for a state's violation of the right to life, a further judicial hearing would have to take place. Within the context of the armed forces this would be a trial by court martial or criminal proceedings in the Crown Court or International Criminal Court. Clearly this would only be relevant in respect of an alleged violation of the substantive element of the right to life.

A public inquiry has no prosecutorial function or mandate to make a determination of criminal wrongdoing. It can, however, make recommendations regarding further criminal investigation of issues that have arisen during the proceedings. Such recommendations were made by Sir William Gage in the Baha Mousa public inquiry and have been endorsed and adopted by the government. In relation to activities of the UK armed forces in Iraq that may have violated the UK's right to life obligations, the investigation and potential prosecution of these allegations is being considered by the Iraq Historic Allegations Team (IHAT) and the Iraq Historic Allegations Prosecution Team (IHAPT) at the Service Prosecuting Authority.

4.13 Iraq Historic Allegations Team—The Role of the Iraq Historic Allegations Team

The establishment of the IHAT was announced to Parliament on 1 March 2010. Its purpose was, inter alia, 'to review and investigate allegations of abuse of Iraqi civilians by UK armed forces personnel in Iraq during the period of 2003 to July 2009'.[324] These allegations included, inter alia, murder and manslaughter, and covered the period during which UK armed forces were in military occupation of Iraq; therefore, both the substantive and procedural elements of the right to life needed to

320 Ibid. 321 *Al-Skeini and Others v the United Kingdom* 176. 322 Ibid 166.

323 s 2(1), Inquiries Act 2005.

324 Purpose of IHAT, cited at <https://www.gov.uk/government/groups/iraq-historic-allegations-team-ihat> (accessed 3 May 2015).

be addressed by the investigations. Beyond the deaths examined in the Baha Mousa public inquiry, evidence had been adduced to support the assertion that several Iraqi citizens died while in UK custody. This evidence included fragmentary orders[325] from UK legal advisers in Iraq at the material time.[326] It is indisputable that there was prima facie evidence to suggest that violations of the right to life had occurred while individuals were within the 'jurisdiction' of UK armed forces. These alleged violations needed to be investigated.

IHAT specifically recognized its human rights obligations to 'work with investigative independence but in partnership with other key organisations to deliver an effective criminal investigation into allegations of murder, abuse and torture. This is a vital constituent part of the UK's obligation to conduct a European Court of Human Rights (ECHR) compliant investigation into these allegations'.[327] The IHAT investigations closed on 30 June 2017 and the remaining investigations were reintegrated into the military police system under the auspices of the Service Police Legacy Investigations (SPLI). At the time of closure there were around 20 cases under investigation.[328]

4.13.1 Composition, independence, and criticisms of IHAT

As a consequence of litigation, the composition of IHAT was modified after its inception. In *Ali Zaki Mousa (No 1)*[329] the Court of Appeal held that the involvement in the IHAT process of Royal Military Police, many of whom had been present in Iraq at the material time, did not comply with the procedural requirement for independence. In their assessment of the scope of independence, the Court of Appeal relied on the ECtHR judgment in *Jordan* that stated: 'it may generally be regarded as necessary for the persons responsible for and carrying out the investigations to be independent from those implicated in the events. This means not only a lack of hierarchical or institutional connection but also a practical independence.'[330]

[325] 'Fragmentary Orders [FRAGO] are used to send timely changes of existing orders to subordinate and supporting commanders while providing notification to higher and adjacent commands. It is an abbreviated form of an operation order (verbal, written or digital) usually issued on a day-to-day basis that eliminates the need for restating information contained in a basic operation order. It may be issued in sections. It is issued after an operation order to change or modify that order or to execute a branch or sequel to that order.' This is the US Department of Defense definition, which is also accepted by NATO forces, including the UK.

[326] Fragmentary Order 152, issued by Lt Col Nicholas Mercer, stated: 'There have recently been a number of deaths in custody where Iraqi civilians have died whilst being held by various units in Theatre. At the same time, the ICRC have advised that they have received a number of complaints about the handling of detainees by coalition forces. A number of these cases are currently being investigated by the SIB [Special Investigation Branch] but all units in Theatre are to ensure that all persons detained by UK Services Personnel are treated with humanity and dignity at all times': <https://www.bahamousainquiry.org/linkedfiles/baha_mousa/baha_mousa_inquiry_evidence/evidence_180310/mod019145.pdf> (accessed 3 May 2015).

[327] Ibid.

[328] Iraq Historic Allegations Team (IHAT) Quarterly Update—October to December 2014, dated 15 February 2015, https://www.gov.uk/government/uploads/system/uploads/attachment_data/file/411437/20150216-Qupdate_Oct_Dec2015.pdf (accessed 3 May 2015).

[329] *R (on the application of Ali Zaki Mousa and Others) v Secretary of State for Defence and another* [2011] EWCA Civ 1334.

[330] *Jordan v the United Kingdom* 106.

The Court of Appeal further refined the issue by focusing on the requirement for independence as a matter of perception, citing Lord Steyn's comment that 'public perception of the possibility of unconscious bias is the key'.[331] In doing so it is arguable that the Court of Appeal elevated the requirement for independence beyond that required by the ECtHR. As a consequence of the judgment in *Ali Zaki Mousa (No 1)*, all Royal Military Police investigators were removed from IHAT and replaced by Royal Navy[332] or civilian police investigators.

Within IHAT there was an investigation team dedicated specifically to the investigation of deaths that are attributable to UK armed forces both within UK-controlled detention facilities and outside. At its inception, the UK government stated that the latter category would be without prejudice to any substantive or procedural right to life obligations. In light of the Divisional Court judgment in *Al-Saadoon and Others*,[333] this position is no longer supportable, as the Divisional Court clearly stated that the UK's jurisdiction at the time under consideration by IHAT extended to circumstances in the British-controlled areas of Iraq outside military compounds and detention facilities.

The independence of IHAT was subject to further scrutiny in *Ali Zaki Mousa (No 2)*,[334] where it was claimed that the reconstituted IHAT was not sufficiently independent due to the presence of military (Royal Navy) investigators and that, even if it were, it was inevitable that a public inquiry would be necessary and thus one should be established immediately.[335] The Court concluded that the reconstituted IHAT was sufficiently independent for the purposes of Article 2, ECHR in that the Royal Navy police were sufficiently independent to discharge their duties as they were outside the military chain of command, they had not served in Iraq at the material time, and their investigations were particularly thorough.[336] In addition, the Court concluded that the prosecutorial function vested in the Director of Service Prosecutions was sufficiently independent, save for a discrete issue in respect of the Royal Navy police disciplinary chain of command that has subsequently been addressed by the Royal Navy.[337]

Despite concluding that the reconstituted IHAT was sufficiently independent for the purposes of Article 2, the Court was critical of the extent to which IHAT has discharged its investigative duty. In order to aid its analysis, the Court divided the cases being investigated by IHAT into three categories, thus:

[331] *Lawal v Northern Spirit Ltd* [2003] ICR 856, 14.

[332] This was communicated by the Minister of State at the Ministry of Defence to Parliament on 26 March 2012 and was complete by 1 April 2012.

[333] *Al-Saadoon and Others v Secretary of State for Defence* 294.

[334] *R (on the application of Ali Zaki Mousa and Others) v Secretary of State for Defence and another No 2* [2013] EWHC 1412 (Admin).

[335] Ibid, 27. [336] Ibid, 108–14.

[337] Royal Navy police assigned to IHAT are now within the disciplinary chain of command of the Provost Martial Navy, who is independent of the Royal Navy command. The Royal Navy IHAT investigators had previously been within the disciplinary chain of command of Royal Navy command and this situation attracted adverse comment by the court in *Ali Zaki Mousa No 2*, at 122–23.

1. cases where there will be no IHAT investigation, and so no prospect of any further prosecution ('Category 1 cases');
2. cases where there has been a previous prosecution and IHAT is now investigating or is about to investigate with a view to considering whether there should be a prosecution ('Category 2 cases');[338]
3. cases where there has been no previous prosecution and IHAT is now investigating or about to investigate whether there should be a prosecution ('Category 3 cases').[339]

In respect of category 1, the Court concluded that there was no impediment to further investigations and this ought to be conducted expeditiously. In respect of category 2, the Court concluded that the likelihood of any further prosecutions was remote due to the ten years that had elapsed since the deaths and the remote prospect of there being any forensic evidence to support any prosecutions. It invited the Director of Service Prosecutions to make an expeditious determination in respect of these cases. In respect of category 3, the Court proposed an inquisitorial framework in which to more efficiently progress these cases and therefore discharge the state's Article 2 obligations.

The Divisional Court further held that, where a prosecution is undertaken, the state's Article 2 duty is complied with. In cases where it has already been determined that there will not be a prosecution, however, the court considered that the state's 'full Article 2 duties would not have been performed'.[340] Despite a coroner's inquest into one of the deaths under consideration (Mr Naheem Abdullah) in which it was concluded there was no case to answer, the Divisional Court held that—as the jurisdiction of UK coroners does not extend to deaths abroad[341]—notwithstanding a coroner's inquest being an ECHR-compliant inquiry, it could not be used to comply with the UK's Article 2 obligations where there was not a prosecution. The Court then provided guidance as to how IHAT could comply with the UK's Article 2 obligations. The Court identified the material factors in respect of the investigations into deaths in Iraq that fell within the UK's jurisdiction as, first, establishment of the facts;[342] second, the very serious nature of the allegations, namely, very serious misconduct by members of the armed forces;[343] third, systemic abuse and lack of training;[344] and, finally, the responsibility of command.[345] Having identified these factors, the Court concluded that IHAT was not discharging the state's Article 2 obligations for the following reasons: first, IHAT had failed to deal expeditiously

[338] This included the court-martial proceedings in respect of Mr Baha Mousa, as well as *R v Payne and Others*.

[339] *R (on the application of Ali Zaki Mousa and Others) v Secretary of State for Defence and another No 2* 152.

[340] Ibid, 169.

[341] *R (Middleton) v West Somerset Coroner* [2004] 2 AC 182, Coroners Act 1988, Coroners Rules 1984.

[342] *R (on the application of Ali Zaki Mousa and Others) v Secretary of State for Defence and another No 2*, 172.

[343] Ibid, 173. [344] Ibid, 174. [345] Ibid, 175.

with the decision to prosecute cases; second, IHAT was not accessible to the public; third, there had been no contact with next of kin during the IHAT process; finally, there was no evidence that IHAT was examining the wider issues of failures in training, supervision, and leadership of armed forces personnel during the Iraq campaign.[346]

4.13.2 Compliance with right to life obligations

In light of the criticisms of the divisional court in *Ali Zaki Mousa No 2*, IHAT was restructured to address the areas of concern. The resources available to IHAT were increased. A specific prosecution team, the IHAPT, was established under the control of the Director of Service Prosecutions to bring to court martial the investigations that have been concluded by IHAT where the evidential sufficiency and service interest tests were satisfied. Greater transparency was included in the process, with quarterly updates from IHAT being published, next of kin being involved, and consideration being given to wider institutional failings in training, supervision, and leadership.[347]

The delay in the overall investigatory process is likely to result in a significant number of cases never being prosecuted at court martial, and therefore the UK cannot be said to have discharged its Article 2 obligations in respect of those matters. IHAT concluded in 2017, some thirteen or fourteen months after the alleged incidents occurred. Furthermore, with respect to the completed investigations,[348] the victim's next of kin have not been involved to the extent necessary to safeguard their interests.[349] Again, any retrospective action in unlikely to rectify this failing, and thus the UK cannot be said to have discharged its Article 2 obligations in respect of these cases.

Where recent allegations have emerged and been reported to IHAT it may be possible to comply with the procedural requirement of Article 2, ECHR if these matters are processed in light of the criticisms in *Ali Zaki Mousa (No 2)*[350] and the guiding principles clearly elucidated by the ECtHR in *Al-Skeini*.[351] Recognizing that the Divisional Court has confirmed the independence of IHAT, it is essential that the outstanding allegations in respect of right to life violations that have been

[346] Ibid, 180–97.

[347] IHAT information is available at <https://www.gov.uk/government/groups/iraq-historic-allegations-team-ihat#baha-mousa-review-team> (accessed 3 May 2015).

[348] Seven allegations of unlawful killing have been closed following a pre-investigation without the next of kin being involved in the process. See <https://www.gov.uk/government/uploads/system/uploads/attachment_data/file/411437/20150216-Qupdate_Oct_Dec2015.pdf> (accessed 3 May 2015). Additionally, see the case of Ahmet Jabbar Kareem Ali referenced in *Ali Zaki Mousa No 2*, 147(i), 190.

[349] By April 2015, IHAT had completed ten investigations. See <https://www.gov.uk/government/uploads/system/uploads/attachment_data/file/421301/20150409-IHAT_work_completed_table_clean.pdf> (accessed 3 May 2015).

[350] *R (on the application of Ali Zaki Mousa and Others) v Secretary of State for Defence and another No 2*, 108–14.

[351] *Al Skeini v the United Kingdom* 167.

transferred into the military justice system are handled expeditiously, allow for the possibility of public scrutiny, and, where possible, involve the victim's next of kin. At the conclusion of IHAT there were around 900 outstanding allegations yet to be accepted by IHAT, of which, based on previous accepted cases, approximately 30 per cent could relate to right to life violations.[352]

4.13.3 IHAT relationship with the prosecutorial function

The prosecutorial function in respect of IHAT cases was conducted by the IHAPT under the control and supervision of the Director of Service Prosecutions at the Service Prosecuting Authority. The entire process was independent of the military chain of command, notwithstanding the involvement of military personnel in an investigatory role. The mere presence of military personnel in IHAT and IHAPT was not sufficient to impugn the independence of the process.[353] Cases under investigation by IHAT proceed directly to the IHAPT and did not involve the military chain of command or the commanding officer of the individual(s) against whom the allegations were made.[354]

4.14 Role of the Iraq Historic Allegation Prosecution Team

The IHAPT was an independent prosecutorial body charged solely with the prosecution of matters emerging from IHAT. The IHAPT was led by a Royal Navy barrister serving in the rank of Captain who was accountable to the Director of Service Prosecutions. The Royal Navy barrister was not in the military chain of command for reporting purposes and not within the Royal Navy chain of command for disciplinary purposes. Recognizing the observations of the Divisional Court in respect of Royal Navy police in *Ali Zaki Mousa No 2*, these measures werre sufficient to ensure the independence of this officer. The remainder of the IHAPT consisted of military lawyers who were outside the military chain of command and civilian lawyers who were not subject to the Armed Forces Act 2006 or military disciplinary procedures. As such, those charged with making prosecutorial decisions at every level were considered sufficiently independent with reference to the requirement for 'hierarchical, institutional, practical'[355] and arguably perceptional[356] independence. Once a case arrived at IHAPT, a standard prosecutorial assessment was made in relation to whether or not there was a realistic prospect of conviction and whether it was in the Service's interest[357] to proceed with the case. Again, the decision-making process within IHAPT

[352] Iraq Historic Allegations Team (IHAT) Quarterly Update—October to December 2014, dated 15 February 2015: <https://www.gov.uk/government/uploads/system/uploads/attachment_data/file/411437/20150216-Qupdate_Oct_Dec2015.pdf> (accessed 3 May 2015).

[353] *R (on the application of Ali Zaki Mousa and Others) v Secretary of State for Defence and another No 2*, 108–14.

[354] Schedule 2, Armed Forces Act 2006.

[355] *Jordan v the United Kingdom* 106.

[356] *Ali Zaki Mousa No 1.*

[357] This is the military equivalent of the public interest test.

complied with the procedural element of the right to life. Similarly, when a case is taken forward for prosecution at court martial the proceedings occur in public, and to this extent comply with an element of the procedural element of Article 2. The limitations of the court martial system are briefly considered at 4.12 and reveal some areas for potential challenge in respect of Article 2 compliance.

4.15 An Inquisitorial Approach at IHAT and the Right to Life

In *Ali Zaki Mousa No 2*, the President of the Queen's Bench Division and Mr Justice Silber extolled the virtues of an inquisitorial approach, adapted from that used in a coronial inquest, to the remaining cases at IHAT.[358] Their approach has much to be commended, as it would comply with the procedural requirements of the right to life by being accessible to next of kin, subject to public scrutiny, and sufficiently independent of the military chain of command. Unfortunately, it is not a panacea. If, during the course of an inquisitorial process, it became apparent that a prosecution should be brought, the process would have to be halted and a criminal investigation commenced. Rather than aiding the expeditious handling of cases, this would create yet further delay. An inquisitorial process could not satisfy the requirement for an individual to be prosecuted for their role in any violation of the right to life, and therefore is of limited utility.

4.16 IHAT's and IHAPT Relationship with the International Criminal Court

On 13 May 2014 the Prosecutor of the International Criminal Court, pursuant to Article 15(2)[359] of the Rome Statute, reopened a preliminary examination into allegations of systematic abuse of Iraq detainees by UK armed forces in Iraq between 2003 and 2008. This decision followed the submission of a communication to the ICC by the European Center for Constitutional and Human Rights and Public Interest Lawyers.[360] In the communication, a series of allegations were made against UK armed forces operating in Iraq at the material time and against the UK government, including conduct that amounted to an alleged violation of the substantive element of the right to life in respect of at least eight Iraq citizens who died in UK custody.[361] Within the context of the communication it was alleged that the actions

[358] *R (on the application of Ali Zaki Mousa and Others) v Secretary of State for Defence and another No 2*, 212–25.

[359] Article 15(2): The Prosecutor shall analyse the seriousness of the information received. For this purpose, he or she may seek additional information from States, organs of the United Nations, intergovernmental or non-governmental organizations, or other reliable sources that he or she deems appropriate, and may receive written or oral testimony at the seat of the Court.

[360] The communication, dated 10 January 2014, can be found at <http://www.publicinterestlawyers.co.uk/go_files/files/ZKHQ6FDDKWA4.pdf> (accessed 3 May 2015).

[361] Ibid, 101–09.

of UK armed forces are categorized as war crimes pursuant to Article 8(2)(a)(i)[362] of the Rome Statute.

Despite Iraq not being a signatory to the Rome Statute, the ICC has jurisdiction over matters alleged pursuant to Articles 12[363] and 13[364] of the Rome Statute as the UK is a signatory,[365] subject to the gravity threshold of Article 8(1) being met[366] and the admissibility provisions of Article 17(a).[367]

[362] For the purpose of this Statute, 'war crimes' means:

(a) Grave breaches of the Geneva Conventions of 12 August 1949, namely, any of the following acts against persons or property protected under the provisions of the relevant Geneva Convention:
(i) Wilful killing.

[363] Rome Statute, Article 12, Preconditions to the exercise of jurisdiction:

A State which becomes a Party to this Statute thereby accepts the jurisdiction of the Court with respect to the crimes referred to in article 5.

In the case of article 13, paragraph (a) or (c), the Court may exercise its jurisdiction if one or more of the following States are Parties to this Statute or have accepted the jurisdiction of the Court in accordance with paragraph 3:

(a) The State on the territory of which the conduct in question occurred or, if the crime was committed on board a vessel or aircraft, the State of registration of that vessel or aircraft;
(b) The State of which the person accused of the crime is a national.

If the acceptance of a State which is not a Party to this Statute is required under paragraph 2, that State may, by declaration lodged with the Registrar, accept the exercise of jurisdiction by the Court with respect to the crime in question. The accepting State shall cooperate with the Court without any delay or exception in accordance with Part 9.

[364] Rome Statute, Article 13, Exercise of jurisdiction:

The Court may exercise its jurisdiction with respect to a crime referred to in article 5 in accordance with the provisions of this Statute if:

(a) A situation in which one or more of such crimes appears to have been committed is referred to the Prosecutor by a State Party in accordance with article 14;
(b) A situation in which one or more of such crimes appears to have been committed is referred to the Prosecutor by the Security Council acting under Chapter VII of the Charter of the United Nations; or
(c) The Prosecutor has initiated an investigation in respect of such a crime in accordance with article 15.

[365] The United Kingdom deposited its instrument of ratification of the Rome Statute on 4 October 2001. The ICC therefore has jurisdiction over war crimes, crimes against humanity, and genocide committed on the territory of the United Kingdom or by UK nationals as of 1 July 2002, representing the date of the entry into force of the Rome Statute.

[366] On 9 February 2006, the then Chief Prosecutor of the ICC considered that, inter alia, this threshold had not been met in respect of the conduct of the UK armed forces in Iraq, and therefore did not order an investigation pursuant to Article 15(3) of the Rome Statute. This decision can be found at <http://www.icc-cpi.int/NR/rdonlyres/04D143C8-19FB-466C-AB77-4CDB2FDEBEF7/143682/OTP_letter_to_senders_re_Iraq_9_February_2006.pdf> (accessed 3 May 2015).

[367] Rome Statute, Article 17, Issues of admissibility:

1. Having regard to paragraph 10 of the Preamble and article 1, the Court shall determine that a case is inadmissible where:
   (a) The case is being investigated or prosecuted by a State which has jurisdiction over it, unless the State is unwilling or unable genuinely to carry out the investigation or prosecution.

It is not necessary to examine the threshold requirement of Article 8(1), Rome Statute in detail here; suffice it to say that it has been contended that it can be applied with a significant degree of discretion and therefore affords a wide margin for interpretation. The ICC considers that:

> For war crimes, a specific gravity threshold is set down in Article 8(1), which states that 'the Court shall have jurisdiction in respect of war crimes in particular when committed as part of a plan or policy or as part of a large-scale commission of such crimes'. This threshold is not an element of the crime, and the words 'in particular' suggest that this is not a strict requirement. It does, however, provide Statute guidance that the Court is intended to focus on situations meeting these requirements. According to the available information, it did not appear that any of the criteria of Article 8(1) were satisfied.[368]

Schabas summarizes the threshold requirement of Article 8(1) as 'an expedient to be invoked opportunistically rather than a meaningful legal norm'.[369] This issue is of significance for SPLI as the successor to IHAT as the Prosecutor of the ICC cannot, pursuant to Article 17(1)[370] of the Rome Statute, assert jurisdiction over a matter that is being investigated and prosecuted by a state party. This clause is not absolute, however, and Article 17(2) reflects the procedural elements of Article 2, ECHR in that the proceedings must be independent[371] and handled expeditiously.[372]

Despite a clear difference in focus and threshold, the framework for the investigation and prosecution of violations of the right to life and the war crime of wilful killing bear remarkable similarities and afford SPLI an opportunity to comply

[368] Chief Prosecutor of the ICC, letter to senders re Iraq, dated 9 February 2006, 8.

[369] William A Schabas, *The International Criminal Court: A Commentary on the Rome Statute* (Oxford University Press 2010) 202.

[370] Rome Statute, Article 17(1) Issues of admissibility:

> Having regard to paragraph 10 of the Preamble and article 1, the Court shall determine that a case is inadmissible where:
>
> (a) The case is being investigated or prosecuted by a State which has jurisdiction over it, unless the State is unwilling or unable genuinely to carry out the investigation or prosecution;
> (b) The case has been investigated by a State which has jurisdiction over it and the State has decided not to prosecute the person concerned, unless the decision resulted from the unwillingness or inability of the State genuinely to prosecute;
> (c) The person concerned has already been tried for conduct which is the subject of the complaint, and a trial by the Court is not permitted under article 20, paragraph 3;
> (d) The case is not of sufficient gravity to justify further action by the Court.

[371] Article 17(2):

> In order to determine unwillingness in a particular case, the Court shall consider, having regard to the principles of due process recognized by international law, whether one or more of the following exist, as applicable:
>
> (a) The proceedings were or are being undertaken or the national decision was made for the purpose of shielding the person concerned from criminal responsibility for crimes within the jurisdiction of the Court referred to in article 5;
> (c) The proceedings were not or are not being conducted independently or impartially, and they were or are being conducted in a manner which, in the circumstances, is inconsistent with an intent to bring the person concerned to justice.

[372] Article 17(2) (b): 'There has been an unjustified delay in the proceedings which in the circumstances is inconsistent with an intent to bring the person concerned to justice.'

with the UK's procedural Article 2, ECHR obligations in respect of the matters yet to be investigated as well as the UK's duties pursuant to the Rome Statute. In order to do so, however, the organization must be properly resourced and adopt the changes in procedure recommended by the Divisional Court[373] and elucidated by the ECtHR.[374]

4.17 NATO Investigation Procedures Following Death in Armed Conflict

Where the UK contributes armed forces to a NATO operation, a NATO-led investigatory procedure can run in parallel to, but independent of, the UK serious incident report and shooting incident review processes.[375] The NATO investigatory process is typically only instigated where there are a significant number of civilian casualties or a 'friendly fire' incident and there is therefore a requirement to independently assess whether the extant rules of engagement were adhered to.[376] In Afghanistan, this process was conducted by a joint initial assessment team (JIAT) composed of both ISAF personnel and, if required, Afghan armed forces or civil servants. The JIAT process was initiated by the military commander, typically a US general, at the ISAF Joint Command Headquarters in Kabul and could be terminated at their command. In reality the report produced by the JIAT is not the result of an investigatory process at all, but merely a fact-finding mission to establish a chronology of events and recommend changes in military tactics, techniques, and procedures to prevent recurrence where it has been determined that there has been a loss of civilian life. The JIAT report was then disclosed to the Afghan government and recommendations taken forward and compensation paid to the families of civilian victims as required.

The JIAT report has no evidential value and is not admissible in any disciplinary proceedings that may be taken against UK armed forces personnel who were involved in the incident under investigation by the UK military chain of command. Additionally, in none of the current[377] or historic[378] missions has NATO had any disciplinary powers over the armed forces assigned to the mission. The military disciplinary process is always vested in the national chain of command. It is clearly apparent, therefore, that any NATO investigation or assessment of an incident does not abrogate the UK of its procedural obligations, or modify them in any way, in respect of Article 2, ECHR and Article 6, ICCPR.

[373] *R (on the application of Ali Zaki Mousa and Others) v Secretary of State for Defence and another No 2*, 171–97.

[374] *Jaloud v the Netherlands* 195–96.

[375] Written evidence to the House of Commons Defence Select Committee from the Ministry of Defence in respect of operations in Afghanistan, 19.5.

[376] An illustrative example can be found at <http://www.rs.nato.int/images/stories/File/Aug2010/2010-08-CA-175-Lashkar%20Gar%20evidence%20points%20to%20ISAF%20caused%20civilian%20casualties%20(1).pdf> (accessed 3 May 2015).

[377] KFOR—Kosovo; Resolute Support—Afghanistan; Operation Active Endeavour; Operation Ocean Shield—http://www.aco.nato.int/ongoingoperations.aspx (accessed 3 May 2015).

[378] For example, ISAF in Afghanistan.

4.18 To What Extent Do Military Investigations Comply with the UK's Procedural Right to Life Obligations?

When procedural right to life obligations arise in armed conflict, the overarching framework used by the UK armed forces to investigate and prosecute these cases does not fully comply with the UK's obligations. Evidence of this can be found in the doctrine used as recently as 2014 in Afghanistan that could not satisfy the requirement for independence, given the pivotal role of the commanding officer of the unit involved in the death. Despite the clear guidance of the ECtHR in *Al-Skeini*,[379] the commanding officer still has a discretion not to commence a formal military police investigation unless an allegation of murder or manslaughter has been made, in which case the matter must be referred to the military police. A similar power is vested in the battlegroup commander, who equally lacks independence. This issue could be easily resolved by the decision on whether to commence a formal military police investigation being taken by a military police officer. This military police officer must be completely detached from the military chain of command, thereby enabling disciplinary, reporting, and functional independence. In order to provide a further check and a more robust process, the military police officer should be advised by a legal adviser who is similarly independent of the military chain of command. Such an approach is supported by the analysis of the Divisional Court in *Ali Zaki Mousa No 2*.

Notwithstanding these functional difficulties, once an investigation has been commenced by the military police, sufficient safeguards are in place to ensure that it complies with the procedural element of the right to life. Structural changes have been made to the Royal Military Police, Royal Navy Police, and Royal Air Force Police to ensure that they are hierarchically, functionally, and, to the extent required, institutionally independent of the military chain of command when investigating allegations that amount to violations of the right to life. In light of the ECtHR judgment in *Al-Skeini*, military police are now governed by a far more comprehensive investigatory code, and their high-profile investigations are overseen by an independent Service Police Assurance Advisor.[380]

Upon completion, a military police investigation is forwarded to the Director of Service Prosecutions at the Service Prosecuting Authority. Both the Director and the Service Prosecuting Authority are sufficiently independent of the military chain of command to comply with the requirements of the procedural element of the right to life. There may, however, be scope to challenge the independence of the court martial system due to the composition of the court and voting regulations. While fully independent itself, the existence of the Court Martial Appeal Court would not obviate the potential lack of independence of the court martial due to the requirement for independence at the first instance tribunal.

[379] *Al-Skeini and Others v the United Kingdom* 166.

[380] At present this is retired Assistant Chief Constable Julian Blazeby.

IHAT was been subject to significant criticism from both the Divisional Court[381] and the Court of Appeal.[382] This criticism focused on IHAT's lack of independence in its investigatory process and, more recently, in relation to the manner in which the investigations are being conducted. While the issue of independence has been resolved to the satisfaction of the Divisional Court,[383] difficulties remain specifically in relation to the ten cases that have been completed and wider structural problems more generally. Given the lack of involvement of the next of kin in, and the lack of opportunity for public scrutiny of, the already completed cases, it is unlikely that these investigations will comply with the procedural element of the right to life. A significant number of cases were not accepted and investigated by IHAT at its conclusion. Any future body charged with investigating similar matters is faced with a choice. Either it can adopt an inquisitorial approach, as recommended by the Divisional Court[384] and as used in coronial inquests, or they adopt the approach used by IHAT, but adapt their procedures to provide greater transparency and include the victim's next of kin where possible. In addition, there would have to be recourse to an independent prosecutorial body on completion of the investigation. Either procedure would comply with the procedural element of the right to life.

Ultimately, the confluence of a number of discrete failings in both the overarching process governing the investigations of deaths in armed conflict and the court martial system leads to the inexorable conclusion that, as presently configured, the UK does not comply with its procedural right to life obligations. These failings are not, however, of such magnitude that they could not be very easily resolved.

4.19 Conclusion

The relationship between international humanitarian law and human rights law during armed conflict is complex and the law is far from settled. It is submitted that attempting to resolve the differences between the two bodies of law with reference to a general all-encompassing theory is not possible due to fundamental incompatibilities in certain areas. With respect to the use of lethal force, notions of necessity/absolutely necessary and proportionality are measured against a different, more permissive, aim in international humanitarian law than in human rights law. Notwithstanding these differences, it is submitted that, in respect of the use of lethal force during armed conflict, the two bodies of law can be interpreted in such a way as to avoid what, on strict interpretation of the provision of the ECHR, represents a fundamental incompatibility.

[381] *R (on the application of Ali Zaki Mousa and Others) v Secretary of State for Defence and another No 2*, 169.

[382] *Ali Zaki Mousa No 1*, 34–38.

[383] *R (on the application of Ali Zaki Mousa and Others) v Secretary of State for Defence and another No 2*,232.

[384] Ibid, 212–25.

A state's substantive right to life obligations do not cease during armed conflict. It is submitted, however, that they are modified by reference to the applicable international humanitarian law, such that a violation of the right to life can only occur where there is a violation of applicable international humanitarian law that regulates the use of lethal force. Despite differences in the right to life provisions of the ICCPR and ECHR, it is further submitted that, both in international and non-international armed conflict, it is possible to interpret these obligations with reference to the applicable international humanitarian law. As an integral part of identifying the applicable international humanitarian law, it is recognized that a state must make a determination in respect of what amounts to membership of the military wing of an armed group and taking a direct part in hostilities in non-international armed conflict. The most convincing analysis of what amounts to membership of the military wing of an armed group, thereby enabling its members to be targeted at any time, is advanced by Sivakumaran.[385] Similarly, despite the creation of a 'revolving door' situation of 'farmer by day and guerrilla by night', the most persuasive analysis of when an individual may be targeted due to their direct participation in hostilities is that an individual loses immunity and may be targeted 'for such time as' they take a direct part in hostilities. What actually amounts to taking a direct part in hostilities is beyond the scope of this study; however, it must be determined by states, and guidance promulgated to armed forces personnel.

It is further recognized that in the case of Article 2, ECHR, interpreting a state's right to life obligations in accordance with the applicable international humanitarian law may result in a violation of treaty interpretation. The ECtHR has, however, been willing to interpret Article 5, ECHR in a way that arguably makes the Article 15 derogation provision redundant, lending a degree of legitimacy to such an approach. It is submitted that current UK doctrine regulating the use of lethal force in armed conflict is sufficient to comply with the state's substantive right to life obligations, if applied correctly. This is the case where the substantive right to life obligations are interpreted with reference to the applicable international humanitarian law or considered independently, relying exclusively on Article 2, as the ECtHR has on occasion done.

A state's procedural right to life obligations also do not cease during armed conflict. Unlike a state's substantive right to life obligations, there does not exist a comprehensive international humanitarian law framework applicable to investigating deaths during armed conflict. As a consequence, procedural right to life obligations assume a greater significance. That said, it is submitted that these procedural right to life obligations are modified to reflect the circumstances present during armed conflict and can be applied in a less stringent manner than in peacetime. At present, it is submitted that the investigatory procedures used by the UK during armed conflict do not fully comply with their procedural right to life obligations. Ensuring compliance would not, however, create an unduly onerous burden for military commanders that would adversely affect their ability to achieve their military objectives.

[385] Sivakumaran, *The Law of Non-International Armed Conflict* 360.

5

The Right to Life of Armed Forces Personnel during Armed Conflict

5.1 Introduction

In order to determine a state's right to life obligations in respect of its armed forces personnel during armed conflict,[1] a number of issues must be considered. First, does the jurisdiction of the UK under Article 1, European Convention on Human Rights (ECHR) extend to securing the protections of Article 2 for armed forces personnel operating overseas in armed conflict? This issue is addressed in this chapter, and, in short, the answer is yes. Second, to what extent are the substantive Article 2 obligations of states applicable during armed conflict? Third, in the event of the death of a member of the UK armed forces during armed conflict, to what extent do the investigatory procedures into the death comply with the procedural element of Article 2? And finally, what effect, if any, does a derogation pursuant to Article 15 have on the state's Article 2 obligations?

To some, the entire notion of members of the armed forces having right to life protection during armed conflict is unrealistic and contrary to the purpose of armed forces.[2] It is submitted, however, that the picture that has emerged as a consequence of recent litigation presents a far more nuanced situation in which the duties undertaken by members of the armed forces, and the circumstances in which they undertake them, are significant determinative factors in assessing the extent of any right to life protections they may have.

[1] The Directorate General of Human Rights and Legal Affairs, Council of Europe has considered this issue (<http://www.coe.int/t/dghl/standardsetting/hrpolicy/publications/cmrec_2010_4en.pdf>) and has recommended the following:

1. Members of the armed forces have the right to life.
2. Members of the armed forces should not be exposed to situations where their lives would be avoidably put at risk without a clear and legitimate military purpose or in circumstances where the threat to life has been disregarded.
3. There should be an independent and effective inquiry into any suspicious death or alleged violation of the right to life of a member of the armed forces.
4. Member states should take measures to encourage the reporting of acts which are inconsistent with the right to life of members of the armed forces and to protect from retaliation those reporting such acts.
5. Members of the armed forces should never be sentenced to death or executed.

[2] Ingrid Detter De Lupis, *The Law of War* (Cambridge University Press 1989) 180.

5.2 Substantive Right to Life Obligations

Having determined that, as a matter of jurisdiction, Article 2, ECHR applies to armed forces operating overseas during armed conflict, the next consideration is the extent to which the substantive obligation applies. As Lord Hope stated in [*Susan*] *Smith*,[3] this will 'vary according to the context'[4] and has not been considered directly by the European Court of Human Rights (ECtHR),[5] yet once the jurisdictional rubicon has been crossed, it is contended that some guiding principles will need to be established.

It is equally important to note that when considering the state's right to life obligations in respect of members of the armed forces during armed conflict, there exists a positive obligation on the state to protect. In other words, the state must take steps to ensure that members of the armed forces are afforded the requisite protection commensurate with the activity they are undertaking. This obligation can be contrasted with a state's right to life obligations in respect of individuals that are affected by the activities of armed forces during armed conflict, where the state has a largely negative duty not to 'arbitrarily' deprive life.

5.2.1 General principles

The Article 2 right to life obligations of states are varied and comprehensive. As an overarching principle, a state must establish a legislative and law enforcement framework to protect life.[6] Significantly, however, a state also has a positive duty to, as Lord Hope describes, 'take preventative operational measures to protect the lives of those within their jurisdiction'.[7] This positive duty occurs at different levels within the state hierarchy. In the context of the armed forces, this can potentially include the decisions made by government ministers and those in the senior echelons of the armed forces and, in the context of armed conflict, military commanders within the operational theatre, as well as, at the lowest level, officers and senior non-commissioned officers issuing orders on the battlefield.[8] This positive duty consists of 'framework' and 'operational' duties.

[3] *Smith and Others v Ministry of Defence* [2013] UKSC 41. When 'Smith' is used, this refers to the Susan Smith case (*Smith and Others v Ministry of Defence* [2013] UKSC 41) as opposed to the Catherine Smith case (*R (Catherine Smith) v Oxfordshire Assistant Deputy Coroner* [2010] UKSC 29; [2011] 1 AC 1). By way of brief factual background, the human rights law element of the Susan Smith case involved the deaths of soldiers during Operation Telic II in Iraq, who were killed by improvised explosive devices while travelling in lightly armoured 'snatch' landrovers. In *Catherine Smith*, the respondent's son, Smith, was a member of the Territorial Army who had been posted to Iraq in June 2003. He had spent eight days in Kuwait for the purpose of acclimatization. The room he occupied in Iraq did not have air conditioning. In August 2003, temperatures in the shade reached in excess of 50 degrees Celsius, which was the maximum that available thermometers could measure. He reported sick, complaining that he could not stand the heat. Some days later he suffered a cardiac arrest and subsequently died.

[4] *Smith and Others v Ministry of Defence* 64. [5] Ibid, 69, 109.

[6] *Osman v the United Kingdom* (1998) 29 EHRR 245, 115.

[7] *Smith and Others v Ministry of Defence* 69.

[8] Support for this position can be found in *Kalender v Turkey* (Application no 4314/02) (unreported), 15 December 2009, where a violation of the substantive element of Article 2 was found in

5.2.2 Framework or operational duties

In his dissenting opinion in *Smith*,[9] Lord Mance categorized substantive right to life duties as a 'systems or framework duty, viz to establish a framework which is appropriately protective of life' and 'an operational duty, viz in appropriate circumstances, a positive duty ... to take preventative operational measures to protect an individual whose life is at risk'.[10] Lord Hope adopted a broadly similar approach and defined the duties thus:

> The first is a systemic duty, to put in place a legislative and administrative framework which will [provide] ... effective deterrence against threats to the right to life. Depending on the facts, this duty could extend to issues about training and the procurement of equipment before the forces are deployed on operations that will bring them into contact with the enemy. The second ... is to ensure that, where there is a real and immediate risk to life, preventative operational measures of whatever kind are adopted to safeguard the lives of those involved so far as this is practicable.[11]

Lord Mance then noted the limitations of such an approach and recognized that 'it is unclear how far the two substantive duties are separated, with middle ground in between them, or form part of a continuum covering almost every aspect of state activity'.[12]

During armed conflict it is rarely possible to neatly compartmentalize the contributory factors that led to the death of a serviceperson. The 'snatch Land Rover' cases considered in *Smith* illustrate the difficulties. By way of brief background, the 'snatch Land Rover claims' arose from the deaths of Private Philip Hewett (the son of the applicant Susan Smith) and Private Lee Ellis. While serving in Iraq, Privates Hewett and Ellis died when the snatch Land Rovers in which they were travelling detonated improvised explosive devices (IEDs), in 2005 and 2006 respectively. The applicants alleged that the UK Ministry of Defence was in breach of its Article 2, ECHR obligation to protect life on the basis that they failed to take reasonable steps to protect soldiers travelling in 'lightly armoured' snatch Land Rovers, given the considerable, and known, threat from IED.

In respect of *Smith*, when assessing the contributory factors that led to the deaths, the relevant considerations include, at the very least, the design, procurement, specification, and deployment of the snatch Land Rovers; the intelligence picture relating to the presence of IEDs and enemies in the specific area of Iraq at the material time; the training, briefing, and competence of the military commanders during the operation; and the tactical decisions made by those directly involved in incidents. Clearly, these issues contain elements of both framework and operational duties. Similarly, the military board of inquiry[13] into the deaths of six Royal Military Police

respect of the procedures for disembarking a train at a specific railway station that led to passengers having to cross the track and being killed: cited by Lord Mance in his dissenting opinion in *Smith*.

[9] *Smith and Others v Ministry of Defence* 103, 138.

[10] *Watts v United Kingdom* [2010] 51 EHRR SE66 82.

[11] *Smith and Others v Ministry of Defence* 68.

[12] Ibid, 104.

[13] A military board of inquiry is the investigative procedure that preceded the service inquiry, but ostensibly performs the same function.

while on routine patrol in Iraq on 24 June 2003 concluded that a significant number of causal factors contributed to their deaths, including inadequate command and control, incomplete intelligence, limited training, and insufficient support while on patrol.[14]

Cognizant of these difficulties, it is not proposed to categorize the duties as 'framework' or 'operational', but rather to consider the relevant factors as forming a continuum of actions a state may take to comply with its substantive right to life obligations. In other words, the circumstances in which armed forces personnel operate (and are killed) become the principal determining factor of the extent of the state's substantive right to life obligations, and not any discrete areas such as procurement decisions. That said, in order to comply with its substantive right to life obligations, a state would still be required to equip soldiers in the most effective way, within obvious financial constraints, to best ensure their safety. For example, if body armour and bulletproof helmets are readily available and can be supplied to frontline soldiers, then they ought to be.

5.2.3 Operational decisions on the battlefield

As a starting point, it is perhaps helpful to attempt to establish the circumstances in which a member of the armed forces is killed and Article 2 would not be engaged. In his dissenting opinion in *Smith*, Lord Mance cited his judgment in *Catherine Smith*[15] and categorized such areas as 'casual errors of judgment or acts of negligence' and 'operational as opposed to systematic failures'.[16] Within the context of armed forces activity overseas, a distinction must be drawn between battlefield operations in the face of the enemy in armed conflict at one end of the spectrum and patrolling in a benign military occupation at the other. It is likely that courts will offer considerable latitude to military commanders in respect of assessing their (ie the state's) right to life obligations during the 'heat of battle' as opposed to within the relative safety of a main operating base.[17] As Lord Hope, citing Lord Rodger in *Catherine Smith*, notes in *Smith*,

> The best laid plan rarely survives initial contact with the enemy. The best intelligence cannot predict with complete accuracy how the enemy will behave, or what equipment will be needed to meet the tactics and devices that he may use to achieve his own ends. Speed may be essential if the momentum of an attack is to be maintained or to strengthen a line of defence. But lines of communication may become stretched. Situations may develop where it is simply not possible to provide troops in time with all they need to conduct operations with the minimum of casualties. Things tend to look and feel very different on the battlefield from the way they look on such charts and images as those behind the lines may have available to them.[18]

14 <https://www.gov.uk/government/uploads/system/uploads/attachment_data/file/83819/rmp_boi.pdf>.

15 *R (Catherine Smith) v Oxfordshire Assistant Deputy Coroner* 201.

16 *Smith and Others v Ministry of Defence* 106.

17 An example of a main operating base is Camp Bastion in Helmand Province, Afghanistan, which was approximately the size of Reading. It was also extremely well protected and safe.

18 *Smith and Others v Ministry of Defence* 64.

Lord Hope concludes that 'the national interest requires that the law should accord the widest measure of appreciation to commanders on the ground who have the responsibility of planning for and conducting operations there'[19] and that 'a court should be very slow indeed to question operational decisions made on the ground by commanders, whatever their rank or level of seniority'.[20] Read in conjunction with Lord Mance's view of errors of judgment and negligence, it can be convincingly argued that genuine mistakes by military commanders and tactical decisions made in the heat of battle are unlikely to amount to substantive violations of Article 2. This is not to suggest that what occurs on the battlefield cannot attract procedural or substantive Article 2 obligations, but rather that the areas likely to attract scrutiny in respect of battlefield operations relate to the way in which military personnel are trained, deployed, and equipped, rather than the decisions taken by military commanders in the heat of battle that might expose their subordinates and colleagues to risk.

5.2.4 Operational decisions not in the face of the enemy

Operational decisions not in the face of the enemy can be defined as those decisions made by military commanders within the operational theatre in respect of the planning and conduct of the military campaign. This will include, inter alia, the deployment and activities of troops in areas such as assessments of troop density within the area of responsibility; use of air assets; discrete missions against the enemy; the provision of reinforcements; medical support; and evacuation capabilities. Within the context of UK military operations in Afghanistan, these are decisions that would be made by the UK commanders physically located in one of the main operating bases at Camp Bastion, Kandahar airfield, or Lashkar Gah. They would therefore be within a secure compound and, in the strictest sense, not directly in the face of the enemy. With reference to this category of decisions, Lord Hope in *Smith* stated that 'even where those directing operations are remote in place and time from the area in which the troops are operating, great care is needed to avoid imposing a burden on them which is impossible or disproportionate'.[21]

What might amount to a burden that is 'impossible or disproportionate' is a significant consideration in determining the right to life obligations of states in respect of their armed forces. By the very nature of military operations there is a significant risk that a serviceperson may lose their life, and it is axiomatic therefore that a degree of risk is accepted by those joining the armed forces. In *Catherine Smith*, Lord Rodger characterized the situation thus: 'the job of members of the armed forces involves their being deployed in situations where, as they well know, opposing forces will be making a determined effort, and using all their resources, to kill and injure them.'[22] It follows that armed forces personnel in whatever service, specialization, or rank must expect to encounter situations where they may be killed by the enemy and placed in situations of mortal danger. In return, it is also a legitimate

[19] Ibid. [20] Ibid, 71. [21] Ibid, 73.
[22] *R (Catherine Smith) v Oxfordshire Assistant Deputy Coroner* 122.

expectation on the part of armed forces personnel that they will be trained, supported, and equipped to an acceptable standard for their tasks, and not deployed into situations where death is inevitable. Naturally, all military decisions are subject to constraints, and this is particularly true in respect of operational decisions not in the face of the enemy. There are, inter alia, a finite number of troops with particular skills; limited intelligence information; time constraints; and limited support provided to the troops conducting the mission. A threshold exists in order to comply with the state's substantive Article 2 obligations in respect of operational decisions made by military commanders not in the face of the enemy, but it is extremely low. Recognizing the judgment in *Smith*, the latitude given to states in the ECtHR judgments in *Finogenov, Giuliani and Gaggio*, and the recognition of the context of military operations in *Hassan*, it is submitted that, provided that the military commander, based on all available intelligence, does not deploy their troops into a situation where their death would be inevitable, then the substantive Article 2 obligation would be complied with.

Evidence suggests that UK military commanders in recent campaigns have exercised far greater caution than this, and, while any loss of life in armed conflict is tragic, the casualty rates in Afghanistan[23] and Iraq[24] support that assertion. In Afghanistan, for example, the threat of IEDs meant that in the areas of greatest threat, patrols were not undertaken at night. Furthermore, each daytime patrol was led by a soldier using a sophisticated detector called a 'vallon' that was specifically designed to detect low metal-content IEDs. Significant resources were allocated to the provision of training both prior to deployment to Afghanistan and upon arrival in theatre. During operations, military commanders had the capability to use significant air assets, including attack helicopters and fighter jets, to minimize the risk to troops on the ground. There is no evidence to suggest that UK military commanders in Afghanistan placed their troops in situations where death would be inevitable.

5.3 Military Planning

All military planning is subject to constraints. These can include, inter alia, limitations on time, numbers of personnel, expertise, equipment, financial resources, intelligence information, and previous campaign experience. Military planning is therefore a particularly imprecise art, the outcome of which cannot be accurately predicted. Prior to Operation Desert Storm,[25] for example, the Pentagon predicted coalition casualties of 30,000–40,000. The overall casualty figure for the entire campaign was 378. As a consequence—and recognizing the latitude the ECtHR

[23] Throughout the military campaign in Afghanistan there were 453 UK deaths: see <https://www.gov.uk/government/fields-of-operation/afghanistan>.

[24] Throughout Operation Telic in Iraq (2003 onwards) there were 136 UK deaths as a result of hostile action: see <https://www.gov.uk/government/fields-of-operation/iraq>.

[25] Operation Desert Storm was the codename for the combat phase (17 January 1991–28 February 1991) of coalition military operations in the Middle East following Iraq's invasion of Kuwait in August 1990.

afforded to the Russian authorities in the planning of the rescue operation following the theatre siege in 2002 in *Finogenov*[26] and to the Italian authorities in *Giuliani and Gaggio*,[27] as well as Lord Hope's view in *Smith* that 'the court must avoid imposing positive obligations on the state in connection with the planning for and conduct of military operations in situations of armed conflict which are unrealistic or disproportionate[28]—what emerges is a requirement for the state to do what is possible with the resources available to protect the lives of their armed forces personnel in armed conflict while best achieving their military objectives. This is, however, subject to further qualification. Without any further elucidation, Lord Hope asserts,

> It will be easy to find that allegations are beyond the reach of article 2 if the decisions that were or ought to have been taken about training, procurement or the conduct of operations were at a high level of command and closely linked to the exercise of political judgment and issues of policy. So too if they relate to things done or not done when those who might be thought to be responsible for avoiding the risk of death or injury to others were actively engaged in direct contact with the enemy.[29]

Absent this qualification, the majority judgment in *Smith* was comprehensible and allowed clear guidance to be incorporated into military training, planning, and procurement that recognizes the state's, albeit low, substantive Article 2 obligations. The inclusion of this sub-clause effectively creates a tiered system in which the state's Article 2 obligations are a function not of the decision made, but rather of the level at which it is made. Lord Mance commented thus:

> I see little attraction in a scheme according to which the acts or omissions of the man on the ground and the policy-maker in Whitehall give rise either to no liability at all or only to liability in egregious cases, but the procurement, training and deployment decisions of a 'middle-rank' commander (query, in Whitehall or in local headquarters or both) are subject to scrutiny under conventional principles of fault-based liability.[30]

Ultimately, this qualification does little to assist in the provision of a coherent framework to aid a state's military planning. Instead, it would be justifiable, with reference to the existing, albeit sparse, ECtHR jurisprudence and the difficult tasks expected of armed forces, to require both government and the armed forces, at all levels, to do what is possible with the resources available to protect the lives of their personnel in armed conflict while best achieving their military objectives. Naturally, this would involve a balancing of risk of the loss of life against achieving the military objective.

5.4 Procurement of Military Equipment

In *Smith*, Lord Hope addressed the issue of the procurement of military equipment and concluded, with reference to Lord Bingham in *A v Secretary of State for the*

26 *Finogenov v Russia*, Application nos 18299/03 and 27311/03, 20 December 2011, 213.
27 *Giuliani and Gaggio v Italy*, Application no 23458/02, 24 March 2011.
28 *Smith and Others v Ministry of Defence* 76. 29 Ibid, 76. 30 Ibid, 149.

Home Department,[31] that '[t]he allocation of resources to the armed services and as between the different branches of the services, is also a question which is more appropriate for political resolution than it is by a court',[32] and further that '[i]t does not follow from the fact that decisions about procurement are taken remote from the battlefield that they will always be appropriate for review by the courts'.[33] Implicit in these remarks is the possibility that these decisions can be 'appropriate for review by the courts' in some instances, even when read in conjunction with Lord Hope's later remarks where he stated: 'it will be easy to find that allegations are beyond the reach of Article 2 if the decisions that were or ought to have been taken about... procurement... were at a high level of command and closely linked to the exercise of political judgment and issues of policy.'[34] As such, the question must again be posed: in what circumstances are these decisions beyond the reach of Article 2 or inappropriate for review by the courts?

A potential course of action might be to adopt the approaches of Lord Bingham in *A v Secretary of State for the Home Department*, Lord Hoffman in *Secretary of State for The Home Department v Rehman*,[35] and Lord Mance[36] in his dissenting opinion in *Smith* and remove the question of procurement from the assessment of Article 2 compliance altogether. As argued by Lord Mance, support for this approach can be found in ECtHR jurisprudence in *Taylor v United Kingdom*[37] and *Banks v United Kingdom*,[38] in which the Commission and Court conclude that in investigating alleged violations of Article 2 and 3, respectively, the procedural element of each right is satisfied without the requirement to examine matters 'for public and political debate which fall outside the scope of Article 2 and the other provisions of the Convention'[39] or that '[t]he wider questions raised by the case as to the background... are, in the Court's opinion, matters for public and political debate which fall outside the scope of article 3 of the Convention'.[40]

[31] *A v Secretary of State for the Home Department* [2005] 2 AC 68, para 29: 'The more purely political (in a broad or narrow sense) a question is, the more appropriate it will be for political resolution and the less likely it is to be an appropriate matter for judicial decision. The smaller, therefore, will be the potential role of the court. It is the function of political and not judicial bodies to resolve political questions.'

[32] *Smith and Others v Ministry of Defence* 65.

[33] Ibid.

[34] *Smith and Others v Ministry of Defence* 76.

[35] *Secretary of State for The Home Department v Rehman* [2001] UKHL 47 62: 'I wrote this speech some three months before the recent events in New York and Washington. They are a reminder that in matters of national security, the cost of failure can be high. This seems to me to underline the need for the judicial arm of government to respect the decisions of ministers of the Crown on the question of whether support for terrorist activities in a foreign country constitutes a threat to national security. It is not only that the executive has access to special information and expertise in these matters. It is also that such decisions, with serious potential results for the community, require a legitimacy which can be conferred only by entrusting them to persons responsible to the community through the democratic process. If the people are to accept the consequences of such decisions, they must be made by persons whom the people have elected and whom they can remove.'

[36] *Smith and Others v Ministry of Defence* 143–51.

[37] *Taylor v United Kingdom*, Application no 23412/94 (unreported) 30 August 1994.

[38] *Banks v United Kingdom* (2007) 45 EHRR SE2.

[39] Ibid.

[40] Ibid.

In adopting this approach, however, it is necessary to distinguish the Article 2 obligations of states during armed conflict from the circumstances examined by the ECtHR in, inter alia, *Osman v United Kingdom*,[41] *Öneryıldız v Turkey*,[42] and *Stoyanovi v Bulgaria*.[43] In *Osman* and *Öneryıldız*, the factual circumstances are vastly different to situations of armed conflict: they involve a state's duties within the public health sphere and regulation of municipal rubbish dumps, respectively. In such circumstances the duty of states to provide a framework to protect the public is correspondingly high, as the situations under examination do not require the affected party to knowingly accept a risk of death. In *Stoyanovi* a death occurred during a military training exercise when a parachutist was unable to open his parachute, having hit his head on the aircraft wheel while exiting the aircraft. A substantive violation of Article 2 was not alleged by the claimants, although the ECtHR addressed this issue briefly as follows: 'positive obligations will vary therefore in their application depending on the context.'[44] It is contended that not only do the obligations of states vary according to the context, but where a substantive or procedural violation of Article 2 is not found in relation to a military training accident, it is extremely unlikely to be found in respect of military procurement decisions that are remote from the death of troops in armed conflict and are only one of many potential contributory factors. As such, a crucial distinction must be made between the de jure applicability of substantive Article 2 obligations and the likelihood that, when considered, a de facto violation would be found.

The ECtHR has repeatedly demonstrated that it is prepared to assess the extent to which the actions of states comply with their Article 2 obligations during armed conflict.[45] As such, procurement decisions, wherever they are made within the military or government hierarchy, would come within the ambit of the substantive element of Article 2. The argument advanced by Lord Mance against such a proposition can be challenged.

In supporting his assertion, Lord Mance relies upon the Commission finding in *Taylor*. It is submitted, however, that *Taylor* must be read in light of subsequent ECtHR judgments, including *Stoyanovi*,[46] *Öneryıldız*,[47] *Grigoriades*,[48] and *Şen*,[49] in which issues concerning the activities of armed forces are specifically considered. In *Taylor*,[50] the Commission acknowledged that the criminal investigations and inquiry into the killings carried out by the hospital nurse

[41] *Osman v United Kingdom*.

[42] *Öneryıldız v Turkey*, Application no 48939/99, 30 November 2004.

[43] *Stoyanovi v Bulgaria*, Application no 42980/04, 9 November 2010.

[44] Ibid, 61.

[45] Numerous cases in respect of the 'Cyprus, Turkey' issue, Turkish military action against the PKK, cases concerning the conflict in Chechnya, cases concerning the war in Bosnia and Herzegovina, interstate cases concerning Georgia–Russia, and cases concerning international military operations in Iraq.

[46] *Stoyanovi v Bulgaria*, Application no 42980/04, 9 November 2010.

[47] *Öneryıldız v Turkey*, Application no 48939/99, 30 November 2004.

[48] *Grigoriades v Greece* (1997) 27 EHHR 464.

[49] *Şen v Turkey*, Application no 45824/99, 8 July 2003.

[50] *Taylor v United Kingdom*, Application no 23412/94 (unreported), 30 August 1994.

Beverley Allitt did not consider the organization and funding of the NHS, and concluded that

> [t]he wider questions raised by the case are within the public domain and any doubts which may consequently arise as to policies adopted in the field of public health are, in the Commission's opinion, matters for public and political debate which fall outside the scope of Article 2 and the other provisions of the Convention.[51]

This must, however, be read within the context of *Stoyanovi*,[52] in which the ECtHR considered that

> The armed forces ... routinely engage in activities that potentially could cause harm; it is, in a manner of speaking, part of their essential functioning. Thus, in the present case, parachute training was inherently dangerous but an ordinary part of military duties. Whenever a State undertakes or organises dangerous activities, or authorises them, it must ensure through a system of rules and through sufficient control that the risk is reduced to a reasonable minimum.[53]

Furthermore, in *Smith*, Lord Hope, citing *Öneryıldız*,[54] concluded that the state's substantive Article 2 obligations 'could extend to issues about ... the procurement of equipment before the forces deploy on operations that will bring them into contact with the enemy'.[55] It is contended, therefore, that fighting in armed conflict is as much 'an ordinary part of military duties'[56] as parachute training and therefore the state must 'ensure ... that the risk is reduced to a minimum'.[57] This in turn would include providing the armed forces with the necessary equipment, subject to obvious financial and practical constraints. Even giving due regard to the nature of armed forces activity as considered by the ECtHR in *Engel*,[58] *Grigoriades*,[59] and *Şen*[60] and recognizing the 'particular characteristics' of military life, there is little support in ECtHR jurisprudence to suggest that procurement decisions made by states cannot, de jure, be considered by the ECtHR.

Second, Lord Mance asserts that as the ECtHR have not considered this discrete issue, and, recognizing that there is 'wholly insufficient guidance' regarding it, the UK Supreme Court should not assume that the ECtHR would consider substantive Article 2 obligations to be applicable in this area. This view is problematic. In *Stoyanovi*, *Al-Skeini*, and *Jaloud*, the ECtHR indicated that it is prepared to examine in significant detail the circumstances surrounding an alleged violation of the right to life. Moreover, Lord Mance himself, in *Catherine Smith*, considered that 'there is nothing that makes the Convention impossible or inappropriate of application to the relationship between the state and its armed forces as it exists in relation to

[51] *Smith and Others v Ministry of Defence* 144, citing *Taylor v United Kingdom*.
[52] *Stoyanovi v Bulgaria*, Application no 42980/04, 9 November 2010.
[53] *Smith and Others v Ministry of Defence* 138 citing *Stoyanovi v Bulgaria* 61.
[54] *Öneryıldız v Turkey*, Application no 48939/99, 30 November 2004.
[55] *Smith and Others v Ministry of Defence* 68. [56] Ibid. [57] Ibid.
[58] *Engel v The Netherlands (No 1)* (1976) 1 EHHR 54.
[59] *Grigoriades v Greece* (1997) 27 EHHR 464.
[60] *Şen v Turkey*, Application no 45824/99, 8 July 2003.

overseas operations, in matters such as, for example, the adequacy of equipment, planning or training'.[61] Ultimately, therefore, in respect of the procurement of military equipment, or lack thereof, it is likely that the ECtHR would consider this issue to fall within the ambit of Article 2. The likelihood of the ECtHR finding a violation in this discrete respect, however, is extremely unlikely.

5.5 Training of Armed Forces Personnel

With regard to military training, it is again necessary to distinguish between the de jure application of Article 2 and the likelihood of a substantive violation being found in respect of inadequate training prior to deployment in armed conflict. It is equally important to disaggregate the right to life obligations of states in respect of deaths in training prior to deployment to an armed conflict and a death in armed conflict that, it is asserted, is due to a lack of sufficient training.

In *Smith*, Lord Hope and Lord Mance make numerous references to military training.[62] This is done within two overlapping contexts. First, military training is used by Lord Mance as a comparator against which a state's substantive right to life obligations during armed conflict can be assessed. Second, the provision of adequate military training is considered within the context of a state's overall right to life obligations during armed conflict.

Lord Mance appears to accept that a state has substantive right to life obligations in respect of military training. With reference to parachute training in *Stoyanovi*,[63] he says the following:

> In the present case, parachute training was inherently dangerous but an ordinary part of military duties. Whenever a state undertakes or organises dangerous activities, or authorises them, it must ensure through a system of rules and through sufficient control that the risk is reduced to a reasonable minimum. If nevertheless damage arises, it will only amount to a breach of the state's positive obligations if it was due to insufficient regulations or insufficient control, but not if the damage was caused through the negligent conduct of an individual or the concatenation of unfortunate events.[64]

Lord Mance then—in contradiction to his previous consideration of the right to life obligations of states in respect of training—asserts:

> That leaves for consideration whether the [state's] duty involves an obligation on the part of the state to exercise due care in the course of planning armed operations, and in equipping and training its armed forces, so as to reduce or limit the risks to life involved in such operations. In my opinion it is not possible to conclude that the Strasbourg court would hold that such matters are justiciable under the Convention.[65]

[61] *R (Catherine Smith) v Oxfordshire Assistant Deputy Coroner* 195.
[62] *Smith and Others v Ministry of Defence*, 63, 64, 68, 71, 72, 75, 141, 142.
[63] *Stoyanovi v Bulgaria* 61.
[64] *Smith and Others v Ministry of Defence* 138, citing *Stoyanovi v Bulgaria*, para 61.
[65] Ibid, 143.

On the basis of Lord Mance's analysis, therefore, military training taken in isolation can create substantive right to life obligations for states, yet training in preparation for a specific 'armed operation' is not justiciable. It is submitted that this approach is both problematic and contradictory—it would be difficult, if not impossible, to disaggregate training that is general and that which is in preparation for an 'armed operation', as all training is ultimately designed to prepare soldiers for 'armed operations' in one form or another. This includes peacekeeping operations where the use of lethal force may only be permitted in self-defence. In respect of training, a more viable alternative would be to imagine the conduct of military operations as a spectrum. At one end of the spectrum would be training in the UK, in the middle training in the operational theatre, and at the other the use of lethal force in the face of the enemy during 'war fighting'. The closer towards the UK 'training' end of the spectrum, the more likely it is that a state has positive right to life obligations in respect of armed forces personnel; the closer towards the 'war fighting' end of the spectrum, the less likely it is.

Lord Hope, in contrast to Lord Mance, takes a more nuanced view of military training in which he considers that, where training decisions are taken at a 'high level of command and closely linked to the exercise of political judgment and issues of policy',[66] it would be 'easy to find the allegations beyond the reach of Article 2'.[67] Lord Hope accurately distinguishes training from active service overseas in the following terms:

> It is hard to see why servicemen and women should not, as a general rule, be given the same protection against the risk of death or injury by the provision of appropriate training and equipment as members of the police, fire and other emergency services. But it is different when the serviceman or woman moves from recruitment and training to operations on active service, whether at home or overseas. It is here that the national interest requires that the law should accord the widest measure of appreciation to commanders on the ground who have the responsibility of planning for and conducting operations there.[68]

Implicit in this statement is a recognition that the substantive Article 2 right exists and therefore ought to be considered by both the ECtHR and domestic courts, albeit recognizing the 'widest measure of appreciation'. It would be unnecessary to make any reference to a 'measure of appreciation' if training were not de jure a relevant consideration when assessing the extent to which a state complies with its substantive Article 2 obligations. It is contended therefore that, in much the same way as procurement of military hardware, it is likely that the ECtHR would consider the provision of adequate military training to fall within the ambit of Article 2. The likelihood of the ECtHR finding a violation in this respect, however, is extremely low, due to very great difficulty in being able to determine that a lack of training directly led to the death of a soldier in armed conflict. This is the case in terms of both factual assessment of the training UK armed forces receive prior to deployment on operations and the obvious difficulties in being able to determine with any accuracy that a lack of training was the reason for a soldier being killed.

[66] *Smith and Others v Ministry of Defence* 76. [67] Ibid. [68] Ibid.

In the UK armed forces, those fighting on the front line receive a significant amount of basic and specialist pre-deployment training. For example, and with reference to the armed conflict in Afghanistan, an infantry soldier in the army would receive twenty-six weeks[69] of basic infantry training, while a Royal Marine Commando receives thirty-two weeks,[70] and all deploying soldiers and marines typically commence additional Afghanistan-specific training twenty-four months prior to deployment.[71] In this respect it would be difficult to successfully argue that the pre-deployment training provided was inadequate. Similarly, individual fitness is assessed regularly by way of basic and battle fitness tests as well as a full medical examination that must be passed before deployment. An RAF, Royal Navy, or army pilot charged with firing missiles or dropping bombs in Afghanistan would receive at least three years of training prior to becoming a 'frontline' pilot. In the event of a 'blue on blue' incident in which they killed members of their own forces, it would, again, be difficult to contend that they had been provided insufficient training.

Where deaths of UK armed forces have occurred in recent armed conflicts, they have often been caused by a multiplicity of factors. Of the 391 fatalities in combat during the armed conflict in Afghanistan, 224 were caused by IEDs, 116 by gunshot, 8 by indirect fire, 21 by grenade, 17 by suicide bomb, and 5 by other causes. In order to counter the IED threat, significant measures were taken to equip the soldiers with the latest detection equipment, and tactics, techniques, and procedures were developed to identify and disarm the IEDs. Patrol routes were also revised to minimize the threat and specific clothing was worn to afford the greatest protection. Despite these considerable efforts, there were still casualties and, while the immediate cause of death was the IED blast, it would be difficult to accurately determine all of the underlying causes. To illustrate yet further, all of the following are relevant factors for the planning of that specific patrol: the patrol route taken; the overall mission in the area; the efforts made to establish and monitor IED-free routes; the likelihood of IEDs in the area and intelligence information available; overall mission and decisions taken by regional commanders or the extent to which each one contributed to the death. Notwithstanding these difficulties, each death of a serviceperson was considered by way of an investigation, as a matter of UK policy. When a court is required to make an objective determination of the extent to which each of these factors may contribute to a state violating their substantive right to life obligations, it faces an extremely difficult task. Recognizing, as Lord Hope asserts in *Smith*, that each case must be considered on its own merits, the multiplicity of relevant factors—each of which, in isolation, may not amount to a violation, although cumulatively they might—places the court in a difficult position in ascribing relative magnitude to each in order that states may better comply with their right to life obligations in future. Moreover, the paucity of guidance exacerbates the difficulty of the task.

[69] <http://www.royalnavy.mod.uk/careers/royal-marines/how-to-join-the-marines/rm-commando-training>.

[70] <https://www.army.mod.uk/rolefinder/role/83/infantry-soldier>.

[71] House of Commons Defence Committee, Operations in Afghanistan, *Fourth Report of Session 2010–12*, 187, 24.2, 24.4.

5.6 Criticism of the Judgment in *Smith*

The Supreme Court judgment in *Smith* has received significant criticism in certain quarters.[72] Those opposing the encroachment of human rights into hitherto uncharted waters have seized upon the dissenting judgments of Lords Mance and Carnwath as evidence of the inapplicability of Article 2, ECHR to armed conflict generally. Clearly this position is unsupportable given the willingness of the ECtHR to decide cases in this area, the UK's compliance with these judgments, and the view of the International Court of Justice (ICJ).[73] Similarly, while in practice the ECtHR may not find a violation of the substantive right to life in respect of military procurement decisions or training, for the reasons set out above, it is nonetheless de jure applicable.

5.7 Procedural Right to Life Obligations in Respect of UK Armed Forces

When UK armed forces personnel are killed during armed conflict each case is investigated by the armed forces by way of review and, if necessary, service inquiry, and is subject to the jurisdiction of a UK coroner who will determine whether a coronial inquiry is required.[74] In many cases where the underlying cause of death is unknown, a coroner will convene an inquiry to investigate. This has occurred on numerous occasions in respect of UK military operations in Iraq and Afghanistan. Equally, if there is an allegation that the cause of death was due to the negligence of any member of the armed forces, then the military police have jurisdiction to investigate pursuant to the Armed Forces Act 2006.

When *Catherine Smith* is considered in the light of the Supreme Court judgment in *Smith*, it would appear that not only is the UK government required to recognize the substantive right to life of armed forces personnel in armed conflict but, significantly, that in circumstances where there are alleged 'systemic' failures, a coroner must convene an inquiry that complies with the procedural element of Article 2. This can be seen both in the judgment of Lord Hope and the partially dissenting opinion of Lord Mance in *Catherine Smith*, where he stated:

> Only if there were sufficient indicia of such a failure or deficiency was it incumbent on the state of its own motion to ensure an effective public investigation by an independent official

[72] Richard Ekins, Jonathan Morgan, and Tom Tugendhat, 'Clearing the Fog of Law: Saving Our Armed Forces from Defeat by Judicial Diktat', <http://www.policyexchange.org.uk/images/publications/clearing%20the%20fog%20of%20law.pdf>.

[73] Advisory Opinion on the Legality of the Threat or Use of Nuclear Weapons, Advisory Opinion on the Legal Consequences of the Construction of a Wall in the Occupied Palestinian Territory (the 2004 *Wall Advisory Opinion*); *Democratic Republic of the Congo v Uganda*.

[74] s 1, Coroners and Justice Act 2009.

body, and incumbent therefore on the coroner to expand the inquest to become a *Middleton* type inquest.[75]

It would appear, therefore, that the procedural right to life obligations of states in respect of armed forces personnel must conform to the classical understanding of the nexus between substantive and procedural right to life obligations. As Lord Bingham characterized it in *Gentle*, the procedural obligation is 'implied in order to make sure that [the substantive right is] effective in practice' and 'is parasitic upon the existence of the substantive right, and cannot exist independently'.[76] As established in *Al-Skeini*, this obligation would apply equally where the death occurred in difficult security conditions or armed conflict. Any coroner would, however, be dependent upon the quality of physical evidence that could be gathered by the armed forces personnel present at the time. This may present some practical difficulties and limitations where the death occurred during a firefight and the primary concern of those involved would not necessarily be the capture and collation of physical evidence. Such difficulties are explicitly referenced by Lord Hope in *Smith* and are likely to fall within the 'measure of appreciation' applied by the ECtHR when it considers such an issue.

Despite criticism by some coroners in respect of the conduct of operations in Afghanistan,[77] in *Smith* Lord Mance took the view that 'the United Kingdom's performance of its investigatory and procedural duties under Article 2 is not in doubt, as attested by the sadly numerous inquests (investigating and recording the circumstances of each death)'.[78] It is therefore likely that the use of criminal investigations where necessary, service inquiries, and coroner's inquests are sufficient to comply with the state's procedural right to life obligations in respect of armed forces personnel killed during armed conflict. In this respect, a distinction can be drawn between the extent to which the UK can comply with its procedural right to life obligations in respect of UK armed forces personnel killed during armed conflict and individuals killed by UK armed forces. The reason for such a distinction is the practical difficulties inherent in investigating the deaths of other individuals when compared to UK armed forces personnel. In the case of UK armed forces personnel, extraordinary efforts are made to recover the body, which facilitates the possibility of a post-mortem examination to establish the cause of death. As a practical matter, it is also easier to interview armed forces personnel who witnessed the death of a colleague and therefore make a determination of the circumstances surrounding it. Investigations following the deaths of non-UK personnel during armed conflict do not always benefit from access to such information.

[75] *R (Catherine Smith) v Oxfordshire Assistant Deputy Coroner* 218.

[76] *R (Gentle) v Prime Minister* [2008] UKHL 20; [2008] AC 1356, 5–6, per Lord Bingham. See also *McCann v United Kingdom; Jordan v United Kingdom; Al-Skeini v United Kingdom*; and most recently Leggatt J in *Al-Saadoon and Others v Secretary of State for Defence* 16–19.

[77] As an illustrative example see <http://www.theguardian.com/uk/2010/mar/09/british-soldiers-afghanistan-inquest>.

[78] *Smith and Others v Ministry of Defence* 146.

5.8 Conclusion

The judgment of the Supreme Court in *Smith* has redrawn the boundaries of the applicability of the right to life in respect of the UK armed forces. While the exact nature of the state's positive right to life obligations owed to their armed forces during armed conflict remains opaque, it is submitted that such obligations do exist. The scope of a state's right to life obligations will only be crystallized through further litigation, yet it is still possible to make some predictions. It is likely that a court will have little difficulty in establishing right to life obligations in respect of deaths in military training in the UK prior to deployment to an armed conflict. Conversely, it is far less likely that a court will consider a state to have right to life obligations in respect of its armed forces when they are killed by the 'enemy' during armed conflict, even where it is asserted that this is as a consequence of inadequate training. The 'middle ground' in respect of procurement decisions is more difficult to predict, although Lord Hope has placed a clear marker down encouraging courts to exercise caution and not encroach into areas of government policy or operational decision-making.

In respect of a state's procedural right to life obligations following the death of UK armed forces personnel during armed conflict, it is submitted that rigorous and comprehensive investigatory procedures exist to ensure the cause of death is determined. Equally, procedures exist to ensure that lessons are learned where applicable and that doctrine and procedures are modified to reduce the likelihood of a recurrence. Ultimately, it is submitted that the UK is able to comply with this aspect of its right to life obligations.

PART III

LIMITATIONS ON THE RIGHT TO LIFE IN ARMED CONFLICT

6

The Effect of Derogation

6.1 Introduction

Derogation from a state's obligations is not permissible in international humanitarian law. International human rights law instruments,[1] on the other hand, contain provisions for the use of derogations in times of 'war', 'public danger',[2] or 'public emergencies that threaten the life of the nation'. Specific provision is made in Article 15, ECHR, [3] that enables states to derogate from their right to life obligations

[1] Article 4, ICCPR:

1. In time of public emergency which threatens the life of the nation and the existence of which is officially proclaimed, the States Parties to the present Covenant may take measures derogating from their obligations under the present Covenant to the extent strictly required by the exigencies of the situation, provided that such measures are not inconsistent with their other obligations under international law and do not involve discrimination solely on the ground of race, colour, sex, language, religion or social origin.
2. No derogation from articles 6, 7, 8 (paragraphs 1 and 2), 11, 15, 16 and 18 may be made under this provision.
3. Any State Party to the present Covenant availing itself of the right of derogation shall immediately inform the other States Parties to the present Covenant, through the intermediary of the Secretary-General of the United Nations, of the provisions from which it has derogated and of the reasons by which it was actuated. A further communication shall be made, through the same intermediary, on the date on which it terminates such derogation.

[2] Article 27, ACHR, Suspension of Guarantees:

1. In time of war, public danger, or other emergency that threatens the independence or security of a State Party, it may take measures derogating from its obligations under the present Convention to the extent and for the period of time strictly required by the exigencies of the situation, provided that such measures are not inconsistent with its other obligations under international law and do not involve discrimination on the ground of race, color, sex, language, religion, or social origin.
2. The foregoing provision does not authorize any suspension of the following articles: Article 3 (Right to Juridical Personality), Article 4 (Right to Life), Article 5 (Right to Humane Treatment), Article 6 (Freedom from Slavery), Article 9 (Freedom from *Ex Post Facto* Laws), Article 12 (Freedom of Conscience and Religion), Article 17 (Rights of the Family), Article 18 (Right to a Name), Article 19 (Rights of the Child), Article 20 (Right to Nationality), and Article 23 (Right to Participate in Government), or of the judicial guarantees essential for the protection of such rights.
3. Any State Party availing itself of the right of suspension shall immediately inform the other States Parties, through the Secretary General of the Organization of American States, of the provisions the application of which it has suspended, the reasons that gave rise to the suspension, and the date set for the termination of such suspension.

[3] Article 15, ECHR:

during armed conflict. Article 6, ICCPR is, on the other hand, non-derogable, pursuant to Article 4(2), ICCPR. It is submitted, however, that the reference to 'arbitrarily deprived of life' in Article 6, ICCPR affords states sufficient latitude to interpret the right to life obligations contained therein in line with international humanitarian law (IHL) standards on the use of lethal force. This chapter will therefore focus on the derogation provision within the ECHR.

Entering a valid derogation does not allow states to act with impunity, free from any right to life obligations. Rather, the use of derogations limits the action state agents may take during armed conflict solely to lawful acts of war as prescribed by IHL. As such, the use of derogations during armed conflict may go some way to resolving the tension that exists when the right to life is applied to situations of armed conflict, provide 'clarity and flexibility'[4] to the development of the law in this area, and 'ensure the coherent co-application'[5] of IHL and international human rights law (IHRL). The use of a derogation from a state's right to life obligations during armed conflict is not, however, a panacea to what some see as the unwelcome encroachment[6] of human rights law and judicial scrutiny into armed conflict. There are several reasons for this. Procedural obligations pursuant to the Article 2, ECHR requirement to investigate alleged violations of a state's right to life obligations remain, even when a derogation is entered, and as such a route to litigation in human rights law remains. Moreover, the European Court of Human Rights (ECtHR) has a significant role in determining whether derogation is permissible with reference to the circumstances existing at the time.[7] Specifically, the Court can consider whether the derogation is required with reference to the 'exigencies of

Derogation in time of emergency

1. In time of war or other public emergency threatening the life of the nation any High Contracting Party may take measures derogating from its obligations under this Convention to the extent strictly required by the exigencies of the situation, provided that such measures are not inconsistent with its other obligations under international law.
2. No derogation from Article 2, except in respect of deaths resulting from lawful acts of war, or from Articles 3, 4 (paragraph 1) and 7 shall be made under this provision.
3. Any High Contracting Party availing itself of this right of derogation shall keep the Secretary General of the Council of Europe fully informed of the measures which it has taken and the reasons therefor. It shall also inform the Secretary General of the Council of Europe when such measures have ceased to operate and the provisions of the Convention are again being fully executed.

[4] Marko Milanovic, 'Extraterritorial Derogations from Human Rights Treaties in Armed Conflict', <https://ssrn.com/abstract=2447183>.

[5] Written evidence submitted from Professor Françoise Hampson, Professor Noam Lubell and Dr Daragh Murray (DRO0010) to the UK Parliament's Joint Committee on Human Rights, 3, <http://data.parliament.uk/writtenevidence/committeeevidence.svc/evidencedocument/human-rights-committee/the-governments-proposed-derogation-from-the-echr/written/49507.html>.

[6] Jonathan Morgan, Richard Ekins, and Guglielmo Verdirame, Derogation from the European Convention on Human Rights in Armed Conflict—Submission to the Joint Committee on Human Rights, 7 April 2017, <http://judicialpowerproject.org.uk/wp-content/uploads/2017/04/JPP-JCHR-submission-on-ECHR-derogation.pdf>.

[7] For example, see *Ireland v the United Kingdom*, 18 January 1978, Series A, Application no 25, 207; *Brannigan and McBride v the United Kingdom*, 26 May 1993, Series A, Application no 258-B, 43; *A. and Others v the United Kingdom* [GC], Application no 3455/05, ECHR 2009, 173.

the situation',[8] whether it is 'not inconsistent with its other obligations under international law',[9] and whether it has been submitted to the Secretary General of the Council of Europe in accordance with the guidance contained within Article 15(3), ECHR.[10]

The issue of the use of derogations during armed conflict has been thrown into particularly sharp relief by proclamations of the UK government. On 10 October 2016, the UK Secretary of State for Defence issued a statement that read:

> The Government will protect our Armed Forces from persistent legal claims by introducing a presumption to derogate from the European Convention on Human Rights (ECHR) in future conflicts, the Prime Minister and the Defence Secretary have announced. Over the past decade a series of court judgments have extended the extra-territorial jurisdiction of the European Convention on Human Rights to the battlefield. Military advisers warn that this risks seriously undermining the operational effectiveness of the Armed Forces ... The intention to derogate from the ECHR, if possible in the circumstances that exist at that time, will protect British troops serving in future conflicts from the kind of persistent legal claims that have followed recent operations in Iraq and Afghanistan on an industrial scale.[11]

The Secretary of State's remarks were amplified by the Chief of the Defence Staff, Air Chief Marshal Sir Stuart Peach, who stated:

> Under the plans, it will remain essential that our Armed Forces operate to the highest standards and are subject to the rule of law at all times. They will continue to operate under a comprehensive legal framework in accordance with International Humanitarian Law (the law of armed conflict including the Geneva Conventions) and with Service Law, which includes UK criminal law of England and Wales regardless of where they are serving.[12]

Notwithstanding that the Defence Secretary's statement was drafted in a way to afford sufficient latitude[13] as to whether the UK will, in fact, enter derogations in respect of future armed conflicts, it is necessary to consider a series of questions in order to assess whether derogations may operate in the way the UK government asserts. First, the issue of whether derogations can be entered at all in respect of an extraterritorial armed conflict must be addressed. Second, assuming extraterritorial derogations are permissible, the associated questions of when derogations to a state's right to life obligations may be entered, and the criteria for such a measure being taken, also arise. Third, how states enter derogations, and finally, the effect of derogations on a state's right to life obligations during armed conflict, must be reviewed.

[8] Article 15(1), ECHR.

[9] Ibid.

[10] *Aksoy v Turkey*, 18 December 1996, Reports of Judgments and Decisions 1996-VI, 85–86.

[11] <https://www.gov.uk/government/news/government-to-protect-armed-forces-from-persistent-legal-claims-in-future-overseas-operations>.

[12] Ibid.

[13] Specifically, the inclusion of the term 'The intention to derogate from the ECHR, if possible in the circumstances that exist at that time.'

6.2 Can Derogations Be Entered in Respect of an Extraterritorial Armed Conflict?

To date, no state has derogated from any human rights law obligations in respect of the operations of its armed forces overseas.[14] With respect to the UK, such an approach may be explained in part by its litigation strategy in a series of cases[15] in which it has denied the applicability of human rights law to military operations overseas. Such a position is looking increasingly untenable and has perhaps prompted a different approach in the form of derogations to human rights law obligations. The fundamental question to be addressed first is: can derogations to a state's right to life obligations be entered in respect of an extraterritorial armed conflict?

On a strict and literal interpretation of the text of Article 15, ECHR, states can derogate from their right to life obligations during an armed conflict overseas. Using the language of the time, specific reference is made to 'war' in Article 15(1) and 'lawful acts of war' in the context of a state's Article 2 right to life obligations in Article 15(2). Such references clearly indicate the possibility of states derogating from their right to life obligations during armed conflict.

6.3 When Can Derogations Be Entered? What are the Criteria for a Derogation to Be Entered?

Any derogation, pursuant to Article 15, ECHR, is subject to four criteria. First, it can only be entered in respect of a state's right to life obligations 'in time of war or other public emergency threatening the life of the nation';[16] second, it is only permissible to 'the extent strictly required by the exigencies of the situation';[17] third, the derogation must not be 'inconsistent with [the state's] other obligations under international law';[18] and finally, a derogation from Article 2 is only permissible in respect of 'lawful acts of war'[19] undertaken by state agents. The difficulty arises, and opinions diverge, in respect of the interpretation of these criteria for a derogation being permissible; or, put another way, the criteria afford significant ambiguity.

[14] *Hassan v the United Kingdom* [GC], Application no 29750/09, ECHR 2014, 101: 'although there have been a number of military missions involving Contracting States acting extra-territorially since their ratification of the Convention, no State has ever made a derogation pursuant to Article 15 of the Convention in respect of these activities. The derogations ... have been rendered necessary as a result of internal conflicts or terrorist threats to the Contracting State.'

[15] See, for example, *R(Al-Jedda) v Secretary of State for Defence* [2007] UKHL 1 AC 332; *Al-Jedda v United Kingdom* [GC], Application no 27021/08, 7 July 2011; *Al-Skeini and others v United Kingdom* [GC], Application no 55721/07, 7 July 2011.

[16] ECHR, Article 15(1). [17] Ibid. [18] Ibid. [19] ECHR, Article 15(2).

6.3.1 'In time of war or other public emergency threatening the life of the nation'

Two issues arise in respect of the requirement that there must exist a 'war or other public emergency threatening the life of the nation' in order to enable states to enter a derogation. First, are the terms 'war' and 'other public emergency threatening the life of the nation' to be read conjunctively or disjunctively? Second, if the terms are to be read conjunctively, is it even possible that an armed conflict overseas into which a state has entered voluntarily can be considered to 'threaten the life of the nation', if the term 'nation' is taken to mean the state entering the derogation?

The ECtHR has not been required to define the archaic term 'war',[20] and it could therefore be subject to several interpretations. Milanovic has proffered three:

1. as a reference to the technical legal concept of 'war' as it existed in classical international law;
2. as a reference to the modern concept of international armed conflict, which is, like 'war', interstate in nature but is objective and factual, and was indeed meant as a replacement for 'war', with perhaps the addition of belligerent occupation as a sub-species of IAC;
3. as a reference to any type of armed conflict regulated by contemporary IHL, thus including both IAC and NIAC, as well as occupation and possibly any third type of armed conflict if it ever evolves through custom or is created by treaty.[21]

If 'war' were considered as an extreme example of a set of circumstances which 'threatened the life of the nation' on a spectrum of conduct that allowed states to enter a derogation to their right to life obligations, this would favour an expansive interpretation of 'war' as set out at 3 above. It would also, as Milanovic argues, 'allow for the most expansive recourse to derogations'[22]—but this interpretation does encounter a potential difficulty where the 'war' must still be considered to threaten the 'life of the nation' in order for any derogation to be valid.

Greene argues that 'war is not just an illustrative example of a public emergency threatening the life of the nation; it is a "core" or paradigmatic example',[23] thereby implying that it is not possible to consider the terms 'war' and 'other public emergency threatening the life of the nation' disjunctively. The consequence of doing so is potentially to create a situation, as advanced by Greene, where if

[20] As Milanovic rightly asserts, the term 'war' has fallen into disuse when considering modern IHL: 'Extraterritorial Derogations from Human Rights Treaties in Armed Conflict', 14. Moreover, states no longer declare 'war' on other states or generally accept that they are at 'war' with another state or states. References to international or non-international armed conflict are now more commonplace.

[21] Milanovic, 'Extraterritorial Derogations from Human Rights Treaties in Armed Conflict' 14.

[22] Ibid, 15.

[23] Written evidence submitted from Dr Alan Greene, Durham Law School (DRO0008) to the UK Parliament's Joint Committee on Human Rights, 9, <http://data.parliament.uk/writtenevidence/committeeevidence.svc/evidencedocument/human-rights-committee/the-governments-proposed-derogation-from-the-echr/written/49456.html>.

'British armed forces overseas are not engaged in an armed conflict that "threatens the life of the nation" then the state cannot lawfully derogate under Article 15'.[24] Greene's position is in line with Lord Bingham's judgment in *Al-Jedda*, given in the following terms:

> It is hard to think that these conditions could ever be met when a state had chosen to conduct an overseas peacekeeping operation, however dangerous the conditions, from which it could withdraw. The Secretary of State does not contend that the UK could exercise its power to derogate in Iraq (although he does not accept that it could not). It has not been the practice of states to derogate in such situations, and since subsequent practice in the application of a treaty may (under article 31(3)(b) of the Vienna Convention) be taken into account in interpreting the treaty it seems proper to regard article 15 as inapplicable.[25]

The extent to which any derogation in respect of a state's right to life obligations during an 'extraterritorial' armed conflict may be valid is therefore dependent upon whether such a conflict threatens the life of the state (nation) seeking to derogate. More specifically, two fundamental questions must be addressed in response to the position advanced by Lord Bingham in *Al-Jedda* and restated by Greene. First, what is meant by 'threaten the life of the nation'—does this mean an existential threat to the entire nation? Second, must the entire nation be affected by the armed conflict or activities prompting recourse to derogation?

The ECtHR has considered that a threat to the life of the nation amounts to 'an exceptional situation of crisis or emergency which affects the whole population and constitutes a threat to the organised life of the community of which the State is composed'.[26] More specifically, 'the crisis or danger should be exceptional in that the normal measures or restrictions permitted by the Convention for the maintenance of public safety, health and order are plainly inadequate'.[27] Closer examination of subsequent judgments does, however, reveal a willingness on the part of the Court to permit derogations where there may not be an existential threat to the 'state's institutions and the existence of a civil community'.[28] It is submitted, for example, that where derogation has been accepted by the Court pursuant to the actions of the IRA[29] and those of the PKK in South-East Turkey,[30] as well as in the aftermath of 9/11,[31] there did not exist an existential threat to the state seeking to derogate. Moreover, such examples suggest that the 'entire nation' need not be affected by circumstances that have necessitated the requirement to derogate. The activities of the IRA were predominately focused on Northern Ireland, despite occasional attacks on the UK mainland, and the activities of the PKK were largely

[24] Ibid. [25] *R(Al-Jedda) v Secretary of State for Defence* 354.

[26] *Lawless v Ireland (no 3)*, 1 July 1961, Series A no 3, 28.

[27] *Denmark, Norway, Sweden and the Netherlands v Greece* (the '*Greek Case*'), Application nos 3321/67 and 3 others, Commission report of 5 November 1969, Yearbook 12, 153.

[28] *A and Others v the United Kingdom* [GC], Application no 3455/05, ECHR 2009, 179.

[29] *Ireland v the United Kingdom*, 18 January 1978, Series A Application no 25; *Brannigan and McBride v the United Kingdom*, 26 May 1993, Series A, Application no 258-B; *Marshall v the United Kingdom* (dec), Application no 41571/98, 10 July 2001.

[30] *Aksoy v Turkey*, 18 December 1996, Reports of Judgments and Decisions 1996-VI.

[31] *A and Others v the United Kingdom* [GC], Application no 3455/05, ECHR 2009.

confined to South-East Turkey. In respect of the post-9/11 landscape, derogation was permitted despite there having been no attack on the UK. If, therefore, the threat to the nation need not be existential and the activities prompting the derogation need not affect the entire nation, then, as Milanovic argues,[32] there appears to be no obvious reason why a derogation cannot be applicable to the activities of armed forces acting overseas. The permissibility of such derogations arises from judgments to date which reveal a willingness on the part of the Court to apply Article 15 with some flexibility. Recognizing this in *Serdar Mohammed*, Leggatt J considered that

> the Convention has been interpreted, however, as having such extraterritorial effect, [and] it seems to me that Article 15 must be interpreted in a way which reflects this. It cannot be right to interpret jurisdiction under Article 1 as encompassing the exercise of power and control by a state on the territory of another state, as the European Court did in the Al-Skeini case, unless at the same time Article 15 is interpreted in a way which is consonant with that position and permits derogation to the extent that it is strictly required by the exigencies of the situation.[33]

However, where the ECtHR has addressed the issue of extraterritorial derogation, it has done so merely to assert that the derogation is only applicable in the areas named in the derogation:

> In the present case the Court would be working against the object and purpose of that provision if, when assessing the territorial scope of the derogation concerned, it were to extend its effects to a part of Turkish territory not explicitly named in the notice of derogation. It follows that the derogation in question is inapplicable *ratione loci* to the facts of the case.[34]

The Court has not addressed the issue of extraterritorial derogation explicitly but has tacitly implied applicability: it has then limited this by allowing extraterritorial derogation only if specifically applied for by states and justified pursuant to the relevant criteria.

As Milanovic and Leggatt assert, to allow the extraterritorial application of certain provisions of the ECHR and not others—particularly when a specific nexus exists between the two, as in the case of Article 2 and Article 15(2)—would be, at best, inconsistent. Equally, in modern warfare, when states use their armed forces overseas there is often a nexus to a threat to the 'life of the nation' at home. The approach of the de facto Taliban government in Afghanistan created the circumstances in which terrorists could train, seek sanctuary, and plan future attacks on Western states from far beyond the borders of such (target) states. Currently, Islamic State groups operate in a similar fashion from territory they control in Iraq and Syria. Cognizant of

[32] Milanovic, 'Extraterritorial Derogations from Human Rights Treaties in Armed Conflict', 18.

[33] *Serdar Mohammed v Ministry of Defence* [2014] EWHC 1369 (QB), 155.

[34] *Sakık and Others v Turkey*, 26 November 1997, Reports of Judgments and Decisions 1997-VII, 39. See also *Sadak v Turkey*, Application nos 25142/94 and 27099/95, 8 April 2004, 56; *Abdülsamet Yaman v Turkey*, Application no 32446/96, 2 November 2004, 69 and *Yurttas v Turkey*, Application nos 25143/94 and 27098/95, 27 May 2004, 58.

the actions of non-state actors, the ECtHR has specifically recognized the need for derogation to be used with flexibility and has allowed states a significant margin of appreciation thus:

> Since the purpose of Article 15 is to permit States to take derogating measures to protect their populations from future risks, the existence of the threat to the life of the nation must be assessed primarily with reference to those facts which were known at the time of the derogation. The Court is not precluded, however, from having regard to information which comes to light subsequently[35]

and

> it falls in the first place to each Contracting State, with its responsibility for 'the life of [its] nation', to determine whether that life is threatened by a 'public emergency'.[36]

In respect of future armed conflict, therefore, it is submitted that states would have significant scope to submit a derogation from their right to life obligations. The extent to which this derogation would be permitted would, of course, be subject to the factual situation at the time. To use the language of Article 15(1), ECHR, a state 'may take measures derogating from its obligations under this Convention to the extent strictly required by the *exigencies of the situation*'. What amounts to the 'exigencies of the situation' will be determined by the factual situation at the time of the derogation, although the Court has stressed that it is not necessary for a state to suffer harm in order to enter a derogation if harm may be imminent.[37]

6.3.2 Strictly required by the exigencies of the situation

In the first instance, it is for a state to decide if the exigencies of a situation require that a derogation be entered. The Court has reasoned thus:

> It falls in the first place to each Contracting State, with its responsibility for 'the life of [its] nation', to determine whether that life is threatened by a 'public emergency' and, if so, how far it is necessary to go in attempting to overcome the emergency. By reason of their direct and continuous contact with the pressing needs of the moment, the national authorities are in principle in a better position than the international judge to decide both on the presence of such an emergency and on the nature and scope of derogations necessary to avert it. In this matter Article 15 § 1 . . . leaves those authorities a wide margin of appreciation.[38]

Yet while a state is the instigator of a derogation, they are not the ultimate arbiters of whether a derogation is valid, as the Court retains the ability to review a state's decision to enter a derogation. When determining if a derogation has 'gone beyond what is strictly required'[39] the Court will consider a range of general factors, namely,

35 *A and Others v the United Kingdom* [GC], Application no 3455/05, ECHR 2009, 177.

36 *Ireland v the United Kingdom* 207.

37 *A and Others v the United Kingdom* 177.

38 *Ireland v the United Kingdom* 207.

39 *Brannigan and McBride v the United Kingdom* 43; *A and Others v the United Kingdom* 173.

'the nature of the rights affected by the derogation, the circumstances leading to, and the duration of, the emergency situation'.[40] The Council of Europe[41] has also promulgated more specific guidance based upon judgments of the ECtHR that particularize criteria that may be relevant in determining whether a derogation is permissible in the circumstances at the time. These criteria are as follows:

1. whether ordinary laws would have been sufficient to meet the danger caused by the public emergency;[42]
2. whether the measures are a genuine response to an emergency situation;[43]
3. whether the measures were used for the purpose for which they were granted;[44]
4. whether the derogation is limited in scope and the reasons advanced in support of it;[45]
5. whether the need for the derogation was kept under review;[46]
6. any attenuation in the measures imposed;[47]
7. whether the measures were subject to safeguards;[48]
8. the importance of the right at stake, and the broader purpose of judicial control over interferences with that right;[49]
9. whether judicial control of the measures was practicable;[50]
10. the proportionality of the measures and whether they involved any unjustifiable discrimination;[51]
11. the views of any national courts which have considered the question: if the highest domestic court in a Contracting State has reached the conclusion that the measures were not strictly required, the Court will be justified in reaching a contrary conclusion only if satisfied that the national court had misinterpreted or misapplied Article 15 or the Court's jurisprudence under that Article, or reached a conclusion which was manifestly unreasonable.[52]

When the above criteria, and the ECtHR's ability to review the decision of states that enter a derogation, are considered in light of the UK government's 'presumption to derogate in times of armed conflict', the UK government's rationale to counter unwelcome judicial encroachment and 'persistent legal claims' looks open to challenge, as a derogation itself is subject to scrutiny by the ECtHR.

[40] *A and Others v the United Kingdom* 173.

[41] Guide on Article 15 of the European Convention on Human Rights—Derogation in Time of Emergency, updated on 30 April 2017, 19, <http://www.echr.coe.int/Documents/Guide_Art_15_ENG.pdf>.

[42] *Lawless v Ireland (no 3)*, 1 July 1961, Series A no 3, 36; *Ireland v the United Kingdom* 212.

[43] *Brannigan and McBride v the United Kingdom* 51.

[44] *Lawless v Ireland (no 3)* 38.

[45] *Brannigan and McBride v the United Kingdom* 66.

[46] Ibid, para 54.

[47] *Ireland v the United Kingdom* 220.

[48] Ibid, 216–19; *Lawless v Ireland (no 3)* 37; *Brannigan and McBride v the United Kingdom* 61–65; *Aksoy v Turkey* 18 December 1996, Reports of Judgments and Decisions 1996-VI, 79 and 84.

[49] *Aksoy v Turkey* 76.

[50] *Brannigan and McBride v the United Kingdom* 59.

[51] *A and Others v the United Kingdom* 190.

[52] Ibid, 174.

6.3.3 Measures are not inconsistent with its other obligations under international law

In addition to the ECtHR's ability to determine if a derogation is permissible given the 'exigencies of the situation', the Court can also determine if a derogation is not inconsistent with a state's other obligations under international law. During armed conflict and with respect to a state's right to life obligations, such obligations under international law are drawn from IHL. In *Hassan*, the ECtHR considered that, despite a derogation not being entered by the UK, the Court could interpret the state's obligations in respect of Article 5, ECHR, in accordance with the principles of IHL, specifically the Third and Fourth Geneva Conventions.[53] The specific issues in respect of a state's Article 2, ECHR obligations are considered at 6.6.

6.3.4 Deaths resulting from lawful acts of war

Article 15(2), ECHR only permits derogation from a state's Article 2 right to life obligations where state agents are responsible for 'deaths resulting from lawful acts of war'. In this context it is generally recognized that 'lawful acts of war' is a reference to the use of lethal force, in both international and non-international armed conflict, being regulated by IHL.[54] As submitted by Hampson, Lubell, and Murray,[55] pursuant to the state's Article 2 obligations, a state's failure to enter a derogation to its right to life obligations during armed conflict would render that state unable to invoke 'lawful acts of war' as a justification for deaths caused by state agents. The justification advanced by Hampson, Lubell, and Murray and by Milanovic is that 'it would render the derogation regime irrelevant if States could invoke the law of armed conflict [to justify their actions in respect of their right to life obligations], without derogating from Article 2'.[56] It is further submitted that the fact that no state has yet entered a derogation in respect of the actions of their armed forces overseas does not invalidate the requirement to do so. This is because it is only relatively recently, through judgments such as *Hassan* and *Serdar Mohammed*, that a more definitive enunciation of the role of derogation in armed conflict has emerged.

6.4 Procedural Requirements for Derogation during Armed Conflict

Article 15(3), ECHR sets out the notification requirement for derogation in the following terms:

> Any High Contracting Party availing itself of this right of derogation shall keep the Secretary General of the Council of Europe fully informed of the measures which it has taken and the

[53] *Hassan v the United Kingdom* 104.

[54] Written evidence submitted from Professor Françoise Hampson, Professor Noam Lubell, and Dr Daragh Murray (DRO0010) to the UK Parliament's Joint Committee on Human Rights, para 26.

[55] Ibid para 22.

[56] Ibid.

reasons therefor. It shall also inform the Secretary General of the Council of Europe when such measures have ceased to operate and the provisions of the Convention are again being fully executed.

The Council of Europe has also issued guidance in respect of the submission of derogations in which the following requirements have been identified:[57]

1. 'The requirement to notify the Secretary General of the measures taken and the reasons therefore is usually met by writing a letter and attaching copies of the legal texts under which the emergency measures will be taken, with an explanation of their purpose.'[58]
2. 'If copies of all relevant measures [set out at (i) above] are not provided, the requirement will not be met.'[59]
3. 'In the absence of an official and public notice of derogation, Article 15 does not apply to the measures taken by the respondent State.'[60]
4. 'The notification [of derogation] did not need to be made before the measure in question had been introduced.'[61]
5. 'Article 15(3) implies a requirement of permanent review of the need for emergency measure.'[62]
6. States must inform the Secretary General of the Council of Europe when the requirement for derogation has ceased, in accordance with Article 15(3).

6.5 What Is the Effect of Derogation during Armed Conflict?

Entering a derogation to a state's right to life obligations during an extraterritorial armed conflict has different effects upon a state's substantive right to life obligations and procedural right to life obligations. Where a state enters a valid derogation, pursuant to Article 15(2), ECHR, this has the effect of declaring that deaths in armed conflict that are the responsibility of the state are not violations of Article 2, ECHR, provided that the action of the armed forces that led to the death is a 'lawful act of war' as determined by IHL—that is to say, that there has been no violation of the substantive element of Article 2, ECHR. The same declaration does not, however, end the state's obligations pursuant to the procedural element of Article 2, ECHR.

The circumstances in which an investigation must be conducted, and how the investigation is conducted, are different in IHRL and IHL. The requirement for a

[57] Guide on Article 15 of the European Convention on Human Rights—Derogation in Time of Emergency, updated on 30 April 2017 paras 31–37, <http://www.echr.coe.int/Documents/Guide_Art_15_ENG.pdf>.

[58] *Lawless v Ireland* 47.

[59] The '*Greek Case*', Commission Report, 81(1) and 81(2).

[60] *Cyprus v Turkey*, no 8007/77, Commission report of 6 October 1983, 66–68.

[61] In *Greece v the United Kingdom* the Commission considered that a period of three months from the measures being taken and the notification being received by the Secretary General of the Council of Europe was excessive. Conversely, in *Lawless v Ireland (no 3)* the Court found that notification twelve days after the measures came into force was acceptable.

[62] *Brannigan and McBride v the United Kingdom* 54.

state to investigate a death in armed conflict arises in a greater range of circumstances in IHRL than in IHL.[63] Moreover, the criteria that are required of an investigation are more onerous in IHRL than in IHL.[64] As a consequence, the ECtHR would still have locus to consider if the investigation itself satisfied the procedural Article 2 requirements as set out in Chapter 2.

6.6 Treaty Interpretation and Article 15, ECHR Derogation Clause

Two further associated issues concerning the derogation from the right to life pursuant to Article 15, ECHR, during armed conflict must be addressed. First, does the lack of a formally entered derogation by a state during an armed conflict prevent the Court from considering provisions of international humanitarian law? Second, does interpreting Article 2 in light of the applicable international humanitarian law regulating the use of lethal force, as the Court in *Hassan* did in respect of Article 5, offend against Article 31, VCLT, in that it makes the Article 15 derogation clause redundant?

As a matter of treaty interpretation[65] and customary international law,[66] a treaty must be interpreted in such a way as to avoid a situation that 'would result in reducing whole clauses or paragraphs to redundancy or inutility'.[67] It therefore follows that if Article 2, ECHR is read to conform to IHL in times of armed conflict, such that killings that do not violate IHL also do not violate Article 2, then Article 15(2) which provides for derogations with respect to lawful acts of war becomes redundant. In turn, this violates the principle established as a corollary to Article 31, VCLT.

In *Hassan* the Court considered the issue of the lack of a formal derogation and noted that:

> the Court accepts the [UK] Government's argument that the lack of a formal derogation under Article 15 does not prevent the Court from taking account of the context and the provisions of international humanitarian law when interpreting and applying Article 5 in this case.[68]

[63] See Chapter 2 for a comparison of IHRL and IHL in respect of the duty to investigate.

[64] See Chapter 2.

[65] Article 31, Vienna Convention on the Law of Treaties (entered into force 27 January 1980) is widely accepted to consider that meaning and effect must be given to all the terms of a treaty: 'an interpreter is not free to adopt a reading that would result in reducing whole clauses or paragraphs of a treaty to redundancy or inutility'. Appellate Body Report, *United States—Standards for Reformulated and Conventional Gasoline (US—Gasoline)*, WT/052/AB/R, adopted 20 May 1996, 21.

[66] Article 31 VCLT is generally recognized as reflecting customary international law: see *Case Concerning the Territorial Dispute (Libyan Arab Jamahiriya/Chad)* Judgment [1994] ICJ Rep 21, 41; *Case Concerning Oil Platforms (Islamic Republic of Iran/United States of America)* Preliminary Objections, Judgment, [1996] (II) ICJ Rep 812, para 23; and specifically in respect of Article 31.3, *Case Concerning Kasikli/Sedudu Island*, Judgment, [1994] ICJ Rep 1045, 48.

[67] World Trade Organisation, *US—Standards for Reformulated and Conventional Gasoline*, Report of the Appellate Body (20 May 1996) WTO Doc WT/DS2/AB/R, 23; See also *Corfu Channel* (UK v Albania) (Merits) ICJ Reports 1949, 24; R Jennings and A Watts (eds) *Oppenheim's International Law* (9th edn, Longman 1992) 1280–1; Vienna Convention on the Law of Treaties (adopted 23 May 1969, entered into force 27 January 1980) 1155 UNTS 331, Article 31.

[68] *Hassan v the United Kingdom* 103.

The Court then proceeded to interpret the UK's human rights law obligations with reference to the applicable IHL, arguably recognizing the potential Article 31, VCLT violation, but opining nonetheless:

> Turning to the criterion contained in Article 31 § 3(c) of the Vienna Convention the Court has made it clear on many occasions that the Convention must be interpreted in harmony with other rules of international law of which it forms part. This applies no less to international humanitarian law. The four Geneva Conventions of 1949, intended to mitigate the horrors of war, were drafted in parallel to the European Convention on Human Rights and enjoy universal ratification. The provisions in the Third and Fourth Geneva Conventions relating to internment, at issue in the present application, were designed to protect captured combatants and civilians who pose a security threat. The Court has already held that Article 2 of the Convention should 'be interpreted in so far as possible in light of the general principles of international law, including the rules of international humanitarian law which play an indispensable and universally-accepted role in mitigating the savagery and inhumanity of armed conflict' and it considers that these observations apply equally in relation to Article 5.[69]

Despite the Court's analysis in *Hassan*, it could be argued that the refusal to permit any reliance on IHL during a non-international armed conflict absent derogation may not adversely affect a state's ability to use lethal force in any event. Noting that no state has yet entered a derogation in respect of a non-international armed conflict and recognizing the approach of the Court in the 'Chechen cases', there is evidence to suggest that the Court is willing to modify the application of Article 2 irrespective of any Article 15(2) derogation being entered or specific reference in pleading to IHL being made.

In summary, and notwithstanding the Court's approach to derogations in *Hassan*, it is submitted that the preferable and more robust way to approach the issue of derogation and Article 2, ECHR, during armed conflict—and the one advocated by Hampson, Lubell, and Murray[70] and Milanovic,[71] among others—is for states to derogate pursuant to Article 15, ECHR, such that their substantive Article 2 obligations consisted of 'lawful acts of war' prescribed by the applicable IHL.[72] Such an approach would allow for a harmonious interpretation of a state's substantive right to life obligations during armed conflict as they would be determined by IHL. It would not, however, exclude the jurisdiction of the ECtHR entirely, or prevent the Court from examining alleged violations of a state's right to life obligations during armed conflict. In other words, the procedural element of Article 2 remains

[69] Ibid, 102.

[70] Written evidence submitted from Professor Françoise Hampson, Professor Noam Lubell, and Dr Daragh Murray (DRO0010) to the UK Parliament's Joint Committee on Human Rights, 22, <http://data.parliament.uk/writtenevidence/committeeevidence.svc/evidencedocument/human-rights-committee/the-governments-proposed-derogation-from-the-echr/written/49507.html>.

[71] Marko Milanovic, 'A Few Thoughts on Hassan v. United Kingdom', *EJIL:Talk!*, 22 October 2014, <https://www.ejiltalk.org/a-few-thoughts-on-hassan-v-united-kingdom/>; Marko Milanovic, 'UK to Derogate from ECHR in Armed Conflict', *EJIL:Talk!*, 5 October 2016, <https://www.ejiltalk.org/uk-to-derogate-from-the-echr-in-armed-conflict/>.

[72] Article 15(2), ECHR.

extant. The Court also retains the power to determine the validity of any derogation entered. Specifically, the Court can consider whether the derogation is required with reference to the 'exigencies of the situation',[73] whether it is 'not inconsistent with its other obligations under international law',[74] and whether it has been submitted to the Secretary General of the Council of Europe in accordance with the guidance contained within Article 15(3), ECHR.[75] Ultimately, therefore, while a derogation would limit the Article 2, ECHR, obligations of states it would not remove them entirely, and a route to ECHR-based litigation would remain.

[73] Article 15(1), ECHR. [74] Ibid.

[75] *Aksoy v Turkey*, 18 December 1996, Reports of Judgments and Decisions 1996-VI, 85–86.

PART VI

THE RIGHT TO LIFE IN FUTURE ARMED CONFLICTS

7

The Right to Life Obligations of States and How to Ensure Compliance

States have significant right to life obligations pursuant to both the ECHR and the ICCPR where they are a party to these human rights instruments. These obligations do not cease during armed conflict, but may be modified by applicable international humanitarian law norms and, in the context of the ECHR, the use of derogations. In order to determine the extent to which the state's armed forces can ensure compliance with their right to life obligations during armed conflict it is necessary to consider three interlinked issues. First, the positive and negative components and substantive and procedural aspects of the right to life must be identified. Second, how the right to life applies during armed conflict must be considered. This requires an examination of the extraterritorial application of the ECHR and ICCPR and how a state's right to life obligations interact with its international humanitarian law obligations during armed conflict. Finally, once these issues have been addressed, the extent to which military doctrine and tactical procedures can ensure compliance with these obligations must be analysed. Current UK military doctrine and tactical procedures are considered as an illustrative example.

As a starting proposition, it is well recognized that states have both positive and negative right to life obligations pursuant to Article 2, ECHR, and Article 6, ICCPR. The positive obligation can be considered as a requirement to adopt measures that allow individuals to live. The negative component is a right of individuals not to be 'arbitrarily' or 'unlawfully' killed by state agents, recognizing that 'arbitrary' is a broader concept than 'unlawful'.[1] Naturally, both the positive and negative obligations can arise simultaneously, and a state can be found to have failed in both respects with reference to a single incident. To illustrate, where there is a death in custody there can be a violation of both a state's positive obligation to protect the life of an individual while they are under the control of the state, and the state's negative obligation not to kill arbitrarily or unlawfully. Such obligations are equally applicable during armed conflict when individuals are held in a military detention facility, and a clear violation was found in the case of Mr Baha Mousa, who died as a result of injuries sustained while detained by UK armed forces in Iraq.

[1] See *Fanny Suárez de Guerrero v Colombia*, Human Rights Committee, Communication no 45/1979: Colombia, 31/03/82, CCPR/C/15/0/45/1979 (Jurisprudence), 31 March 1982.

A state's positive and negative right to life obligations are inextricably linked to their substantive and procedural right to life obligations. A state's substantive right to life obligations are found in the text of Article 2, ECHR and Article 6, ICCPR and relate specifically to the circumstances in which a death occurs. The texts of the ECHR and ICCPR differ in that the ECHR is prescriptive in enumerating the exceptions to the right to life and the ICCPR less so, stating merely that no person shall be 'arbitrarily' deprived of their right to life. On the face of the texts, therefore, it is easier to interpret the right to life provisions in the ICCPR in line with a state's international humanitarian law obligations. Significantly, however, Article 2, ECHR can also be read to reflect a state's international humanitarian law obligations in respect of the use of lethal force, both during international and non-international armed conflict. Support for this assertion can be found in both ECtHR[2] and domestic jurisprudence.[3]

A state's procedural right to life obligation to investigate an alleged violation of its substantive right to life obligation has been interpreted in a similar fashion by both the Human Rights Committee and the ECtHR. Any investigation must be independent, impartial, and conducted expeditiously. Mechanisms to ensure accountability must also exist.

While the exact circumstances in which the ECHR and ICCPR apply extraterritorially is still keenly debated and far from settled, some conclusions can be drawn. Despite the protestations of certain states, it can be said that both instruments are capable of having extraterritorial effect and create obligations for armed forces operating overseas. With respect to the ECHR, these obligations can arise in circumstances where armed forces exercise control over territory and/or individuals, or exercise certain 'public powers' normally undertaken by the state within which they operate. The rights to be guaranteed can be 'divided and tailored' according to the manner in which the control is exercised, namely over territory, over individuals, or through the exercise of public powers. With respect to the ICCPR, a compelling proposition is that jurisdiction can arise in circumstances where 'the State exercises authority or effective control over a particular person or context without regards to territory'.[4] This approach does, however, create a distinction between how jurisdiction arises between the ECHR and ICCPR. This potential discrepancy can be resolved by understanding jurisdiction as arising in circumstances where a state agent(s) exercise(s) control over individuals and not necessarily by the control of territory or by exercising 'public powers'.

Notwithstanding recent ECtHR judgments that appear to indicate that jurisdiction can arise when and wherever armed forces have the power to kill individuals, it can be argued that some residual reasoning from *Banković* remains due to

[2] See *Hassan v the United Kingdom*, Application no 29750/09 (ECtHR, 16 September 2014); *Al-Skeini and Others v United Kingdom* [GC], Application no 55721/07, 7 July 2011, 90–94.

[3] *Al-Saadoon and Others v Secretary of State for Defence*, [2015] EWHC 715, 111; *Serdar Mohammed v Ministry of Defence* [2017] UKSC 2, 68(1).

[4] Harold Hongju Koh, United States Department of State Office of the Legal Adviser, 'Memorandum Opinion on the Geographic Scope of the International Covenant on Civil and Political Rights', 19 October 2010, 55.

the ECtHR's unwillingness to directly and explicitly depart from this judgment. Ultimately, this means that where there is the application of lethal force absent any exercise of 'public powers' or control of territory, then there may be no jurisdiction.[5] This lack of clarity is unsatisfactory, clashes with the concept of exercising control over individuals, and ought to be resolved. The Divisional Court in *Al-Saadoon* proposed a solution when it concluded that 'whenever and wherever a state which is a contracting party to the Convention purports to exercise legal authority or uses physical force, it must do so in a way that does not violate Convention rights.'[6] While not without difficulty, this approach would provide a clear basis upon which a state could assess its human rights obligations during armed conflict. Merely that jurisdiction is established in such a manner does not necessarily create onerous obligations for a state that would adversely affect the ability of armed forces to achieve its military objectives. Once jurisdiction is established, the next step is to examine how international humanitarian law may modify a state's right to life obligations during armed conflict.

As previously contended, the interpretation of the substantive and procedural right to life provisions by the Human Rights Committee and ECtHR has been broadly similar. Where there has been some divergence, however, is in the approach taken by the ICJ and ECtHR in respect of the interaction between international human rights law and international humanitarian law during armed conflict. The ICJ has favoured an approach, albeit modified slightly between the *Nuclear Weapons* and *Wall* cases, in which a human rights law norm should be interpreted in light of the applicable international humanitarian law norm.[7] The ECtHR has, on the other hand, been less consistent and has been prepared, in certain circumstances, to consider a state's substantive right to life obligations absent any direct reference to international humanitarian law.[8] This difference in approach does not, however, inextricably lead to a fundamental incompatibility between the two bodies of law, for four reasons. First, in the 'Chechen cases', the ECtHR made only indirect reference to international humanitarian law, in that the use of lethal force must be proportionate to the achievement of 'permitted aims'. It is submitted that within the context of these cases the 'permitted aims' relate to international humanitarian law principles regulating the conduct of an armed conflict. Second, the Court further stated that 'the obligation to protect the right to life must be interpreted in a way which does not impose an impossible or disproportionate burden on the authorities'.[9] Third, the Court has expressly stated that 'Article 2 must be interpreted so

[5] Marco Milanovic, 'Al-Skeini and Al-Jedda in Strasbourg' (2012) 23 *Eu J Int Law* 126, at 139.

[6] *Al-Saadoon and Others v Secretary of State for Defence* 106.

[7] ICJ, *Legal Consequences of the Construction of a Wall in the Occupied Palestinian Territory, Advisory Opinion*, 9 July 2004, 106.

[8] See *Isayeva v Russia*, Application no 57950/00 (ECtHR, 24 February 2003); *Isayeva, Yusopova and Bazayeva v Russia*, Application nos 57947/00, 57948/00, 57949/00 (ECtHR, 24 February 2003); *Albekov et al v Russia*, Application no 68216/01 (ECtHR Chamber, 2006); *Arzu Akhmadova et al v Russia*, Application no 13670/01 (ECtHR, 8 January 2009); *Umayeva v Russia*, Application no 1200/03 (ECtHR, 4 December 2004).

[9] See *Isayeva v Russia*, Application no 57950/00, (ECtHR, 24 February 2003); *Isayeva, Yusopova and Bazayeva v Russia*, Application nos 57947/00, 57948/00, 57949/00 (ECtHR, 24 February 2003).

far as possible in light of the general principles of international law, including the rules of international humanitarian law which play an indispensable and universally accepted role in mitigating the savagery and inhumanity of armed conflict.'[10] Finally, subsequent judgments of the Court, such as in *Hassan*, clearly indicate a willingness to recognize and reflect international humanitarian law in the Court's analysis of a state's human rights obligations.[11]

While it is recognized that there are differences between the concepts of (military) necessity and proportionality in international humanitarian law and international human rights law, it may be possible to reconcile these differences in a way that allows armed forces to ensure compliance with their right to life obligations. With reference to the right to life, necessity in human rights law is considered to mean the use of lethal force as a last resort pursuant to a lawful or non-arbitrary purpose. On a strict interpretation, therefore, this would prohibit the use of lethal force against combatants in armed conflict, which is permissible under the international humanitarian law 'military necessity' construct, where they did not pose an imminent threat to life. If a state's human rights obligations are, however, interpreted in light of the relevant international humanitarian law, this would enable state agents to use lethal force in a way that did not contravene the state's substantive right to life obligations. To illustrate, in non-international armed conflict and with reference to Article 2, ECHR, the use of lethal force would be permissible in self-defence or to quell a riot or insurrection. This, when read in conjunction with the ECtHR's judgments in the 'Chechen cases', would provide significant latitude to armed forces in the use of lethal force. In respect of international armed conflict, a similar case can be made on the basis of the analysis of the Court in *Hassan*, supported by the Divisional Court in *Serdar Mohammed*. In respect of Article 6, ICCPR it is submitted that there is sufficient latitude in the term 'arbitrarily' when read in conjunction with the ICJ's judgment in the '*Wall* case' to again allow a state to comply with its right to life obligations in international armed conflict by interpreting these obligations in light of the relevant international humanitarian law.

There are significant difficulties in advocating an alternative position whereby the applicable human rights law framework is determined by the intensity or nature of the armed conflict. Such an approach is not only contrary to the view of the ICJ, but also risks having different and fluid legal regimes being applicable in the same military theatre of operations both geographically and temporally. Rather than protecting non-combatants, this approach may lead to confusion among military commanders that results in risks to both non-combatants and armed forces personnel.

As with 'necessity', the notion of proportionality has a different and more permissive meaning in international humanitarian law than in international human rights law. The ECtHR have referred to proportionality in, inter alia, *McCann* and the 'Chechen cases' with reference to the use of lethal force being 'strictly proportionate to the achievement of permitted aims'. While this is a different standard to proportionality in international humanitarian law requiring that 'the losses resulting

[10] *Varnanva and Others v Turkey*, [GC] Application no 16064/90, (ECtHR, 2009) 185.

[11] See also Lord Sumption in *Serdar Mohammed v Ministry of Defence* [2017] UKSC 2, 68(1).

from a military action should not be excessive in relation to the expected military advantage', the two notions should not be viewed as entirely incompatible. Where the ECtHR has found violations of a state's substantive right to life obligations by armed forces acting as state agents, their actions, if conducted during an armed conflict, would have equally offended against the international humanitarian law principle of proportionality.[12] Given the ECtHR's recent recognition of international humanitarian law when considering alleged violations of human rights in *Hassan*, it can be persuasively argued that, when considering alleged violations of the substantive element of the right to life during armed conflict, the Court may be willing to make any proportionality assessment, if required to do so, in line with international humanitarian law.

In considering the extent to which the UK government can ensure its armed forces comply with the state's substantive right to life obligations during international and non-international armed conflict, it is important to recognize that in modern warfare, armed forces use lethal force in broadly three main ways:[13] first, when engaging planned targets from land, sea, or air using weapon systems designed to be operated at a significant distance from the target; second, when conducting a planned attack using forces on the ground against a known target; and finally, in individual or group self-defence. In each case the use of force is governed by rules of engagement underpinned by tactical directives, military doctrine, UK domestic law, and international humanitarian law. Human rights law obligations generally and the right to life specifically are not reflected in UK military doctrine. Despite this omission, the rules of engagement governing the use of lethal force in respect of planned attacks and in self-defence would comply with the UK's substantive right to life obligations, if properly adhered to. The planned targeting process applicable in international and non-international armed conflict is particularly thorough and an extremely high degree of certainty is required prior to a combatant being lethally targeted. During a planned attack using forces on the ground, similar safeguards are in place through training and planning to ensure that only lawful targets are deliberately attacked. Similarly, when armed forces personnel use lethal force in self-defence such action is permitted by both the ECHR and ICCPR, provided that the generally recognized criteria for the use of lethal force in self-defence are complied with. The use of lethal force by armed forces personnel in self-defence applies equally during international and non-international armed conflict.

While it can be persuasively argued that current UK military doctrine and procedures ensure compliance with the state's substantive right to life obligations during armed conflict, the same cannot be said of their procedural right to life obligations to, inter alia, investigate alleged right to life violations by state agents. While

[12] For example see *Isayeva, Yusopova and Bazayeva v Russia* 199; *Isayeva v Russia* 10–28; *Güleç v Turkey* 71–72, 76, 83.

[13] This does not include the potential application of cyber activity to the right to life. For the legal framework in respect of cyber operations see Michael Schmitt (ed), *Tallinn Manual 2.0 on the International Law Applicable to Cyber Warfare* (2nd edn, Cambridge University Press 2017).

in the area of substantive right to life obligations, international humanitarian law has well-established and understood rules governing the use of lethal force, the same cannot be said of procedural right to life obligations and the corresponding requirement to investigate in international humanitarian law. Clearly, the Geneva Conventions,[14] Additional Protocol I,[15] and the Rome Statute require the investigation and prosecution of grave breaches of international humanitarian law and 'war crimes'. Additional obligations are also placed upon military commanders of 'armed forces under their command and other persons under their control, to prevent and, where necessary, to suppress and to report to competent authorities breaches' of the Geneva Conventions and AP I. The Turkel Commission,[16] citing the Rome Statute,[17] also persuasively argues that these obligations apply equally during non-international armed conflict. Nonetheless, the 'investigatory' obligations of international humanitarian law would not encompass all the individual violations of the right to life during armed conflict that have been considered by the ECtHR in cases such as *Jaloud*. As a consequence, there is arguably a far greater role for international human rights bodies to consider alleged violations of a state's procedural right to life obligations.

Despite there being numerous methods available to UK armed forces to investigate the use of lethal force by armed forces personnel during armed conflict, very few comply with the requirements established by the ECtHR and the Human Rights Committee. Even allowing latitude for the difficulties inherent in investigating alleged right to life violations on the battlefield, structural problems exist with regard to serious incident reports and shooting incident reviews that result in a lack of independence. These issues were recognized by Sir Thayne Forbes in the *Al-Sweady* inquiry and ought to be addressed by the UK Ministry of Defence. It must be recognized, however, that doing so would require greater numbers of independent military police deployed during armed conflict. This requirement would not, it is submitted, adversely affect a military commander's ability to achieve their military objectives, as this investigatory requirement does not impede a commander's ability or authority to use lethal force against legitimate targets.

With regard to derogations, if a state's substantive right to life obligations are seen to conform to international humanitarian law standards, an argument could be advanced that this makes the requirement to derogate unnecessary. It is recognized that such an approach may risk violating a principle of treaty interpretation in that Article 2, ECHR would be read in such a way as to make Article 15(2), ECHR redundant. The ECtHR has, however, implicitly endorsed such a situation in its judgment in *Hassan* by interpreting Article 5, absent any derogation by the state, in light of international humanitarian law principles during armed conflict, thereby making the Article 15(1) requirement to derogate redundant. In respect of

[14] See, inter alia, GCI Article 52, GCII Article 53, GCIII Article 132, GCIV Articles 131, 146, 147.

[15] API, Article 87.

[16] The Public Commission to Examine the Maritime Incident of 31 May 2010, Israel's Mechanism for Examining and Investigating Complaints and Claims of Violations of the Law of Armed Conflict According to International Law, The 'Turkel Commission' Second Report, February 2013, 27.

[17] Rome Statute 6.

the right to life, it is submitted that such an approach could apply equally during international and non-international armed conflict. Ultimately, however, entering a derogation must be considered to be the preferred option, as it would ensure clarity and allow a harmonious interpretation of IHL and IHRL in respect of the substantive element of the right to life. In doing so, however, states that have hitherto litigated on the basis that the ECHR has no extraterritorial effect and is therefore not applicable during armed conflict must accept that, by entering a derogation, such a position is no longer tenable.

The ability of states, including the UK, to derogate from their ECHR right to life obligations in respect of lawful acts of war has been lauded by some as a panacea to restrict the unwelcome encroachment, as they see it, of human rights law and judicial scrutiny into armed conflict. This belief is misplaced for several reasons. First, any derogation would only be effective in so far as it permitted 'lawful acts of war' as defined by international humanitarian law. Where allegations were made that armed forces personnel acted in a way that violated international humanitarian law, then the state would be required to investigate such allegations pursuant to its procedural right to life obligations. In this sense, the derogation would not prevent ECHR-based litigation should the relevant act be found not to have constituted a 'lawful act of war'. Second, the ECtHR has a significant role in determining whether derogation is permissible with reference to the circumstances existing at the time.[18] Specifically, the Court can consider whether the derogation is required with reference to the 'exigencies of the situation';[19] if the derogation is 'not inconsistent with its other obligations under international law';[20] and whether the derogation has been submitted to the Secretary General of the Council of Europe in accordance with the guidance contained within Article 15(3), ECHR.[21] It is apparent, therefore, that the Court has a significant role in determining the validity of any derogation that is entered. Finally, it has been argued that an effective derogation would remove the requirement to conduct an investigation pursuant to the state's procedural right to life obligation, thereby conserving valuable resources during armed conflict. This proposition is only partially accurate. First, as has been submitted, any derogation would only be effective in respect of 'lawful acts of war' that resulted in a death; a requirement would remain to investigate deaths that resulted from 'unlawful acts of war', in addition to whether the action of armed forces personnel did, in fact, amount to a 'lawful act of war'. Second, the UK investigates all allegations of 'unlawful killing' in any event. Ultimately, as a matter of the de jure effect of Article 15, ECHR and the *lex lata*, a derogation may not prevent the requirement to investigate all deaths in armed conflict that fall outside a strict interpretation of Article 2.

When considering the right to life protections to be afforded UK armed forces personnel during armed conflict, it is important to recognize the vastly different

[18] For example, see *Ireland v the United Kingdom*, 18 January 1978, Series A, Application no 25, 207; *Brannigan and McBride v the United Kingdom*, 26 May 1993, Series A, Application no 258-B, 43; *A and Others v the United Kingdom* [GC], Application no 3455/05, ECHR 2009, 173.

[19] Article 15(1), ECHR. [20] Ibid.

[21] *Aksoy v Turkey*, 18 December 1996, Reports of Judgments and Decisions 1996-VI 85–86.

roles they can undertake and the changeable nature of any armed conflict. Put simply, the further removed, both geographically and temporally, an individual is from the risk of loss of life due to enemy action, the greater the likelihood that the state will be required to protect their right to life. It is incorrect to assert that all armed forces personnel in an operational theatre forgo any right to life protection. That said, the Supreme Court in *(Susan) Smith* was not prepared to extend the protections of Article 2 to those directly engaged in combat, fearful of the potential negative effect on combat effectiveness that such a ruling would have.

Ultimately, in respect of substantive right to life obligations pursuant to the ECHR and ICCPR, the relationship between international humanitarian law and human rights law continues to evolve and a settled position is yet to be determined. Nonetheless, there is evidence to suggest that it is possible to reach a situation in which the requirements of international humanitarian law and human rights law during armed conflict can mutually complement each other. Such a situation would neither unduly restrict armed forces in pursuit of legitimate military aims nor expose combatants and non-combatants to unnecessary risk. At present, it is submitted that in terms of the use of lethal force during armed conflict, the UK can, through the safeguards it has in place, ensure compliance with its substantive right to life obligations. Alas, the same cannot be said of its procedural right to life obligations. These shortcomings are not, however, insurmountable, and can be easily rectified without adversely affecting a military commander's ability to achieve their military objectives.

In sum, in order to best comply with their right to life obligations during armed conflict, states ought to enter a derogation pursuant to Article 15, ECHR, and properly resource the investigative function of armed forces during armed conflict overseas. In doing so, states would provide clarity to their armed forces in respect of their substantive and procedural right to life obligations, and while it is recognized that the use of derogation and ECHR-compliant investigations would never eliminate the possibility of future litigation, it is submitted that they would significantly reduce its likelihood.

Select Bibliography

BOOKS

Bossyut, M, *Guide to the 'Travaux Preparatioires' of the International Covenant on Civil and Political Rights* (Nijhoff 1987)

Bothe, Michael, Partsch, Karl-Josef, and Solf, Waldemar A, *New Rules for Victims of Armed Conflicts: Commentary on the Two 1977 Protocols Additional to the Geneva Conventions of 1949* (Nijhoff 1982)

Brownlie, Ian, *Principles of Public International Law* (6th edn, Oxford University Press 2003)

Brownlie, Ian and Goodwin-Gill, Guy S, *Basic Documents on Human Rights* (5th edn, Oxford University Press, 2006)

Burgers, JH and Danelius, H, *The United Nations Convention against Torture* (Nijhoff 1988)

Cassese, A, *International Law* (2nd edn, Oxford University Press 2005).

Coomans, F and Kamminga, M (eds), *Extraterritorial Application of Human Rights Treaties* (Intersentia 2004)

Denza, E, *Diplomatic Law* (3rd edn, Oxford University Press 2008)

Detter, Ingrid, *The Law of War* (Cambridge University Press 2000)

Dinstein, Yoram, *The Conduct of Hostilities under the Law of International Armed Conflict* (Cambridge University Press 2004)

Dinstein, Yoram, *The International Law of Belligerent Occupation* (Cambridge University Press 2009)

Donnelly, J, *Universal Human Rights in Theory and Practice* (2nd edn, Cornell University Press 2003)

Doswald-Beck, Louise, *Human Rights in Times of Conflict and Terrorism* (Oxford University Press 2011)

Evans, Malcolm (ed), *International Law* (2nd edn, Oxford University Press 2006)

Forsythe, David, *The Humanitarians: The International Committee of the Red Cross* (Cambridge University Press 2005)

Fox, G, *Humanitarian Occupation* (Cambridge University Press 2008)

Fox, H, *The Law of States Immunity* (2nd edn, Oxford University Press 2008)

Gardiner, R, *Treaty Interpretation* (Oxford University Press 2008)

Gondek, M, *The Reach of Human Rights in a Globalising World: Extraterritorial Application of Human Rights Treaties* (Intersentia 2009)

Green, Leslie C, *The Contemporary Law of Armed Conflict* (Manchester University Press 2008)

Gross, Oren and Ni Aolain, Fionnuala, *Law in Times of Crisis: Emergency Powers in Theory and Practice* (Cambridge University Press 2006)

Henkin, L, *Age of Rights* (Columbia University Press 1996)

International Institute of Humanitarian Law, *The Manual on the Law of Non-International Armed Conflict* (Sanremo: International Institute of Humanitarian Law 2006)

Jennings, R and Watts, A (eds), *Oppenheim's International Law* (9th edn, Longman 1992)

Kalin, Walter and Kunzli, Jorg, *The Law of International Human Rights Protection* (Oxford University Press 2009)

Kamminga, M and Scheinin, M (eds), *The Impact of Human Rights Law on General International Law* (Oxford University Press 2009)

Kolb, Robert and Hyde, Richard, *An Introduction to the International Law of Armed Conflict* (Hart 2008)

Lauterpacht, H, *International Law and Human Rights* (Archon Books, 1968; earlier editions 1930 and 1950)

Lubell, Noam, *Extraterritorial Use of Force against Non-State Actors* (Oxford University Press 2010)

Meessen, K (ed), *Extraterritorial Jurisdiction in Theory and Practice* (Kluwer 1996)

Melzer, Nils, *Targeted Killing in International Law* (Oxford University Press 2008)

Meron, Theodor, *Human Rights in Internal Strife: Their International Protection* (Grotius 1987)

Meron, Theodor, *Human Rights and Humanitarian Norms as Customary Law* (Oxford University Press 1989)

Meron, Theodor, *The Humanization of International Law* (Nijhoff 2006)

Mertus, Julie, *The United Nations and Human Rights: A Guide for a New Era* (2nd edn, Routledge 2009)

Milanovic, Marko, *Extraterritorial Application of Human Rights Treaties: Law, Principles, and Policy* (Oxford University Press 2011)

Moir, Lindsay, *The Law of Internal Armed Conflict* (Cambridge University Press 2002)

Mowbray, A., *The Development of Positive Obligations under the European Convention on Human Rights by the European Court of Human Rights* (Hart Publishing 2004)

Nowak, Manfred, *UN Covenant on Civil and Political Rights: CCPR Commentary* (2nd edn, Engel 2005)

Oberleitner, Gerd, *Human Rights in Armed Conflict: Law, Practice, Policy* (Cambridge University Press 2015)

Pictet, Jean (ed), *Commentary on the First Geneva Convention for the Amelioration of the Condition of the Wounded and Sick in Armed Forces in the Field* (International Committee on the Red Cross 1952)

Pictet, Jean (ed), *Commentary on the Fourth Geneva Convention Relative to the Protection of Civilian Persons in Time of War* (International Committee of the Red Cross 1952)

Pictet, Jean, *The Principles of International Humanitarian Law* (International Committee of the Red Cross 1967)

Provost, Rene, *International Human Rights and Humanitarian Law* (Cambridge University Press 2002)

Ramcharan, Bertrand, *Contemporary Human Rights Ideas* (Routledge 2008)

Roberts, Adam and Guelff, Richard, *Documents on the Law of War* (3rd edn, Oxford University Press 2000)

Robertson, AH (ed), *3 Collected Edition of the 'Travaux Préparatoires' of the European Convention on Human Rights* (Nijhoff 1976)

Rowe, Peter, *The Impact of Human Rights Law on Armed Forces* (Cambridge University Press 2006)

Shaw, Malcolm, *International Law* (6th edn, Cambridge University Press 2008)

Sivakumaran, Sandesh, *The Law of Non-International Armed Conflict* (Oxford University Press 2012)

Smith, Rhona K, *Textbook on International Human Rights* (4th edn, Oxford University Press 2010)

Solis, Gary D, *The Law of Armed Conflict* (Cambridge University Press 2010)

Teitel, Ruti G, *Humanity's Law* (Oxford University Press 2011)

Thurer, Daniel, *International Humanitarian Law: Theory, Practice, Context* (Hague Academy of International Law 2011)

UK Ministry of Defence, *The Manual of the Law of Armed Conflict* (Oxford University Press 2004)
van Dijk, P et al, *Theory and Practice of the European Convention on Human Rights* (4th edn, Intersentia 2006)
White, Nigel D and Henderson, Christian (eds), *Research Handbook on International Conflict and Security Law: Jus ad Bellum, Jus in Bello and Jus post Bellum* (Edward Elgar Publishing 2013)
Wicks, Elizabeth, *The Right to Life and Conflicting Interests* (Oxford University Press 2010)

ALLIED JOINT DOCTRINE PUBLICATIONS (AJPS)

AJP-01: Allied joint doctrine
AJP 2.5(A): Captured persons, materiel and documents
AJP 3(B): Allied joint doctrine for the conduct of operations
AJP 3.1: Allied joint maritime operations
AJP 3.2: Allied joint doctrine for land operations
AJP 3.2.3.3: Allied joint doctrine for military police
AJP 3.3(A): Allied joint doctrine for air and space operations
AJP 3.3.1(B): Allied joint doctrine for counter-air
AJP 3.3.2(A): Allied joint doctrine for close air support and air interdiction
AJP 3.3.3(A): Air-maritime co-ordination
AJP 3.3.5(B): Doctrine for joint airspace control
AJP 3.4.1(A): Allied joint doctrine for the military contribution to peace support operations
AJP 3.4.4: Allied joint doctrine for counterinsurgency (COIN)
AJP 3.4.9(A(1)): Allied joint doctrine for civil–military cooperation
AJP 3.5: Allied joint doctrine for special operations
AJP 3.9: Allied joint doctrine for joint targeting
AJP 3.9.2: Land targeting
AJP 3.10: Allied joint doctrine for information operations
AJP 3.13: Allied joint doctrine for the deployment of forces
AJP 3.14(A): Allied joint doctrine for force protection
AJP 4.5(B): Allied joint doctrine for host nation support
AJP 5: Allied joint doctrine for operational-level planning with UK national elements
AJP 6: Allied joint doctrine for communication and information systems

JOINT DOCTRINE PUBLICATIONS (JDPS)

JDP 0-01: UK defence doctrine
JDP 0-01.1: United Kingdom supplement to the NATO terminology database
JDP 0-10: British maritime doctrine
JDP 0-30: UK air and space doctrine
JDP 01: UK joint operations doctrine
JDP 1-10: Captured persons (CPERS)
JDP 2-00: Understanding and intelligence support to joint operations (third edition incorporating Change 1)
Change 1 to JDP 2-00: Understanding and Intelligence support to joint operations (third edition)
JDP 3-00: Campaign execution

JDP 3-24.1: Use of helicopters in land operations (UK supplement to ATP-49)
JDP 3-40: Security and stabilisation: the military contribution
JDP 3-40: Security and stabilisation: the military contribution
JDP 3-46: Legal support to joint operations
JWP 3-63: Joint air defence
JWP 3-63.1: Ground based air defence
JWP 3-63.1.1: Joint ground based air defence fighting book
JDP 3-70: Battlespace management
JWP 3-80: Information operations
JTTP 4-05: Operational infrastructure
JDP 6-00: Communications and information systems support to joint operations

ARTICLES AND BOOK CHAPTERS

Abresch, William, 'A Human Rights Law of Internal Armed Conflict: The European Court of Human Rights in Chechnya' (2005) 16 *EJIL* 741–67

Akande, Dapo, 'Clearing the Fog of War? The ICRC's Interpretive Guidance on Direct Participation in Hostilities', *EJIL: Talk!*, 4 June 2009, available at <http://www.ejiltalk.org/clearing-the-fog-of-war-the-icrcs-interpretice-guidance-on-direct-participation-in-hostilities/>.

Akehurst, M, 'Jurisdiction in International Law' (1972–73) 46 *BYBIL* 145

Akehurst, M, 'The Hierarchy of the Sources of International Law' (1974–75) 47 *BIBIL* 273

Aldrich, George H, 'Human Rights and Armed Conflict: Conflicting Views' (1973) 67 *AJILP* 141–42

Aldrich, George H, 'Human Rights in Armed Conflict: Development of the Law' (1973) 68 *Department of State Bulletin* 876–82

Aldrich, George H, 'The Laws of War on Land' (2000) 94(1) *AJIL* 31–41

Allott, P, 'The Concept of International Law' (1999) 10 *EJIL* 31

Alston, Philip, Morgan-Foster, Jason, and Abresch, William, 'The Competence of the UN Human Rights Council and Its Special Procedures in Relation to Armed Conflicts: Extrajudicial Executions in the "War on Terror"' (2008) 19 *EJIL* 183–209

Altiparmak, Kerem, 'Bankovic: An Obstacle to the Application of the European Convention on Human Rights in Iraq?' (2004) 9(2) *JC&SL* 213–51

An-Na'im, Abdullah Ahmed, 'Toward a Universal Doctrine of Reparation for Violations of International Human Rights and Humanitarian Law' (2003) 5(1) *ILF* 27–35

Anderson, K, 'Predators over Pakistan', *The Weekly Standard*, 8 March 2010, available at <http://ssrn.com/abstract-1561229>

Aust, A, 'Treaties, Territorial Application', *Max Planck Encyclopedia of Public International Law*, available at <http://www.mpepil.com>

Bailin, A, 'Case Preview—R (Smith) v Secretary of State for Defence—on appeal from [2009] EWCA Civ 441', *UKSCblog*, 13 March 2010, available at <http://ukscblog.com/case-preview-r-smith-v-secretary-of-state-for-defence-on-appeal-from-2009-ewca-civ-441>

Balendra, Natasha, 'Defining Armed Conflict' (2008) 29(6) *Cardozo L Rev* 2461–516

Balendra, Natasha, 'International Human Rights Law and International Humanitarian Law: Alternative Frameworks for Interaction' in Christoffer C. Eriksen and Marius Emberland (eds), *The New International Law* (Nijhoff 2010), pp 117–37

Bell, C, 'Capitulations', *Max Planck Encyclopedia of Public International Law*, available at <http://www.mpepil.com>

Bellinger, John B II, 'Legal Issues in the War on Terrorism: A Reply to Silja N. Voneky' (2007) 8(9) *GYIL* 871–78

Ben-Naftali, Orna, 'Introduction: International Humanitarian and International Human Rights Law: Pas de Deux' in Orna Ben-Naftali (ed), *International Humanitarian and International Human Rights Law* (Oxford University Press 2011), pp 3–10

Ben-Naftali, Orna and Shany, Yuval, 'Living in Denial: The Application of Human Rights in the Occupied Territories' (2004) 37(1) *Isr Law Rev* 17–118

Bennoune, Karima, 'Toward a Human Rights Approach to Armed Conflict: Iraq 2003' (2004) 11(1) *UCDavisJIntL&Pol'y* 171–228

Benvenisti, E, 'Occupation, Pacific', *Max Planck Encyclopedia of Public International Law*, available at <http://opil.ouplaw.com/view/10.1093/law:epil/9780199231690/law-9780199231690-e360?rskey=Y4jkf&result=1&prd=EPIL>

Benvenuti, Paolo and Guilio Bartolini, 'Is There a Need for New International Humanitarian Law Implementation Mechanisms?' in Robert Kolb and Gloria Gaggioli (eds), *Research Handbook on Human Rights and Humanitarian Law* (Edward Elgar 2013), pp 590–627

Besson, Samantha, 'The Extraterritoriality of the European Convention on Human Rights: Why Human Rights Depend on Jurisdiction and What Jurisdiction Amounts To' (2012) *LJIL* 857–84

Bhuta, N, 'The Antinomies of Transformation Occupation' (2005) 16 *EJIL* 721

Bhuta, N, 'Conflicting International Obligations and the Risk of Torture and Unfair Trial' (2009) 7 *JICJ* 1133

Blum, Gabriella, 'The Dispensable Lives of Soldiers' (2012) 2(1) *Legal Analysis* 69–124

Borgen, C, 'Resolving Treaty Conflicts' (2005) 37 *Geo Wash Int'l Rev* 573

Bowring, Bill, 'Fragmentation, Lex Specialis and the Tensions in the Jurisprudence of the European Court of Human Rights' (2010) 14(3) *JC&SL* 485–98

Bruscoli, Francesco, 'The Rights of Individuals in Times of Armed Conflict' (2002) 6(1) *IJHR* 45–60

Buergenthal, T, 'To Respect and to Ensure: State Obligations and Permissible Derogations' in L Henkin (ed), *The International Bill of Rights: The Covenant on Civil and Political Rights* (Columbia University Press, 1981)

Buyse, A, 'A Legal Minefield—The Territorial Scope of the European Convention' (2008) 1 *IAEHRJ* 269

Cassese, Antonio, 'The *Nicaragua* and *Tadić* Test Revisited in Light of the ICJ Genocide Judgment in Bosnia' (2007) 18 *EJIL* 649

Cassimatis, A, 'International Humanitarian Law, International Human Rights Law, and the Fragmentation of International Law' (2007) 56 *ICLQ* 623

Cerna, Christina, 'Human Rights in Armed Conflict: Implementation of International Humanitarian Law Norms by Regional Intergovernmental Human Rights Bodies' in Frits Kalshoven and Yves Sandoz (eds), *Implementation of International Humanitarian Law* (Nijhoff, 1989), pp 31–67

Cerna, Christina, 'Extraterritorial Application of the Human Rights Instruments of the Inter-American System' in Coomans, F and Kamminga 141, M (eds), *Extraterritorial Application of Human Rights Treaties* (Intersentia 2004) 141–74

Cerone, J, 'The Application of Regional Human Rights Law Beyond Regional Frontiers: The Inter-American Commission on Human Rights and US Activities in Iraq', *ASIL Insights*, 25 October 2005, available at <www.asil.org/insights051025.cfm>

Cerone, J, 'Jurisdiction and Power: The Intersection of Human Rights Law and the Law of Non-International Armed Conflict in an Extraterritorial Context' (2007) 40 *Isr Law Rev* 72

Chinkin, Christine, 'International Humanitarian Law, Human Rights and the UK Courts' in Laurence Boisson de Chazournes and Marcelo G Kohen (eds), *International Law and the Quest for Its Implementation* (Nijhoff 2010), pp 239–60

Clapham, Andrew, 'Human Rights Obligations of Non-State Actors in Conflict Situations' (2006) 88(863) *IRRC* 491–523

Cleveland, Sarah, 'Embedded International Law and the Constitution Abroad' (2010) 110 *Colum L Rev* 225

Conderman, P, 'Status of Armed Forces on Foreign Territory Agreements (SOFA)', *Max Planck Encyclopedia of Public International Law*, available at <http://www.mpepil.com>

Coomans, F, 'Some Remarks on the Extraterritorial Application of the International Covenant on Economic, Social and Cultural Rights', in Coomans, F and Kamminga, M (eds) *Extraterritorial Application of Human Rights Treaties* (Intersentia 2004) 183–200

Corn, Geoffrey, 'Mixing Apples and Hand Grenades: The Logical Limit of Applying Human Rights Norms to Armed Conflicts' (2010) 1(1) *IHLS* 52–94

Craven, M, 'Legal Differentiation and the Concept of the Human Rights Treaty in International Law' (2000) 11 *EJIL* 489

Crawford, James, 'Multilateral Rights and Obligations in International Law' (2006) 319 *Recueil des Cours* 325

Cross, M and Williams, S, 'Between the Devil and the Deep Blue Sea: Conflicted Thinking in the Al-Saadoon Affair' (2009) 58 *ICLQ* 689

Cryer, Robert, 'The Interplay of Human Rights and Humanitarian Law: The Approach of the ICTY' (2009) 14(3) *JC&SL* 511–27

Czuik, P and Szwedo, P, 'Consular Jurisdiction', *Max Planck Encyclopaedia of Public International Law*, available at <http://www.mpepil.com>

Davis, H, 'Public Authorities as "Victims" under the Human Rights Act' (2005) 64 *CLJ* 315

de Hoogh, A, 'Article 4 and 8 of the 2001 ILC Articles on State Responsibility, the Tadić Case and Attribution of Acts of Bosnian Serb Authorities to the Federal Republic of Yugoslavia' (2001) 72 *BYBIL* 255

De Schutter, O, 'Globalization and Jurisdiction: Lessons from the European Convention on Human Rights' (2006) 6 *BalticYIL* 183

Del Mar, K, 'The Requirement of "Belonging" under International Humanitarian Law' (2010) 21 *EJIL* 105

Dennis, Michael J, 'Application of Human Rights Treaties Extraterritorially in Times of Armed Conflict and Military Occupation' (2005) 99(1) *AJIL* 119–41

Dennis, Michael J, and Surena, Andre M, 'Application of the International Covenant on Civil and Political Rights in Times of Armed Conflict and Military Occupation: The Gap between Legal Theory and State Practice' (2008) 6 *EHRLR* 714–31

Dimitrijevic, V, 'Customary Law as an Instrument for the Protection of Human Rights' (2006) ISPI 7 Working Papers, available at www.ispionline,it/it/documents/wp_7_2006.pdf

Dinstein, Yoram, 'The International Law of Inter-State Wars and Human Rights' (1977) 7 *Isr Yb Hum Rts* 139–53

Doswald-Beck, Louise, 'The Right to Life in Armed Conflict: Does International Humanitarian Law Provide All the Answers?' (2007) 88(864) *IRRC* 881–904

Doswald-Beck, Louise and Vite, Sylvain, 'International Humanitarian Law and Human Rights Law' (1993) 33(293) *IRRC* 94–119

Downes, Chris, ' "Targeted Killings" in an Age of Terror: The Legality of the Yemen Strike' (2004) 9(2) *JC&SL* 277–94

Droege, Cordula, 'The Interplay between International Humanitarian Law and International Human Rights Law in Situations of Armed Conflict' (2007) 40(2) *Isr Law Rev* 310–55

Droege, Cordula, 'Elective Affinities? Human Rights and Humanitarian Law' (2008) 90(871) *IRRC* 501–48

Dugard, John, 'Bridging the Gap between Human Rights and Humanitarian Law' (1998) 38(324) *IRRC* 445–53

Eden, Paul and Happold, Matthew, 'Symposium: The Relationship between International Humanitarian Law and International Human Rights Law' (2010) 14(3) *JC&SL* 441–47

Fallon, R and Meltzer, D, 'Habeas Corpus Jurisdiction, Substantive Rights, and the War on Terror' (2007) 120 *HarvLRev* 2029

Ferraro, Tristan, 'The Law of Occupation and Human Rights Law: Some Selected Issues' in Robert Kolb and Gloria Gaggioli (eds), *Research Handbook on Human Rights and Humanitarian Law* (Edward Elgar 2013), pp 273–93

Gaggioli, Gloria and Kolb, Robert, 'A Right to Life in Armed Conflict? The Contribution of the European Court of Human Rights' (2007) 37 *Isr Yb Hum Rts* 115–63

Gardam, Judith, 'The Contribution of the International Court of Justice to International Humanitarian Law' (2001) 14(2) *LJIL* 349–65

Garraway, Charles HB, 'Occupation Responsibilities and Constraints' in Howard M Hensel (ed), *The Legitimate Use of Force: The Just War Tradition and the Customary Law of Armed Conflict* (Ashgate 2008), pp 263–82

Garraway, Charles HB, 'The International Humanitarian Fact-Finding Commission' in Aldo Zammit Borda (ed), *International Humanitarian Law and the International Red Cross and Red Crescent Movement* (Routledge, 2010), pp 74–77

Gioia, Andrea, 'The Role of the European Court of Human Rights in Monitoring Compliance with Humanitarian Law in Armed Conflict' in Orna Ben-Naftali (ed), *International Humanitarian Law and International Human Rights Law, Pas de Deux* (Oxford University Press 2011), pp 201–49

Goldstone, R and Hamilton, R, '*Bosnia v. Serbia*: Lessons from the Encounter of the International Court of Justice with the International Criminal Tribunal for the Former Yugoslavia' (2008) 21 *LJIL* 95

Goodwin-Gill, Guy S, 'The Extra-Territorial Reach of Human Rights Obligations: A Brief Perspective on the Link to Jurisdiction' in L Boisson de Chazournes and M Kohen (eds), *International Law and the Quest for Its Implementation/Le droit international et la quête de as mise en œvre, Liber Amicorum Vera Gowlland-Debbas* (Brill/Martinus Nijhoff 2010), p 293

Gondek, Michal, 'Extraterritorial Application of the European Convention on Human Rights: Territorial Focus in the Age of Globalization?' (2005) 52(3) *NethILR* 349–87

Goddard, David, 'Applying the European Convention on Human Rights to the Use of Physical Force: Al-Saadoon' (2015) 91 *Int'l L Stud* 402–24

Gowland-Debbas, Vera and Gaggioli, Gloria, 'The Relationship between International Human Rights Law and Humanitarian Law: An Overview' in Robert Kolb and Gloria Gaggioli (eds), *Research Handbook on Human Rights and Humanitarian Law* (Edward Elgar 2013), pp 77–103

Green, Leslie C, 'The Contemporary Law of Armed Conflict and the Protection of Human Rights' in Gerald L Gall (ed), *Civil Liberties in Canada: Entering the 1980s* (Butterworths 1982), pp 166–90

Green, Leslie C, 'Human Rights and the Law of Armed Conflict' in Leslie C Green (ed), *Essays on the Modern Law of War* (Transnational 1999), pp 40–58

Green, Leslie C, 'Human Rights Law and International Humanitarian Law: A Historical Overview' in Susan C Breau and Agnieszka Jachec-Neale (eds), *Testing the Boundaries of*

International Humanitarian Law (British Institute of International and Comparative Law 2006), pp 49–83

Greenwood, Christopher, 'The Administration of Occupied Territory in International Law' in Emma Playfair (ed), *International Law and the Administration of Occupied Territories: Two Decades of Israeli Occupation of the West Bank and Gaza Strip* (Clarendon Press 1992), pp 241–66

Greenwood, Chris, 'The Development of International Humanitarian Law by the International Criminal Tribunal for the Former Yugoslavia' (1998) 2 *MaxPlanckYBUNL* 97–140

Greenwood, Chris, 'Historical Development and Legal Basis' in Dieter Fleck (ed), *The Handbook of International Humanitarian Law* (Oxford University Press 2008), pp 1–43

Greer, S, 'Reflections of a Former President of the European Court of Human Rights,' (2010) *EHRLR* 169

Guilfoyle, Douglas, 'Counter-Piracy Law Enforcement and Human Rights' (2010) 59 ICLQ 141

Guilfoyle, Douglas, 'ECHR Rights at Sea: Medvedyev and Others v. France', *EJIL: Talk!*, 19 April 2010, available at <www.ejiltalk.org/echr-rights-at-sea-medvedyev-and-others-v-france/>

Hampson, Francoise, 'Fundamental Guarantees' in Elizabeth Wilmshurst and Susan Breau (eds), *Perspectives on the ICRC Study on Customary International Humanitarian Law* (Cambridge University Press 2007), pp 282–301

Hampson, Francoise, 'The Relationship between International Humanitarian Law and Human Rights Law from the Perspective of a Human Rights Treaty Body' (2008) 90(871) *IRRC* 549–72

Happold, Matthew, 'Bankovic v. Belgium and the Territorial Scope of the European Convention on Human Rights' (2003) 3 *HRLR* 1

Joseph, Sarah, 'Scope of Obligations' in Daniel Moeckli, Sangeeta Shah, and Sandesh Sivakumaran (eds), *International Human Rights Law* (Oxford University Press 2010), pp 150–70

Kavanagh, A, 'The Elusive Divide between Interpretation and Legislation under the Human Rights Act 1998' (2004) 24 *OJLS* 259

Kaye, David, 'International Decision (Comment on *Khasyivev and Akayeva v Russia; Isayeva, Yusupova and Bazayeva v Russia; Isayeva v Russia*)' (2005) 99(4) *AJIL* 873–78

King, H, 'The Extraterritorial Human Rights Obligations of States' (2009) 9 *HRLR* 521

King, H, 'Unravelling the Extraterritorial Riddle: An Analysis of *R (Hassan) v Secretary of State for Defence*' (2009) 7 *JICJ* 633

Kolb, Robert, 'The Relationship between International Humanitarian Law and International Human Rights Law: A Brief History of the 1948 Universal Declaration of Human Rights and the 1949 Geneva Conventions' (1998) 38(324) *IRRC* 409–19

Kolb, Robert, 'Occupation in Iraq since 2003 and the Powers of the UN Security Council' (2008) 90 *IRRC* 29

Krahenmann, Sandra, 'Positive Obligations in Human Rights Law during Armed Conflicts' in Robert Kolb and Gloria Gaggioli (eds), *Research Handbook on Human Rights and Humanitarian Law* (Edward Elgar 2013), pp 170–87

Kretzmer, David, 'Targeted Killing of Suspected Terrorists: Extra-Judicial Execution or Legitimate Means of Defence' (2005) 16(2) *EJIL* 171–212

Lawson, Rick, 'Life after Bankovic: On the Extraterritorial Application of the European Convention on Human Rights' in Fons Coomans and Menno T Kamminga (eds), *Extraterritorial Application of Human Rights Treaties* (Intersentia 2004), pp 83–123

Leach, Philip, 'The British Military in Iraq—the Applicability of the *Espace Juridique* Doctrine under the European Convention on Human Rights' (2005) *PL* 448

Leach, Philip, 'The Chechen Conflict: Analysing the Oversight of the European Court of Human Rights' (2008) *EHRLR* 732

Lindroos, A, 'Addressing Norm Conflicts in a Fragmented Legal System: The Doctrine of *Lex Specialis*' (2005) 74 *NordicJIL* 27–66

Loucaides, L, 'Determining the Extra-Territorial Effect of the European Convention: Facts, Jurisprudence and the *Banković* Case' (2006) 4 *EHRLR* 391

Lowe, V, 'Jurisdiction', in Evans 335

Lubell, Noam, 'Challenges in Applying Human Rights Law to Armed Conflict' (2005) 87(860) *IRRC* 737–54

Lubell, Noam, 'Parallel Application of International Humanitarian Law and International Human Rights Law: An Examination of the Debate' (2007) 40(2) *Isr Yb Hum Rts* 648–60

Lubell, Noam, 'Human Rights in Military Occupation' (2012) 94(885) *IRRC* 317–37

McCarthy, Conor, 'Legal Conclusion or Interpretative Process? Lex Specialis and the Application of International Human Rights Standards' in Roberta Arnold and Noelle Quenivet (eds), *International Humanitarian Law and Human Rights Law: Towards a Merger in International Law* (Nijhoff 2008), pp 102–18

McCarthy, Conor, 'Legal Reasoning and the Applicability of International Human Rights Standards during Military Occupation' in Roberta Arnold and Noelle Quenivet (eds), *International Humanitarian Law and Human Rights Law: Towards a Merger in International Law* (Nijhoff 2008), pp 122–32

McGoldrick, Dominic, 'Extraterritorial Application of the International Covenant on Civil and Political Rights' in Coomans, F and Kamminga, M (eds), *Extraterritorial Application of Human Rights Treaties* (Intersentia 2004), pp 41–72

McLaughlin, Rob, 'The Law of Armed Conflict and International Human Rights Law: Some Paradigmatic Differences and Operational Implications' (2010) 13 *YIntlHL* 213–43

Melzer, Nils, 'Bolstering the Protection of Civilians in Armed Conflict' in Antonia Cassese (ed), *Realizing Utopia: The Future of International Law* (Oxford University Press 2012), pp 508–18

Meron, Theodor, 'On the Inadequate Reach of Humanitarian and Human Rights Law and the Need for a New Instrument' (1983) 77(3) *AJIL* 589–606

Meron, Theodor, 'Convergence of International Humanitarian and Human Rights Law' in Daniel Warner (ed), *Human Rights and Humanitarian Law: The Quest for Universality* (Nijhoff 1997), pp 97–105

Milanovic, M, 'State Responsibility for Genocide' (2006) 17 *EJIL* 553

Milanovic, M, 'Lessons for Human Rights and Humanitarian Law in the War on Terror: Comparing Hamdan and the Israeli Targeted Killings Case' (2007) 89 *IRRC* 373.

Milanovic, M, 'From Compromise to Principle: Clarifying the Concept of State Jurisdiction in Human Rights Treaties' (2008) 8 *HRLR* 411

Milanovic, M, 'A Norm Conflict Perspective on the Relationship between International Humanitarian Law and Human Rights Law' (2009) 14 *JCSL* 459

Milanovic, M, 'Norm Conflict in International Law: Whither Human Rights?' (2009) 20 *DukeJComp&IntlL* 69

Milanovic, M, 'Al-Saadoon and Mufdhi Merits Judgment', *EJIL: Talk!*, 2 March 2010, available at <www.ejiltalk.org/al-saadoon-and-mufdhi-merits-judgment/>

Milanovic, M, 'Grand Chamber Hearings and Preview of Al-Skeini and Al-Jedda', *EJIL: Talk!*, 9 June 2010, available at <www.ejiltalk.org/grand-chamber-hearings-and-preview-of-al-skeini-and-al-jedda/>

Milanovic, M, 'More on Drones, Self-Defense, and the Alston Report on Targeted Killings', *EJIL: Talk!*, 5 June 2010, available at <www.ejiltalk.org/more-on-drones-self-defense-and-the-alston-report-on-targeted killings/>

Milanovic, M, 'Al-Skeini and Al-Jedda in Strasbourg' (2012) 23 *EJIL* 121–39

Milanovic, Marko and Papic, Tatjana, 'As Bad as It Gets: The European Court of Human Rights' Behrami and Saramati Decision and General International Law' (2008) 58(2) *ICLQ* 267–96

Miller, Sarah, 'Revisiting Extraterritorial Jurisdiction: A Territorial Justification for Extraterritorial Jurisdiction under the European Convention' (2009) 20(4) *EJIL* 1233–46

Modirzadeh, Naz, 'The Dark Sides of Convergence: A Pro-Civilian Critique of the Extraterritorial Application of Human Rights Law in Armed Conflict' (2010) 86 *U.S. Naval War College International Law Studies* (Blue Book) Series 349

Moir, Lindsay, 'The European Court of Human Rights and International Humanitarian Law' in Robert Kolb and Gloria Gaggioli (eds), *Research Handbook on Human Rights and Humanitarian Law* (Edward Elgar 2013), pp 480–502

O'Boyle, Michael, 'The European Convention on Human Rights and Extraterritorial Jurisdiction: A Comment on "Life After Bankovic"' in Fons Coomans and Menno T Kamminga (eds), *Extraterritorial Application of Human Rights Treaties* (Intersentia 2004), pp 125–39

Orakhelashvili, Alexander, 'Legal Consequences of the Construction of a Wall in the Occupied Palestinian Territory: Opinion and Reaction' (2006) 11(1) *JC&SL* 119–39

Orakhelashvili, Alexander, 'Legal Stability and Claims of Change: The International Court's Treatment of Jus Ad Bellum and Jus in Bello' (2006) 75(3–4) *NordicJIL* 371–407

Orakhelashvili, Alexander, 'The Interaction between Human Rights and Humanitarian Law: Fragmentation, Conflict, Parallelism, or Convergence?' (2008) 19(1) *EJIL* 162–82

Pejic, Jelena, 'The European Court of Human Rights' Al-Jedda Judgment: The Oversight of International Humanitarian Law' (2012) 93(838) *IRRC* 837–51

Prud'homme, Nancy, 'Lex Specialis: Oversimplifying a More Complex and Multifaceted Relationship?' (2007) 40(2) *Isr Law Rev* 357–93

Quenivet, Noelle, 'The Right to Life in International Humanitarian Law and Human Rights Law' in Roberta Arnold and Noelle Quenivet (eds), *International Humanitarian Law and Human Rights Law: Towards a Merger in International Law* (Nijhoff 2008), pp 331–53

Quenivet, Noelle and Arnold, Roberta, 'Conclusions' in Noelle Quenivet and Roberta Arnold (eds), *International Humanitarian Law and Human Rights Law: Towards a Merger in International Law* (Nijhoff 2008), pp 591–92

Roberts, Adam, 'Transformative Military Occupation: Applying the Laws of War and Human Rights' in Michael N Schmitt and Jelena Pejic (eds), *International Law and Armed Conflict: Exploring the Faultlines* (Nijhoff 2007), pp 439–95

Rodley, Nigel S, 'Integrity of the Person' in Daniel Moeckli, Sangeeta Shah, and Sandesh Sivakumaran (eds), *International Human Rights Law* (Oxford University Press 2010), pp 209–32

Rogers, APV, 'The Principle of Proportionality' in Howard M. Hensel (ed), *The Legitimate Use of Military Force: The Just War Tradition and the Customary Law of Armed Conflict* (Ashgate 2008), pp 189–218

Rowe, Peter, 'The Application of the European Convention on Human Rights during an Armed Conflict' in Richard Burchill, Nigel D White, and Justin Morris (eds), *International Conflict and Security Law, Essays in Memory of Hilaire McCoubrey* (Cambridge University Press 2005), pp 185–208

Rowe, Peter, 'Non-International Armed Conflict and the European Court of Human Rights: Chechnya from 1999' (2007) 4 *NZYIL* 205–26

Sassoli, Marco, 'The Role of Human Rights and International Humanitarian Law in New Types of Armed Conflicts' in Ben-Naftali (ed), *International Humanitarian and International Human Rights Law* (Oxford University Press 2011), pp 34–94

Sassoli, Marco and Olson, Laura M, 'The Relationship between International Humanitarian Law and Human Rights Law Where It Matters: Admissible Killing and Internment of Fighters in Non-International Armed Conflicts' (2008) 90(871) *IRRC* 599–627

Schabas, William, 'Lex Specialis? Belts and Suspenders? The Parallel Operation of Human Rights Law and the Law of Armed Conflict, and the Conundrum of Jus ad Bellum' (2007) 40(2) *Isr Law Rev* 592–613

Schmitt, Michael N, 'Targeted Killings and International Law: Law Enforcement, Self-Defense and Armed Conflict' in Roberta Arnold and Noelle Quenivet (eds), *International Humanitarian Law and Human Rights Law: Towards a Merger in International Law* (Nijhoff 2008), pp 525–53

Schondorf, Roy S, 'Extra-State Armed Conflicts: Is There a Need for a New Legal Regime?' (2004) 37(1) *NYUJIntL&P* 1–78

Scobbie, Iain, 'Principle or Pragmatics? The Relationship between Human Rights Law and the Law of Armed Conflict' (2009) 14(3) *JC&SL* 449–57

Sivakumaran, Sandesh, 'Binding Armed Opposition Groups' (2006) 55 *ICLQ* 369–94

Sivakumaran, Sandesh, 'International Humanitarian Law' in Daniel Moeckli, Sangeeta Shah, and Sandesh Sivakumaran (eds), *International Human Rights Law* (Oxford University Press 2010), pp 521–39

Sivakumaran, Sandesh, 'Re-Envisaging the International Law of Armed Conflict: A Rejoinder to Gabriella Blum' (2011) 22 (1) *EJIL* 273–75

Tomuschat, Christian, 'Human Rights and International Humanitarian Law' (2010) 21(1) *EJIL* 15

Tomuschat, Christian, 'The Right to Life: Legal and Political Foundations' in Christian Tomuschat, Evelyne Lagrange, and Stefan Oeter (eds), *The Right to Life* (Nijhoff, 2010), 3–18

Turns, David, 'Droning On: Some International Humanitarian Law Aspects of the Use of Unmanned Aerial Vehicles in Contemporary Armed Conflicts' in C Harvey, J Summers, and ND White (eds), *Contemporary Challenges to the Laws of War: Essays in Honour of Professor Peter Rowe* (Cambridge University Press 2014), 191–215

Turns, David, 'The Law of Armed Conflict (International Humanitarian Law)' in MD Evans (ed), *International Law* (4th edn, Oxford University Press 2014), 821–53

Turns, David, 'Targets' in Nigel D White and Christian Henderson (eds), *Research Handbook on International Conflict and Security Law: Jus ad Bellum, Jus in Bello and Jus post Bellum* (Edward Elgar Publishing 2013), 342–74

Van Schaak, Beth, 'The United States' Position on the Extraterritorial Application of Human Rights Obligations: Now Is the Time for Change' (2014) 90 *Int'lLStud* 20–65

Verdirame, Guglielmo, "Human Rights in Wartime: A Framework for Analysis" (2008) 6 *EHRLR* 689–705

Watkin, Kenneth, 'Assessing Proportionality: Moral Complexity and Legal Rules' (2005) 8 *YIntlHL* 3–53

Watkin, Kenneth, '21st Century Conflict and International Humanitarian Law: Status Quo or Change?' in Michael N. Schmitt and Jelena Pejic (eds), *International Law and Armed Conflict: Exploring the Faultlines* (Nijhoff 2007), pp 295–96

Weissbrodt, David, 'The Role of the Human Rights Committee in Interpreting and Developing Humanitarian Law' (2010) 31(4) *UnivPaJIntLaw* 1185–1237

Wilde, Ralph, 'Legal "Black Hole"? Extraterritorial State Action and International Treaty Law on Civil and Political Rights' (2005) 26 *MichJIntlL* 739–806

Wilde, Ralph, 'Triggering State Obligations Extraterritorially: The Spatial Test in Certain Human Rights Treaties' (2007) 40(2) *Isr Law Rev* 503–26

Wilde, Ralph, 'Are Human Rights Norms Part of the Jus Post Bellum, and Should They Be?' in Carsten Stahn and Jann K. Kleffner (eds), *Jus Post Bellum: Towards a Law of Transition from Conflict to Peace* (TMC Asser 2008), pp 163–86

Zimmermann, A, 'Extraterritorial Application of Human Rights Treaties—The Case of Israel and the Palestinian Territories Revisited' in I Buffard, J Crawford, A Pellet, and S Wittich (eds), *International Law between Universalism and Fragmentation: Festschrift in Honour of Gerhard Hafner* (Brill 2008), p 747

WEBSITE BIBLIOGRAPHY

The Al-Sweady Public Inquiry—<http://webarchive.nationalarchives.gov.uk/20150115114702/http://www.alsweadyinquiry.org/linkedfiles/alsweadyinquiry/theal-sweadyinquiryreport-volume2part2.pdf> [accessed 3 May 2015]

Armed Forces Act 2006, Schedule 2 update—<http://www.legislation.gov.uk/ukpga/2006/52/schedule/2> [accessed 3 May 2015]

Baha Mousa Public Inquiry—terms of reference are at <http://webarchive.nationalarchives.gov.uk/20120215203912/http://www.bahamousainquiry.org/index.htm> [accessed 3 May 2014]

British Army information—http://www.army.mod.uk/agc/provost/23207.aspx [accessed 9 April 2015]

Richard Ekins, Jonathan Morgan, and Tom Tugendhat, Clearing the Fog of Law: Saving Our Armed Forces from Defeat by Judicial Diktat, Policy Exchange, London (2015), <http://www.policyexchange.org.uk/images/publications/clearing%20the%20fog%20of%20law.pdf> [accessed 5 May 2015]

EJILTALK

Aurel Sari, Jaloud v Netherlands: New Directions in Extraterritorial Military Operations, 24 November 2014 <http://www.ejiltalk.org/jaloud-v-netherlands-new-directions-in-extra-territorial-military-operations/> [accessed 19 December 2015]

The Guardian Newspaper—<http://www.theguardian.com/world/2015/sep/07/drone-british-citizens-syria-uk-david-cameron> [accessed 16 Sep 15]

Operations in Afghanistan—Defence Committee, House of Commons—Written evidence to the House of Commons Defence Select Committee from the Ministry of Defence in respect of operations in Afghanistan, <http://www.publications.parliament.uk/pa/cm201012/cmselect/cmdfence/554/554we02.htm> para 19 [accessed 6 April 2015]

Letter from the Chief Prosecutor of the ICC regarding the situation in Iraq—dated 9 February 2006 ICC—<http://www.icc-cpi.int/NR/rdonlyres/04D143C8-19FB-466C-AB77-4CDB2FDEBEF7/143682/OTP_letter_to_senders_re_Iraq_9_February_2006.pdf> [accessed 3 May 2015]

ICRC IHL and Human Rights Law—An overview—<https://www.icrc.org/eng/war-and-law/ihl-other-legal-regimes/ihl-human-rights/overview-ihl-and-human-rights.htm> [accessed 25 October 2014]

IHAT website—<https://www.gov.uk/government/groups/iraq-historic-allegations-team-ihat> [accessed 3 May 2015]

Ministry of Defence police information—https://www.gov.uk/government/uploads/system/uploads/attachment_data/file/380044/20141121_MDP_Recruitment_Patterns_Redacted.pdf [accessed 9 April 2015]

NATO Operations information—KFOR—Kosovo, Resolute Support—Afghanistan, Operation Active Endeavour, Operation Ocean Shield—<http://www.aco.nato.int/ongoingoperations.aspx> [accessed 3 May 2015]

NATO ISAF Tactical Directive example—<http://www.nato.int/isaf/docu/official_texts/Tactical_Directive_090706.pdf> [accessed 3 May 2015]

Royal Air Force information—<http://www.rafpa.com/RAFP%20Factsheet%20Jan12.pdf> [accessed 9 April 2015]

Royal Marines information—<http://www.royalnavy.mod.uk/our-organisation/the-fighting-arms/royal-marines/3-commando-brigade/42-commando> [accessed 3 May 2015]

Royal Navy information—<http://www.royalnavy.mod.uk/About-the-Royal-Navy/~/media/Files/Navy-PDFs/About-the-Royal-Navy/Future%20Navy%20Vision.pdf> [accessed 18 December 2014]

Service Inquiry information—<https://www.gov.uk/government/collections/service-inquiry-si> [accessed 18 December 2014]

unchr.org Digital record of the UDHR, February 2009 <http://www.ohchr.org/EN/NEWSEVENTS/Pages/DigitalrecordoftheUDHR.aspx> [accessed 15 May 2014]

UK Parliament—Joint Committee on Human Rights <http://www.parliament.uk/business/committees/committees-a-z/joint-select/human-rights-committee/> [accessed 18 July 2017]

Index